Y0-CZQ-206

ANALYTICAL URBAN GEOGRAPHY

Spatial Patterns and Theories

MARTIN T. CADWALLADER

University of Wisconsin – Madison

Prentice-Hall, Inc., Englewood Cliffs, New Jersey 07632

Library of Congress Cataloging in Publication Data

Cadwallader, Martin T. (date)
Analytical urban geography.

Bibliography: p.
Includes index.
1. Cities and towns. 2. Sociology, Urban.
3. Land use, Urban. 4. Urban economics. 5. Social sciences—Statistical methods. I. Title.
HT151.C318 1985 910'.09172'4 84-16083
ISBN 0-13-034950-X

For

Lorraine, Evan, and Meredith

Printed in the United States of America

10 9 8 7 6 5 4 3 2 1

Editorial/production supervision and interior design: Paul Spencer
Cover design: Diane Saxe
Manufacturing buyer: John Hall

ISBN 0-13-034950-X 01

Prentice-Hall International, Inc., *London*
Prentice-Hall of Australia Pty. Limited, *Sydney*
Editora Prentice-Hall do Brasil, Ltda., *Rio de Janeiro*
Prentice-Hall Canada Inc., *Toronto*
Prentice-Hall of India Private Limited, *New Delhi*
Prentice-Hall of Japan, Inc., *Tokyo*
Prentice-Hall of Southeast Asia Pte. Ltd., *Singapore*
Whitehall Books Limited, *Wellington, New Zealand*

Contents

Preface

This book is intended primarily for the use of undergraduates in urban geography courses, although it will also be of interest to students of urban planning, urban economics, and urban sociology. It is particularly appropriate for semester-length courses that focus on the internal structure of cities. The approach parallels the spatial positivist theme that has dominated most of the contemporary research in urban geography, although the closely related behavioral perspective is also explicitly considered. More specifically, the scientific method is stressed throughout the book. This methodological stance is adopted for two main reasons. First, it has been the primary methodological vehicle for developing and evaluating theory in urban geography. Second, it is this approach that is of the greatest value to those students wishing to pursue employment opportunities, or graduate training, in the professional fields, such as urban and regional planning or marketing.

The major theme of the book, and the feature that distinguishes it from other texts in the field, is the *integration of substantive and methodological material.* The substantive material is arranged in such a manner as to allow the statistical techniques to be introduced in an orderly fashion, beginning with the simplest and following through to the more complex. No previous training in statistics is required, equations are kept to a minimum, and the various techniques are explained in conjunction with the empirical testing of particular models and theories. It is the author's experience that the majority of students can easily grasp the major elements of these concepts if they are not burdened with mathematical proofs, and are provided with appropriate schematic diagrams. More important, there is such a fine line between theory and methodology in contemporary urban geography that it is almost impossible to appreciate one without the other. The traditional device of relegating methodological and technical discussions to an appendix is no longer appropriate, as theory development is integrally related to the calibration and testing of models via statistical techniques.

Three other themes are also represented in the book. First, the approach is *multidisciplinary*, in the sense that appropriate theory is culled from the major social science disciplines of economics, geography, psychology, and sociology. In all cases, however, these theories are discussed from a geographical perspective, as it is not just the processes themselves, but also their spatial manifestations, that are of primary interest. For example, particular attention is paid to the spatial patterns associated with the urban land market and to the spatial outcome of the decision-making process involved in residential mobility.

Second, the *model building* paradigm is emphasized throughout the book, and the ways in which mathematical or symbolic models can be used to represent processes and associated spatial patterns are discussed in detail. For example, models to explain the distribution of land values, the distribution of housing values, and the choice process in consumer spatial behavior are all examined at some length. It is in conjunction with the discussion of models such as these that the statistical procedures are introduced and that the mutual reinforcement of theory and methodology is exemplified.

Third, specific *urban problems* are discussed in each chapter, to alert the student to the applied component of most contemporary urban research. These problems, such as governmental fragmentation and urban sprawl, are discussed in three ways: first, the problem is identified and described; second, the processes responsible for generating that problem are discussed; and third, possible solutions are suggested.

The first chapter introduces the student to the overall orientation of the book. Chapters 2 through 6 deal with the internal structure of cities, especially with respect to the underlying socioeconomic processes and their spatial manifestation. Chapter 2 explores land use and land value theory, using the traditional approach of neoclassical economics, and bivariate correlation and regression techniques are introduced in order to test the major hypotheses generated by that theory. More complex, multivariate models of land values are developed in Chapter 3, and the calibration of these models necessitates an introduction to multiple correlation and regression. The characteristics of the urban housing market are also examined at this juncture, as a prelude to discussing multivariate housing value models. These models are couched within the framework of causal models and path analysis, and so provide a natural methodological extension of the previously described multiple correlation and regression models. In particular, the notion of indirect effects between explanatory variables is explored.

Chapter 4 deals with two components of urban spatial structure that are inextricably linked to the underlying pattern of land values. First, the urban retail structure is described, and central place theory is used as a conceptual framework for analyzing the spatial distribution of shopping centers within cities. Second, the spatial pattern of population density is considered, and the use of trend surface analysis, a form of multiple regression analysis, is explored. Having discussed the distribution of people in general, Chapter 5 addresses the question of whether different kinds of people tend to live in different parts of the city. The process of spatial sorting, according to social and economic differentiation, involves the generation of distinctive social areas within cities, and the characteristics of these social areas are identified through the use of factor analysis. Finally, Chapter 6 is concerned with the industrial structure of cities, and the economic base concept and input–output analysis are used to describe and calibrate the various interrelationships within an urban economy.

Chapter 7 introduces the ideas of environmental perception and cognitive maps. With these concepts as a backdrop, Chapters 8 and 9 discuss various approaches to understanding movement patterns within cities. More specifically, the discussion of psychological concepts such as imagery and preferences provides a fuller understanding of human behavior within an urban setting, and leads quite naturally to the issue of spatial choice. Different approaches to choosing between alternatives within the context of shopping behavior are discussed in Chapter 8, while Chapter 9 addresses the decision-making process involved in residential mobility. It is in Chapter 9 that the elaboration of multivariate statistics is brought to a logical conclusion by the introduction of simultaneous equation models, which include not only indirect effects between sets of variables, but also feedback effects, or reciprocal relationships, between those variables. Chapter 10 concludes the book by discussing the role of urban planning.

I would like to thank John Adams, Larry Bourne, William Clark, Rodney Erickson, John Everitt, Larry Ford, Reginald Golledge, Peter Haggett, Truman Hartshorn, Paul Knox, Peter Muller, Robert Sack, and David Ward, who all made helpful comments on previous drafts of the manuscript. I am also indebted to my colleagues in the Department of Geography at the University of Wisconsion-Madison, for creating an exceptionally stimulating and congenial environment in which to live and work.

Martin T. Cadwallader

1

Urban Geography

1.1 SYSTEMS OF CITIES AND THEIR INTERNAL STRUCTURE

One way of understanding the evolution of cities is to think of the urban future as being a response to the present pattern of socioeconomic forces, plus the intervention of government agencies and factors outside the urban system itself (Figure 1.1). Within this context, the urban system can be conceived of as containing two components: the system of cities and the internal structure of cities. Investigations of the system of cities focus on cities as points in space, generally at either a national or regional level, while investigations of the internal structure of cities focus on the spatial arrangement of places and activities within those cities. In Figure 1.1 the squares representing these two components overlap, as what happens at one level within the urban system is partly dependent on what happens at the other.

Governmental intervention in the operation of this system occurs via the activities of various local urban and regional planning departments, and federal agencies such as the Department of Housing and Urban Development. These departments and agencies use devices such as land use zoning and environmental pollution standards to influence the distribution and characteristics of activities within cities. Generally beyond their control, however, are certain forces whose impact is generated outside the system. Examples of these outside factors are various natural phenomena, such as earthquakes and volcanoes, and the socioeconomic policies and problems of other countries.

Within this conceptual framework, the present book is concerned with the internal structure of cities, and in particular, with statements that apply to cities in

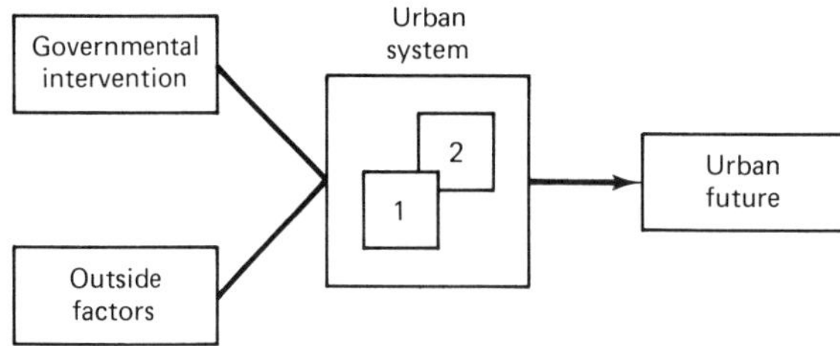

Figure 1.1 The urban future as a response to the present pattern of socio-economic forces, governmental intervention, and outside factors. (1) System of cities. (2) Internal structure. (Based on L. S. Bourne, *Urban Systems: Strategies for Regulation*, Clarendon Press, Oxford, 1975, Fig. 3.1, p. 44.)

general rather than to specific, individual cities. The information used to identify these generalizations is usually collected in matrix form. A city is first divided into subareas, using spatial units such as blocks, census tracts, or traffic zones (Figure 1.2a). The most popular spatial unit tends to be census tracts, as these are used for reporting data in the U.S. Census of Population and Housing. Generally, a city of 250,000 people will have somewhere between 40 and 60 such census tracts.

Interest is then focused on various attributes, or characteristics, of these census tracts, such as the predominant type of land use, the average land value, and the population density. The information relating to these attributes is represented in a matrix by having the rows correspond to census tracts, and the columns correspond to attributes (Figure 1.2b). For example, the cell labeled A might contain the average land value for census tract 2, while the cell labeled B might contain the population density for census tract 3. It is customary to designate the total number of cases, or census tracts, as N, and the total number of attributes as M, thus creating an $N \times M$ matrix.

The organizational structure of the present text revolves around the characteristics of the columns within this matrix, as we are interested in the different attributes, especially with respect to how their values vary from one census tract, or one part of

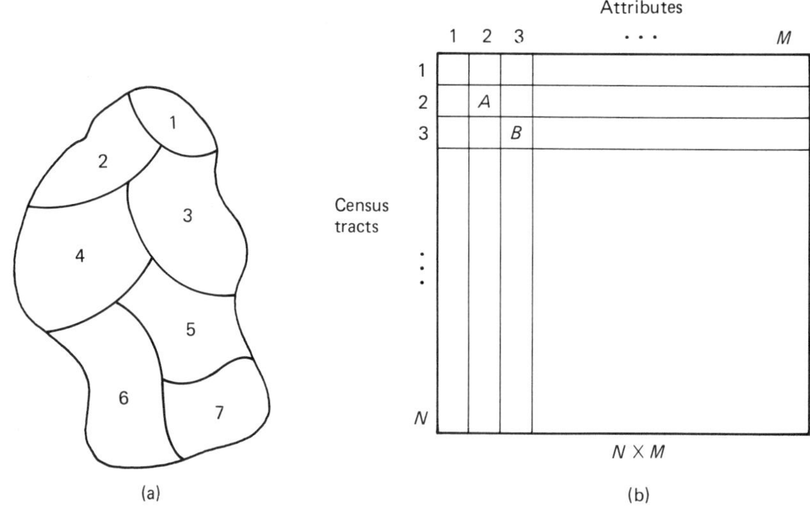

Figure 1.2 Representation of information in matrix form.

the city, to another. For example, Chapter 2 is concerned with the characteristic patterns of land use and land value within cities. Chapter 3 investigates, among other things, the pattern of housing value; Chapter 4 is concerned with the distribution of population density; and so on. In contrast, an overriding interest in the rows within the matrix would entail the examination of a single census tract at a time, and such an approach would become excessively encyclopedic.

1.2 APPROACHES TO URBAN GEOGRAPHY

Within this organizational framework it is possible to consider a variety of disciplinary perspectives on the city. These perspectives are not mutually exclusive, however, and are best represented by a series of overlapping sets (Figure 1.3). Each set represents a subdiscipline, such as urban economics or urban sociology, and each of these subdisciplines has its own particular perspective on the city. For example, urban economics (Mills, 1980) is concerned with the allocation of scarce resources in cities, such as land, labor, and capital, and how these resources are combined to produce goods and services. Urban sociology (Mann, 1965) is concerned with the characteristics of urban society, such as community organizations and class structure. Urban politics (Saunders, 1979) involves the distribution of political power within cities and the various forms of urban government. Urban psychology (C. Mercer, 1975) deals with the experience of living in cities, and the psychological reactions to high density, and often stressful, environments. Urban history (Dyos, 1968) is concerned with the historical evolution of cities, while urban geography, as we shall see, is particularly concerned with spatial patterns and processes within cities.

Where these subdisciplinary sets intersect is the discipline of urban planning. Urban planning lies within the area of overlap because it involves applying the theoretical insights of the various subdisciplines to urban problems, such as governmental

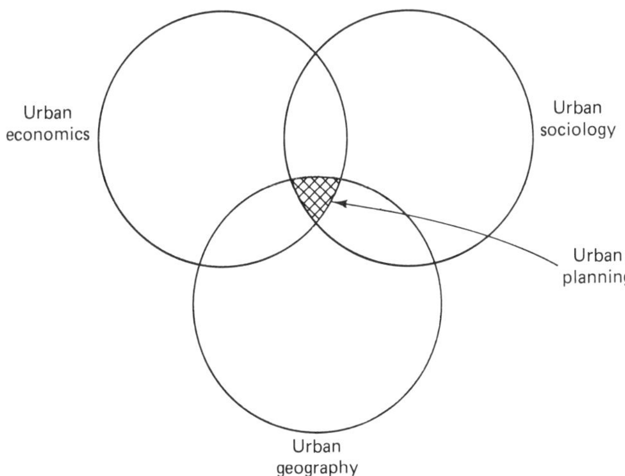

Figure 1.3 Overlap of disciplinary approaches to cities. (Adapted from Fig. 1.1 (p. 2) from *The North American City*, Third Edition by Maurice Yeates and Barry Garner. Copyright © 1980 by Maurice Yeates and Barry J. Garner. Reprinted by permission of Harper & Row, Publishers, Inc.)

fragmentation, urban renewal, and traffic congestion (Catanese and Synder, 1979). The present text parallels this diagram, in that theories are culled from a variety of disciplines and there is also a concern for urban problems. Particular attention, however, is paid to the perspective of urban geography. Urban geography is comprised of at least three major dimensions of inquiry: positivist, behavioral, and structuralist (Johnston, 1977). These three research orientations are by no means exhaustive, nor are they mutually exclusive, as there is considerable overlap, especially betwen the positivist and behavioral approaches. They are the three most important, however, with the positivist tradition representing the mainstream of current urban geography.

The Positivist Approach

The positivist approach was originally developed by the natural sciences, and forms the basis of the *scientific method* (Harvey, 1969). It is characterized by the search for generalizations and laws as a means of explaining and predicting the phenomena of interest. Abstract modes of thought, especially the use of statistics and mathematics, are invoked to assist with the identification and representation of these generalizations. In this sense, positivism assumes that there is a material world, and that there is an identifiable order to that material world (Johnston, 1980a).

Within this context, the positivist approach to urban geography tends to emphasize the *spatial patterns* of urban phenomena, both in terms of spatial distribution and spatial interaction. Patterns of *spatial distribution* can be categorized into four major groups: point patterns, networks, surfaces, and regions (Unwin, 1981). A *point pattern* is formed when the phenomenon of interest is represented as a series of points (Figure 1.4a). The distribution of banks, hotels, or supermarkets within a city constitutes a set of point patterns, and these patterns can be arranged along a continuum going from completely clustered at one end to completely dispersed at the other. Clustered patterns are generally produced by contagious processes. A measles epidemic, for example, would produce a spatially clustered pattern of victims. Dispersed patterns, on the other hand, are generated by competitive processes. For example, the distribution of supermarkets within a city generally conforms to a dispersed pattern, as the supermarkets are competing for customers.

A *network*, or line pattern, is used to represent such linear features as roads and railways (Figure 1.4b). We can quantitatively investigate the flow of traffic through the network, the relative accessibility of the different nodes (a, b, c), and the overall connectivity of the network. Network connectivity, for example, is amenable to analysis via the branch of mathematics known as graph theory.

Surfaces are formed by isolines, which join together points of equal value. The most common form of isoline is a contour, which joins together points of equal elevation. Within the urban context, population density can be represented as a surface. Such a surface would be cone-shaped, with the highest densities toward the center of the city and the lowest densities toward the periphery (Figure 1.4c). Alternatively, if the values of the isolines are reversed, the surface might represent the distribution of income within a city, which is generally lowest at the center and increases toward the suburbs.

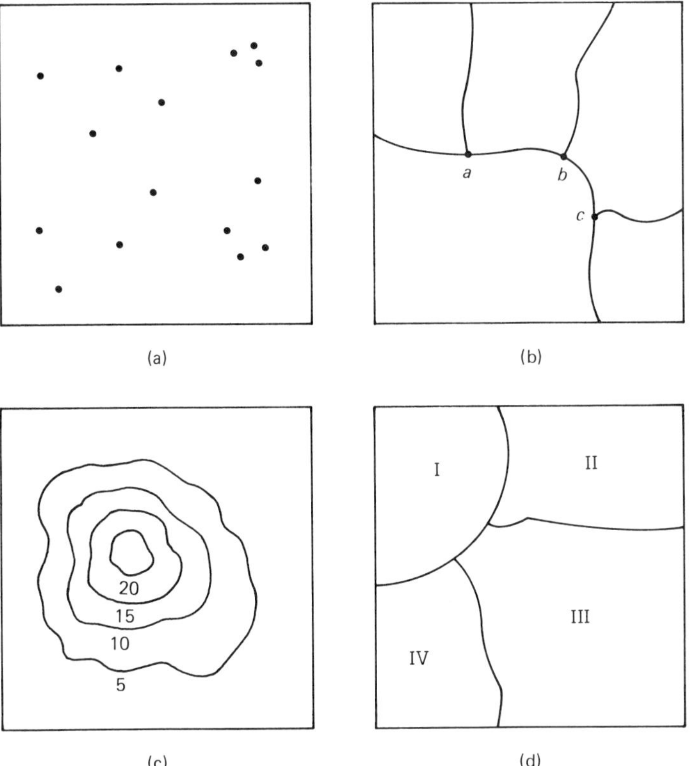

Figure 1.4 Patterns of spatial distribution: (a) point; (b) network; (c) surface; (d) region.

The final kind of spatial distribution is composed of *regions* within a city (Figure 1.4d). Geographers distinguish between two types of regions: uniform regions, and functional, or nodal regions. Uniform regions are areas that are relatively homogeneous with respect to certain specified characteristics. Social areas in a city constitute uniform regions, since they are relatively homogeneous with respect to the kind of people living in them, as measured by such variables as income, education, and family size. Functional regions, on the other hand, are characterized by a high degree of interaction. The market areas around supermarkets, for example, which circumscribe the areas within which people travel to purchase their weekly groceries, would be classified as functional regions.

In addition to these patterns of spatial distribution, geographers are also interested in describing and explaining patterns of *spatial interaction*, or movement patterns, within cities. These movement patterns might be of a temporary nature, such as with the journey to work or the journey to shop, or they might be of a more permanent nature, as with residential mobility or the changing of residence within cities. Within the context of these different kinds of spatial patterns, the initial chapters in this book deal with the spatial distributions of particular variables, such as land use, land value, and housing value, while the later chapters are more concerned with patterns of spatial interaction, as represented by consumer behavior and residential mobility in particular.

The positivist approach to urban geography, with its emphasis on spatial patterns, has not been immune from criticism, especially with respect to three of its major assumptions: first, the assumption that social science can generate scientific laws that are well-confirmed empirical regularities (Sayer, 1982); second, the assumption that scientific discourse can somehow be value-free or neutral (Gregory, 1978); and third, the assumption that peculiarly spatial laws can be generated in which space is considered independently from time and matter (Sack, 1980). Although these criticisms are certainly valid, however, they are to a certain extent caricatures of the positivist position, as most practitioners have tended to argue for a less dogmatic form of positivism (Hay, 1979).

The Behavioral Approach

As previously mentioned, two other approaches to the study of urbanism have also found favor within urban geography: the behavioral and the structural (Johnston, 1983). Although involving significant overlap with the spatial positivist perspective, the behavioral approach puts greater emphasis on the decision-making processes that generate the various kinds of spatial patterns. This approach was introduced to urban geography through the study of movement patterns, especially those associated with intraurban migration and the journey to shop (Herbert and Johnston, 1978). Models describing the individual decision-making process in various kinds of choice situations are now commonplace, and are built on such behavioral concepts as place utility, stress, and information space, as discussed in Chapters 8 and 9.

A second major strand within the behavioral approach relates to the notion of individual cognitions of the urban environment. Urban dwellers possess cognitive, or mental, maps of their surrounding environment, and these maps are far from identical to the actual physical structure of the city. It is the distortions contained in such maps, however, that are of primary interest, as they shed light on the behavioral context within which decisions concerning spatial choices are reached. These cognitive maps, and the related concept of cognitive distance, are discussed in Chapter 7.

The behavioral approach has been viewed as merely an appendage to the spatial-positivist tradition because of its preoccupation with measurement and highly formalized methodology (Ley, 1981). In all fairness, however, behavioral geographers never intended to produce a different disciplinary subfield, but rather to incorporate behavioral variables and concepts within the explanatory schema (Golledge, 1981b). In particular, behavioral geographers argue for a more process-oriented approach, incorporating such concepts as learning, cognition, information processing, and attitude formation (Gold, 1980). Thus the behavioral approach is not concerned primarily with the spatial manifestation of behavior itself, but rather with the processes responsible for that behavior.

Criticisms of such an approach have tended to focus on the implied assumption of subject–object separation (Cox, 1981). That is, the world can be separated into the objective world of things and the subjective world of the mind, and thus the observer is somehow separate from the observed. Such criticisms have given rise to a more humanistically oriented behavioral geography, which focuses on human feelings and values, such as the sense of place (Tuan, 1977), and on participant observation methodologies (Rowles, 1978). This "humanistic geography" (Ley and Samuels, 1978), however, with its illustrative use of facts and anecedotes, tends to concentrate on the unique rather than the general, and so does not fully participate in the development of verifiable theory. Rather, the humanist philosophy can be interpreted as a form of criticism that helps to counter some of the extreme abstractive tendencies of the positivist tradition (Entrikin, 1976).

The Structuralist Approach

The behavioral viewpoint in general has also been attacked for neglecting the societal constraints on individual human behavior. These societal constraints form an integral part of what is known as the structuralist approach, which emphasizes the politico-economic environment in which decisions are made (Gray, 1975). Thus an understanding of the urban housing market, and residential differentiation, cannot be concerned only with consumer preferences, but should also take into account the behavior of such institutions as mortgage lending companies (Boddy, 1976) and real estate agents (Palm, 1979), as we discuss in Chapter 3. Within this managerialist perspective (Pahl, 1975), it is argued that a variety of urban managers, or gatekeepers, have an effect on the allocation of housing, and it is these managers, and the institutions they represent, that should be the focus of much urban research.

The structuralist viewpoint clearly entails an interest in the role of the state in urban affairs (Dear and Scott, 1981) and the development of theories of the state, as we shall see in Chapter 10. The idea of conflict is also central to structuralism (Eyles, 1974), as sectional interests are seen as being the basis of social life, with political power being the key to understanding how scarce resources are allocated. Finally, an increasing number of scholars have turned to Marxist theories of political economy, in order to relate urban patterns explicitly to the wider organization of society (Castells, 1977). Such scholars contend that all social phenomena are inextricably linked to the prevailing mode of production, so that any understanding of American cities, for example, cannot be divorced from an analysis of the capitalist mode of production.

In general, then, urban geography involves a multiplicity of approaches (Bourne, 1982), in which no particular paradigm is completely dominant (Johnston, 1979, p. 188). The present text reflects the philosophy that a combination of the spatial positivist and behavioral traditions, together with an appreciation of societal constraints, is needed to understand fully the spatial structure of contemporary cities, and the behavior patterns that both create and respond to that structure (Johnston, 1980a). As Ley (1981) has eloquently stated, the time has come to abandon dogmatic claims to universalism on the part of any particular approach in order to begin the necessary integration of perspectives that will lead to a higher order of synthesis. Within the context of urban geography, the present book attempts to move toward such a synthesis, although the major emphasis lies within the positivist and behavioral traditions.

1.3 THE SCIENTIFIC METHOD

Within the philosophical framework of the positivist approach to urban geography, or indeed to social science in general, the pursuit of explanation involves trying to identify interrelationships between significant variables. These interrelationships are often represented by statements of the following kind:

$$Y = f(X) \tag{1.1}$$

where Y is the dependent variable and X is the explanatory, or independent variable. This equation states that the values of variable Y are in some way dependent on the values of variable X. The precise nature of this dependency is represented by the term f, which indicates the functional relationship linking X and Y.

Three major questions are asked about these relational statements. First, is there a relationship between the two variables? Second, if there is a relationship, what is the strength of that relationship? Third, what is the precise form of the relationship? The answer to the third question involves ascertaining whether the relationship is linear, curvilinear, or more complex.

Imagine, for example, that the two variables Y and X represent income and education, respectively. That is, we are postulating that a person's income level is determined, to a certain extent at least, by his or her level of education. If the relationship between these two variables is linear, it means that for every extra year of schooling, income increases by a certain, constant amount (Figure 1.5a). If, however, level of education increases income quite sharply at first, but then diminishing returns begin to set in, we have a curvilinear relationship (Figure 1.5b). Finally, if increasing levels of education first cause an increase in income, then a decrease, followed by another increase, and so on, the relationship between the two variables is more complex (Figure 1.5c).

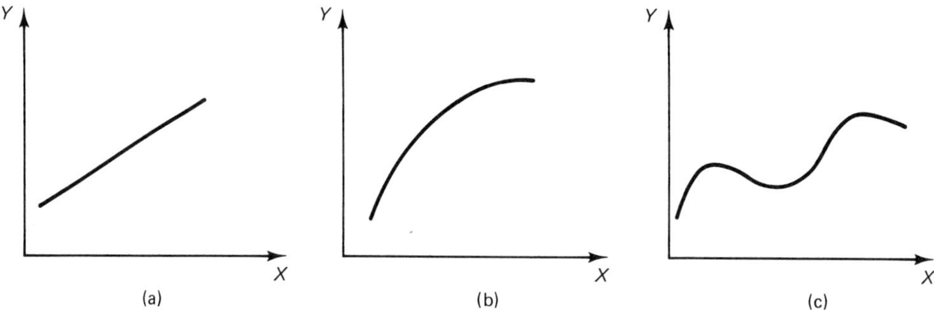

Figure 1.5 (a) Linear, (b) curvilinear, and (c) complex relationships.

Given the introductory nature of the present text, only the first two kinds of relationships, linear and curvilinear, will be formally expressed by equations. In fact, curvilinear relationships are sometimes referred to as being intrinsically linear, as they can often be logarithmically transformed into simple linear functions. Such a transformation is described in Chapter 2, when we discuss the relationship between land value and distance from the central business district.

Stages in the Scientific Method

In simplest terms, the scientific method is merely a strategy, or series of steps, for uncovering relationships between variables. There are five main stages in this process: problem identification, hypothesis formulation, data collection, data analysis, and a statement of conclusions. The nature of these steps can be illustrated by using the example of residential mobility within cities.

The process of *problem identification* involves asking a particular question about the phenomenon under investigation. For example, we might ask why there is more migration between some pairs of neighborhoods within a city than between others. It often helps to conceptualize the problem by drawing a picture of it (Figure 1.6a). In this representation five neighborhoods have been identified, and we are interested in investigating the amount of migration between one neighborhood and each of the other four. The actual volume of migration is represented by the thickness of the lines, so the research problem reduces to explaining why some of the lines are thicker than others.

The next step is to *formulate an hypothesis*. Hypotheses are tentative answers to the original question, so we might speculate that the amount of migration between neighborhoods depends on the distance separating them. Specifically, the amount of migration should decrease as distance increases, thus producing a negative, or inverse relationship between the two variables.

After formulating an hypothesis, *data are collected* in order to test that hypothesis. Because the hypothesis contains two variables, migration and distance, the associated data matrix will have two columns (Figure 1.6b). In addition, there are four rows, one for each of the potential destinations. At this juncture, decisions have to be made with respect to how the variables should be measured. What time period, for example, is most appropriate for measuring the amount of migration? A week, a year, or perhaps some even longer period? Also, how should distance be measured? As straight-line distance, road distance, or in some other way?

Once such measurement issues have been satisfactorily resolved, and the appropriate data collected, the process of *data analysis* begins. The precise details of this process will vary from study to study, but in this particular instance we can at least draw a graph, or picture of the relationship (Figure 1.6c). A graph involves plotting out the data in a two-dimensional space, where the dependent variable, migration, is placed on the vertical axis, and the independent variable, distance, is placed on the horizontal axis. Four data points are represented on the graph, as there are four cases, or pairs of neighborhoods, in the data matrix. A dashed line has been "eye-

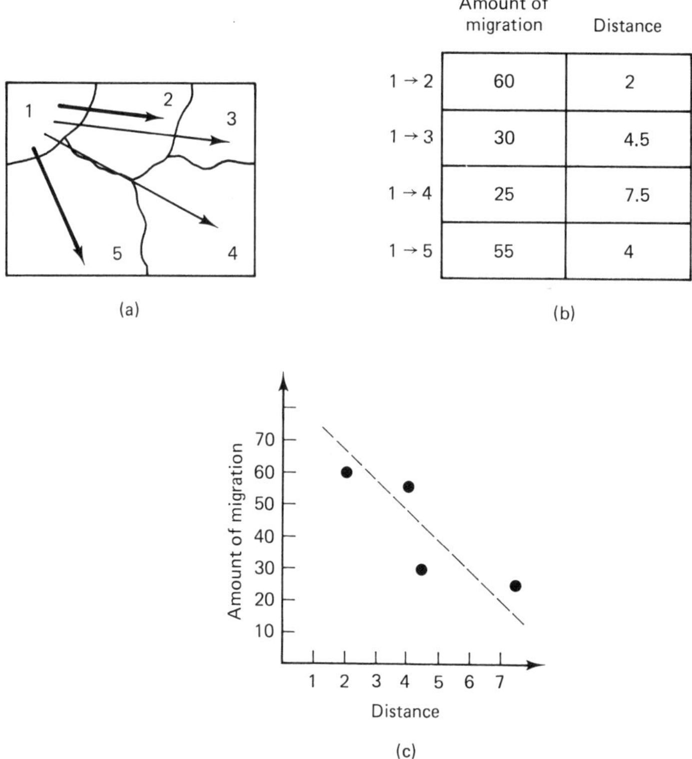

Figure 1.6 (a) Schematic representation of intraurban residential mobility, with (b) the associated data matrix and (c) graph.

balled" through the four points, in order to indicate that there is a generally negative relationship.

The final step is to arrive at some *conclusion* concerning the validity of the original hypothesis. In this instance, although there is some evidence of the hypothesized negative relationship between migration and distance, that relationship is not exceptionally strong, as the points do not all lie on, or close to, the dashed line. If all the points were exactly on the line, the amount of migration between any two neighborhoods could be predicted exactly by merely knowing the distance between them. As it is, however, other variables must obviously be involved. Perhaps the population sizes of the neighborhoods, and their relative income levels, should also be included in the analysis, thus requiring the hypothesis to be reformulated in terms of a multivariate rather than a bivariate equation. A multivariate equation has more than two variables, so the new hypothesis is expressed as follows:

$$Y = f(X_1, X_2, X_3) \tag{1.2}$$

where Y is the amount of migration, X_1 is distance, X_2 is population size, and X_3 is median income. In this equation there are three explanatory variables, so the data matrix expands to four columns. Also, more cases, or neighborhoods, will be needed if any kind of formal statistical analysis is to be undertaken.

This search for the interrelationships between variables often involves the *hypothetico-deductive spiral.* Initial hypotheses are usually found wanting when tested with appropriate data, so scientists repeatedly return to the stage of hypothesis formulation and begin anew the whole process of data collection and data analysis. It is only in this way that hypotheses, and their associated generalizations, become increasingly refined and useful in an explanatory and predictive sense.

Scientific Terms

There are a variety of technical terms that are commonly used in conjunction with the scientific method. A *hypothesis*, which as we have seen plays an important role when identifying relationships between variables, can be formally defined as a statement whose truth or falsity is capable of being asserted. This condition of testability is crucial, as it allows us to evaluate the empirical validity of competing hypotheses.

If a hypothesis is tested and found to be correct, a *scientific law* is established. These laws are of two major types: deterministic and probabilistic. A *deterministic law* can be stated as follows:

$$\text{If A, then } P(B) = 1.0 \tag{1.3}$$

This statement signifies that if event A occurs, the probability of event B occurring is 1.0, or 100 percent, as probabilities run between 0 and 1.0. Alternatively, a *probabilistic law* would take the following form:

$$\text{If A, then } P(B) < 1.0 \tag{1.4}$$

In other words, if event A occurs, the probability of event B occurring is something less than 1.0. This situation entails a probabilistic relationship, because the presence or absence of event B is not completely determined by the presence or absence of event A.

An example will help to make this distinction clearer. Suppose that we imagine a person living in the suburbs who can choose between three possible routes when commuting to work in the central city (Figure 1.7). These routes are labeled A, B, and C. Over a lengthy period of observation, we might note that this person uses route A 33 percent of the time, route B 50 percent of the time, and route C 17 percent of the time. In other words, the probabilities associated with using routes A, B, and C, are

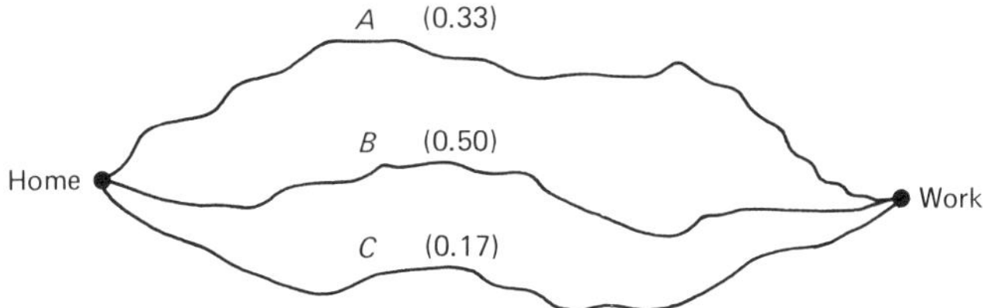

Figure 1.7 Journey to work in probabilistic terms.

0.33, 0.50, and 0.17, respectively. Thus, on any given day, if we predicted that our commuter would be using route *B*, for example, we would have a 50 percent chance of being correct.

These probabilities are also useful in an aggregate context. If there are 100 commuters who need to travel to the central city every day, and we assume that they all have similar behavioral characteristics, we would expect 33 of them to use route *A*. Of course, we cannot say with any certainty which particular 33 persons will be involved, as this will change from day to day. Note that if one of the routes is assigned the value 1.0, it means that a person uses that route to the exclusion of all others, so his or her behavior is completely predictable and thus describable in terms of a deterministic law. If all 100 commuters exhibit the same behavioral pattern, we also have a deterministic relationship at the aggregate level.

Most relationships between variables that have been identified by social scientists are probabilistic. In other words, social scientists deal with generalizations; event *A* is generally related to event *B*, but not in every instance. In contrast, physical scientists have identified some truly deterministic relationships, as exemplified by the statement that pure water freezes at a temperature of 32 degrees Fahrenheit.

When a series of laws are interconnected in some way they create a *theory*, and like the laws on which they are based, theories can be either deterministic or probabilistic. Empirically validated theories represent the culmination of the scientific method, as they integrate previously isolated generalizations into broader systems of knowledge. The hypothetico-deductive spiral is never completed, however, as theories can also serve as vehicles for generating new hypotheses (Amedeo and Golledge, 1975, p. 39).

Models

Many of the "theories" developed by social scientists are more accurately described as *models*, as they consist of a series of interconnected hypotheses, rather than a set of empirically validated laws. A model is often an idealized representation of reality, in order to demonstrate certain of its properties. Such idealized representations are abstractions of reality, and thus omit certain unimportant details. The process of model building, therefore, represents a procedure for making these abstractions (Thomas and Huggett, 1980).

There are three general categories of models: iconic models, analog models, and symbolic models (Taylor, 1977, p. 3). An *iconic model* is one in which reality is transformed primarily in terms of scale. Examples of such models include the scale models of buildings used by architects and the relief models of physical landscapes used by geographers. In both cases the models involve a reduction in scale.

Analog models transform the properties of the real object or event, as well as changing the scale. The most common form of analog model is a map, where elevation is usually represented by brown contour lines, for example. Sometimes physical analogs are used to analyze social systems, as when stream networks are compared with transportation networks.

Finally, *symbolic models* represent the real world in terms of symbols. A mathematical equation is an example of a symbolic model. For example, in the equation depicting the relationship between income and education depicted in Fig. 1.5, the symbol Y was used to represent income and the symbol X was used to represent education. These symbolic models are the most abstract of the three main types of models, and thus the most easily manipulated.

Wherever possible, the models described in this book are expressed in equation form, and then empirically calibrated and tested using appropriate data and statistical techniques (Figure 1.8). For example, we might construct the following multivariate model to explain the distribution of housing values in a city:

$$HV = f(HA, HQ, D) \tag{1.5}$$

where HV is housing value, HA is housing age, HQ is housing quality, and D is distance from the city center. To test this model data might be collected at the census tract level, so housing value, housing age, and housing quality could be taken from the U.S. Census of Population and Housing. The distance from the city center of each census tract can be measured using a map.

For this particular type of model, the most appropriate statistical techniques for testing and calibration are multiple correlation and regression analysis. The multiple correlation coefficient indicates the extent to which the three explanatory, or independent variables account for variations in housing value, while the regression coefficients indicate the relative importance of the individual explanatory variables. A complete test of the model involves comparing its performance across a whole series of cities.

The fully tested and calibrated model can then be used for three major purposes: structural analysis, forecasting, and policy evaluation (Intriligator, 1978, p. 5). *Structural analysis* involves an attempt to understand the model for its own sake, simply in terms of what it tells us about the quantitative relationships between variables. *Forecasting* involves using a mathematical model to predict future values for particular variables, while *policy evaluation* involves using a model to simulate the outcomes of alternative policy formulations. In the latter context, for example, we might be interested in estimating what will happen to the housing values of a given neighborhood if the overall housing age is substantially altered by some kind of urban renewal project.

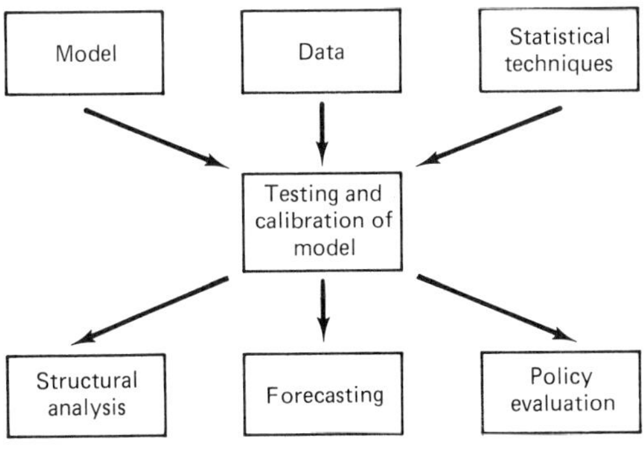

Figure 1.8 Model-building approach. (Based on Michael D. Intriligator, *Economic Models, Techniques, and Applications*, © 1978, p. Reprinted by permission of Prentice-Hall, Inc., Englewood Cliffs, N.J.)

1.4 THE PROCESS OF MODEL BUILDING

Although the construction and testing of mathematical models has been a central theme in much contemporary urban research (Wilson, 1974), the process of model building is comparatively difficult to teach, as it represents a creative endeavor that is in many ways more reflective of the artist than the scientist. The personal perspective that the model builder brings to his or her craft means that there are no hard and fast "rules" of model building. In most situations, however, the model-building process consists of a series of steps. Six such steps, or stages, are common to most models: (1) identifying the problem, (2) constructing a conceptual model, (3) translating this into a symbolic model, (4) making the model operational, (5) testing, and (6) evaluation (Cadwallader, 1978a). These six steps will be illustrated by way of a simple model of consumer behavior.

Problem Identification

The initial step in any kind of model construction is to specify the purpose for which the model is being built. This involves, first, identifying a *scientific problem* and then posing a *question* designed to clarify that problem. For example, considering consumer behavior we might ask: On what basis do consumers choose between alternative supermarkets? This question provides a good starting point for a general investigation, but the problem is not yet posed precisely enough for model-building purposes.

At this juncture, it is often a useful strategy to draw a picture of the problem. In the present context, one way to draw such a picture is to identify the group of consumers in whose behavior we are interested and to note that within a certain radius around them there are a finite number of supermarkets. These supermarkets represent the opportunity set, the boundary of which is defined by the greatest distance consumers are likely to travel in order to buy groceries (Figure 1.9). If five supermarkets lie within the chosen radius, the problem becomes one of analyzing how the consumers choose among these five alternatives. More specifically, the aim is to construct a model that is capable of predicting the proportion of consumers who patronize each supermarket. Accomplishment of this goal suggests that the major variables involved in the decision-making process have been successfully identified.

If we can proceed thus far, the problem has been formulated in sufficiently abstract terms for it to apply to a variety of types of behavior, not simply consumer behavior. For example, it could be used to represent a situation where a group of pro-

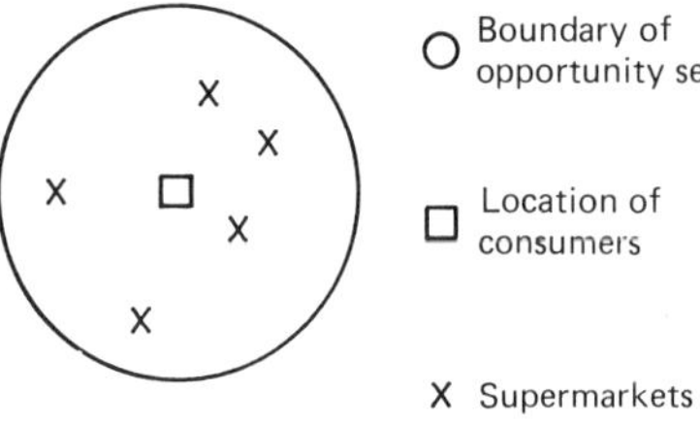

Figure 1.9 Opportunity set. (From M. T. Cadwallader, "The model-building process in introductory college geography: An illustrative example," *Journal of Geography*, 77, 1978, Fig. 1, p. 101.)

spective migrants are faced with choosing among alternative destinations, or where a group of intending vacationers must choose among various recreational areas.

The Conceptual Model

After specifying the purpose for which the model is to be built, the next step is to select the main ingredients of the model. This involves *selecting the most important variables* in the process under investigation. These variables are chosen on the basis of either previous research or intuition. In the case of consumer behavior, conventional wisdom suggests that store attractiveness and distance to the supermarket are two of the major variables.

After the major variables have been chosen, it is often helpful to diagram the proposed model (Figure 1.10). The behavior to be accounted for, in this case the choice of a supermarket, is placed on the right-hand side of the diagram, and the two major variables governing this decision, supermarket attractiveness and distance from the consumers, are placed on the left-hand side. The arrows represent the hypothesized causal connections between the variables.

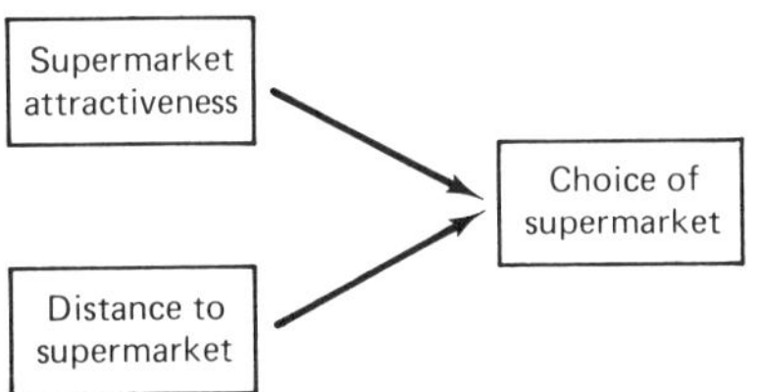

Figure 1.10 Conceptual model. (From M. T. Cadwallader, "The model-building process in introductory college geography: An illustrative example," *Journal of Geography*, 77, 1978, Fig. 2, p. 101).

This particular model is very simple, and there are a variety of ways in which it could be made more elaborate. For example, the possibility of change over time could be represented by a feedback effect between supermarket choice and supermarket attractiveness, as the perceived attractiveness of a supermarket may change after each visit. Similarly, an intervening variable representing the amount of information known about each of the supermarkets might be inserted between the major variables and the choice of a supermarket.

The Symbolic Model

After the proposed model has been understood in this rather general fashion, it should be written in a more precise mathematical form, using symbols rather than words. In this case, the symbolization might be as follows:

$$P_i = f(A_i, D_i) \tag{1.6}$$

where P_i is the proportion of consumers patronizing supermarket i, A_i is the attractiveness of supermarket i, and D_i is the distance to supermarket i. The symbolic model should then be rewritten to reflect the expected relationships between the variables:

$$P_i = \frac{A_i}{D_i} \tag{1.7}$$

where the notation is the same as in equation (1.6). This second formulation indicates that a positive, or direct relationship is postulated between P and A, while a negative, or inverse relationship is postulated between P and D.

At this point, following the precise specification of the model, the *assumptions* that have been incorporated into the model should be explicitly recognized. In this particular instance, two of the most obvious assumptions are first, that the consumers are aware of all five supermarkets, and second, that no consumer will choose a supermarket that lies outside the opportunity set. Assumptions like these simplify the real situation, but this is often a necessary part of model construction. The hope is that these assumptions can be relaxed when more insight has been gained into the process under investigation.

Operationalizing the Model

Once the model has been couched in symbolic terms, it should be tested against reality. In order to do this, however, the model builder must provide empirical values for each of the constituent variables. Generally, there are a number of ways in which any model can be made operational, and the following procedure represents merely one of the many possible ways in which the three variables in the present model might be calibrated.

Supermarket *attractiveness* is measured in terms of four attributes: parking facilities, prices, quality of goods sold, and range of goods sold. Each consumer assesses each store on each of these evaluative dimensions by using a seven-point rating scale ranging from very unsatisfactory to very satisfactory. The resulting scale values for each store are then aggregated, using the median scale values, into an attractiveness matrix (Figure 1.11). Each element in the matrix represents the rating that the corresponding supermarket has been given with respect to one of the four attributes. For example, the value a_{12} is the rating given supermarket B with respect to parking facilities.

Each supermarket's overall attractiveness measure can be derived by simply adding the values in each column. However, such a procedure implies that the four attributes are equally important. If this assumption is thought to be too unrealistic, a *weighting vector*, indicating the relative importance of the attributes, can be obtained by asking the consumers to rank the attributes in order of their importance to them

	Supermarket				
	A	*B*	*C*	*D*	*E*
Parking facilities	a_{11}	a_{12}	a_{13}	a_{14}	a_{15}
Prices	a_{21}	a_{22}	a_{23}	a_{24}	a_{25}
Quality of goods	a_{31}	a_{32}	a_{33}	a_{34}	a_{35}
Range of goods	a_{41}	a_{42}	a_{43}	a_{44}	a_{45}

Figure 1.11 Attractiveness matrix. (From M. T. Cadwallader, "The model-building process in introductory college geography: An illustrative example," *Journal of Geography*, 77, 1978, Fig. 3, p. 101.)

when selecting a supermarket. Each time an attribute is ranked first it is given four points, each time it is ranked second it is given three points, and so on. The sum of the points associated with each attribute comprises the weighting vector. If the attractiveness matrix is premultiplied by this weighting vector, the resulting vector describes the relative attractiveness of each supermarket, taking into account the varying importance of the four attributes. This particular form of weighting vector assumes that the intervals between the ranks are equal. If this assumption is felt to be too simplistic, however, a more sophisticated weighting procedure could be devised.

The *distance* variable can be measured in a variety of ways, including cost, time, or mileage distance. It might also be measured in terms of cognitive distance, which represents how far people think the distance is. In this case, each consumer is asked to estimate the distance in miles to each supermarket, and then the average estimate for each supermarket is computed.

Finally, the *actual behavioral patterns* of the consumers can be determined by simply asking them where they usually do their grocery shopping and then standardizing these values to reveal the proportion of consumers who normally patronize each of the five supermarkets. It is inadvisable to ask the subject which supermarket they used on their most recent shopping expedition because that may represent only a minor fluctuation in their overall shopping strategy.

Testing

When each variable in the model has been measured, all that remains is to determine how closely the predicted proportion of consumers patronizing each supermarket approximates the actual proportion. In this case, the predicted proportions have been derived by dividing the attractiveness value by the distance value for each supermarket and then standardizing so that the values add to 1. Normally, such a comparison between the observed and the predicted involves a statistical test of some kind, and a wide variety of such tests are currently available. It is also interesting to test how well the model works in comparison with others that have been designed for the same purpose, and in the present instance the gravity model, which is discussed later in the book, would provide a suitable point of reference.

If the model does not perform as well as expected, it can usually be traced to one or more of three major *sources of error*. First, it might be due to sampling error, which would occur if the subjects chosen for the study were not representative of the general population. In this event the model should be retested by selecting further samples. A second source of error is measurement error, which occurs when the variables in the model have not been accurately calibrated. In the present example, the use of seven-point scales to measure supermarket attractiveness might be inappropriate, and the investigator would need to experiment with different ways of measuring supermarket attractiveness. Finally, the model might not perform satisfactorily because of specification error. This type of error occurs when the variables themselves, or their hypothesized relationships, are incorrectly specified. For example, in the present model some significant variable, such as the influence of advertising, might have been inadvertently omitted from the analysis.

Evaluation

Throughout this book the model-building approach to understanding urban processes and phenomena is emphasized. Although a rather catholic view of models is maintained, most of the models are presented in symbolic, or equation form. These analytical models are only selective approximations of reality, in that incidental detail is omitted in order to generalize certain fundamental relationships. They are also representative of a structured, or pattern-seeking viewpoint (Symanski and Agnew, 1981) that emphasizes recurrent connections and interrelationships.

Such analytical models can serve a variety of functions (Haggett and Chorley, 1967). First, they are constructional in that they form stepping stones to the development of theory, in a systematic progression of understanding. Second, models, by explicating the interrelationships between exogenous and endogenous variables, allow one to predict future values of the endogenous variables. Third, models perform an organizational function with respect to data acquisition, in that they provide a framework for defining, collecting, and ordering information. Fourth, models can be used to generate hypotheses that both substantiate and extend the original theoretical structure. Finally, as it is hoped this book will exemplify, models can be used as pedagogical devices, in that they allow complex phenomena to be visualized and understood more easily.

It is nevertheless true, however, that the model-building approach also entails certain disadvantages. In particular, despite the recent advances involving dynamic models (Clarke and Wilson, 1983; Wilson, 1981), models can present an overly simplified view of reality which leads to unsuccessful predictions. Interestingly enough, however, Haggett (1978) suggests that increasing model complexity often leads to diminishing returns in terms of predictive capability or model fidelity, the ability to replicate faithfully a real-world system (Figure 1.12). It is also noteworthy, in this context, that most models are merely calibrated rather than tested. Calibration is usually achieved by searching for parameter values that optimize the goodness of fit between the model's predictions and observed behavior. This procedure is obviously rather different from validating the model, so two sets of data are required, one for calibration and the other for testing (Batty, 1978).

More important, in addition to these somewhat technical problems, analytical models fail to take into account certain influential determinants of urban structure. First, the effect of the overall political economy on urban patterns is very difficult to

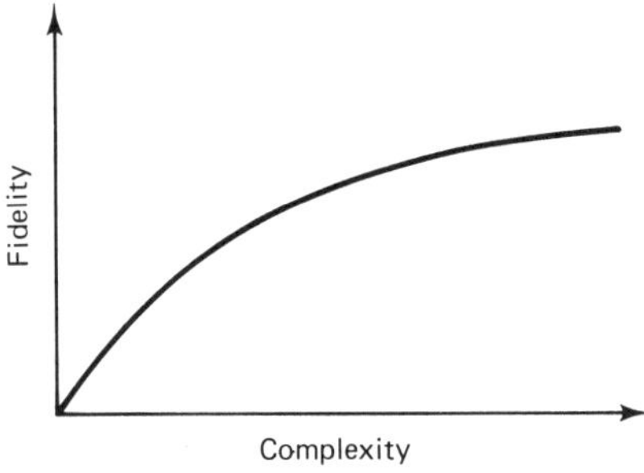

Figure 1.12 Trade-off between complexity and fidelity in model-building. (From P. Haggett, "Spatial forecasting—a view from the touchline," in R. L. Martin, N. J. Thrift, and R. J. Bennett, Eds., *Towards the Dynamic Analysis of Spatial Systems*, Pion, London, 1978, Fig. 1, p. 210.)

capture in any kind of formal model. In particular, the residential morphology of individual American cities is partly a reflection of the class system within capitalist society and the associated mechanism by which housing is assigned a value (Johnston, 1982). Second, the model-building approach can only pay lip service to the importance of different institutional structures and their associated constraints. For example, Canadian and U.S. cities can be partly distinguished on the basis of their institutional structures, which have led to marked variations in patterns of investment and disinvestment (Mercer, 1979). Similarly, cross-cultural comparisons are only rather poorly developed within the model-building paradigm (Griffin and Ford, 1980). Finally, analytical methods seldom incorporate the historical context of urban development, thus failing to appreciate the role of changing patterns of land ownership, legislation, and government or institutional policy (Gordon, 1981).

Despite these obvious shortcomings, however, models perform the invaluable task of helping us to formalize our knowledge of urban areas, and throughout the present text an effort has been made to supplement the insights obtained from models with the other, more informal insights that can be derived from considering the historical and institutional contexts. In this respect, a pluralistic view of urban geography is encouraged (see Section 1.2), in which a variety of approaches are acceptable (Herbert, 1979a).

1.5 PROBLEMS OF URBAN DEFINITION

The subject matter of this book is not easily defined, as it is sometimes difficult to distinguish between rural and urban settlements. This difficulty is reflected by the wide variation in population sizes used by different countries in order to categorize urban as opposed to rural settlements. In Sweden and Denmark, for example, settlements of only 200 people are counted as urban, whereas in Japan settlements have to contain at least 30,000 people before they are designated as urban. These different definitions make it difficult to compare levels of urbanization across countries.

Perhaps the most meaningful approach for discussing the difference between urban and rural settlements is to think of them being arranged along a *continuum*, going from rural at one end to urban at the other. The settlement types along this continuum can be sequentially categorized as hamlets, villages, towns, cities, and metropolitan areas. At the rural end of this continuum, settlements such as hamlets are characterized by relatively low-density living and agrarian-related occupations, whereas settlements at the other end of the continuum, such as metropolitan areas, are characterized by relatively high-density living, and non-agrarian-related occupations.

Once it has been decided which settlements are urban, there still remains the problem of defining the *spatial extent* of those settlements. How far east does Los Angeles extend, for example? In most cases the corporate boundary, or legal definition of a city, does not represent the true extent of that city. This problem has led to the identification of *underbounded cities*, where the legal city lies inside the real, or physical city, and *overbounded cities*, where the reverse is true.

Most cities in the United States are of the underbounded variety, as the corporate, or central city, is usually surrounded by a ring of suburbs. These suburbs use the facilities of the corporate city, such as museums and schools, but are not within the jurisdiction of that city. As one can imagine, this situation leads to severe problems in terms of governmental fragmentation and fiscal imbalance, as it is exceedingly difficult to coordinate the wide variety of local governments that represent the interests of individual communities.

Local Government Fragmentation

The primary mechanism responsible for the evolution of underbounded cities is the *suburbanization process*, which dates back to the years immediately following World War II. The move to the suburbs, of both people and jobs, was precipitated by a variety of factors, including transportation improvements and a growing dissatisfaction with the quality of life in central cities. The housing boom of the late 1940s, fueled partly by cheap government loans, helped reinforce this decentralization process.

As the suburbs grew in population, and the volume of industrial and commercial activity intensified, a whole range of government services were required. These services usually came to be supplied by local authorities rather than by the corporate city, and local government units proliferated at a rapid pace. For example, by 1972 the Chicago Standard Metropolitan Statistical Area had a total of 1172 local government units.

This multiplicity of government units entails a wide variety of individual jurisdictons. Besides the elected governments of the various municipalities and counties, there are a whole range of special districts. These special districts are responsible for such services as fire protection, police protection, education, health facilities, and libraries, and they often overlap both each other and the underlying political districts.

A variety of problems are created by these underbounded cities and their associated plethora of local governments, perhaps the most critical of which is the problem of *fiscal imbalance*. In most cities the tax base of the central city has been steadily eroding in real terms as people and industry have moved out to the suburbs. Coincidental with these rapidly falling revenues is the equally rapid rise in central city expenditures. The old and dilapidated building stock of these areas entails increased costs for fire protection, the higher crime rates require greater police protection, and the general poverty and high rates of unemployment induce increased demand for social services. In sum, there is a conspicuous disparity between the revenue resources and expenditure needs of the different political units within large cities. Central cities tend to have the greatest disparity between revenues and expenditures, especially when compared to the generally high revenue–expenditure ratios characteristic of most suburban municipalities.

A second major problem arising from the fragmented pattern of local government is that often there are many districts administering *overlapping programs* of social services. The special districts set up to provide such services as water, gas, hospitals, libraries, and parks, are generally unifunctional, and it is very difficult to coordinate their individual policies and interests. As a result, many of the larger issues in urban areas, such as land use planning and conservation, are neglected due to the inability to coordinate policy decisions made at the local level by very specialized administrative boards. It should be noted, however, that recent literature has suggested that fragmentation is not necessarily inefficient (Cox and Nartowicz, 1980).

Possible Solutions

Solutions to these twin problems of fiscal imbalance and government fragmentation are not readily forthcoming, but responsible efforts have begun to be made. Central cities receive increasing amounts in grant money from federal, state, and provincial governments, as part of an overall policy of *revenue sharing*. Local governments are also attempting to develop additional *sources of revenue*. The present system of prop-

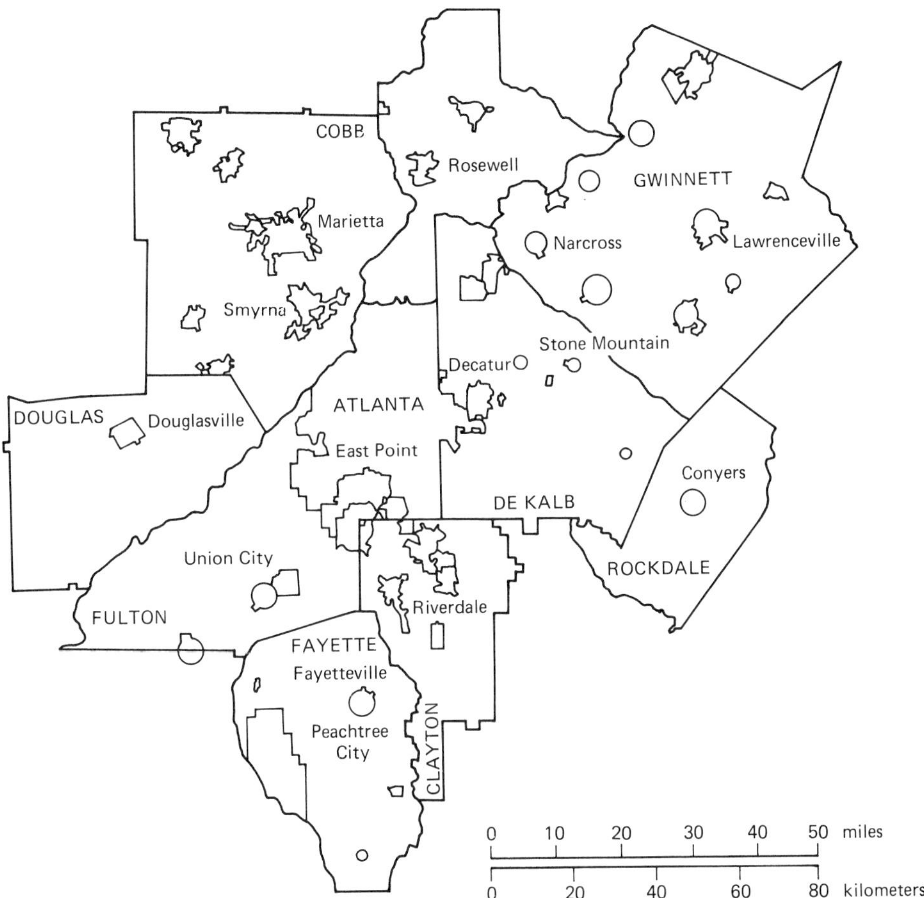

Figure 1.13 Atlanta region political boundaries. (From R. D. Honey, "Metropolitan governance," in J. S. Adams, Ed., *Urban Policymaking and Metropolitan Dynamics: A Comparative Geographical Analysis*, Ballinger, Cambridge, Mass., 1976, Fig. 11.6, p. 447.)

erty taxation, for example, includes a provision for the value of improvements, which tends to discourage reinvestment in inner cities, thus contributing to the declining tax base. An alternative system of taxation might involve primarily taxing the value of the land. Such a system would force the owners of high-valued central-city land with deteriorated property to either sell or to improve the rent-producing potential of their property by making appropriate improvements.

Solutions to the coordination problems generated by the multiplicity of special districts have been sought by administrative reform involving various types of *government consolidation*. In Atlanta, for example, the Atlanta Regional Commission coordinates planning and special-purpose district activity in the area. The Commission expanded from five to seven counties in 1973 (Figure 1.13) and currently acts as a kind of umbrella government, overseeing the operation of local governments within the area, acting as the integrated grant administrator, and generally trying to achieve what is best for the whole region (Honey, 1976). Although the Commission lacks zoning powers of its own, it is responsible for coordinating the region's overall zoning policy and has been successful in initiating the development of a rapid transit system, something which the individual government units lacked the jurisdiction to build.

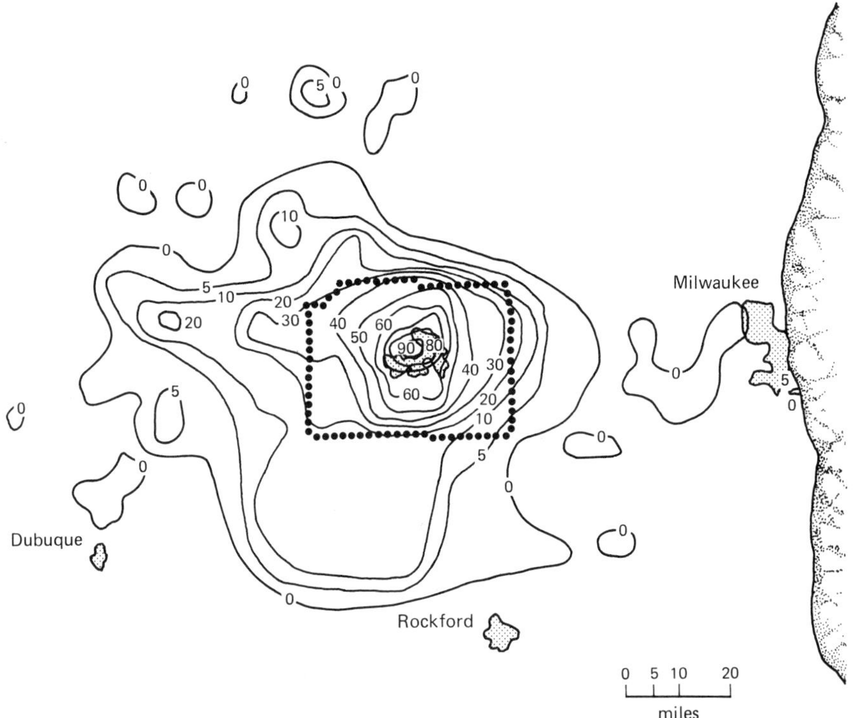

Figure 1.14 Commuting to the central city of Madison, Wisconsin. (Reprinted from Berry and Gillard's *The Changing Shape of Metropolitan America: Commuting Patterns, Urban Fields, and Decentralization Processes: 1960–1970*, Copyright 1977, Ballinger Publishing Company.

Some metropolitan areas have attempted to consolidate by merging city and county governments. In those cases where *city–county consolidation* has been approved, however, the unification does not usually extend beyond the core county. Such city–county consolidation is similar to the concept of a federation, where a two- or three-tiered local government system is developed in those situations where the metropolitan region spreads over a number of counties as well as municipalities.

It has also been suggested that *daily commuting patterns* might provide the basis for local government consolidation. This suggestion is attractive in the sense that those people who commute to the central city also use the services of the central city, and therefore should be part of the tax base supporting those services. In practice, however, we are still faced with the overriding problem of where to actually draw the boundary. In the case of Madison, Wisconsin, for example, a small percentage of commuters travel to the corporate city from as far away as Milwaukee, while many of the residents of Dane County do not use Madison on a daily basis (Figure 1.14).

In general, Honey (1976) suggests a series of ways in which both the federal and state governments could strengthen the role of government at the metropolitan level. First, he contends that the federal government should (1) continue and augment metropolitan review of local government applications for federal funds; (2) provide revenue sharing for the metropolitan area; (3) assist in the creation and development of more powerful regional agencies in multistate metropolitan areas; and (4) institute a national land use planning policy that prevents the coalescence of individual metropolitan areas.

Second, he suggests that, among other things, state governments should (1) provide financial assistance for metropolitan governments; (2) make local government participation in regional planning compulsory; (3) institute procedures to allow for the orderly amalgamation, incorporation, and annexation of urban areas; and (4) cooperate in the organization and planning of multistate metropolitan areas.

2

Patterns of Land Use and Land Value

2.1 AGRICULTURAL LAND USE THEORY

The theoretical framework for explaining the distribution of land use and land value in urban areas is derived from the pioneering work of Johann Heinrich Von Thünen in agricultural land economics (Hall, 1966). Von Thünen was a German farmer in the early nineteenth century, and many of his ideas were generated by this practical experience and the associated cost accounting on his estate. He was concerned primarily with analyzing the patterns of land use and land value in agricultural areas, and the basic principle underlying his theory, or model, was the concept of economic rent, which later came to be known as location rent. In the present chapter we first outline Von Thünen's agricultural model, and then apply the same kind of reasoning to urban areas. After discussing the effects of relaxing the simplifying assumptions, and various other modifications, we conclude the chapter by considering the related problem of urban sprawl.

Assumptions

Like many economic theories, Von Thünen's agricultural land use theory is based on a set of simplifying assumptions. There are four major assumptions (Amedeo and Golledge, 1975, p. 299). First, it is assumed that there is an agricultural area isolated from all other such areas; called the *isolated state*. Within this area there is a single city, or market, which is centrally located. This city is the only market for all surplus agricultural products produced within the region, and no products are imported from outside the region. The market price for a given product, or commodity, is the same for all farmers.

Second, it is assumed that this isolated state occupies a *uniform plain* that is completely homogeneous with respect to the physical environment. Topography, soil fertility, rainfall, and the like, are assumed to be the same everywhere. As a result, the yield per unit area for any particular crop, and the production costs associated with that crop, are the same for all farmers throughout the region.

Third, it is assumed that transportation is equally available in all directions from the central city, and that *transportation costs* are directly proportional to distance. That is, there is a positive, linear relationship between transportation costs and distance from the market, and the slope of the line is invariant across different directions of travel. Furthermore, transportation costs are a constant for any given agricultural product, although they vary from product to product and are borne by the farmer.

Finally, it is assumed that all farmers wish to *maximize profits*, and are blessed with complete information and perfect decision-making abilities. Also, they are assumed to be capable of adjusting their agricultural operations in response to changing economic conditions. This concept of profit maximization and complete information is in stark contrast to the more behaviorally oriented satisficing concept. According to this latter conceptualization, men and women are assumed to be satisfied with less than optimal profits, and their decision-making ability is constrained by a lack of complete and accurate information.

Location Rent

Given these simplifying assumptions, the major mechanism behind the distribution of land use within the isolated state is represented by the concept of location, or economic, rent. *Location rent* is the total revenue received by a farmer for a particular product on a particular parcel of land, minus the production and transportation costs associated with that same product and parcel of land. Location rent reflects, therefore, the economic utility of a particular site for a particular product. Note that the term "rent," as used in this context, does not correspond to its more popular usage as contract rent, which is the actual payment tenants make to others for the use of their land or property.

The location rent associated with any plot of land, for any particular crop or commodity, is calculated as follows:

$$LR = Y(p - c) - Ytd \tag{2.1}$$

where LR is the location rent per unit of land, Y is the yield per unit of land, p is the market price per unit of commodity, c is the production cost per unit of commodity, t is the transportation rate per unit of commodity per unit of distance, and d is distance from the market.

This equation contains only two variables, location rent and distance from the market. All the other terms are constants that correspond to the initial simplifying assumptions. Because of the assumption of a homogeneous physical environment, the yield per unit of land and the production cost per unit of commodity will be the same everywhere. The assumption of a single market, and a single price for each

TABLE 2.1 DIFFERENCES IN THE LOCATION RENT FOR WHEAT AT VARIOUS DISTANCES FROM THE MARKET

Distance (miles)	0	10	20	30	40
Location rent (dollars)	400	300	200	100	0

commodity, ensures that the market price per unit of commodity is a constant, and finally, the transportation cost is assumed to be a constant function of distance.

Imagine that we are interested in the location rent associated with a particular crop, say wheat, at a series of different distances from the market. Let the constants in the equation take the following values; Y is 100 bushels per acre; p is \$10 per bushel, c is \$6 per bushel, and t is 10 cents per mile per bushel. These values are then substituted into the location rent equation in order to determine the location rent at various distances from the market (Table 2.1). The relationship between location rent and distance (Figure 2.1) represents a *marginal rent curve*, as it reflects, for any given distance from the market, the rent that would accrue to an infinitesimal unit of land (Lloyd and Dicken, 1972, p. 17). In the present example, wheat will not be cultivated beyond a distance of 40 miles, as at that distance the transportation costs equal the net revenue resulting from the difference between market price and production costs.

Bid-Rent Curves

The location rent associated with a particular parcel of land represents a surplus to the farmer as long as the production costs include a payment for the farmer's labor and skills. This surplus can be paid to the landowner for the use of the land, and the farmer can afford to bid the full amount of the surplus and still remain in business in the long run. In this sense, the line expressing the relationship between location rent

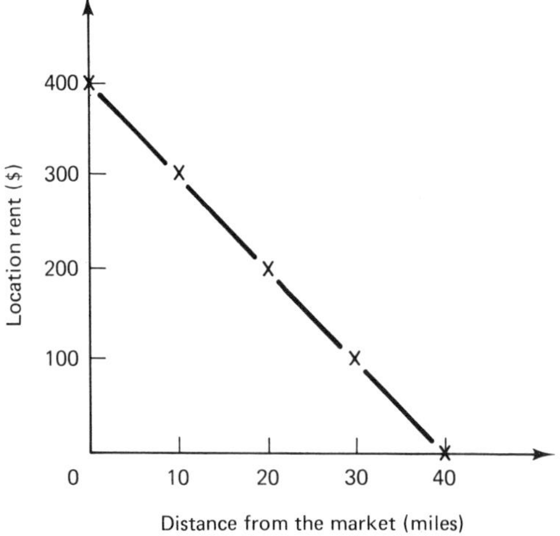

Figure 2.1 Relationship between location rent and distance from the market.

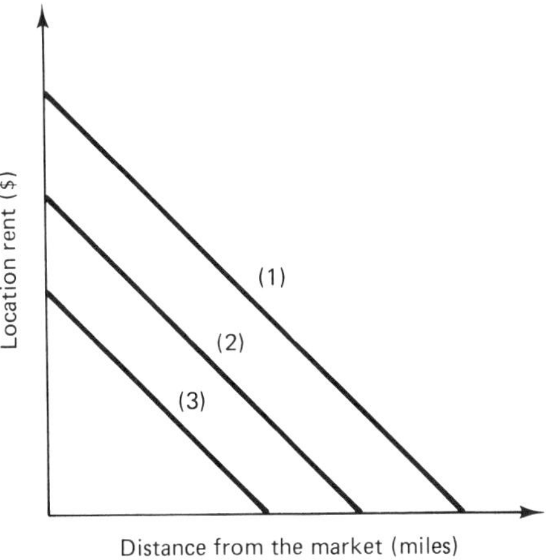

Figure 2.2 Family of bid-rent curves associated with high (1), medium (2), and low (3) market prices for wheat.

and distance can also be looked upon as a *bid-rent curve* (Figure 2.1). The farmer is prepared to bid quite high amounts for the land right next to the market, as that land generates a large surplus, but he or she is prepared to bid far less for land farther away, as that land generates a far smaller surplus.

If the market price for wheat were to decrease for some reason, a new bid-rent curve would come into operation, with lower values than the previous one, as the location rent would be less everywhere. In other words, a whole series, or family, of bid-rent curves can be conceived of, with each one being related to a different market price for wheat (Figure 2.2). These curves are examples of *indifference curves*, as the farmer is indifferent with respect to the various possibe locations on each particular curve, because his or her profits will be exactly the same at any point along the line.

We can now consider the situation where there are a number of competing crops, or land uses, such as wheat, barley, and oats. Assume that the constants associated with these three types of land use, for substitution in the location rent equation, are as shown in Table 2.2. For the sake of simplicity, the yield for all three crops has been made exactly the same, although this condition is not necessary for the operation of the model. Given these values, the location rent for each crop can be determined for different distances from the market. For example, the location rent for barley at 10 miles from the market can be calculated by making the following

TABLE 2.2 HYPOTHETICAL YIELDS, MARKET PRICES, PRODUCTION COSTS, AND TRANSPORTATION RATES FOR THREE DIFFERENT CROPS

	Yield (bushels per acre)	Market price (dollars per bushel)	Production cost (dollars per bushel)	Transportation rate (dollars per mile, per bushel)
Wheat	100	10	5	0.20
Barley	100	8	4	0.08
Oats	100	6	3	0.02

TABLE 2.3 LOCATION RENTS FOR WHEAT, BARLEY, AND OATS AT DIFFERENT DISTANCES FROM THE MARKET, BASED ON THE HYPOTHETICAL DATA IN TABLE 2.2

	Distance (miles)		
	0	10	20
Wheat	$500	$300	$100
Barley	400	320	240
Oats	300	280	260

substitutions in the location rent equation:

$$LR = 100(8 - 4) - 100(0.08)(10) \tag{2.2}$$

The location rent is $320, and this substitution procedure can be undertaken for all three crops, at distances of 0, 10, and 20 miles from the market (Table 2.3).

The bid-rent curves for the three land uses are generated by plotting the relationships between location rent and distance (Figure 2.3). Wheat has the steepest bid-rent curve because, in this hypothetical example, the transportation costs associated with wheat are the highest. Oats are the least sensitive of the three crops to transportation costs, so they have the gentlest bid-rent curve.

Assuming that each plot of land is used by the highest bidder, the land closest to the market will be used for wheat, the intermediate land will be used for barley, and the land farthest from the market will be used for oats (Figure 2.4). More precisely, the land between the market and distance A, which represents the intersection of the wheat and barley bid-rent curves, will be devoted to wheat, while the land

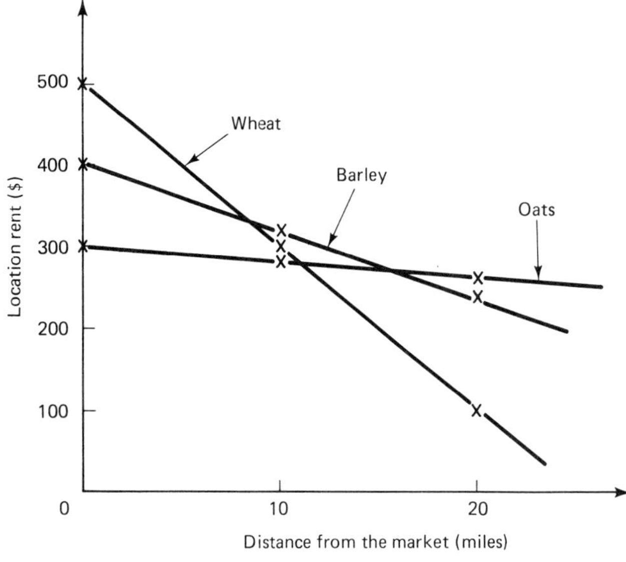

Figure 2.3 Bid-rent curves for wheat, barley, and oats, based on the hypothetical data in Table 2.2.

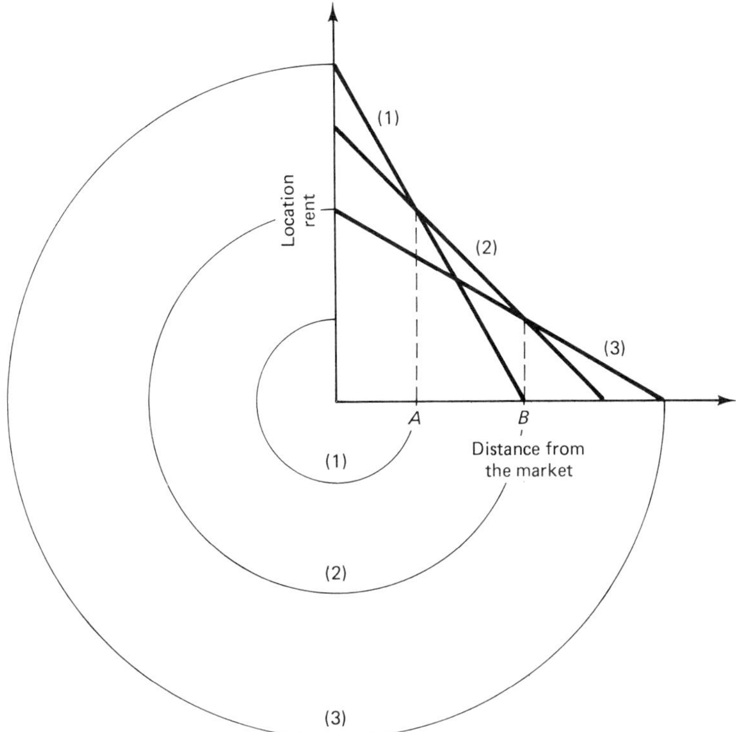

Figure 2.4 Concentric land use zones generated by the bid-rent curves for wheat (1), barley (2), and oats (3). Distances A and B represent the intersections of pairs of bid-rent curves.

between distances A and B will be used for barley, and the land beyond B as far as distance C, will be used for oats. The resulting land use pattern can be expressed diagrammatically by swinging the graph around on its vertical axis and letting the distances A, B, and C trace out a series of three concentric land use zones.

It is instructive at this point to determine how the bid-rent curves will change if the constants in the location rent equation are altered in some way. For example, what if, due perhaps to some kind of government intervention, the market price for wheat rose from \$10 per bushel to \$11 per bushel? The location rent for wheat would increase to \$600 right next to the market, \$400 at a distance of 10 miles, and \$200 at a distance of 20 miles. The new bid-rent curve would be to the right of its previous position, and the land use pattern would adjust accordingly (Figure 2.5). In particular, the amount of land devoted to wheat production would increase at the expense of that devoted to barley.

Also, in this context, we might ask what would happen if the transportation cost associated with wheat is increased from 20 to 25 cents per mile, per bushel. The location rent for wheat would then be \$500 right next to the market, \$250 at a distance of 10 miles, and \$0 at a distance of 20 miles. In other words, the bid-rent

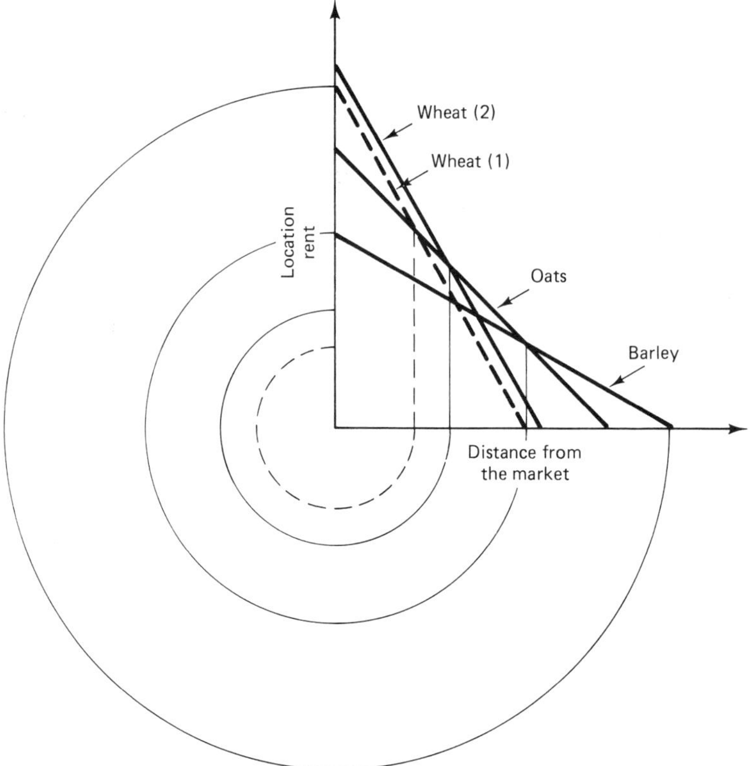

Figure 2.5 Land use pattern resulting from an increase in the market price of wheat. Wheat (1) represents the bid-rent curve for wheat before the price increase, and wheat (2) represents the bid-rent curve for wheat after the price increase.

curve would move to the left of its former position and have a steeper slope. (Figure 2.6). This leftward shift of the bid-rent curve entails a corresponding decrease in the amount of land devoted to wheat, and an increase in that devoted to barley. Note that, unlike changing the market price, the effect of changing transportation costs varies with distance from the market. Obviously, the farmers close to the market will be affected very little, while those farther away will be affected quite substantially. It is because of this varying sensitivity to changes in transportation costs that the new bid-rent curve is not parallel to the previous one.

Relaxing the Assumptions

Having analyzed the effect of changing the values of some of the constants, we can also determine what will happen if those constants are allowed to become variables. In other words, what happens if the simplifying assumptions on which the preceding analysis is based are relaxed? First, it was assumed that there is a *single market* at which all surplus agricultural products are sold. If a second market is introduced,

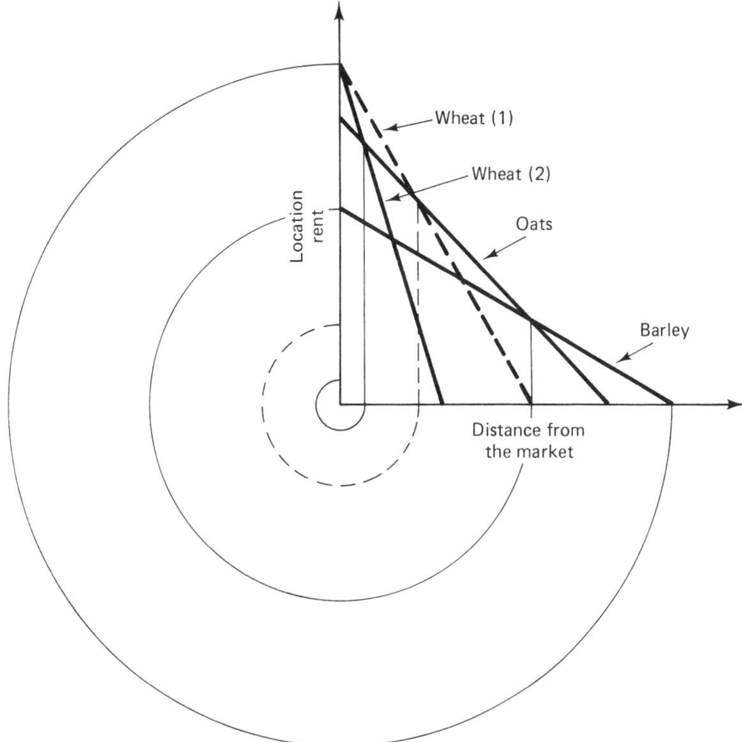

Figure 2.6 Land use pattern resulting from an increase in the transportation costs associated with wheat. Wheat (1) represents the bid-rent curve for wheat before the increase in transportation costs, and wheat (2) represents the bid-rent curve for wheat after the increase in transportation costs.

the land use pattern will conform to a series of intersecting zones (Figure 2.7). Some of the land previously devoted to crop number 4 is now devoted to crop number 3, as the higher transportation costs associated with the latter crop are offset by the fact that it can be sold at the new market.

Second, it was assumed that the agricultural area under discussion occupies a *uniform plain* which is homogeneous with respect to the physical environment, and thus contains no internal variation in terms of such attributes as soil fertility. If this assumption is relaxed, the bid-rent curve associated with any particular crop is unlikely to decline as a simple, linear function of distance from the market (Figure 2.8). Those areas containing fertile soils will produce a higher yield per unit area, and thus generate higher location rents. On the other hand, those areas characterized by infertile soils will produce lower yields per unit area, or the yields will have to be increased by the use of fertilizers, and thus involve an increase in production costs. In either situation, the location rent is lower than that in the fertile areas, and is reflected by a trough in the bid-rent curve. Of course, soil fertility

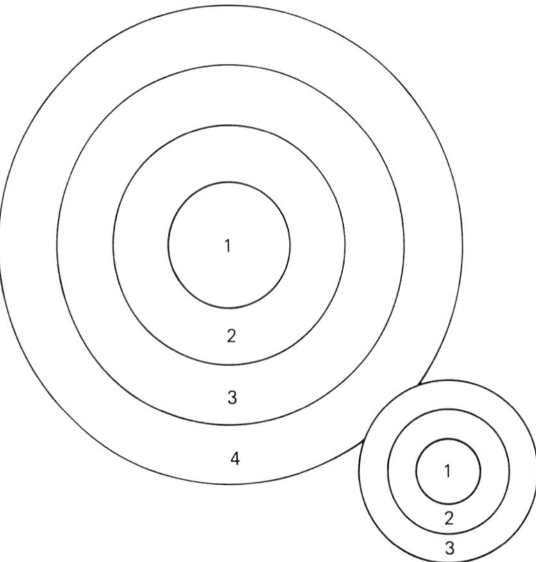

Figure 2.7 Effect on the land use pattern of competing markets.

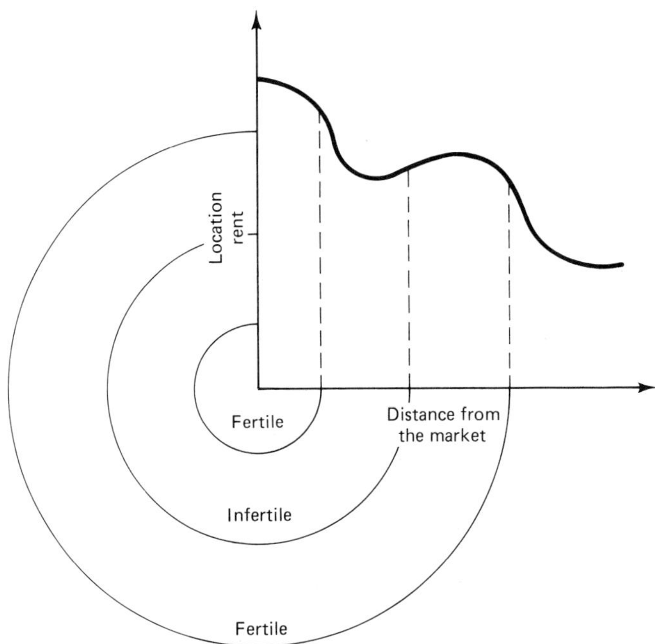

Figure 2.8 Relationship between bid-rent curves and soil fertility.

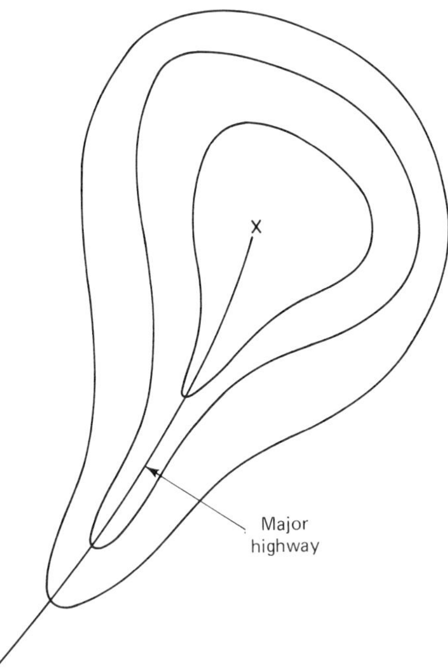

Figure 2.9 Effect of varying transportation costs in different directions from the market.

is not usually a simple function of distance from the market, so variations in soil fertility tend to create a fragmented type of land use pattern.

Third, it was assumed that *transportation costs* are directly proportional to distance, and that travel is equally easy in all directions from the market. In reality, however, transportation costs vary in response to such factors as the availability of roads or railways, and the characteristics of the physical landscape. The bid-rent curves will be less steep in the direction of cheaper travel, meaning that the land use zones are no longer concentric circles, but are elongated in the direction of such features as major highways (Figure 2.9).

Finally, if the assumption of *profit maximization* is relaxed, the agricultural landscape will reflect a variety of irrational economic behavior. Farmers will not necessarily know which crop is the most profitable, and even if they do, they might not choose to grow that particular crop due to some kind of personal preference. Such idiosyncratic behavior tends to produce a highly segmented land use pattern.

In sum, the overall impact of relaxing the various simplifying assumptions is to create a land use pattern that is far more complex, and thus closer to reality, than the concentric land use zones generated by the concept of location rent. This difference between the model and reality, however, does not necessarily deny the validity of Von Thünen's argument. Beneath the apparent confusion of the agricultural landscape, the principle of location rent may well be in operation. However, the spatial pattern associated with this economic concept varies from place to place due to the great variety of physical and socioeconomic environments.

Empirical Testing

Any empirical test of Von Thünen's model of land use distribution is rather problematical, as there is no region on earth where the simplifying assumptions are completely met. One can only look for signs of concentric land use zones, rather than conclusive proof. In this context, the distribution of land use around the Sicilian village of Canicatti seems to be based on accessibility considerations (Chisholm, 1979, p. 49).

Canicatti is a settlement of approximately 30,000 inhabitants, located 18 miles from the nearest settlement of similar size. The percentage of land devoted to different commodities varies with distance from Canicatti (Table 2.4). In particular, the production of vines is concentrated within the inner zone, between 0 and 4 kilometers, olives are more concentrated in the intermediate zone, between 2 and 5 kilometers, while unirrigated arable farming is especially prevalent in the area beyond 5 kilometers.

The rationale behind this land use sorting, and the resultant land use zones, seems to be related to the labor input associated with the different types of crops. This labor input can be measured by the average number of person-days per hectare expended on each crop. Values of 90, 45, and 35, for vines, olives, and unirrigated arable farming, respectively, strongly suggest that the crops with the highest transportation costs are located closest to the village. Note that transportation costs can be thought of either in terms of transporting the crop to market, or in terms of getting labor to the crop, as is the case here.

Actually, the relationship between labor input and distance is probably even greater than that indicated by Table 2.4, for two reasons. First, the data are based on the assumption that labor input is a constant for each crop, although the labor

TABLE 2.4 PERCENTAGE OF LAND AREA IN VARIOUS USES, AND ANNUAL LABOR REQUIREMENTS PER HECTARE, FOR CANICATTI, SICILY

Distance from Canicatti (km)	Percentage of land area:		
	In vines	In olives	Unirrigated arable
0–1	15.8	—	19.7
1–2	18.0	8.4	15.9
2–3	2.3	14.4	23.6
3–4	13.3	0.6	18.1
4–5	5.1	2.4	43.4
5–6	6.3	1.6	64.1
6–7	3.3	—	68.7
7–8	4.0	—	62.4
Average number of person-days per hectare	90	45	35

Source: M. Chisholm, *Rural Settlement and Land Use: An Essay in Location*, 3rd ed., Hutchinson, London, 1979, Table 8, p. 50.

input, within any one crop type, probably decreases with increasing distance. Second, the unirrigated arable land is left fallow more frequently at distances farther from the market, which would also be reflected by less labor input.

2.2 URBAN LAND USE AND LAND VALUE THEORY

The ideas of Von Thünen have been formally applied in the urban context by William Alonso (1964b). Like Von Thünen, Alonso based his analysis on the concept of economic, or location rent, and generated a series of land use zones from the intersections of different bid-rent curves. Also like Von Thünen, however, Alonso began his theoretical analysis by postulating a set of simplifying assumptions.

Assumptions

For the most part, the assumptions associated with urban land use theory parallel those of agricultural land use theory. First, it is assumed that the city has *one center*, or central business district. All employment opportunities are located within the central business district, and the buying and selling of goods also takes place at the city center. These last two points have the same effect as assuming a single market for all goods in the case of agricultural products.

Second, it is assumed that the city is located on a *flat, featureless plain*, which is similar to the assumption concerning a homogeneous physical environment in the agricultural case. No sites within the city have particular advantages, or disadvantages, with respect to such attributes as the underlying geology, or an attractive view.

Third, it is assumed, as in the agricultural context, that *transportation costs* are linearly related to distance. More specifically, transportation costs increase with increasing distance from the city center, and the rate of that increase is the same in all directions. In this way the central business district is the most accessible location in the city, and accessibility decreases as one moves away from that location.

Finally, it is also assumed that each plot of land is sold to the *highest bidder*. This assumption implies that all land users have equal access to the land market, so there are no monopoly situations in terms of either buyers or sellers. Furthermore, there is assumed to be no intervention in the market economy on the part of government planning agencies, and no restrictions due to legislation associated with land use zoning or environmental pollution standards.

Bid-Rent Curves

Given these simplifying assumptions, the urban land market operates in a similar fashion to its agricultural counterpart. Those uses that have the greatest to gain by locating on a particular plot of land will be able to bid highest for the use of that land. Thus each plot of land is sold to the *highest and best use:* highest in the sense of being the highest bidder, and best in the sense of being the type of land use that is best able to take economic advantage of that particular plot. The term "best," in this context, is used in a purely economic rather than a social sense.

The bid-rent curves, and associated land use pattern, can be analyzed in terms of three major types of urban land use: retailing, industrial, and residential (Figure 2.10). *Retailing* has the steepest bid-rent curve, as it is the most sensitive to accessibility considerations. The importance of high turnover rates makes a central location especially attractive, and the location rent declines with increasing distance from the central business district in response to decreasing accessibility and potential profits. As in the agricultural context, the bid-rent curve can be thought of as an indifference curve. Individual retailers are indifferent with respect to their location along the line, as their profits will be the same everywhere. Toward the center of the city, where potential profits are high, they can afford to bid a great deal for the use of the land, whereas toward the edge of the city, where potential profits are much less, they can only afford to bid relatively little.

The bid-rent curve for *industry* also decreases with increasing distance from the city center, but at a slower rate than that for retailing. It is argued that industry is less susceptible to accessibility considerations than retailing, because many industrial products are sold outside the city, thus reducing the relative importance

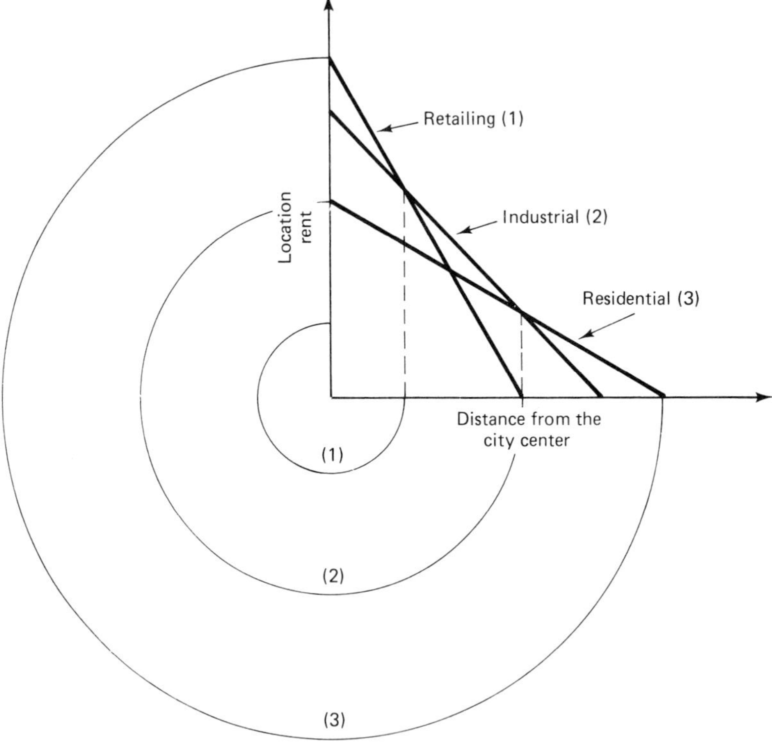

Figure 2.10 Concentric land use zones generated by the bid-rent curves for retailing, industrial, and residential land uses.

of location within the city. Industry still has some incentive to be close to the central business district, however, as in the present hypothetical city, that is the most convenient location for their employees.

The bid-rent curve for *residential* use is the shallowest of the three, with the primary advantage accruing to central locations being associated with the shorter journey to work. This advantage, however, is not such that residential land use is able to outbid either retailing or industry. Those residential areas that are located toward the center of the city involve a greater capital investment than those farther out, and will be characterized by higher-density living. This situation arises because, in order to obtain a satisfactory return on their investments, residential developers need to use intensively the more expensive land.

In some respects, however, the residential sector of the urban economy fits this type of analysis less well than do its retailing or industrial counterparts. Individual households are presumed to behave in a way that maximizes overall satisfaction, as the assumption of profit maximization is not entirely appropriate in this context. It is argued that households make a trade-off between more living space and greater commuting costs. The poor, with relatively little disposable income, consume small amounts of space at the center of the city, where commuting costs are negligible. The rich, on the other hand, with much larger disposable incomes, can pay the same amount of money for a large plot of land near the edge of the city, and still have enough left to cover commuting costs. This argument explains the apparent contradiction of relatively poor people living on relatively expensive land, as it points out that the poor use only small parcels of that expensive land.

As a corollary of the configuration of bid-rent curves, *land values* decrease with increasing distance from the city center. The thick line in Figure 2.11 denotes the highest price offered for any particular plot of land, and this line slopes away from the central business district in a curvilinear fashion, with land values decreasing quite rapidly at first, and then more gradually.

In summary, five major points can be made concerning the interrelationships among bid-rent curves, land use, and land value (Alonso, 1971). First, a family of bid-

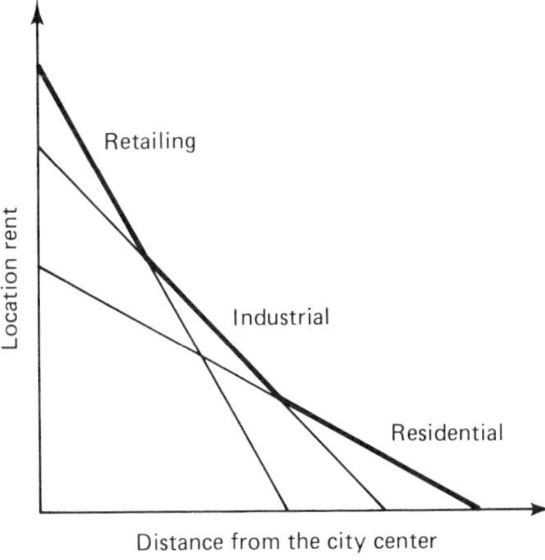

Figure 2.11 Relationship between land value and distance from the city center.

rent curves can be derived for each user of land such that the user is indifferent to his or her location along any one of those curves. Second, the equilibrium rent for any location is determined by choosing the highest bid from among the various potential users. Third, because each plot of land goes to the highest bidder, those land uses with the steeper bid-rent curves capture the central locations. Fourth, through this competitive bidding among potential users, land uses determine values. Fifth, and finally, land values also determine land uses, as the latter are distributed according to their ability to pay for the land.

2.3 RELAXING THE ASSUMPTIONS AND OTHER MODIFICATIONS

As with agricultural land use theory, it is instructive to determine what happens to the pattern of land use and land value when the original simplifying assumptions are relaxed. If it is no longer assumed that the city has a *single center*, or central business district, then one can imagine a series of subcenters, each generating its own set of concentric land use zones. The land use pattern in such a polynuclear city will be quite fragmented, as the zones surrounding individual subcenters will intersect each other. Los Angeles is perhaps the classic example of a polynuclear settlement, as it is really a series of cities within a city. Culver City, Century City, and Santa Monica, for example, each have their own distinctive land use patterns, which merge with each other to provide the overall pattern for Los Angeles. Recent research has attempted to place such polycentric cities within the same theoretical structure as that constructed for single-center, or monocentric cities (Griffith, 1981; Papageorgiou and Casetti, 1971).

If the assumption that the city is located on a *uniform plain* is relaxed, the land use and land value patterns will respond to variations in such things as the local topography and underlying geology. The nature of this response depends on what particular kind of land use is being considered. For example, if a plot of land is to be used for a multistoried office complex, it is important to have a suitable underlying geology. If, on the other hand, one is planning to construct a set of high-priced condominiums, the presence of an attractive view might be a more important consideration. In general, of course, such attributes as the underlying geology and the location of scenic views are not distributed in any regular fashion within cities. In fact, cities tend to be highly idiosyncratic with respect to the spatial distribution of these attributes, and that is why the latter are best treated as constants within the overall theory.

The assumption concerning *transportation costs* can be at least partially relaxed by imagining a city that is composed of a series of major highways radiating out from the center, with a second set of highways forming concentric circles, or ring roads (Figure 2.12). This transportation network is much more realistic than that implied by the original assumption that accessibility simply decreases with increasing distance from the central business district. In the present network, accessibility is greatest along the major radial and ring roads, with minor peaks of accessibility occurring at the intersections.

The associated pattern of land values has three main elements (Figure 2.12). First, in accordance with the original theoretical formulation, land values generally decrease as one moves away from the city center. Second, there are ridges of higher-valued land associated with both the ring roads and radials. Third, there are local peaks of higher land value that are coincidental with the intersections of the major traffic arteries.

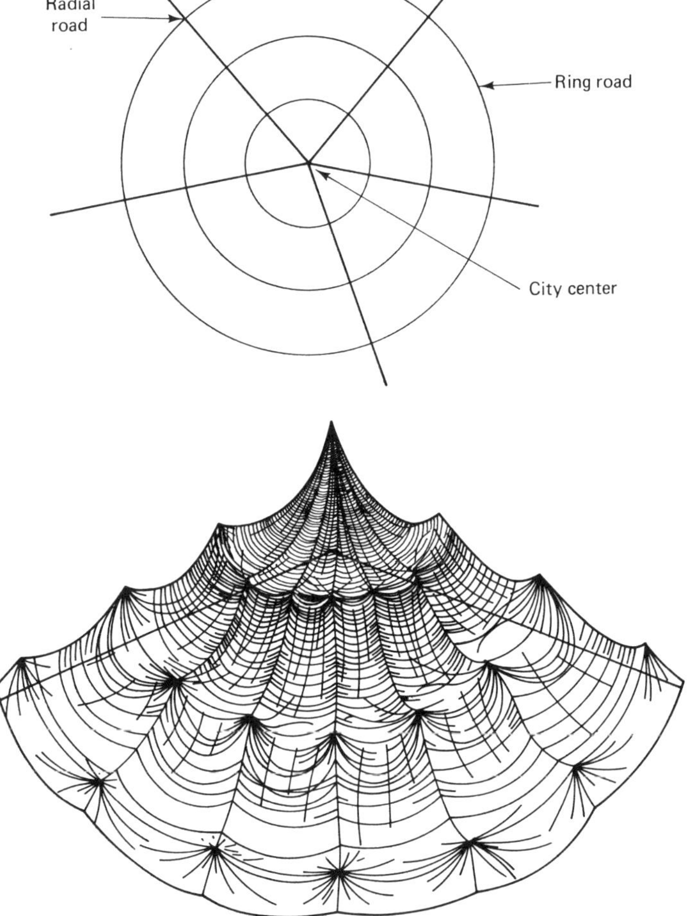

Figure 2.12 Transportation network based on radial and ring roads, and the corresponding land value surface. (The land value surface is from B. J. L. Berry, *Commercial Structure and Commercial Blight: Retail Patterns and Processes in the City of Chicago*, Department of Geography Research Paper 85, University of Chicago, Chicago, 1963, Fig. 3, p. 14.)

In turn, the land use pattern responds to this new distribution of accessibility and land values. Retailing activity emerges at the intersections, often in the form of planned shopping centers, and along the major highways. These outlying shopping centers often become surrounded by apartment buildings and other kinds of multi-family dwelling units, as residential developers adjust to the increased cost of land by using it more intensively. In sum, a series of mutual readjustments take place within the system, due to the complex interrelationships among accessibility, land use, and land value.

These adjustments are not instantaneous, however, so at any given point in time the land use pattern reflects a certain amount of *inertia*. In general, urban land is less flexible than rural land in terms of being adjusted to changing conditions. The short seed-to-harvest cycle of most agricultural crops is much more conducive to land use changes than is the lengthy effective life of the urban building stock. This comparative inflexibility of urban land, at least in the short run, means that a certain percentage of the city's land area is always underutilized, in the sense that it is not occupied by the highest and best use as defined previously.

Externalities present a second major difference between the urban and rural contexts. The value of a particular farm, for example, will not ordinarily depend on what is being produced in adjacent fields, whereas the value of an urban lot may depend quite significantly on the adjacent land uses (Berry, et al., 1976, p. 134). At one extreme, obnoxious facilities, such as meat-packing plants, tend to lower the value of the surrounding land. At the other extreme, the concentration of similar industries may generate positive externalities, as such concentrations reduce costs by facilitating subcontracting.

Because the assumption of a free-market economy does not hold for the urban land market, imperfections occur in the land use allocation process. A variety of different types of rent can be identified, one of the most important of which is *monopoly rent* (Harvey, 1973, p. 179). Monopoly rent occurs when the ownership of land becomes concentrated in the hands of a few individuals or corporations. In this situation, the amount of rent associated with a particular plot of land is not determined primarily by a competitive bidding process, but rather by the price at which the monopoly owner is willing to sell.

Finally, the process of land use allocation discussed by Alonso and others assumes the absence of *government intervention*. Such intervention, however, is of course fairly common, and can sometimes have quite a profound impact on the distribution of land use and land value. For example, the presence of tax breaks just beyond corporate city limits has tended to encourage the suburbanization of industry and the development of outlying industrial parks. Of even greater importance, however, has been the compartmentalization of land uses associated with the proliferation of zoning ordinances.

Land Use Zoning

Comprehensive land use zoning first appeared in New York City in the early part of this century. In 1916 the New York State legislature delegated authority to the city of New York, which then enacted the first comprehensive zoning ordinance in North America (Goldberg and Horwood, 1980, p. 3). This ordinance allowed the city to designate certain areas for specific types of land use, such as residential or industrial, whereas prior to 1916, land use control was mainly limited to private actions related to the laws of nuisance. Since this initial legislation, the overwhelming majority of zoning cases that have been decided by federal and state appellate courts have involved suburbs rather than central cities (Weaver and Babcock, 1979, p. 14). In this context, it is symptomatic that when the U.S. Supreme Court decided its first zoning case, in 1926, the justices chose a case challenging a zoning ordinance in a suburb of Cleveland. This celebrated case, involving the village of Euclid, extended to zoning enactments a presumption of validity that they had not formerly received (Babcock and Bosselman, 1973, p. 26).

The demand for zoning arose because property owners were concerned about externalities in the land market, whereby the value of land, and property on it, was often significantly influenced by the characteristics and uses of adjacent land. High-rise office buildings or apartment structures, for example, often had a negative impact on neighboring properties because they blocked out the daylight. Zoning was a means by which negative externalities could be minimized, while positive externalities, such as the clustering of compatible land use types, could be maximized.

A variety of zoning concepts have been developed to promote specific land use planning goals (Hartshorn, 1980, p. 226). *Transfer zoning*, for example, is designed to promote historic preservation. *Impact zoning* is used to manage urban growth. *Percentage zoning* encourages a certain prespecified mix of land use types, and *agricultural zones* are used to designate areas for agricultural use, thus preventing speculative development, especially at the edge of the city within the rural-urban fringe.

Recently, the practice of *exclusionary zoning* has been particularly closely scrutinized. Exclusionary zoning is associated with specific performance standards, and is frequently used in suburban areas to ensure high levels of economic and land use uniformity. This kind of zoning tends to screen lower-income families from certain neighborhoods by regulating such things as lot size, floor space, and even the number of bedrooms. Equally troublesome is the potential use of exclusionary zoning for purposes of racial discrimination. Indeed, one judge maintained that zoning was nothing but a vast plan for segregation, while it has been more recently claimed that the single major effect of zoning legislation has been to exclude lower-income classes from certain neighborhoods, especially lower-income blacks. (Babcock and Bosselman, 1973, p. 4).

As one might imagine, the administrative structure associated with land use regulation is often exceedingly complex. Zoning activity in a typical community may involve a planning board, a zoning commission, an appeals board, a zoning enforcement officer, a building inspector, and so on. Delays are inevitable when these agencies, or individuals, have a backlog of work, and the role of independent planning commissions has been subject to increasing attacks. These lay planners, who often administer the subdivision regulations and recommend zoning changes, have been criticized on two main grounds. First, they lack the expertise of professional planners. Second, unlike the city council, or other legislative bodies, they lack political accountability.

In any event, all types of land use zoning tend to fragment the regular pattern of land use predicted by Alonso's model. In particular, each plot of land is no longer necessarily sold to the highest and best use. Due to some local zoning ordinance, for example, land that would ordinarily be used for industrial activity might instead be developed for housing (Figure 2.13). In other words, land that cannot be used by the highest bidder, or the land use with the highest bid-rent curve at that location, has to be used by the next highest bidder, or the land use with the second highest bid-rent curve at that location. The associated land value will drop accordingly, creating a discontinuity in the land value surface.

Because each plot of land is no longer utilized by the highest and best use, zoning tends to reduce the overall tax base of the city, and land use zoning has also been criticized on a number of other grounds (Goldberg and Horwood, 1980, pp. 26–29). First, zoning creates a rigid division of uses that are unable to cope with the variety of tastes and demands that occur in modern society. Second, zoning has begun to dominate the planning function as a whole. Third, zoning ordinances tend to preserve the status quo, and thus impede change in the land use system. Fourth, zoning can encourage monopoly situations in the urban land market.

On the other hand, it can be argued that zoning is a very beneficial form of land use regulation (Goldberg and Horwood, 1980, pp. 24–26). First, zoning protects property values by minimizing negative externalities. Second, zoning helps to maximize the public good by ensuring that sufficient amounts of land are available for different kinds of uses. Third, by identifying areas of historical importance, zoning can preserve the architectural character of a city. Fourth, zoning ensures that the majority of residents are in control of land use, such that one or two people cannot threaten the property values of their neighbors by indiscriminately adjusting their land use.

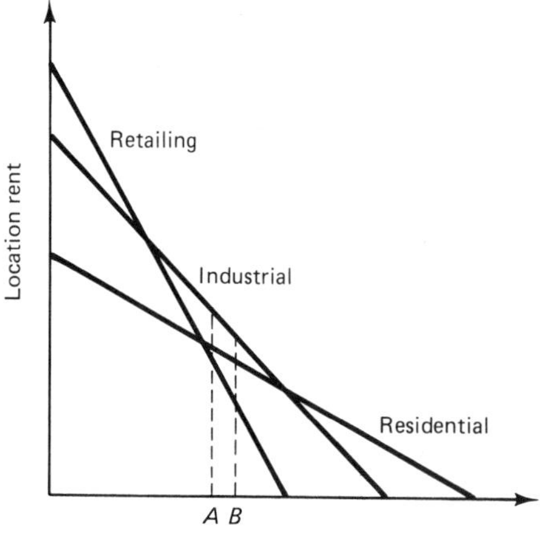

Figure 2.13 Effect of land use zoning on bid-rent curves. The land between distances A and B is zoned against industrial use, and is therefore used for residential purposes.

2.4 EMPIRICAL TESTING

The urban land use and land value theory discussed above generates two testable propositions. First, it postulates that land values decrease in a curvilinear fashion with increasing distance from the city center. Second, it argues that land uses will be arranged in a series of concentric zones radiating out from the city center. It is possible to test both these propositions by the use of bivariate, or simple, correlation and regression analysis, and thus come to some conclusions concerning their empirical validity.

Introduction to Bivariate Correlation and Regression Analysis

Correlation analysis indicates the strength of the relationship between two variables, while regression analysis identifies the form of that relationship. Although one would ordinarily wish to know something about the strength of a relationship before becoming overly concerned about its form, for the purposes of exposition it is easier to begin with the rudiments of regression analysis.

The first step involves drawing a *scatter diagram*, whereby all the cases, or observations, are placed on a graph according to their values for the two variables, X and Y (Figure 2.14). The *least-squares* line is placed through the center of these points, such that the sum of the squared deviations around that line is minimized. The deviations referred to are the vertical distances between each point and the line, two of which are shown in Figure 2.14. These deviations are then squared, thus eliminating all negative values. Finally, the squared deviations are summed, and that value is minimized.

Appropriate formula are available to solve for the unknowns in the following *least-squares equation*, thus determining the position of the least-squares line (Blalock, 1979, p. 392):

$$Y = a + bX \tag{2.3}$$

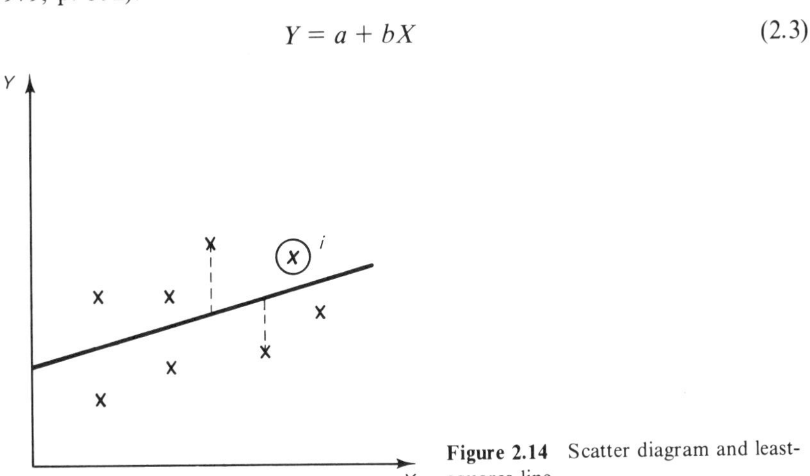

Figure 2.14 Scatter diagram and least-squares line.

where Y is the dependent variable; X is the independent, or explanatory variable; a is a constant representing the value of Y when X is zero; and b is a constant representing the slope of the line. Note that the equation contains two variables, X and Y, and two constants, a and b. The term a is a constant because there is only one point at which the least-squares line intercepts the Y axis, and b is a constant because the line is straight, and therefore has the same slope throughout the relationship.

In the same way that this equation expresses the form of the overall relationship, each individual case can be represented by its own particular equation. The value for any inidvidual case i is described as follows:

$$Y_i = a + bX_i + e_i \tag{2.4}$$

where the terms are the same as in equation (2.3), except that the subscript i has been added and an error term, denoted by the symbol e, has also been included. The *error term* expresses the degree to which any case i is removed from the least-squares line and so is not exactly predicted by the least-squares equation. In Figure 2.14, for example, the error term associated with case i, or the *residual*, as it is often called, is positive because i lies above the line. In other words, the predicted value of i, based on the least-squares equation, must have something added to it in order to equal the actual value of i. Similarly, those cases lying below the line have negative error terms, or residuals.

A variety of factors are represented by the error term. First, it might include measurement error in variable Y, although least-squares analysis is based on the assumption that there is no measurement error in variable X. Second, the error term might reflect the fact that the relationship is not really linear, although again, least-squares analysis is based on the assumption of a linear relationship. Third, and most important, the error term includes all the other variables, in addition to variable X, that influence the dependent variable Y in some way.

In sum, the least-squares equation, representing the least-squares line, is a predictive equation relating the two variables X and Y. Once the two constants in this equation have been solved for, values of Y can be predicted for particular values of X simply by inserting the value of X in the right-hand side of the equation. The accuracy of these predictions will depend partly on the strength of the relationship between the two variables, as determined by correlation analysis.

The *correlation coefficient* (r), which measures the strength of the relationship between two variables, runs between -1.0 and $+1.0$. A negative value indicates a negative, or inverse relationship, while a positive value indicates a positive, or direct relationship. Note that, for any pair of variables, the signs associated with b, the slope of the line, and r are always the same. A negative slope is always reflected by a negative correlation, and vice versa.

The strength of the relationship, and the associated correlation coefficient, is measured by the degree to which the points are scattered around the least-squares line (Figure 2.15). If all the points lie exactly on the line, the relationship is perfect, and the value of r will be $+1.0$ if the slope is positive, and -1.0 if the slope is negative. The greater the scatter of points around the line, or the larger the residuals, the closer the correlation coefficient will be to zero. Due to the linearity assumption in

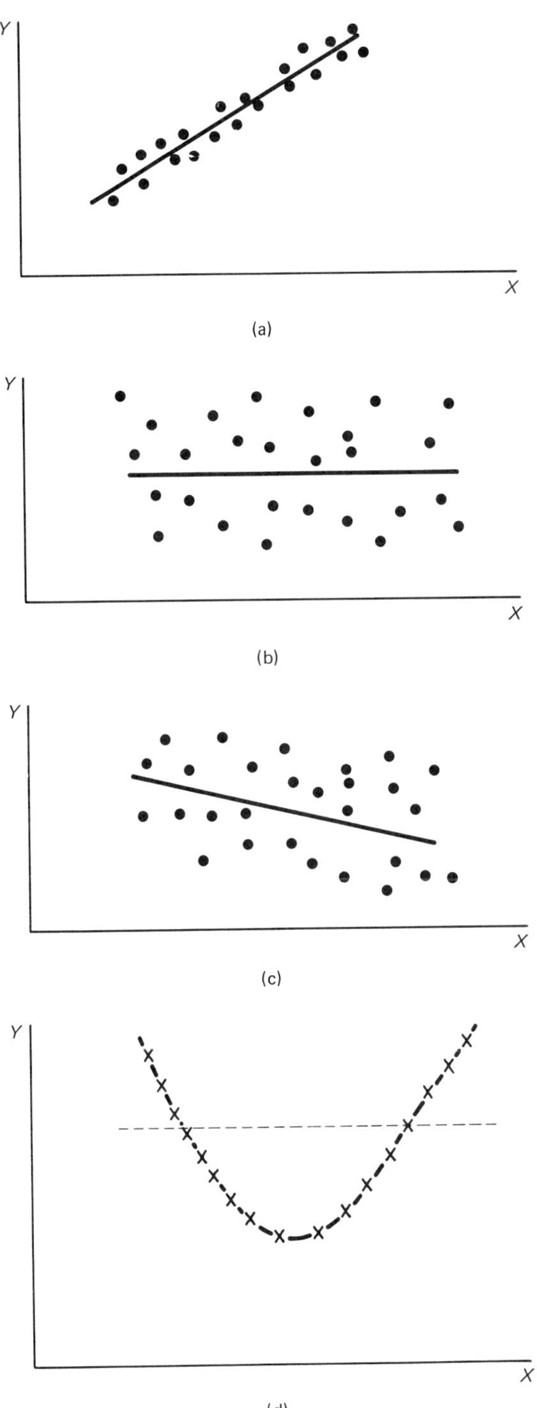

Figure 2.15 Examples of the relationship between the scatter diagram and the associated correlation coefficient: (a) strong positive relationship; (b) no relationship; (c) weak negative relationship; (d) perfect nonlinear relationship for which $r = 0$. (From H. M. Blalock, Jr., *Social Statistics*, Revised Second Edition, McGraw-Hill, New York, 1979, Fig. 17.7, p. 397 and Fig. 17.8, p. 398. Reproduced with permission.)

least-squares analysis, however, a low correlation coefficient does not necessarily signify the absence of a relationship. A perfect curvilinear relationship would not be reflected by an r of 1.0 unless some transformation of the variables had previously been undertaken (Figure 2.15).

A related statistic to the correlation coefficient is the *coefficient of determination* (r^2), which is simply the square of the correlation coefficient. The coefficient of determination runs between 0 and 1.0 and represents the amount of variation in variable Y that is accounted for, or statistically explained, by the variation in variable X. If the variation in Y is completely accounted for by the variation in X, the coefficient of determination will be 1.0.

The use of a bucket-and-sponge analogy helps to clarify the interpretation of the coefficient of determination (Figure 2.16). Imagine that the water in the bucket represents the amount of variation associated with Y, while the sponge represents the amount of variation associated with X. When dipped into the bucket the sponge soaks up a certain amount of water, and this represents the percentage of variation in Y accounted for by the variation in X, that is, the coefficient of determination. The water remaining in the bucket represents the variation in Y that is left unaccounted for by X, or, in other words, the residual variation in Y. This residual variation must be explained by other variables not presently being considered.

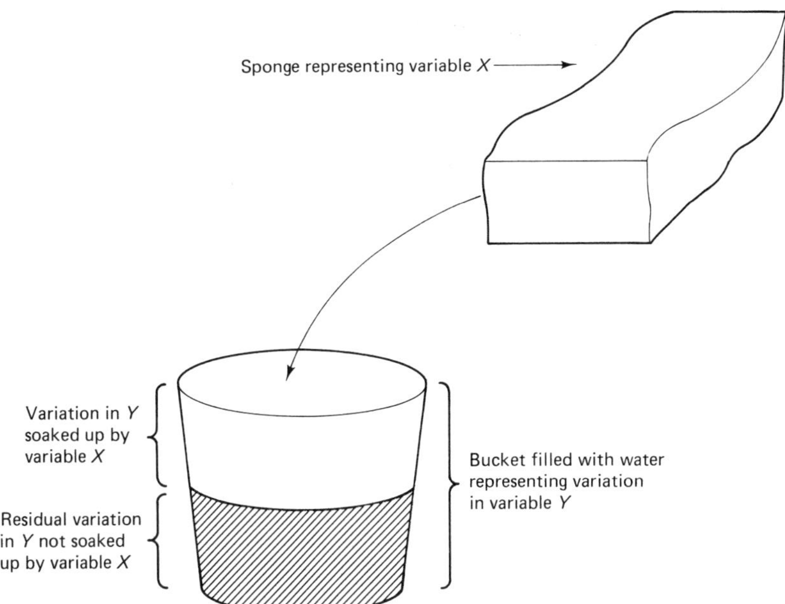

Figure 2.16 Bucket-and-sponge analogy for interpreting the coefficient of determination. (Based on R. Abler, J. Adams, and P. Gould, *Spatial Organization: The Geographer's View of the World*, © 1971, Fig. 5.23, p. 129. Reprinted by permission of Prentice-Hall, Inc., Englewood Cliffs, N.J.)

The Pattern of Land Value

Alonso's proposition that land values decrease with increasing distance from the city center has been empirically tested for Seattle, Washington, by Warren Seyfried (1963). Seyfried considered a variety of functional relationships, but of greatest interest are the results associated with a simple linear function, and a power function. The *linear function*, in this particular context, can be expressed as follows:

$$LV = a - bD \tag{2.5}$$

where LV is land value, D is distance, and a and b are constants, representing the value of the intercept, and the slope of the line, respectively. The unknowns in this equation, and the strength of the relationship between land value and distance, can be determined via the previously described least-squares analysis.

The *power function*, on the other hand, is expressed as follows:

$$LV = aD^{-b} \tag{2.6}$$

where the notation is the same as in equation (2.5). This power function provides a closer representation of Alonso's prediction as it describes land values as decreasing at a decreasing rate. In other words, it is a curvilinear, rather than linear function. In order for equation (2.6) to be investigated using least-squares analysis, however, it must first be transformed into a linear equation by taking the common logarithms, to the base 10, of both variables. The new equation is as follows:

$$\log LV = \log a - b(\log D) \tag{2.7}$$

where the notation is the same as in equation (2.6), and log represents common logarithms to the base 10.

To evaluate the relative appropriateness of the linear and power functions, Seyfried collected data on the mean assessed value per square foot for street intersections radiating outward from the central business district of Seattle. The gradients associated with these assessed values were determined for the four major compass directions, and the results provide strong support for Alonso's hypothesis (Table 2.5). First, all the b values, representing the slopes of the lines, or land value gradients,

TABLE 2.5 CORRELATION AND REGRESSION RESULTS FOR LAND VALUE GRADIENTS IN SEATTLE, WASHINGTON

	North	South	East	West
Linear function				
r	−0.275	−0.356	−0.454	−0.959
b	−0.240	−0.048	−0.244	−8.610
Power function				
r	−0.795	−0.928	−0.895	−0.914
b	−0.807	−1.078	−1.576	−2.343

Source: W. R. Seyfried, "The centrality of urban land values," *Land Economics*, 39 (1963), Table I, p. 280.

are in the expected negative direction. Second, the correlation coefficients suggest that the curvilinear, or power function, is more appropriate than its linear counterpart. Indeed, the correlation coefficients associated with the power function are exceptionally high, indicating that, at least in three of the four directions, approximately 80 percent of the variation in land values is accounted for by distance from the city center.

The results obtained for the westerly direction are rather surprising, in that the correlation coefficient for the linear function is as high as that for the power function. On closer inspection, however, this apparent anomaly is explained by the fact that both these coefficients are based on only six observations, due to the proximity of the ocean. In general, a small sample size tends to inflate the correlation coefficient. At the extreme, when dealing with bivariate correlation, a sample size of 2 will always yield a perfect correlation of 1.0, as one can always draw a straight line through two points.

Recent research has suggested that the relationship between land value and distance from the central business district can be described by more complex curvilinear functions than the power function utilized by Seyfried. McDonald and Bowman (1979), for example, using data from Chicago, conclude that a fourth-degree polynomial best fits the relationship between land value and distance. It is noteworthy that this functional form implies that land values initially increase with distance from the city center, and then begin to decrease, at a distance of somewhere between 4 and 8 miles.

The Pattern of Land Use

Alonso's second proposition, that land uses will be sorted into concentric zones radiating out from the city center, has been investigated by the economist Edwin Mills (1972, p. 40). Mills analyzed the density gradients associated with different types of land use patterns for a sample of 18 U.S. Metropolitan Areas. This sample was not chosen randomly, but rather with four major factors in mind. First, the cities had to be approximately circular, or semicircular in shape, thus excluding those cities with highly irregular political boundaries. Second, a wide range of population sizes was included. Third, the cities were chosen from different regions of the country, and fourth, a variety of historical growth rates were included.

A negative *exponential function* was used to identify and compare these density gradients. This function is expressed as follows:

$$Y = ae^{-bD} \tag{2.8}$$

where Y is the dependent variable, such as employment density in retailing; D is distance from the city center; a and b are the empirically derivable constants; and e is the base of natural logarithms. The negative exponential function is extremely similar to the previously described power function, and like the power function, it must be logarithmically transformed before it can be analyzed via the least-squares analysis. In this instance, the transformation is acheived by taking the natural logarithm of the dependent variable, thus generating the following equation:

TABLE 2.6 AVERAGE DENSITY GRADIENTS ASSOCIATED WITH DIFFERENT TYPES OF LAND USE

Land use	1948	1954	1958	1963
Population	−0.58	−0.47	−0.42	−0.38
Manufacturing	−0.68	−0.55	−0.48	−0.42
Retailing	−0.88	−0.75	−0.59	−0.44

Source: E. S. Mills, *Studies in the Structure of the Urban Economy*, The Johns Hopkins University Press, Baltimore, 1972, Table 12, p. 42. Published for Resources for the Future by the Johns Hopkins University Press.

$$\ln Y = \ln a - bD \tag{2.9}$$

where the notation is the same as in equation (2.8), and ln represents natural logarithms.

Mills averaged the density gradients associated with each type of land use, based on the value of b in equation (2.9), across the 18 cities (Table 2.6). The values were computed for four different time periods, in order to assess the change over time. Two major points emerge from this analysis. First, for all four time periods, as predicted by Alonso, the density gradient associated with retailing is the steepest, while that associated with population is the gentlest. In other words, retailing dominates the central locations, while residential land use dominates the peripheral locations. Second, all three density gradients have become less steep over time, and also less distinguishable from each other. The declining gradients are due to the postwar suburbanization process, while the increasing similarity between the gradients reflects the fact that both retailing and manufacturing have become more peripherally located in recent years, as witnessed by the growing number of outlying shopping centers and industrial parks.

Criticisms

In summary, Alonso's hypotheses, concerning the spatial arrangement of land use and land value within cities, seem to enjoy substantial empirical support. The patterns could never be exactly as hypothesized, as no city completely conforms to the various simplifying assumptions upon which the theoretical analysis is based. Despite this empirical support, however, Alonso's overall approach to understanding urban spatial structure has been subjected to increasing criticism. In large part these criticisms can be applied to neoclassical economics in general, of which Alonso's model is a representative example. Before considering these specific criticisms, therefore, it is useful to summarize the major features of neoclassical economics.

Neoclassical economics was originally a reaction to the classical economics of Ricardo, whereby the emphasis was shifted away from the circumstances and conditions of production toward the preferences of individual consumers. In particular, neoclassical economics suggests that the nature of the economy, and society, is shaped by the preferences of persons within that society. The individual behavioral units upon which the approach is based are households and firms. Households demand certain amounts of goods and services in order to maximize their overall utility, or level of satisfaction, while firms produce a certain amount of goods, and demand certain amounts of land, labor, and capital, in order to maximize their profits.

Neoclassical economics involves four major assumptions (Bassett and Short, 1980, p. 26). First, all households and firms have perfect information with respect to the state of the market. Second, within the context of this perfect information, all households attempt to maximize utility, while all firms attempt to maximize profits. Third, the production of certain goods and services is a direct reflection of consumer preferences. Fourth, the factors of production, land, labor, and capital, can be interchanged. As a consequence of this conceptual framework, with its particular emphasis on equilibrium conditions, the market economy is viewed as a harmonious and self-regulating mechanism for allocating scarce resources. Moreover, such features as unemployment and excess profits are regarded as mere deviations from the norm that occur in times of economic disequilibrium, and conflicts between such interest groups as entrepreneurs and workers, or tenants and landlords, are ignored.

Within this general framework, at least six major criticisms have been leveled at the neoclassical approach to understanding land use and land value patterns within cities. First, buyers and sellers in the urban land market do not really posssess perfect information. Also, the emergence of powerful corporations, and the increasing intervention of urban governments, cast serious doubt on the idea of a free market in land. Second, little is known about how households actually make the complex trade-offs between housing expenditures, travel expenditures, and the many other household budget items. Indeed, it has been shown that income and race are often more important determinants of residential location than accessibility to work (Granfield, 1975). Third, Alonso's approach tends to ignore the supply side of the equation, as under the assumptions of profit maximization and perfect competition, supply is deemed to follow automatically from the structure of demand (Evans, 1983). Such considerations are not beyond the scope of the general approach, however, as Muth (1969) has been able to incorporate the production of housing into his more sophisticated version of the trade-off model. Fourth, neoclassical models tend to be ahistorical in nature, and overlook the inertia from the past that has left many activities in suboptimal locations. In this respect, such models provide no insight into the process of historical change, and thus do not directly address the question of how we came to our present urban condition (Walker, 1978). Fifth, the neoclassical theory of consumer choice pays insufficient attention to the constraining influence of the larger political-economic structure in which the land and housing markets are embedded. For some, the social relations of production must obviously precede, in academic discourse, the system of consumption (Scott, 1980, p. 76). Finally, the neoclassical paradigm reduces the factors of production, such as labor and capital, to the status of abstract and mutually substitutable technical inputs, and thus assumes that they are politically neutral (Scott, 1980, p. 81).

2.5 URBAN SPRAWL

The phenomenon of urban sprawl is one of the major problems associated with efficient land use utilization in contemporary American cities, and this problem can be usefully analyzed within the context of urban land use and land value theory. Urban sprawl refers to the continuous expansion around large cities, whereby there is always a zone of land that is in the process of being converted from rural to urban use. There are three major forms of sprawl (Harvey and Clark, 1971). The first, and perhaps least offensive is the low-density *continuous development* that surrounds most large cities (Figure 2.17). Second, *ribbon development sprawl* is characterized by segments of development that extend axially from the city. Third, *leapfrog or checkerboard sprawl*, is characterized by discontinuous patches of urban development, and it is usually this type of sprawl that is attacked as being economically inefficient and aesthetically unattractive.

Causes

A variety of factors have been held responsible for the proliferation of urban sprawl (Harvey and Clark, 1971). Perhaps the most obvious of these is that sprawl is sometimes a response to the *physical terrain* surrounding a city. Mountains, rivers, and swamps, for example, often necessitate discontinuous urban development.

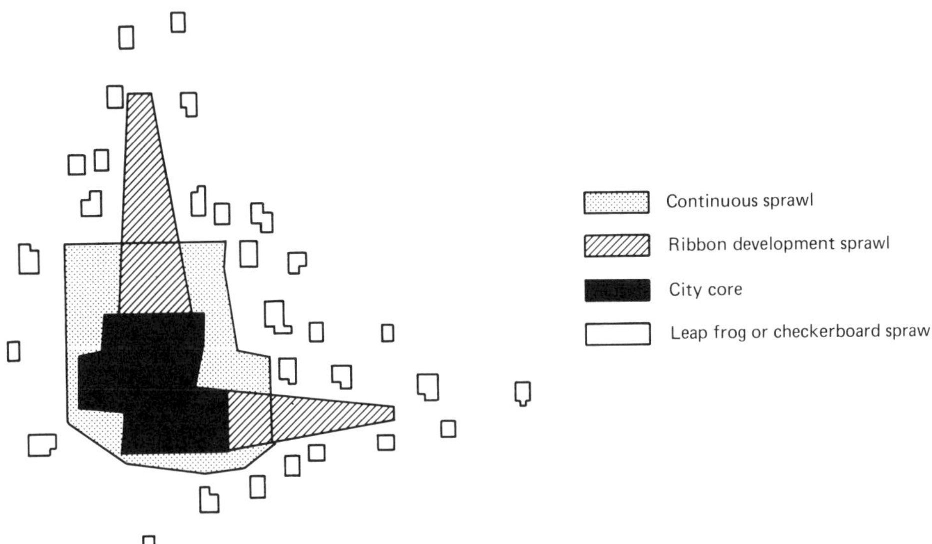

Figure 2.17 Forms of urban sprawl. (From C.S. Sargent, Jr., "Land speculation and urban morphology," in J. S. Adams, Ed., *Urban Policymaking and Metropolitan Dynamics: A Comparative Geographical Analysis*, Ballinger, Cambridge, Mass., 1976, Fig. 2.8, p. 41.)

Sprawl is also encouraged by different *administrative policies* in the rural-urban fringe, as opposed to the core of the city. If building codes are stricter within the corporate city than outside it, residential developers tend to be attracted to suitable locations just beyond the city limits. Similarly, land use zoning regulations are often more stringent within the city than outside it.

The leap-frog, or checkerboard type of sprawl, appears to be particularly related to the number of *independent land developers*. The greater the number of independent firms operating within a given area, the greater the number of fragmented projects. More collusion among these developers, or greater guidance from the local planning agencies, would lead to a more ordered progression of development.

The process of *land speculation* is also sometimes blamed for sprawl, as speculation results in some land being withheld from development, while other land is developed prematurely. Land values at the edge of an expanding uban area are composed of two major components: a value for agricultural use and a speculative value associated with potential urban development (Figure 2.18). The speculative component decreases with increasing distance from the central city, until at distance *A* it is effectively zero. Within this speculative zone the land is developed at different rates and intensities, according to a multitude of individual decisions on the part of independent developers. Generally speaking, entrepreneurs attempt to buy relatively cheap land, retain possession while it gains in value, and then sell it just as the pace of appreciation begins to slacken (Figure 2.19). The exact timing of this sale, and any subsequent developments, depends on the varying calculations and predictions of the individual entrepreneurs.

The *tax laws* in the United States also tend to encourage discontinuous urban development. The real property tax ensures that as soon as agricultural land is platted it is taxed at urban rates, thus encouraging subdivision developers to avoid excess platting in advance of actual development. In addition, income tax methods

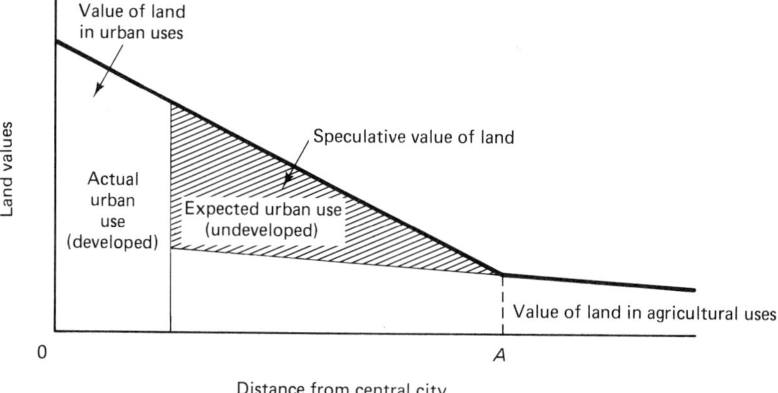

Figure 2.18 Components of land value. (From C. S. Sargent, Jr., "Land speculation and urban morphology," in J. S. Adams, Ed., *Urban Policymaking and Metropolitan Dynamics: A Comparative Geographical Analysis*, Ballinger, Cambridge, Mass., 1976, Fig. 2.2, p. 27.)

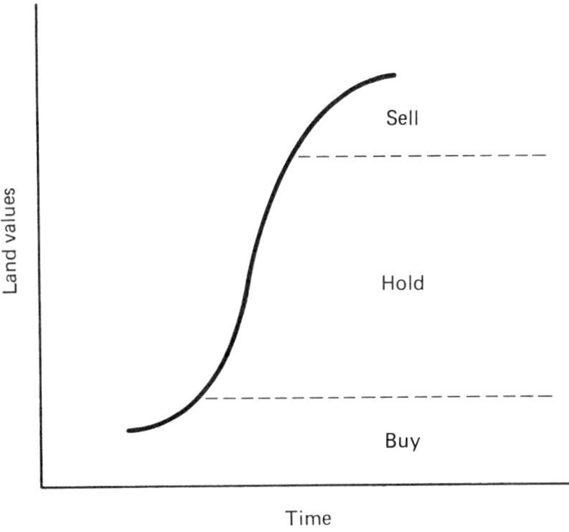

Figure 2.19 Land value appreciation curve. (From C. S. Sargent, Jr., "Land speculation and urban morphology," in J. S. Adams, Ed., *Urban Policymaking and Metropolitan Dynamics: A Comparative Geographical Analysis*, Ballinger, Cambridge, Mass., 1976, Fig. 2.6, p. 34.)

also encourage this kind of piecemeal development, as developers tend to spread their building programs over a number of years to avoid occupying a particularly high tax bracket for any single year.

Finally, *transportation routes* are catalysts of urban sprawl, and historically, trolley and bus lines were largely responsible for the ribbon development within the rural-urban fringe. More recently, freeway construction has generated ribbon-type sprawl at the edge of cities, and these ribbons have been extended and reinforced when associated with rapid transit lines. Closely related to these freeways and rapid transit lines is the development of outlying shopping centers. Such shopping centers are often constructed before the surrounding area is fully developed, in order to take advantage of cheap land. Once in existence, however, they add impetus to the residential development process.

Consequences

Unchecked urban sprawl has a variety of undesirable consequences (Sargent, 1976). One of the major drawbacks of urban sprawl, especially the checkerboard type, is that potentially productive *agricultural land* is often left idle. Parcels of land at the urban fringe tend to be used inefficiently, or sometimes left completely unused, if their main value lies in speculation.

Sprawl can sometimes have a deleterious effect on *inner-city neighborhoods*, as commercial and industrial enterprises are syphoned off into the urban fringe. Not only is the tax base of the central city decreased, but the distribution of employment opportunities is also profoundly altered. At the same time, access to public land surrounding the city is made more difficult, as residential developments reduce the number of entry points to parks, forests, and beaches.

The costs of providing various kinds of *public services* are also generally much higher in areas of low density, or discontinuous development. For example, the costs associated with police and fire protection are greater per person, as are the costs of constructing sewer, gas, and electricity lines. It is also argued that low-density sprawl is a major impediment to the development of economically viable mass transit systems.

Possible Solutions

A number of different strategies have been suggested as possible solutions to the problem of urban sprawl (Sargent, 1976). First, *tax reforms* might be instituted to reduce the present comparative advantage of land speculators. In particular, the capital gains provision might be modified, and local communities should consider taxing vacant land more heavily and structures less heavily.

Second, *local planning agencies* could make greater efforts to control the expansion of cities by manipulating the location and availability of such services as water lines, sewage lines, and roads. This manipulation could be construed as an "orderly growth" rather than a "no growth" strategy, although there are certain drawbacks. The unethical influencing of local politicians, for example, would probably increase, and the restrictions on new housing development would inflate the price of existing housing.

Third, *zoning ordinances* and *subdivision controls* might be modified and strengthened. Such modification and strengthening, however, would require the cooperation of all the local administrative agencies, so it should be preceded by some kind of governmental consolidation.

Fourth, a fairly radical strategy would be to increase substantially the amount of *local government purchased land* within the rural-urban fringe. This land could be acquired from the present owners, held, and then sold at a later date to private developers who would have to adhere to certain conditions concerning its use. Federal loans and subsidies might be created to facilitate the initial acquisition of the land.

Fifth, the delicate balance between public and private interests should be monitored by a sophisticated *information system*. Major land transactions, and associated prices, should be immediately recorded and made publicly available, so that buyers and sellers are more fully aware of the prevailing market situation. By maximizing the potential success of individual development decisions, unnecessary or premature subdivision, and the related loss of agricultural land, would be minimized.

In summary, this chapter began by outlining the basic arguments involved in Von Thünen's agricultural land use theory. These arguments were then adapted to the urban context, and the effects of relaxing the simplifying asumptions, and considering other factors such as externalities and inertia, were considered. Simple bivariate correlation and regression analysis was then introduced in order to assess the empirical validity of the major theoretical propositions, and the chapter was concluded by discussing one of the major problems associated with the urban land market, the phenomenon of urban sprawl.

3

Multivariate Land Value and Housing Models

3.1 MULTIVARIATE LAND VALUE MODELS

The land value theory described in Chapter 2 is essentially bivariate in nature, as it addresses the relationship between land values and distance from the city center, while assuming that other variables are held constant. The present chapter extends this discussion in a number of ways: first, by investigating the relationships between land values and a set of other variables within the context of multiple correlation and regression analysis; second, by discussing the idea of a housing market, and associated multivariate housing value models; third, by introducing the idea of causal models, and using them in the context of housing quality and size; and fourth, by analyzing certain problems connected with the urban housing market. Before the multivariate models can be described in detail, however, the basic elements of multiple correlation and regression analysis must be considered.

Introduction to Multiple Correlation and Regression

Multiple correlation and regression analysis is used in those situations where one is investigating the interrelationships between more than two variables. In this particular multivariate context, there is one dependent variable, and a series of explanatory, or independent variables. The general relationships are expressed as follows:

$$Y = f(X_1, X_2, \ldots, X_m) \tag{3.1}$$

where Y is the dependent variable and X_1 through X_m are the independent variables. Two major questions, with respect to equation (3.1), can be answered by multiple

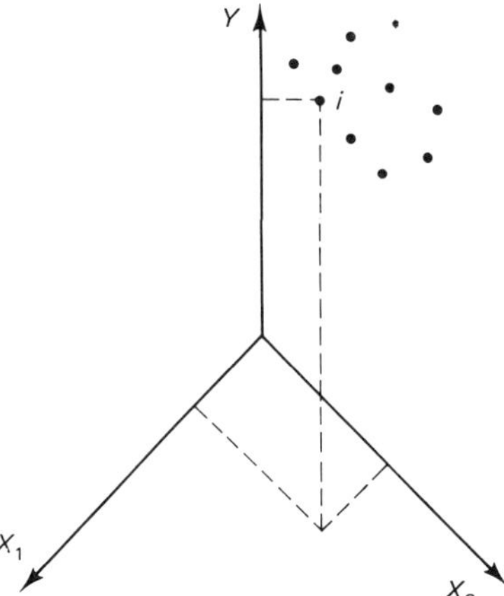

Figure 3.1 Scatter diagram for the three-variable case.

correlation and regression analysis. First, how strong is the overall relationship between the independent variables and the dependent variable? Or, in other words, how well, in combination, do they account for the variation in Y? Second, what is the relative importance of the independent variables in terms of accounting for the variation in Y?

As in the bivariate situation, a *scatter diagram* can be conceptualized, and this is most easily thought of in the three-dimensional case where there is one dependent variable and two independent variables (Figure 3.1). Each axis represents an individual variable, and all three axes are at right angles to each other. The individual case, or observation, i has a particular value for each of the three variables, giving it a unique location in this three-dimensional space. Obviously, when more than three variables are involved it is impossible to draw the associated scatter diagram, although the location of observations in a multidimensional space can still be described algebraically.

A plane is fitted through the observations in three-dimensonal space such that the sum of the squared deviations around this plane is minimized (Figure 3.2). This

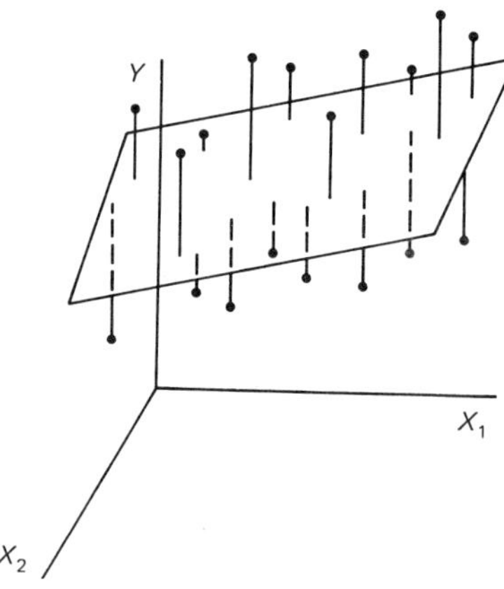

Figure 3.2 The least-squares plane minimizing the sum of the squared deviations in the vertical (Y) dimension. (From H. M. Blalock, Jr., *Social Statistics*, Rev. Ed., McGraw-Hill, New York, 1979, Fig. 19.2, p. 454. Reproduced with permission.)

least-squares plane is analogous to the least-squares line in the bivariate case, and is represented as follows:

$$Y = a + b_1X_1 + b_2X_2 \tag{3.2}$$

where Y is the dependent variable, X_1 and X_2 are independent variables, and a, b_1, and b_2 are constants. The constant a represents the value at which the plane intercepts the Y axis, and b_1 and b_2 represent the slopes of the plane in the directons of X_1 and X_2, respectively. Note that, in the $(m + 1)$-dimensional space corresponding to m independent variables we would be fitting an m-dimensional hyperplane, although such a figure can hardly be imagined.

The *multiple correlation coefficient* measures the goodness of fit of the points to the least-squares plane, and thus reflects the explanatory power of the independent variables taken together. It runs between zero and 1, with a coefficient of 1 indicating that all the points lie exactly on the least-squares plane. The greater the scatter of points about the least-squares plane, the lower the multiple correlation coefficient.

It is perhaps helpful, in this context, to note that the multiple correlation coefficient can be thought of as representing the bivariate correlation between the actual values of the dependent variable and those predicted by the least-squares equation (Blalock, 1979, p. 483). The square of the multiple correlation coefficient is termed the *coefficient of multiple determination*, and this coefficient expresses the amount of variation in the dependent variable that is accounted for by the explanatory, or independent variables.

Besides determining the goodness of fit of the whole equation, it is equally important to ascertain the relative importance of the individual explanatory variables. These individual contributions can be assessed in two different ways, the first of which involves computing *partial correlation coefficients.* Partial correlations refer to the relationship between each independent variable and the dependent variable, while controlling for one or more of the remaining independent variables. In the three variable case, for example, one could calculate the partial correlation between Y and X_1, while controlling for the influence of X_2. This relationship can be expressed in symbolic form as $r_{12.3}$, where 1 is the dependent variable Y, 2 is the first independent variable X_1, and 3 is the second independent variable X_2. When a single variable is controlled for, as in the present example, the resulting correlation is called a *first-order partial;* when two variables arc controlled for, the resulting correlation is called a *second-order partial;* and so on. In keeping with this terminology, a simple bivariate correlation, with no controls, is sometimes referred to as a *zero-order correlation.*

The intuitive meaning of a partial correlation coefficient can best be grasped by first imagining that the variables Y and X_1 are, in turn, related to the control variable X_2. The residuals associated with these two relationships are than correlated in order to obtain a measure of the relationship between Y and X_1 that is independent of the effects of X_2. In other words, the partial correlation coefficient expressing the relationship between Y and X_1, while controlling for X_2, can be defined as the correlation between the residuals of the regressions of Y on X_2, and X_1 on X_2. As a result of this kind of analysis, the independent variables can be rank-ordered on the basis of the strength of their relationship with the dependent variable Y, with those variables with the highest partial correlation coefficients being the most important, and those variables with the lowest partial correlation coefficients being the least important.

A similar rank ordering, in terms of relative importance, can also be achieved by investigating the *regression coefficients.* If the independent variables are all measured in the same units, their relative importance can be immediately ascertained by reference to the regression coefficients b_1 and b_2 in equation (3.2). Recall that the coefficient b measures the change in Y associated with a unit change in X. A high value for b indicates that Y is very sensitive to changes in X, while a low value for b indicates that Y is not unduly sensitive to changes in X.

In those instances, however, where the independent variables are not measured in the same units, a direct comparison of the associated regression coefficients is unrewarding, as their magnitudes will not be independent of the units being used. For example, how does one compare the change in Y associated with a change of one dollar, on the one hand, and a change of one mile, on the other? In such situations it is necessary to calculate the *standardized regression coefficients*, or beta weights.

To understand what is meant by the term "standardized regression coefficient," it is necessary to rewrite equation (3.2) a little more formally, as follows:

$$X_1 = a + b_{12.3}X_2 + b_{13.2}X_3 \tag{3.3}$$

where X_1 is the dependent variable, X_2 and X_3 are independent variables, and a, $b_{12.3}$, and $b_{13.2}$ are constants. The regression coefficient $b_{12.3}$ indicates the relationship between X_1 and X_2, while controlling for X_3, while the regression coefficient $b_{13.2}$ indicates the relationship between X_1 and X_3, while controlling for X_2. Note that this subscript notation is the same as that used for partial correlations, and that we have departed from the usual practice of denoting the dependent variable as Y merely in order to simplify the notation system.

The standardized regression coefficients associated with equation (3.3) can be obtained in either of two ways. First, each variable in the original data matrix can be converted to standardized form by expressing it in terms of standard deviations from its mean. Second, the unstandardized regression coefficients can be converted to standardized regression coefficients by simply multiplying the particular unstandardized coefficient by the ratio of the standard deviation of its associated variable to the standard deviation of the dependent variable. Either way, the resulting standardized regression coefficients associated with each independent variable are now directly comparable, thus allowing the independent variables to be rank-ordered in terms of relative importance.

It should be remembered that the partial correlations and standardized regressions represent different measures of the relationships between variables, and therefore give different results, although they usually rank variables in the same order of importance. The partial correlation coefficient indicates the amount of variation explained by one independent variable after the others have explained all they can. The standardized regression coefficient, on the other hand, indicates the change in the dependent variable that is associated with a standardized unit of change in one of the independent variables, while controlling for all the remaining independent variables.

A few final notes of caution are in order. First, the multiple correlation coefficient will ordinarily be larger than any of the zero-order, or bivariate correlations, since it is impossible to explain less variation by adding further variables. Second, the magnitude of the multiple correlation coefficient, for a given set of variables, will usually be maximized in those situations where there are no intercorrelations between the independent variables. It is prudent, therefore, to search for independent variables that are relatively unrelated, with each accounting for a different portion of the total variation. Finally, where the independent variables are highly intercorrelated, both the partial correlations and standardized regressions will be sensitive to sampling and measurement errors. This problem is referred to as *multicollinearity* (Blalock, 1979, p. 485).

A Multivariate Land Value Model for Chicago

One of the best illustrative examples of a multivariate land value model has been provided by Yeates and Garner (1971) for the city of Chicago, based on an earlier study by Yeates (1965), and it is instructive to summarize this model in terms of the model-building process outlined in Chapter 1. The *research problem* was to account for the spatial variation in land values within Chicago for the years 1910 and 1960, with two time periods being chosen to assess any significant change over time. Yeates and Garner expressed this research problem in visual form by producing land value surfaces for 1910 and 1960. A close inspection of these two maps suggested a number of variables to be included in the land value model. In particular, land values seem to decrease with increasing distance from the central business district, as predicted by Alonso's theory, and distance from Lake Michigan appeared to play a similar role.

In all, the model contains five variables, and the interrelationships among these five variables can be represented by means of a *conceptual model* (Figure 3.3). The variable to be explained, land value, is placed on the right-hand side of the diagram, and the explanatory variables are on the left-hand side. All of the explanatory variables—distance from the central business district, distance from Lake Michigan, distance from the nearest elevated-subway station, and distance from the nearest regional shopping center—are directly linked to the dependent variable.

This conceptual model can be translated into the following *symbolic model:*

$$V_i = f(C_i, M_i, E_i, S_i) \tag{3.4}$$

where V_i is the land value at site i, C_i is the distance from the central business district, M_i is distance from Lake Michigan, E_i is distance from the nearest elevated-subway station, and S_i is distance from the nearest regional shopping center. More specifically, Yeates and Garner hypothesized the following relationships:

$$V_i = a - b_1C_i - b_2M_i - b_3E_i - b_4S_i \tag{3.5}$$

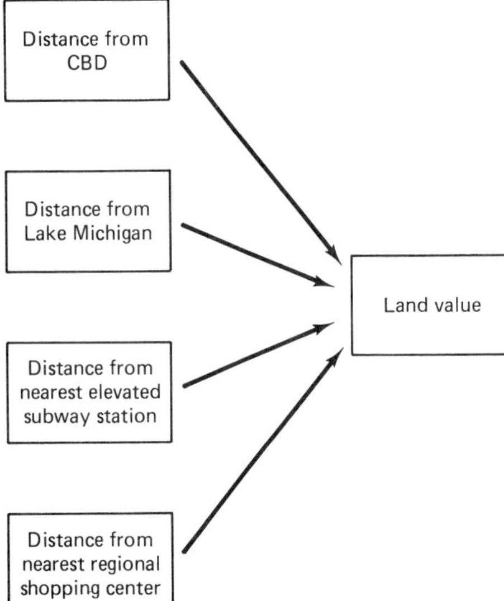

Figure 3.3 Conceptual model to explain the spatial distribution of land values in Chicago. (Based on M. H. Yeates, "Some factors affecting the spatial distribution of Chicago land values, 1910–1960," *Economic Geography*, 41, 1965, pp. 55–70.)

where the notation is the same as in equation (3.4), and $a, b_1, \ldots, b_4$ are constants. In other words, land values were expected to be inversely related to each of the independent variables.

The model was *operationalized* by using data from Olcott's *Blue Book of Chicago Land Values*, which gives a front-foot land value for every block in the city. Rather than use all these data, however, a sample of 484 front-foot land values was chosen, using a systematic, stratified, random sample procedure (Berry and Baker, 1968). This procedure is designed to ensure an adequate spatial coverage of sample points, thus reducing the risk of having a cluster of sample points in one particular part of the city. For purposes of the statistical analysis, all the data were transformed into logarithms.

Multiple correlation and regression analysis were chosen as the appropriate techniques for *testing* the overall goodness of fit of the model, and for assessing the relative importance of the explanatory variables (Table 3.1). For 1910 the coefficient of multiple determination was comparatively high, indicating that, in combination, the four explanatory variables accounted for over 75 percent of the variation in land values. Also, the signs of all the regression coefficients are negative, as hypothesized, and these regression coefficients are direct indicators of the relative importance of the explanatory variables, because all those variables were measured in common distance units. Distance from the central business district was the most important determinant of land values, followed, in order, by distance from Lake Michigan, distance from the nearest elevated-subway station, and distance from the nearest regional shopping center.

By 1960, however, the situation was rather different. First, the coefficient of multiple determination indicates that only just over 10 percent of the variation in

TABLE 3.1 CHICAGO LAND VALUES: COEFFICIENTS OF DETERMINATION (R^2), AND REGRESSION COEFFICIENTS, FOR 1910 AND 1960

Year	R^2	C	M	E	S
1910	.762	−.935	−.469	−.300	−.035
1960	.112	−.250	−.120	+.029	−.124

Source: Table 9.4 (p. 256) from *The North American City*, First Edition by Maurice H. Yeates and Barry J. Garner. Copyright © by Maurice H. Yeates and Barry J. Garner. Reprinted by permission of Harper & Row, Publishers, Inc.

land values was accounted for. In other words, the model was far more successful with respect to the 1910 data than with respect to the 1960 data. Second, the regression coefficient associated with distance from the nearest elevated-subway station is positive in 1960, reflecting the declining importance of this form of rapid transit. Third, although the other regression coefficients remained negative, the individual contribution of each variable is considerably less than it was in 1910.

In general, then, because of highway improvements and the increased use of private automobiles, accessibility considerations were far less important as a determinant of land values in 1960 than they were in 1910. Other variables, besides these location factors, must obviously be included in contemporary land value models. In particular, site factors, representing the intrinsic attributes of the individual site, should be taken into account together with the more traditional situation, or location factors.

A Multivariate Residential Land Value Model for Los Angeles

A multivariate residential land value model that incorporates both site and situation factors has been developed for Los Angeles by Brigham (1965). The conceptual model states that residential land values are a function of three major factors: accessibility to economic activities, amenities, and topography (Figure 3.4). This conceptual model can be expressed in symbolic form as follows:

$$V_i = f(P_i, A_i, T_i) \tag{3.6}$$

where V_i is the residential land value at site i, P_i is accessibility to economic activities, A_i is amenities, and T_i is topography.

The *accessibility to economic activities* factor is operationalized in two different ways. First, it is measured simply by calculating the distance to the central business district. Such an operationalization assumes that the central business district is the major workplace, and that it is equally accessible in all directions. Second, accessibility to economic activities is also measured by what is called *accessibility potential.* This concept is especially valuable when there are a variety of major workplaces in

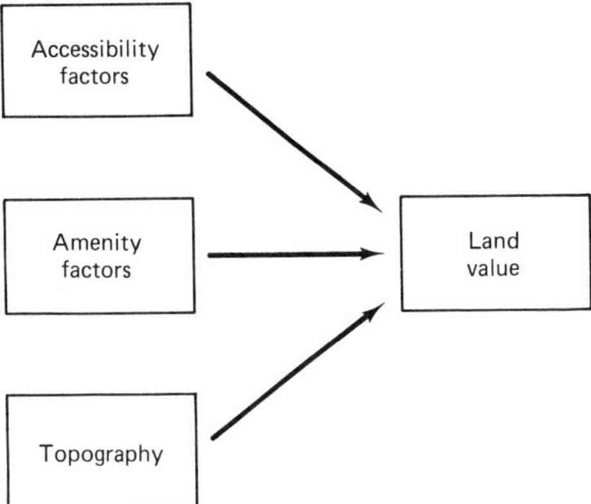

Figure 3.4 Conceptual model to explain the spatial distribution of residential land values in Los Angeles. (Based on E. F. Brigham, "The determinants of residential land values," *Land Economics*, 41, 1965, pp. 325–334.)

the city, as the accessibility potential of any given site is a direct function of the magnitude of surrounding employment opportunities, and an inverse function of the distances to those opportunities.

The *amenity value* associated with a particular site depends on the local neighborhood characteristics. In this instance, amenity value is measured by median family income, the percentage of dwelling units with more than 1.01 persons per room, and median single family housing value. Income and housing value should be positively related to land value, while crowding should be negatively related to land value.

Finally, *topography* is treated as a binary variable, with relatively hilly sites being assigned the value 1 and relatively flat sites the value 0. Topography should have a bearing on land values through its effect on development costs. Generally speaking, flat land can be comparatively easily subdivided into residential lots, whereas the costs associated with developing hilly land are far greater, due to the extra expenses incurred when putting in access roads, grading slopes, and providing utilities.

The data to calibrate the model, and to determine how well these three factors account for the variation in land values, were obtained from tax assessment appraisal records. Two arbitrary rays, or lines, were extended out from the Civic Center to the county boundaries. The first ray ran to the northwest of the Civic Center, through Hollywood, the Santa Monica Mountains, and out through the San Fernando Valley to the Ventura County boundary. The second ray ran to the northeast through South Pasadena to the base of the San Gabriel Mountains. Each block that these rays passed through was treated as a sample point.

As some of the explanatory variables are highly intercorrelated, two equations are used to test the model for each ray (Table 3.2). For both rays, distance from the central business district (CBD) is used in equation 1, while accessibility potential is used in equation 2, as these variables are too highly correlated to be used in unison. Overall, the coefficients of multiple determination suggest that the general model is very successful in terms of accounting for the variation in residential land values.

Both accessibility variables behave as expected, as the partial correlation coef-

TABLE 3.2 LOS ANGELES RESIDENTIAL LAND VALUES: COEFFICIENTS OF DETERMINATION (R^2) AND PARTIAL CORRELATION COEFFICIENTS

Ray 1:	Distance to CBD	Accessibility potential	Median income	Housing value	Topography	R^2
Equation 1	−.89		−.12	.44	−.64	.87
Equation 2		.53	−.01	.33	−.53	.79
Ray 2:	**Distance to CBD**	**Acessibility potential**	**Crowding**	**Housing value**	**Topography**	**R^2**
Equation 1	−.68		−.83	.17	−.69	.87
Equation 2		.73	−.87	.20	−.76	.89

Source: E. F. Brigham, "The determinants of residential land values," *Land Economics*, 41 (1965), Table 1, p. 331.

ficients indicate that land values are negatively related to distance from the central business district, and positively related to accessibility potential. The magnitudes of the partial correlation coefficients are different for the two rays, however. So, although there is clearly a relationship between land values and accessibility, the strength of that relationship varies from sample to sample. Housing value, one of the amenity variables, also behaves as expected in that it is in all cases positively correlated with land values. The median income variable, however, has an unexpected negative partial correlation for both equations, which is probably due to the high correlation between median income and housing value. Crowding is substituted for median income in the second ray, and here the result is exactly as expected, with the crowding variable exhibiting comparatively strong negative partial correlations. Finally, the binary level variable measuring topography also behaves as expected. For all four equations the partial correlation coefficient is negative, indicating that residential land values are relatively lower in the hilly areas.

In sum, Brigham's model successfully incorporates a variety of variables beyond the accessibility measures used by Yeates and Garner. The validity of the results, however, could be improved in at least two important ways. First, the sample could be made more representative by including more than two transects, and these transects should be chosen on the basis of some type of random sample design. Second, the stability of the relationships needs to be investigated by calibrating the model for a variety of different cities.

The two multivariate land values models that have just been described represent a rather different approach to the study of urban land values than that followed by Alonso. Alonso's model is based on a series of simplifying assumptions, and thus is not directly testable, as no single city can meet all these assumptions. In contrast, although the models of Yeates and Garner, and Brigham, are not constrained by such simplifying assumptions, they are directly applicable only to Chicago and Los Angeles, whereas the level of abstraction involved in Alonso's model makes it generally appropriate for all cities.

3.2 MULTIVARIATE HOUSING VALUE MODELS

As with land values, the intraurban variation in housing values is also amenable to investigation via multiple correlation and regression analysis. Before discussing examples of such housing value models, however, it is worthwhile considering the general nature of the urban housing market. In particular, we will focus our attention on the demand and supply of housing, and the various kinds of individuals and institutions that comprise the major elements in the urban housing market.

The Urban Housing Market

There are at least three major factors that determine the *demand for housing*. First, the overall demographic structure of the population plays a vital role in generating housing demand. The pressure on housing resources is especially severe when a large proportion of the population is concentrated within the age group between 30 and 40. Similarly, the rate of family formation is a critical determinant of housing demand, and this rate tends to vary in concert with the demographic profile of households.

Second, the demand for housing is closely tied to family income levels. The rapid rise in real income that has occurred in the United States since World War II has greatly spurred the demand for new single-family housing. Rises in real income have also increased the replacement demand, which involves a demand for new housing based on changing tastes and rising aspirations. When replacement demand is high, and yet there is no growth in the number of households, certain portions of the housing stock are simply abandoned. The income elasticity of demand for housing is defined as the proportional change in the demand for housing which results from a unit change in the level of real income. So if, for example, a 20 percent increase in real income leads to a 10 percent increase in the quality of housing demanded, the income elasticity is 0.5. In the United States, estimates of the magnitude of this income elasticity have ranged from 0.55 to 1.63, with a figure of 1.0 often being quoted as the average (Bourne, 1981, p. 127). More important, however, income elasticities tend to vary according to age, income, and ethnicity. For example, Moore and Clatworthy (1978) have suggested that a given increase in income produces a smaller increase in housing consumption among low-income than among high-income households. Also, elasticities appeared to be higher among families with children.

Third, the demand for housing is also significantly influenced by the availability of credit, and associated interest rates. Often the magnitude of the interest rate is of more immediate concern to a prospective homeowner than the price of the house itself, as monthly mortgage payments can vary quite substantially depending on the prevailing interest rates. When credit restrictions are comparatively severe, the number of new housing starts diminishes accordingly.

The *supply of housing* is also influenced by at least three major factors. First, the activity of private developers is of prime importance. Residential developers are especially responsive to vacancy rates as a means of monitoring the housing market and gauging its ability to absorb new dwelling units at appropriate prices. From the point of view of the buyer, of course, vacancies ensure a degree of choice and mobility, but housing suppliers hope for as low vacancy rates as possible.

Second, like the demand for housing, the supply of housing is also affected by the availability of cheap credit. Builders normally need to borrow large amounts of money in order to cover the initial construction costs. The money lenders, therefore, such as banks and savings and loan associations, can significantly influence the housing market, as they are able to regulate the flow of capital.

Finally, the federal government plays an important role in determining the supply of housing in the United States. The Housing Act of 1949 was of particular significance in this respect, as its stated goal of providing a decent home and suitable living environment for every American family led to programs of inner-city slum clearance and public housing construction, and stimulated single-family housing construction in the suburbs through mortgage guarantees (Palm, 1979). Since that time, urban renewal and low-rent public housing schemes have been significant instruments of direct government intervention in the urban housing market. The subsidies for new construction and slum clearance are administered by the Department of Housing and Urban Development, and more recently subsidies on the demand side have also been instituted. The latter subsidies often take the form of vouchers that are intended to increase the purchasing power of low-income families.

Besides considering the demand and supply of housing, the operation of the housing market can also be analyzed in terms of the actors involved, the behavior of some of which, such as residential developers and the federal government, has already been alluded to. These actors, or elements, in the housing market have been identified and categorized by Harvey (1972). Perhaps the most prevalent of these "actors" are the *occupiers* of housing, who act, for the most part at least, on the basis of use value rather than exchange value. There are two major categories of occupiers, owners and tenants, and the latter do not ordinarily receive any exchange-value benefit when they improve the use value of a property by modernizing or altering it in some way. Most tenants wish to become owner-occupiers eventually, mainly because of the tax advantages and security of tenure associated with home ownership.

Landlords, on the other hand, tend to be involved primarily with considerations of exchange value. How much they will invest in terms of improvements to their properties, however, depends on a variety of external factors, such as threats of highway clearance, urban renewal, vandalism, and general neighborhood deterioration. Also, the behavior of other, neighboring landlords is critical. It is only in those situations where all landlords decide to improve their properties that an individual landlord will maximize the economic returns to his or her investment. For this reason, landlords are generally reluctant to make improvements unless they are sure that their peers will behave in a similar fashion. It is to the benefit of an individual landlord in the housing market to slightly underinvest relative to other landlords in the neighborhood. However, if all landlords react this way, the housing stock will deteriorate quite rapidly. Note also that this kind of underinvestment is rational only for those landlords interested in the exchange value of housing, and does not apply to owner-occupiers concerned with the use value of housing. As a consequence, the housing stock of an area tends to deteriorate more rapidly under the exchange-value system than under the use-value system, unless landlords cooperate with each other.

As already mentioned, *residential developers*, and the construction industry in general, play an important role in determining the overall supply of housing, with respect to both the type and quantity of that housing. The residential development process has three major stages. First, a potentially profitable site must be identified and purchased. This process requires establishing the general nature and scale of the project, examining large areas to determine the probability of finding suitable sites, and evaluating specific sites in the chosen areas (Baerwald, 1981). Second, the site must be prepared for development, which involves such things as clearance and the provision of water, road, and sewage facilities. In this context, it is usually cheaper to develop new land on the urban fringe than it is to clear and redevelop land toward the center of the city. The third stage involves the housing construction itself. Throughout these stages the developers are concerned with whether or not they will obtain permission to build, financing will be available, and they will sell for a profit. As a result, most new construction is based on the demands of upper-income groups, as they are the groups most able to afford new housing. Low-income groups obtain housing via the "filtering of housing process," by which older housing is successively passed down to lower-income families.

Real estate agents play an important intermediary role in the housing market. They make a profit by charging for their services as coordinators between buyers and sellers, and for this reason, they tend to encourage turnover in the housing stock. Realtors also significantly influence migration patterns, as they are a major source of information about the housing market. In particular, of course, they tend to over-recommend areas in which they list homes, and thus have the potential for creating localized imbalances between supply and demand (Palm, 1979).

The major role of *financial institutions*, such as banks, savings and loan associations, and insurance companies, is to regulate the flow of money into the housing market (Doling and Williams, 1983). These financial institutions tend to avoid areas of housing that are preceived to have high risks and low rates of return associated with them. The resulting lack of mortgage money in certain parts of a city seriously hampers the purchase and improvement of housing in those areas. Harvey (1977) reports that commercial institutions prefer to provide mortgage money to households involved in purchasing higher-priced homes, as the servicing costs on mortgage loans are constant, and therefore the larger the mortgage, the greater the profit margin for the institution servicing it. State-chartered savings and loan associations are less profit oriented, and more interested in financing housing in the lower price ranges. As a result, there is a clear relationship between different types of financial institutions and different segments of the housing market.

Finally, it is in those areas of the city that lack adequate mortgage money that the *federal and local government* tend to play an important part in the operation of the housing market. Generally speaking, most governments have three major purposes in mind when intervening in the private market (Bourne, 1981, p. 192). First, they try to ensure that the productive resources of society are allocated as effectively as possible. Second, they try to stabilize the economic system such that major fluctuations are minimized. Third, they encourage continuing economic growth and a reduction in the level of social inequality. Within this context, besides directly providing housing through various types of public housing programs, the government also influences the character of the current housing stock by means of zoning and housing code legislation. Also, some kinds of government agencies, such as the Veterans' Administration, are directly involved in the provision of mortgage money.

A Multivariate Housing Value Model for Chicago

Berry and Bednarz (1975) have constructed and tested a multivariate housing value model for the city of Chicago. Selling prices of a sample of single-family homes in Chicago in 1971 was the dependent variable, while the explanatory variables were grouped into three general categories: location, housing characteristics, and neighborhood characteristics. The location variable represented an attempt to capture accessibility, and was measured by the distance of the home from downtown Chicago. Housing characteristics were subdivided into housing characteristics per se, measured by floor space, lot size, and the age of the house, and housing improvements, measured by four dummy variables indicating the presence or absence of air conditioning, a garage, an improved attic, and an improved basement, plus the number of bathrooms. The neighborhood characteristics were also subdivided into two groups. First, median family income, the percentage of multiple-family dwelling units, and the amount of migration were grouped together to represent neighborhood socioeconomic status and mobility characteristics. Second, percent blacks, percent Cubans and Mexicans, and percent Irish were used as racial and ethnic variables.

Data on the housing characteristics and housing improvement variables were obtained from the Society of Real Estate Appraisers' Market Data Center for a sample of 275 single-family homes. All the neighborhood characteristics were generated from census data, with figures corresponding to the census tract in which the property was located. Finally, the accessibility variable was calculated in terms of straight-line distance.

The results of the multiple regression analysis are reported in Table 3.3, and as the variables were in logarithmic form, the coefficients can be interpreted as elasticities. Overall, the 15 explanatory variables account for just under 80 percent of the total variation in house prices, and nearly all the relationships are in the the expected directions. With respect to the housing characteristics, floor space and lot size are both positively related to price, while age of the dwelling unit has a negative coefficient. Also, all the housing improvement variables exhibit the expected positive relationships.

In terms of the neighborhood characteristics, median family income has a positive influence on selling price, whereas migration, or the amount of population turnover, has a negative impact. A somewhat surprising result, however, is the positive relationship between the percentage of multiple-family dwelling units, or apart-

TABLE 3.3 CHICAGO HOUSING VALUES: COEFFICIENT OF DETERMINATION (R^2) AND REGRESSION COEFFICIENTS

Variable	Regression coefficient
Housing characteristics	
Floor space	.344
Age	−.123
Lot size	.123
Housing improvements	
Air conditioning	.078
Garage	.071
Improved attic	.124
Improved basement	.074
Number of baths	.130
Neighborhood characteristics	
Median family income	.720
Multiple family dwellings	.061
Migration	−.034
Race and ethnicity	
Percent blacks	−.022
Percent Cubans and Mexicans	−.013
Percent Irish	−.016
Acessibility	
Distance to CBD	.023
R^2	.787

Source: Adapted from B. J. L. Berry and R. S. Bednarz, "A hedonic model of prices and assessments for single-family homes: Does the assessor follow the market or the market follow the assessor?" *Land Economics*, 51 (1975), Table 4, p. 31.

ments, and house price. Ordinarily, one might expect proximity to apartments to bring down the housing value. In this context it should be noted that the rather unexpected behavior of the apartment variable might be due to its relatively high correlation with some of the other variables in the model. Such multicollinearity among the independent variables tends to result in rather unstable coefficients and makes it difficult to determine the true relationship between the independent and dependent variables involved.

The regression coefficients indicate negative relationships between house price and each of the three racial and ethnic variables; percent black, percent Cuban or Mexican, and percent Irish. These coefficients imply, then, that housing prices tend to be lower in those areas characterized by large racial or ethnic minorities. This result appears to be at odds with those obtained by some previous researchers, who have found, for example, that black households in U.S. cities tend to pay more than whites for comparable housing (see Section 3.4). It should be remembered, however, that the racial and ethnic variables are measured at the census tract level rather than for the individual houses. Finally, the coefficient for the accessibility variable reflects

TABLE 3.4 INCREASES IN EXPLANATORY POWER WITH THE ADDITION OF VARIABLE GROUPS

Variable group added	R^2
Housing characteristics	.474
Housing improvements	.568
Neighborhood characteristics	.741
Race and ethnicity	.772

Source: Adapted from B. J. L. Berry and R. S. Bednarz, "A hedonic model of prices and assessments for single-family homes: Does the assessor follow the market or the market follow the assessor?" *Land Economics*, 51 (1975), Table 3, p. 30.

the fact that housing price tends to increase with increasing distance from the central business district.

Table 3.4 reports the results obtained when successively entering the different groups of variables into the overall regression model. The housing characteristics and improvements were entered first, as it was felt that they are the most important variables in determining the value of housing. Similarly, the neighborhood characteristics were entered before the racial and ethnic variables in order to reflect their relative importance. The results indicate the increase in the coefficient of multiple determination (R^2) as each of the variable groups is added to the model.

Multivariate Housing Value Models for St. Louis

In a study similar to that of Berry and Bednarz, Jonathan Mark (1977) attempted to identify the determinants of housing value in St. Louis, Missouri. He developed four different models, although some of the variables appear in more than one model. The first model is a *housing characteristics model*, containing such variables as housing age, number of rooms, housing size, and presence or absence of central air conditioning. The second model is termed a *spatial model*, and contains a variable measuring distance from the central business district and a series of dummy variables representing location in terms of direction from the central business district. Third, an *accessibility model* was constructed, using such variables as distance from the central business district, distance from the airport, and the number of bus routes passing through the census tract. Finally, an *area preference model* was developed to measure characteristics of the local neighborhood, including median income, percent nonwhite, and expenditure per pupil in public schools.

The housing value data are actual sales prices for 6533 owner-occupied single-family dwelling units in St. Louis, and the ability of each of the four models to account for the variation in these sales prices is reported in Table 3.5. Corrected coefficients of determination are calculated to take into account the different number of variables in each model; otherwise, it would be difficult to tell whether a particular

TABLE 3.5 ST. LOUIS HOUSING VALUES: CORRECTED COEFFICIENTS OF DETERMINATION ASSOCIATED WITH FOUR DIFFERENT MODELS

Model	R^2
Housing characteristics	.647
Spatial	.345
Accessibility	.407
Area preference	.449

Source: J. Mark, "Determinants of urban house prices: A methodological comment," *Urban Studies*, 14 (1977), Table 2, p. 362.

model worked best due to having a greater number of explanatory variables or due to the inclusion of variables that are more important in terms of representing the causes of variation in housing values. These corrected coefficients indicate that the housing characteristics model works best, while the strictly spatial model has the least explanatory power.

3.3 CAUSAL MODELS OF HOUSING QUALITY AND SIZE

The multivariate models considered thus far have represented rather simplistic causal structures. In the present section more sophisticated causal structures are investigated, and then exemplified by two models of housing quality and housing size. These causal models allow one to distinguish between direct and indirect effects among the constituent variables.

Introduction to Causal Models

The land value and housing value models described previously are based on the assumption that only direct relationships exist between each of the explanatory variables and the associated dependent variable, as expressed in Figures 3.3 and 3.4. Such an assumption is overly simplistic, however, in two important ways. First, it does not allow for interrelationships between the explanatory variables. Second, it does not allow for feedback relationships, either between the dependent variable and the explanatory variables, or between the explanatory variables themselves.

In contrast, if it is hypothesized that each variable in a particular causal system is dependent on all the other variables in that system (Figure 3.5), a separate equation for each of the variables can be written as follows:

$$X_1 = a_1 + b_{12.3}X_2 + b_{13.2}X_3 + e_1 \tag{3.7}$$

$$X_2 = a_2 + b_{21.3}X_1 + b_{23.1}X_3 + e_2 \tag{3.8}$$

$$X_3 = a_3 + b_{31.2}X_1 + b_{32.1}X_2 + e_2 \tag{3.9}$$

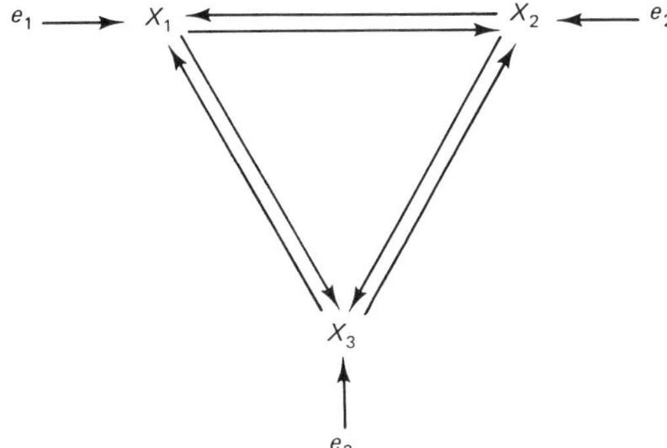

Figure 3.5 Three-variable nonrecursive model.

where the error terms e_1, e_2, and e_3 represent the effect of all variables outside the system on X_1, X_2, and X_3, respectively. Note that all possible interrelationships between the three variables are represented, and that each variable, in turn, is treated as the dependent variable.

When dealing with systems involving two-way causation, however, ordinary least-squares analysis should not be used to estimate the regression coefficients, as the error terms cannot be assumed to be uncorrelated with the independent variables in each equation. In these situations, when estimating *nonrecursive models*, other techniques such as two- or three-stage least-squares analysis should be adopted. As a result, we will postpone consideration of these more complex causal structures until later, and concentrate instead on *recursive models*, models that involve only one-way causation and thus do not allow for feedback effects.

A simple three-variable recursive model is represented in Figure 3.6. In this case all the arrows indicate one-way causality, and X_1 is an *exogenous* variable, determined by forces outside the system, while X_2 and X_3 are *endogenous* variables, as their values are at least partially determined by variables within the system itself. This causal structure can be described mathematically by the following three equations:

$$X_1 = e_1 \tag{3.10}$$

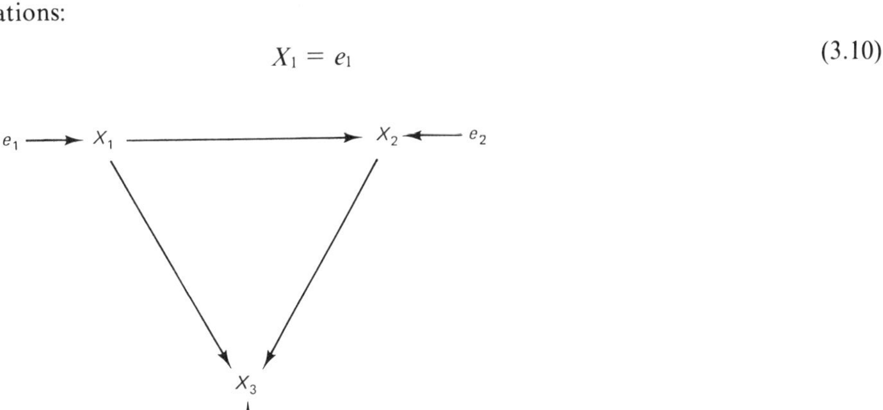

Figure 3.6 Three-variable recursive model.

$$X_2 = b_{21}X_1 + e_2 \tag{3.11}$$

$$X_3 = b_{31.2}X_1 + b_{32.1}X_2 + e_3 \tag{3.12}$$

Note that the a terms can be omitted by simply assuming that each variable is measured in standardized form, thus ensuring that the least-squares line passes through the origin, and that the a terms, or intercepts, are therefore zero.

In general, any kind of causal structure can be described by an appropriate set of equations. For example, the four-variable recursive model represented by Figure 3.7a can be expressed as follows:

$$X_1 = e_1 \tag{3.13}$$

$$X_2 = b_{21}X_1 + e_2 \tag{3.14}$$

$$X_3 = b_{31.2}X_1 + b_{32.1}X_2 + e_3 \tag{3.15}$$

$$X_4 = b_{41.23}X_1 + b_{42.13}X_2 + b_{43.12}X_3 + e_4 \tag{3.16}$$

The empirical adequacy of this causal structure is best understood by successively removing individual causal arrows from Figure 3.7a (Blalock, 1964, p. 66). If the arrow between X_1 and X_3 is eliminated (Figure 3.7b), it means that X_1 only has an indirect effect on X_3 via X_2. In other words, we are really saying that $r_{31.2} = 0$, meaning that when the intervening variable X_2 is controlled for, the partial correlation be-

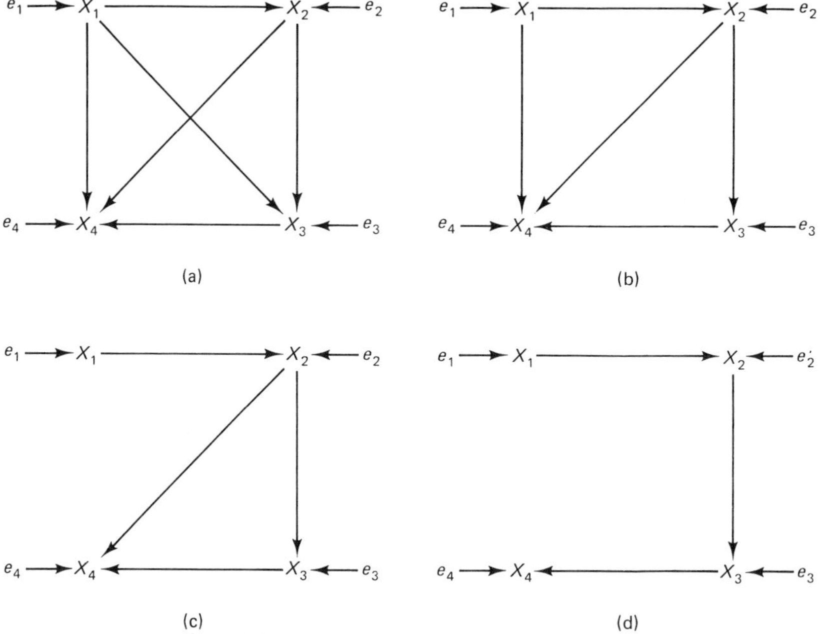

Figure 3.7 Examples of four-variable recursive models. (Based on H. M. Blalock, Jr., *Causal Inferences in Nonexperimental Research*, University of North Carolina Press, Chapel Hill, N.C., 1964, p. 66.)

tween X_1 and X_3 should be approximately zero. Also, if $r_{31.2} = 0$, the associated standardized regression coefficient $b_{31.2} = 0$, and thus disappears from equation (3.15).

If we next omit the arrow linking X_1 and X_4 (Figure 3.7c), we are saying that X_1 will only influence X_4 via X_2 and X_3. We are therefore predicting that $r_{41.23} = 0$ and that the associated standardized regression coefficient $b_{41.23}$ will disappear from equation (3.16). Finally, if the arrow linking X_2 and X_4 is removed (Figure 3.7d), we are hypothesizing that X_2 only influences X_4 via X_3, thus creating a simple causal chain going from X_1 to X_2, to X_3, to X_4. If this hypothesis is true, $r_{42.13} = 0$ and $b_{42.13} = 0$.

Many verbal theories in social science can be usefully stated in terms of causal models and their associated equations. Such statements tend to highlight any ambiguities, or inconsistencies, in the original verbal theory, and also cast that theory in a form that is empirically testable. An excellent example of this approach is represented by J. Mercer's (1975) application of causal modeling to metropolitan housing quality.

A Causal Model of Housing Quality

J. Mercer (1975) uses the causal modeling approach to evaluate a causal structure suggested by Richard Muth (1969). Generally speaking, Muth's thesis is as follows: Given that poor people tend to live in poor-quality housing, and given that a disproportionate number of black Americans are poor, the observed relationship between blacks and poor-quality housing can be explained largely in terms of income. The associated causal model is represented in Figure 3.8. In particular, it is hypothesized that there is no direct link between X_1 and X_3, only an indirect link via X_2. This causal structure is of interest, as it implies, for example, that racial discrimination in the housing market is not a major factor.

Mercer tested the adequacy of this causal structure by using data for the Chicago Metropolitan Area, as reported in the 1950 and 1960 U.S. Censuses of Population and Housing. The data were collected at the census tract level, with 1060 observations for 1950, and 1216 observations for 1960. Housing quality was measured by determining the percentage of blighted dwelling units in each census tract, where blight is represented by the percent of dwelling units that had no private bath or were dilapidated in 1950, and by the percent of dwelling units dilapidated, deteriorating

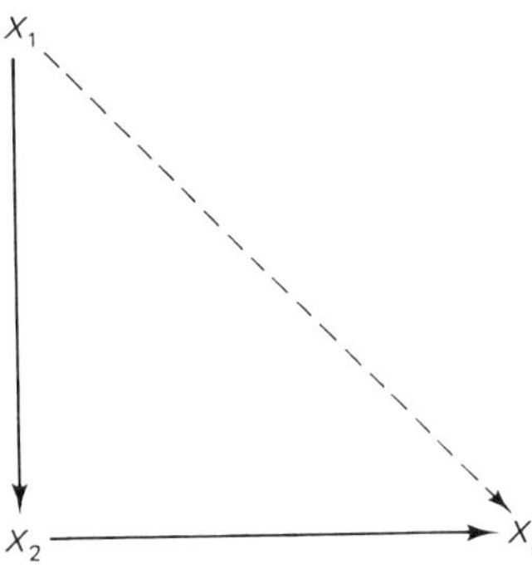

Figure 3.8 Hypothesized relationships between black Americans, income, and poor-quality housing. X_1, percent blacks in a census tract; X_2, median income; X_3, percent blighted dwelling units in a census tract. (Adapted by permission from John Mercer, "Metropolitan housing quality and an application of causal modeling," *Geographical Analysis*, 7 (July 1975), pp. 295–302. Copyright © 1975 by the Ohio State University Press.

TABLE 3.6 EMPIRICAL RELATIONSHIPS BETWEEN BLACK AMERICANS, INCOME, AND POOR-QUALITY HOUSING, IN CHICAGO

Year	r_{31}	$r_{21}r_{32}$
1950	.59	.39
1960	.45	.33

Source: Reprinted by permission from John Mercer, "Metropolitan housing quality and an application of causal modeling," *Geographical Analysis*, 7 (July 1975), Table 1, p. 298. Copyright © 1975 by the Ohio State University Press.

and lacking in plumbing facilities, or sound and lacking in plumbing facilities, in 1960.

The model predicts that there is no direct relationship between X_1 and X_3, meaning that $r_{31.2} = 0$. This partial correlation coefficient is computed as follows:

$$r_{31.2} = \frac{r_{31} - r_{21}r_{32}}{[(1 - r_{12}^2)(1 - r_{23}^2)]^{1/2}} \tag{3.17}$$

If, however, $r_{31.2} = 0$, then

$$r_{31} - r_{21}r_{32} = 0 \tag{3.18}$$

and therefore,

$$r_{31} = r_{21}r_{32} \tag{3.19}$$

In other words, in order for the partial correlation between X_1 and X_3, while controlling for X_2, to be zero, the zero-order correlation between X_3 and X_1 should be equal to the product of the zero-order correlations between X_2 and X_1, and between X_3 and X_2.

The results of this analysis are reported in Table 3.6. The differences between the values are sufficiently large to raise questions with respect to the acceptability of a Muth-type causal structure. The smaller gap between the values for 1960, however, suggests that income may be beginning to play a more important role.

A Causal Model of Housing Size

As a second example of the causal modeling approach, we can look at a causal model of housing size, although the version presented here is a substantial simplification of the original formulation by Guest (1972). The model is represented in Figure 3.9, and it can be seen that there is one exogenous variable, distance from the central business district, while the other four variables are endogenously determined. In particular, size of housing is determined both directly and indirectly by all the other variables in the model.

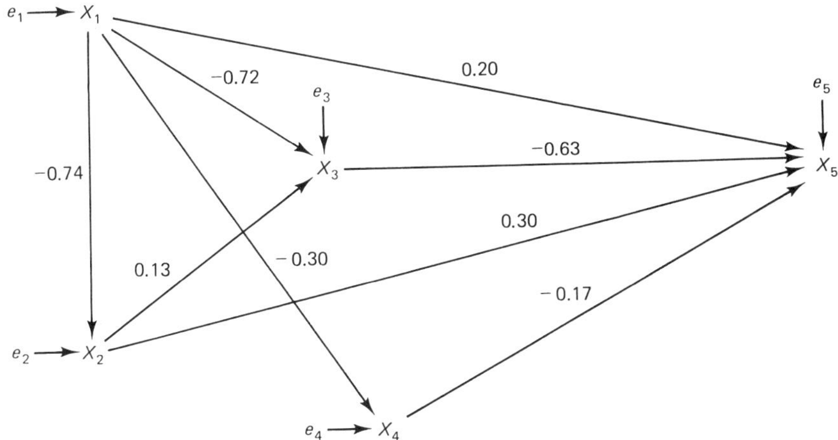

Figure 3.9 Causal model to explain variations in house size. X_1, distance from the central business district; X_2, housing age; X_3, housing density; X_4, industrial activity; X_5, housing size. (Based on A. M. Guest, "Patterns of family location," *Demography*, 9, 1972, Fig. 2, p. 165.)

The equations describing this recursive model are as follows:

$$X_1 = e_1 \tag{3.20}$$

$$X_2 = -b_{21}X_1 + e_2 \tag{3.21}$$

$$X_3 = -b_{31.2}X_1 + b_{32.1}X_2 + e_3 \tag{3.22}$$

$$X_4 = -b_{41}X_1 + e_4 \tag{3.23}$$

$$X_5 = b_{51.234}X_1 + b_{52.134}X_2 - b_{53.124}X_3 - b_{54.123}X_4 + e_5 \tag{3.24}$$

where X_1 is distance from the central business district, X_2 is age of housing, X_3 is housing density, X_4 is industrial acitivity, and X_5 is housing size. Note that values for the intercepts are not represented, as the data are in standardized form.

The model was tested using census tract data for the Cleveland, Ohio, Standard Metropolitan Statistical Area. Distance from the central business district, as defined by the U.S. Bureau of the Census, was measured in terms of 1-mile concentric zones. Age of housing was measured by the proportion of household units built before 1940. Housing density was represented by the natural logarithm of the number of household units per acre of residential land. Industrial activity was the natural logarithm of the proportion of the land area in industrial uses, and housing size was measured by the mean number of rooms per household unit.

All of the standardized regression coefficients in this model, as expressed in equations (3.20) to (3.24), can be thought of as *path coefficients*, measuring the strengths of the links in the causal structure. The values for these path coefficients have been included in Figure 3.9. They indicate, for example, that the link between distance from the central business district and housing age is fairly strong, whereas the link between industrial activity and housing size is comparatively weak.

The path coefficients also allow us to determine the *direct versus indirect* effect of variables on each other. For example, we can calculate the direct and indirect effect of distance from the central business district on each of the other variables in the system (Table 3.7). The zero-order correlation between distance from the CBD and housing age (r_{21}) can be decomposed into direct and indirect effects. However, in this particular model, there is only a direct path between these two variables (p_{21}), so the zero-order correlation is the same as the path coefficient. A similar situation occurs in the case of distance from the CBD and industrial activity, as again there is no indirect effect.

The relationship between distance from the CBD and housing density, however, can be decomposed into direct and indirect effects. The direct effect is represented by the path coefficient p_{31}. There is also an indirect effect via the chain from housing density, to housing age, to distance from the CBD. In other words, housing age acts

TABLE 3.7 DIRECT VERSUS INDIRECT EFFECTS OF DISTANCE FROM THE CBD ON EACH VARIABLE IN THE HOUSING SIZE CAUSAL MODEL

Housing age:

$$r_{21} = p_{21}$$

$$-.74 = -.74$$

Housing density:

$$r_{31} = p_{31} + p_{32}p_{21}$$

$$-.82 = -.72 + (.13)(-.74)$$

$$= -.72 + (-.10)$$

$$= -.82$$

Industrial activity:

$$r_{41} = p_{41}$$

$$-.30 = -.30$$

Housing size:

$$r_{51} = p_{51} + p_{52}p_{21} + p_{53}p_{31} + p_{53}p_{32}p_{21} + p_{54}p_{41}$$

$$.55 = .20 + (.30)(-.74) + (-.63)(-.72) + (-.63)(.13)(-.74) + (-.17)(-.30)$$

$$= .20 + (-.22) + .45 + .06 + .05$$

$$= .20 + .34$$

$$= .54$$

Source: Based on A. M. Guest, "Patterns of family location," *Demography* 9 (1972), Table 2, p. 164, and Figure 2, p. 165.

as an intervening variable. This indirect effect is calculated by obtaining the product of the two constituent path coefficients, p_{32} and p_{21}. In this way the zero-order correlation coefficient of −.82 can be decomposed into a direct effect of −.72 and an indirect effect of −.10.

Finally, the relationship between distance from the CBD and housing size is more complex still, as there are a number of causal chains connecting these two variables. The direct effect is represented by the path coefficient p_{51}. In addition, there are four different indirect effects, whose values are calculated by multiplying the constituent path coefficients. One of these indirect effects involves a three-link chain, going from housing size to housing density, from housing density to housing age, and from housing age to distance from the CBD. This particular indirect effect is measured by obtaining the product of the three path coefficients, p_{53}, p_{32}, and p_{21}. Overall, the zero-order correlation coefficient of .55 between housing size and distance from the CBD can be decomposed into a direct effect of .2, and an indirect effect of .34, although these two values do not exactly sum to .55 because of rounding errors.

In summary, the idea of being able to decompose relationships into direct and indirect effects, based on the existence of intervening variables, is a very seductive one. The complexity of both social and physical systems is such that unanticipated indirect effects are often produced when one tries to intervene or tamper with the system. Efforts to direct the national economy, for example, are often thwarted by unanticipated indirect effects. In the context of medicine, these indirect effects are commonly called side effects, although there impact on the patient can be quite substantial.

3.4 PROBLEMS IN THE URBAN HOUSING MARKET

A variety of problems are associated with contemporary urban housing markets, and two of these problems are discussed in the present section: discrimination and abandoned housing. Although this sample is by no means exhaustive, it accurately reflects the varied nature of the "housing problem."

Discrimination

A great deal has been written about housing submarkets and the fact that some of them might be biased against certain segments of the population. The issue of racial discrimination has been of particular concern, as there is evidence that black households in U.S. cities pay more than whites for comparable housing (Kain and Quigley, 1972; King and Mieszkowski, 1973). The evidence is by no means completely consistent, however, as others have found no statistical difference between black and white housing costs (Lapham, 1971). One of the difficulties in comparing the results obtained from different studies is that any price differential must be due solely to discrimination rather than differences in housing quality. In other words, great care must be taken when controlling for housing quality differences to ensure essentially identical housing bundles for the purpose of price comparison. Adding to this difficulty, empirical conclusions in such studies are also probably influenced by the short-run supply of housing in various neighborhoods, the relative numbers of black and white home buyers during the study period, and the availability of mortgage money within the study areas (Palm, 1979).

There are a variety of reasons why blacks might pay more than whites for similar-quality housing (Bourne, 1981, pp. 176–177). First, the combination of restricted housing choices due to segregation, and the rapid growth of the black population in certain parts of the city, has exerted upward pressure on prices and rents. Second, landlords may hesitate to rent to black households because they fear that racial change may lead to increased social problems and maintenance costs. Higher rents are charged, therefore, to cover these expected costs. Third, blacks might have less access to information concerning the housing market, due to discriminatory practices by real estate agents.

More generally, there are two extreme schools of thought as to why black households are concentrated in certain parts of the city and occupy lower-quality housing than do their white counterparts (Straszheim, 1974). One viewpoint assumes the existence of free choice in the housing market, and therefore attributes differences in black and white housing consumption to socioeconomic differentials. Specifically, it is argued that blacks have lower incomes than whites, and that they prefer to invest a smaller proportion of that income in housing. The idea of blacks preferring segregated neighborhoods, called self-segregation, is used to explain why middle- and high-income black households also tend to congregate together.

The alternative viewpoint emphasizes that the segregation of blacks is not merely due to income differences, but also occurs as a result of racial discrimination in the housing market. It is argued that blacks have been discouraged from entering certain submarkets, especially by the activities of realtors, who are sometimes unwilling to help them locate suitable housing, and financial institutions, who may refuse to provide adequate mortgage money. According to this view, the self-segregation hypothesis is inappropriate, because blacks have remained far more segregated than other immigrant or ethnic groups that also have strong cultural traditions.

Historically, one of the major tools for discimination in the housing market has been the practice of *redlining*, which can be traced back at least to the 1930s (Darden, 1980). In its extreme form, redlining refers to the alleged policy of financial institutions whereby they refuse to make mortgage funds available to certain high-risk neighborhoods within a city. The term "redlining" was coined because it was believed that lending officials actually drew a red line on a map around the borders of such neighborhoods. Less extreme forms of redlining can include the requirement of higher down payments in certain neighborhoods, the requirement of particularly short loan maturities, the requirement of higher interest rates than would be charged in other neighborhoods, and the under appraising of property so that the loan is smaller. These last three practices increase the monthly payments that the buyer has to make.

Those neighborhoods that are typically earmarked for redlining tend to have one or more of the following characteristics: older housing; lower- or middle-class income groups; racially integrated, white ethnic, or black populations; and a location near other poorer or declining neighborhoods (Darden, 1980). Once the process of redlining has been initiated, neighborhoods often tend to decline in a self-reinforcing cycle of decay. Home improvement loans and property insurance are difficult to obtain, resulting in poor maintenance and the development of abandoned housing. Neighborhood businesses begin to leave, and property values decline at an increasing rate. Eventually, the deteriorating physical structure of the area creates negative spillover effects, or externalities, for the surrounding neighborhoods.

Dennis Dingemans (1979) has noted a strong association between the racial and ethnicity characteristics of neighborhoods and mortgage lending behavior in Sacramento, California. The level of lending is low in the areas of black and Chicano concentration, and in general tends to increase with increasing distance from the census tracts with significant minority populations. Similarly, there is a strong association between the socioeconomic status of neighborhoods and mortgage lending behavior. As Dingemans is careful to point out, however, there are at least two major lines of reasoning that could be used to account for these relationships. First, it can be argued that mortgage lenders initiate neighborhood decline by refusing to lend money in certain neighborhoods. Alternatively, it can also be argued that lenders follow, rather than initiate, the cycle of neighborhood deterioration. According to this interpretation, few mortgages are issued in declining neighborhoods merely because there are few qualified buyers.

Abandoned Housing

Abandoned housing is a conspicuous problem in contemporary cities, and it is important to analyze the spatial distribution of abandoned housing, the processes responsible for its occurrence, and any possible solutions. Within this context, an abandoned house is a housing unit that has been withdrawn from the housing market and will not be returned to that market in the same use. There is, of course, great variation within the national pattern of abandoned housing, with the older cities in the Northeast being particularly susceptible to this problem. Of greater significance, however, is the uneven distribution of abandoned housing within cities. Dear (1976) has suggested that there are two stages associated with the *spatial pattern of abandoned housing*, and has illustrated these stages with data from Tioga, in central North Philadelphia.

Tioga is an area of six census tracts, and in December 1969 a survey revealed that 369 residential structures of the area's 12,549 residential units, or approximately 2.9 percent, had been abandoned. The spatial pattern of these abandonments had two main characteristics. First, at the macrolevel, there were large clusters of abandoned housing, each consisting of about 10 to 12 blocks. Second, at the microlevel, there were many clusters of two or three individual units within the larger clusters. Between December 1969 and February 1971, a further 155 residential structures were abandoned. The pattern in 1971 was very similar to that in 1969, except that the distribution appeared to have intensified. The large macrolevel clusters were still very much in evidence, but the microlevel clusters within them had grown to include more individual units, sometimes as many as five or six.

This two-stage process of initial abandonment and later consolidation is represented schematically in Figure 3.10. The spatial pattern suggests that the process is a contagious one, with a leader–follower sequence that resembles the diffusion of a plant species. A more detailed understanding of the processes responsible for this pattern is necessary, however, if urban planners are to make informed decisions concerning appropriate types of intervention in the housing market.

Dear (1976) has suggested an explanation for abandonment that involves four separate levels (Figure 3.11). First, the major force underlying abandonment is explained. Second, the process by which this underlying force becomes localized, and is manifested within particular neighborhoods, is explored. Third, the precise cause of abandonment within these neighborhoods is identified. Fourth, the internal dynamic of abandonment is discussed.

The *major force* underlying the process of housing abandonment is the suburbanization of population and economic activity. As discussed in Chapter 1, this suburbanization process has resulted in the declining tax base of central cities, and the flow of migrants into the inner city has diminished to a point at which many central cities have experienced a net loss of population. As a result, the traditional functions of the inner city have changed. In particular, it is no longer the major source of industrial employment, especially since the emergence of industrial parks at the edge of cities. This changing land use function would not ordinarily be cause for concern, except that in the inner city context no successor function has appeared on the scene. In other words, no major land use has come forward to take over the land that is being released from the inner-city housing market. The normal succession of land use functions, dictated primarily by economic concerns, does not appear to be operating, thus leaving a "functional vacuum."

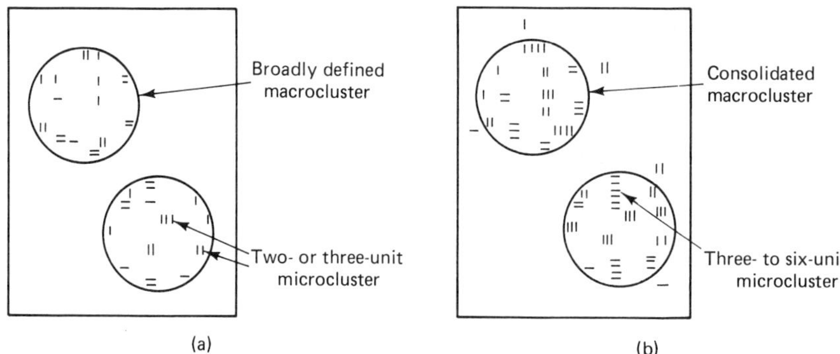

Figure 3.10 Diagrammatic representation of a two-stage process of housing abandonment: (a) initial abandonment (leaders); (b) consolidation (followers). (From M. J. Dear, "Abandoned housing," in J. S. Adams, Ed., *Urban Policymaking and Metropolitan Dynamics: A Comparative Geographical Analysis*, Ballinger, Cambridge, Mass., 1976, Fig. 3.3, p. 67.)

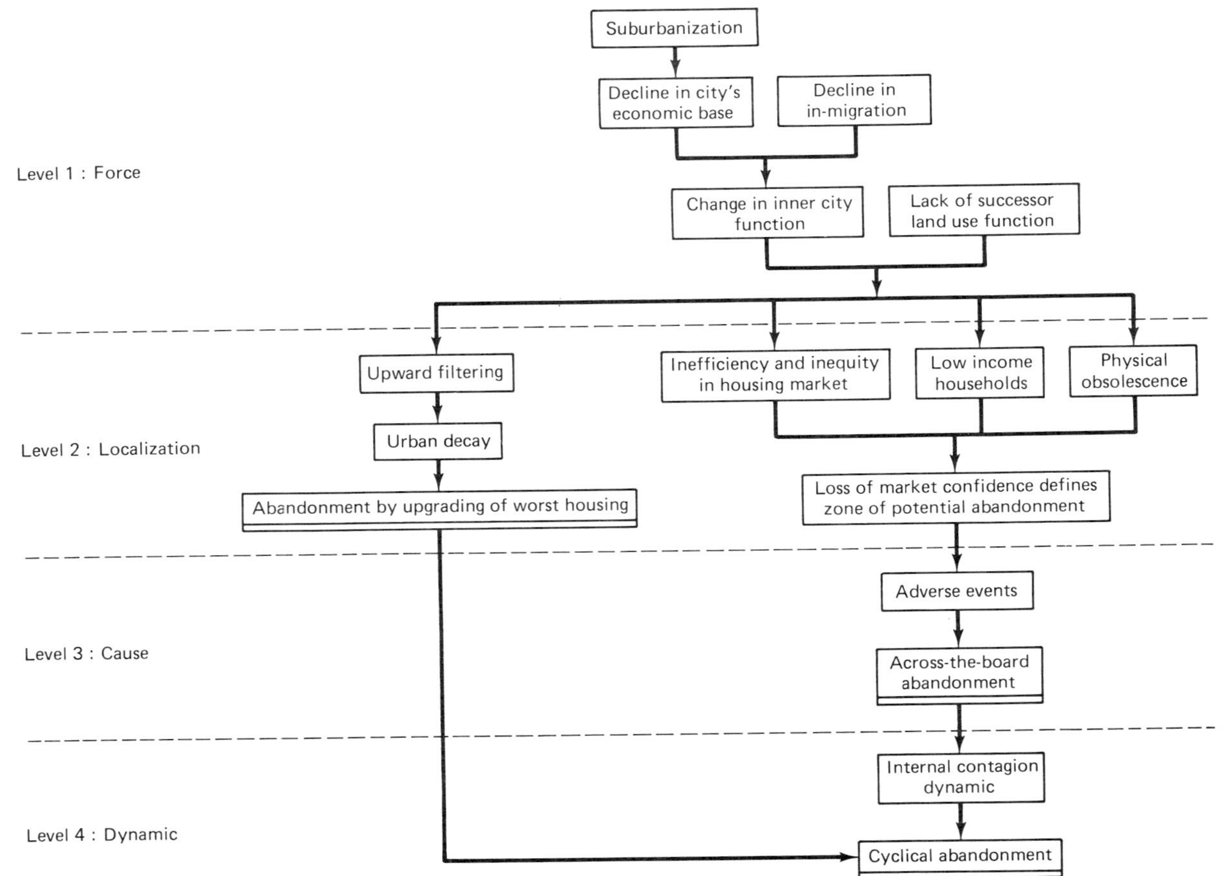

Figure 3.11 An explanation for abandoned housing. (From M. J. Dear, "Abandoned housing," in J. S. Adams, Ed., *Urban Policymaking and Metropolitan Dynamics: A Comparative Geographical Analysis*, Ballinger, Cambridge, Mass., 1976, Fig. 3.11, p. 91.)

There are two ways in which this general process of abandonment is *localized within particular neighborhoods*. First, as the housing stock in a neighborhood becomes old and dilapidated, there is an upward filtering of households into better housing units in other parts of the city. Given the general decline in demand for inner-city housing, however, the worst housing at the end of the filtering chain is abandoned. A second cause of the localization of abandoned housing is related to the incidence of poverty. An extremely low-income household is financially unable to participate in the filtering process or improve its present house. The increasing obsolescence of the housing stock leads to a situation in which there is a loss of confidence in that particular submarket, as manifested by declining property values. Such submarkets, or neighborhoods, constitute zones of potential abandonment.

The *actual cause of abandonment*, within one of these zones, is often related to some adverse event that befalls a particular property owner, such as an extreme case of vandalism. Outside the zones of potential abandonment, where confidence in the housing market remains high, these adverse events would be absorbed by the property owner, but within these zones investments in housing maintenance are not financially rewarding. Individual adverse events explain the initial abandonments in a neighborhood, but once begun, the contagious process of abandonment alluded to previously tends to take on an *internal dynamic* all its own, resulting in a form of cyclical abandonment. The presence of abandoned property in a neighborhood encourages landlords to undermaintain there own property, and decay is further accelerated by the fact that such neighborhoods become prime targets for vandalism and arson.

Dear (1976) suggests a series of possible strategies for reducing the incidence of abandoned housing. First, *public corporations* could be established and charged with the specific responsibility of rehabilitating the inner city. Such a body would acquire land and property in the neighborhood under its jurisdiction, and administer any federal, state, or local grants that might have been targeted for that particular neighborhood.

Second, *plans for neighborhood revitalization* should be developed involving local community cooperation. These plans would pay particular attention to the preferred overall function and land use pattern of the local area, and suggest ways in which that land use pattern might be achieved by zoning regulations.

Third, a *public works labor force* might be established to renovate the local housing stock. This labor force could be organized and operated by the previously mentioned public corporation. It would be concerned primarily with improving publicly owned housing, but could also be used to renovate private property, for appropriate fees.

Fourth, current government housing subsidies to help the supply side of the housing market could be at least partially realigned into a *housing allowance program*. A scheme of direct housing allowances for low-income families would provide them with greater purchasing power in the housing market, and help to reduce the inordinate power of large landlords within the inner-city housing market.

4

Urban Retail Structure and Population Density Patterns

4.1 ELEMENTS OF THE URBAN RETAIL STRUCTURE

Two of the spatial distributions most closely associated with that of land values are the patterns of retailing and population density. In the present chapter we discuss the elements of the urban retail structure, the spatial organization of shopping centers, and the issues of commercial blight and downtown redevelopment. Then we will turn our attention to the pattern of population density, including the idea of density surfaces, and conclude with a discussion of the relationship between population density and social pathology.

The retail structure of urban areas is composed of three main elements: specialized areas, ribbons, and retail nucleations (Herbert and Thomas, 1982, p. 207). These elements, and their associated subtypes, are represented in Figure 4.1, although not all cities contain every subtype. In particular, smaller cities are often lacking in terms of ribbon developments and specialized areas, or they might not contain all levels in the hierarchy of retail nucleations. After describing the major characteristics of these three elements, we will examine their relationship to the pattern of land values discussed in Chapters 2 and 3.

Specialized Areas

Specialized areas are concentrations of retail or service establishments that have something in common. Such concentrations make it easier for consumers to compare prices and quality, and also allow the retailers to use each other's facilities. For exam-

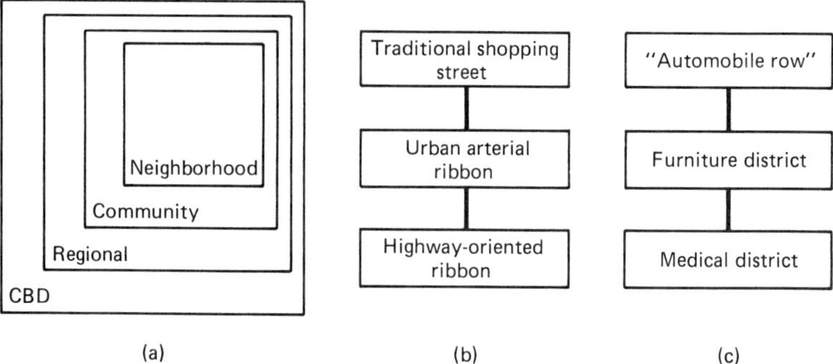

Figure 4.1 Elements of the urban retail structure: (a) retail nucleations; (b) ribbons; (c) specialized areas. (Based on B. J. L. Berry, *Commercial Structure and Commercial Blight: Retail Patterns and Processes in the City of Chicago*, Department of Geography Research Paper 85, University of Chicago, 1963, Table 2, p. 20.)

ple, major medical centers often have one central laboratory for analyzing blood samples, or a central x-ray testing facility.

One of the best examples of a specialized area is "*automobile row*," where one finds new- and used-car showrooms, plus associated facilities such as body shops, service stations, and spare parts outlets. Buying a car involves a major outlay of money, so consumers wish to compare prices and quality carefully before coming to a final decision. This kind of comparative shopping is facilitated by the clustering of car showrooms.

Furniture districts are also a relatively common feature of larger urban areas. Such districts usually include a variety of different types of furniture stores, plus ancillary activities such as furniture repairs and rental furniture stores. As with automobiles, the purchase of furniture is a relatively expensive, but infrequent event. Therefore, consumers generally wish to evaluate their options carefully, and are willing to travel to some specialized area of the city in order to compare products.

Similarly, *medical districts* also represent a clustering of linked activities. Doctors, dentists, hospitals, and pharmacies are often located together in medical centers. Here the clustering tendency reflects not so much a desire to facilitate comparative shopping, but a desire to concentrate related activities and functions. For example, including a pharmacy in a medical center or clinic reduces the amount of time patients spend traveling.

In general, then, these specialized areas are associated with the provision of higher-order goods and services, that is, goods and services that are quite expensive but are not required on a daily basis. Because such areas often cater to the whole city, they require very accessible locations, near freeways or major highways. Originally, these specialized areas arose from the informal clustering of similar establishments or related functions, but increasingly they are being developed according to a formal set of plans, especially in the case of complex medical centers.

Ribbons

Ribbon developments are composed of retail and service activities that are associated with automobile traffic. Such establishments include fast-food restaurants, drive-in banks, motels, and service stations. As the demand for these goods and services is generated by the flow of automobile traffic, it is those highways with the greatest traffic volume that tend to be the most densely developed. Freeways would not be included in this category, as their accessibility is restricted to a series of relatively widely spaced intersections and off-ramps.

The *traditional shopping street* is perhaps the most common form of ribbon development, especially in the older parts of cities. Such streets are generally associated with low-order convenience goods and services, such as groceries, laundromats, and drugstores. These goods and services are described as being low-order because they are relatively inexpensive and are demanded on a day-to-day basis. Often such streets are the scene of multipurpose trips, as one can be doing the groceries while washing the clothes in the laundromat.

The *urban arterial ribbons* are similar in many ways to the specialized areas, as they are composed of facilities associated with infrequent demand. They are different from the specialized areas, however, in that the individual establishments generally function independently of each other and are often large consumers of space. Lumberyards, funeral parlors, housing supplies, and television repairs and services exemplify the types of activities that are found along arterial ribbons.

Highway-oriented ribbons contain business types that are most closely related to traffic generated demand. These ribbons represent the classic type of ribbon development, involving gas stations, motels, ice-cream parlors, drive-in banks, and other kinds of financial institutions. As with the arterial ribbons, but unlike the traditional shopping streets, there is usually very little functional linkage between the individual establishments. Highway-oriented ribbons are different from arterial ribbons, however, in that the goods and services they sell are less specialized and in more frequent demand.

Ribbon development in general is often accused of being a major contributor to visual blight in cities. This is because such ribbons are only haphazardly planned, especially in comparison with some of the large, modern shopping centers. They are also usually adorned with large billboards, and most cities do not have effective policies or ordinances concerning the size and spacing of these billboards. The problem of visual blight has received especially critical attention when it is associated with major highways leading out to suburban communities.

Retail Nucleations

The third component of the urban retail structure is made up of various kinds of retail nucleations that are usually quite widely dispersed within cities. Some of these nucleations are unplanned, often at the intersection of two strips of ribbon development, while others, especially in younger cities, are planned shopping centers. Whether planned or unplanned, however, these retail nucleations form a hierarchy of shopping centers, with the smaller centers providing low-order goods and services that are required on a daily basis, while the larger centers provide more specialized high-order goods and services that are required at more infrequent intervals.

The top of this hierarchy is represented by the *central business district* (CBD). As the name implies, the CBD is usually located toward the center of the city and attracts consumers from all parts of the city. In smaller cities, the CBD is still the major retailing, entertainment, and financial center, although in some larger cities these functions have been progressively usurped by outlying regional shopping centers. This latter situation has created serious problems of commercial abandonment in central cities, a topic that will be taken up later when we discuss various problems associated with the urban retail structure.

The CBD in very large cities can be subdivided into smaller functional regions, creating a core area surrounded by a frame area (Herbert and Thomas, 1982, p. 215). The *core area* is characterized by very intensive land use, as manifested by multistoried buildings, or "skyscrapers," of various kinds, and is usually the focus of a city's mass transit and freeway systems. It is dominated by (1) very specialized retailing activity; (2) financial institutions, such as savings and loan associations, banks, and insurance companies; and (3) the main offices of large companies.

By contrast, the *fringe area*, or frame, is characterized by less intensive land use, such as warehouses, transportation facilities, and light manufacturing. These are the activities that cannot afford the high-priced land at the core, partly because they are less sensitive to accessibility considerations and so have lower bid-rent curves, as discussed in Chapter 2, and also because they are space-consuming kinds of activities. Mixed in with these commercial activities are clusters of low-quality multifamily residences that are often in the process of becoming abandoned and being converted into other more profitable uses.

The next level in the hierarchy of retail nucleations is represented by *regional shopping centers*, which contain such specialized functions as department stores, camera shops, and music stores. As mentioned previously, in some cities these outlying regional shopping centers have taken over some of the functions traditionally associated with the CBD, and they often contain cinemas, banks, legal offices, and real estate agents. As these shopping centers are very similar to each other in terms of level of specialization and the variety of goods and services provided, each one tends to attract its consumers from a particular subregion within the city.

The *community centers* and *neighborhood centers* are responsible for providing less specialized goods and services that are required more frequently. Variety stores, clothing stores, and jewelers are often found in the community centers, while the neighborhood centers are occupied by even lower-order functions, such as supermarkets, bakeries, and laundromats. The neighborhood centers are responsible for serving the needs of very localized areas within the city, while the community centers serve somewhat larger subregions, although these are still smaller than the subregions served by the regional shopping centers. The exact nature of this hierarchy of retail nucleations will be examined in greater detail after we have considered the interrelationships between the overall urban retail structure and the pattern of land values.

The Urban Retail Structure and the Pattern of Land Values

As described in Section 2.3, the generalized urban land value surface has three major components (Figure 2.12). First, land values reach a peak toward the center of the city. Second, there are ridges of higher-valued land associated with major highways. Third, there are local peaks of higher land value at the intersections of those major highways. These three components are closely related to the elements of the urban retail structure that we have just discussed. Specifically, the CBD is located on the highest-valued land at the center of the city, the various outlying shopping centers are located at the local peaks, while the ribbons are associated with the ridges in the land value surface.

This close correspondence between the pattern of land values, on the one hand, and the pattern of retailing, on the other, should come as no surprise, as both land values and retailing are heavily dependent on accessibility considerations. We have already discussed how the various bid-rent curves associated with different types of land use respond to differing accessibility, thus ensuring that the land value pattern is similarly influenced. Retailing is equally sensitive to accessibility considerations, as retail establishments depend on a steady flow of customers.

4.2 THE SPATIAL ORGANIZATION OF SHOPPING CENTERS

The spatial pattern of shopping centers in cities can be explained by central place theory, although this theory was originally applied to settlement patterns (Warnes and Daniels, 1979). Within the context of the intraurban structure of cities, central place theory attempts to account for the number, size, and spacing of shopping centers, or retail nucleations. The theory will be examined in three parts: a conceptual overview, the formal theory, and empirical tests of that theory.

Conceptual Overview

Imagine that we have a small bakery store located somewhere in the city. In order to stay in business, the baker must earn "normal" profits. These normal profits are just sufficient to cover the operating costs associated with the bakery, including a reasonable wage for the baker, or entrepreneur. To realize these normal profits, the baker must reach a certain threshold sales volume. In other words, he or she must serve a certain minimum population or market area.

This concept of a threshold, or minimum market area, is expressed diagrammatically in Figure 4.2. More formally, the *threshold of a good or service* is the minimum population required to support that good or service. If, in the long run, the

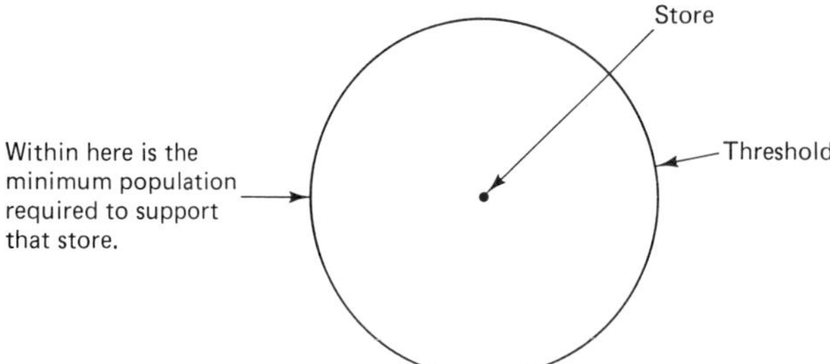

Figure 4.2 Threshold of a good or service.

entrepreneur fails to reach the threshold sales volume, he or she will go out of business. The size of the required threshold will vary from good to good, with jewellers, for example, needing a larger minimum population, or market area, than bakers. The calculation of these different threshold sizes will be discussed a little later, however.

A second concept that is of fundamental importance to central place theory is the *range of a good or service*. The price the consumer must pay for a particular good or service will vary according to how far away from the store he or she lives. In general, the farther away a person lives, the more the good will cost, as transportation costs must be added to the original price of the good. In other words, there will be a positive relationship between delivered price and distance from the store (Figure 4.3a).

According to microeconomic theory, as the price, or in this case delivered price, of a good or service increases, the demand for that good or service will generally decrease (Figure 4.3b). Just how quickly the demand decreases depends on the elasticity associated with the product in question. Where the decrease in demand is quite small, as reflected by a gently sloping demand curve, it means that the demand for the good is relatively elastic, and therefore comparatively insensitive to changes in price. On the other hand, where the decrease in demand is quite dramatic, as reflected by a steeply sloping demand curve, it means that the demand for the good is relatively inelastic, and therefore very sensitive to changes in price.

It follows from these two relationships that there must be a negative relation-

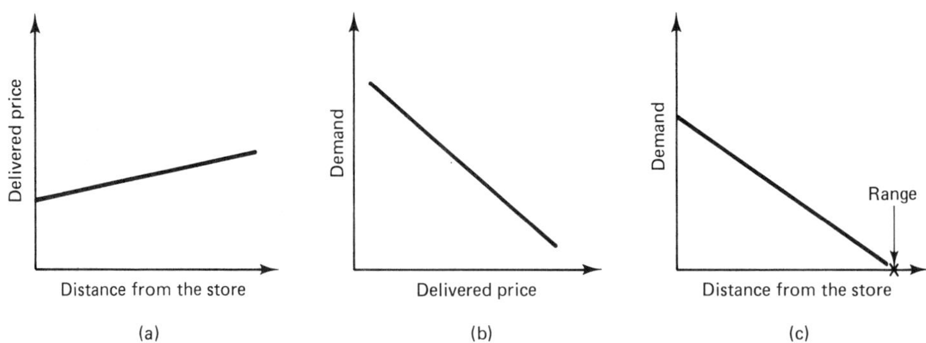

Figure 4.3 Range of a good or service.

ship between demand and distance from the store (Figure 4.3c). As delivered price increases with increasing distance, and demand decreases with increasing delivered price, demand must also decrease with increasing distance. In fact, at a certain distance, the demand curve will intersect the horizontal axis, indicating that demand is effectively zero beyond that point. This particular distance corresponds to the range of a good or service, so we can state more formally that the range of a good or service is the maximum distance people will travel to purchase that good or service.

If the threshold and range are superimposed on each other, it is possible to see how bakers, or any other kind of entrepreneur, might earn greater than normal, or excess profits (Figure 4.4a). In those situations where the range lies outside the threshold, the area between the threshold and the range represents excess profits that accrue to the entrepreneur. In other words, all the people living in the area between the threshold and the range are over and above the minimum population required to earn normal profits. Over the long run, we can expect other bakers to move into the area and thus soak up the excess profits (Figure 4.4b). Conversely, if stores are earning less than normal profits, we can expect some of them eventually to go out of business, thus increasing the market areas of those remaining. In this sense the system always tends to be moving toward an equilibrium position in which all entrepreneurs earn normal profits.

As mentioned earlier, threshold size will vary across different types of goods and services. The threshold populations contained in Table 4.1 are from a study based upon Snohomish County, Washington. Specific values like these are most easily obtained by simply dividing the total population by the number of filling stations, for example. In this particular case, then, there are 196 people per filling station. Such a simple methodology for computing threshold sizes does involve certain problems, however. First, if some of the filling stations are earning less than normal profits, the true threshold is somewhat higher than 196. Conversely, if some filling stations are earning excess profits, the true threshold is somewhat lower. Second, we are not really dealing with a closed economic system. Some people from Snohomish County will travel outside the county to purchase their gasoline, while others living outside

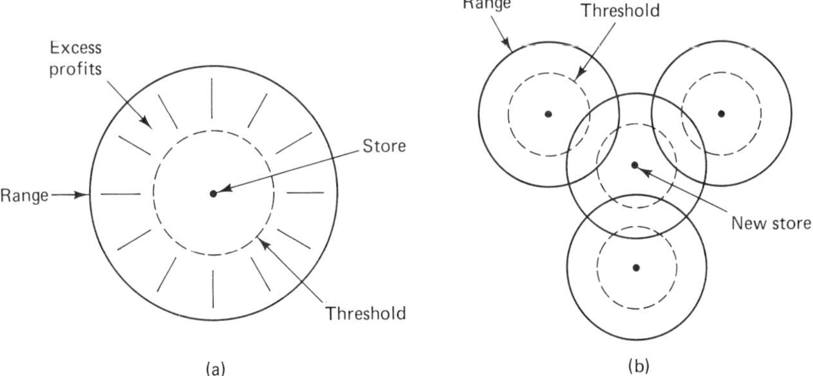

Figure 4.4 Threshold and range combined.

TABLE 4.1 THRESHOLD SIZES FOR SELECTED CENTRAL FUNCTIONS IN SNOHOMISH COUNTY, WASHINGTON

Central functions	Threshold size
Filling stations	196
Food stores	254
Restaurants	276
Appliance stores	385
Hardware stores	431
Drugstores	458
Furniture stores	546
Apparel stores	590
Florists	729
Jewelry stores	827
Sporting goods stores	928
Department stores	1083

Source: B. J. L. Berry and W. L. Garrison, "The functional bases of the central place hierarchy," *Economic Geography*, 34 (1958), Table 2, p. 150.

the county will purchase gasoline while traveling through it. If there are more people living within the county but purchasing gasoline outside the county than vice versa, the threshold size is overestimated. Finally, the threshold size will vary according to the size of the filling station and the income of the surrounding population. All other things being equal, larger filling stations will require larger threshold sales populations, or market areas. Also, those filling stations surrounded by low-income households will require a larger market area than those surrounded by high-income households, as the latter have greater disposable incomes and are therefore likely to use more gasoline.

In any event, despite these methodological shortcomings, Table 4.1 is worth close inspection, as it provides the basis for the *central place hierarchy* within cities (Berry and Garrison, 1958). It should be remembered, however, given the previous discussion, that it is only the ordering of central place functions that will remain relatively stable from city to city, not the absolute threshold values themselves. The functions with the lowest thresholds, such as filling stations and food stores, are referred to as low-order functions, while those with higher thresholds, such as jewelry stores and department stores, are referred to as high-order functions. Following from this distinction, the smallest shopping centers, or neighborhood shopping centers, are characterized by low-order functions, while the regional shopping centers are characterized by higher-order functions (Table 4.2).

Furthermore, the size of the market area associated with each class of shopping center will be related to the kinds of functions contained within that center. More specifically, neighborhood centers will have comparatively small market areas, whereas regional centers will serve much larger areas. As a result, in any given city, we should expect to find fewer regional centers than neighborhood centers. The overall hierarchy of centers, according to the size and number of them at each level, com-

TABLE 4.2 SELECTED BUSINESS TYPES TYPICAL OF SHOPPING CENTERS IN CITIES

Neighborhood shopping centers
Barbers
Cleaners/laundry
Drugs
Hardware
Beauty
Bakery
Real estate and insurance
Community shopping centers
Variety
Clothing
Dairy
Lawyer
Jewelry
Post office
Regional shopping centers
Department stores
Shoes
Sporting goods
Banks

Source: B. J. L. Berry, "Ribbon developments in the urban business pattern," *Annals of the Association of American Geographers*, 49 (1959), Table 1, p. 147.

prises a series of steps (Figure 4.5). In a medium-sized city, for example, there might be one CBD, four regional shopping centers, and so on.

Finally, in terms of this conceptual overview of central place theory, it should be noted that the market areas associated with the different levels in the hierarchy of shopping centers will tend to nest inside each other, thus reflecting the *nesting principle* (Figure 4.6). Inside the market area for the CBD will be a series of regional cen-

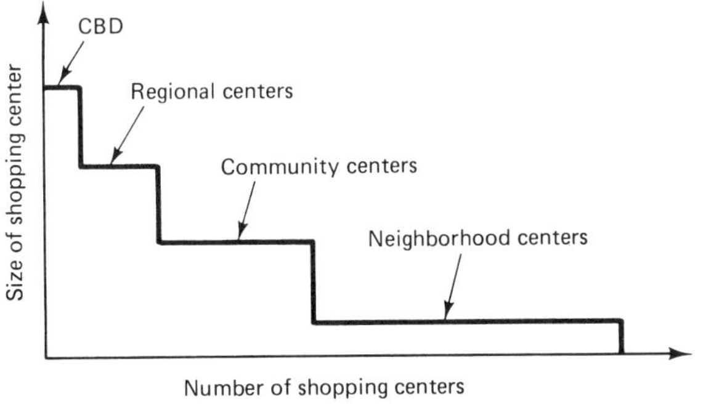

Figure 4.5 Hierarchy of shopping centers.

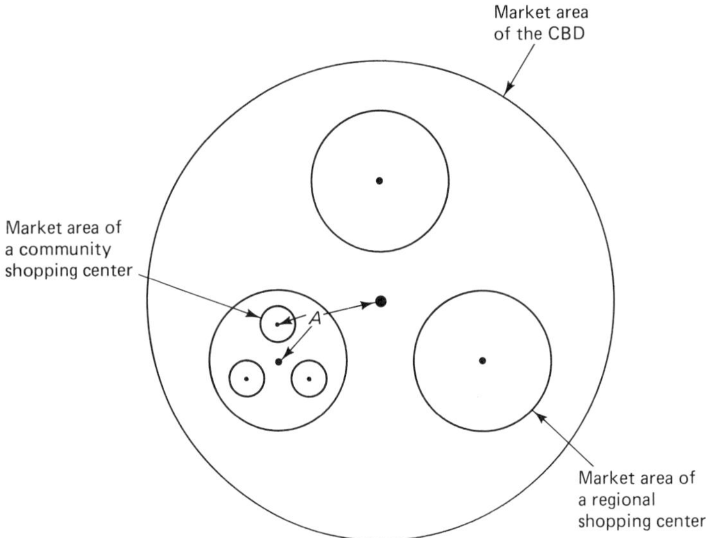

Figure 4.6 Nesting principle.

ter market areas, while inside each of the regional market areas will be a series of community market areas, and so on. As a result, a person located at *A* in Figure 4.6 might go to the nearest community shopping center for low-order goods, to the nearest regional shopping center for higher-order goods, and to the CBD for the most specialized goods.

The Formal Theory

Like many theories based on economic principles, central place theory contains a series of *simplifying assumptions* (Beavon, 1977). After examining these simplifying assumptions and the associated spatial patterns, we will discuss what happens when the assumptions are relaxed. The first assumption is that we have a uniform distribution of population and a uniform distribution of purchasing power within our hypothetical city. That is, population density and income are everywhere the same. Second, it is assumed that the city is characterized by an isotropic transportation surface. There are no barriers to movement, such as rivers or mountains, and movement is equally possible in all directions. Furthermore, the transportation cost per unit distance is the same in all directions. Third, it is assumed that consumers always patronize the nearest store offering the desired good. That is, consumers are interested only in minimizing transportation costs and are insensitive to variations in the price or quality of goods. Finally, it is also assumed that no excess profits are being earned by entrepreneurs. In other words, the thresholds and ranges associated with the various individual businesses will always coincide.

Given these assumptions, and the previously discussed concepts of the threshold, range, and nesting principle, we would expect the *spatial pattern of shopping*

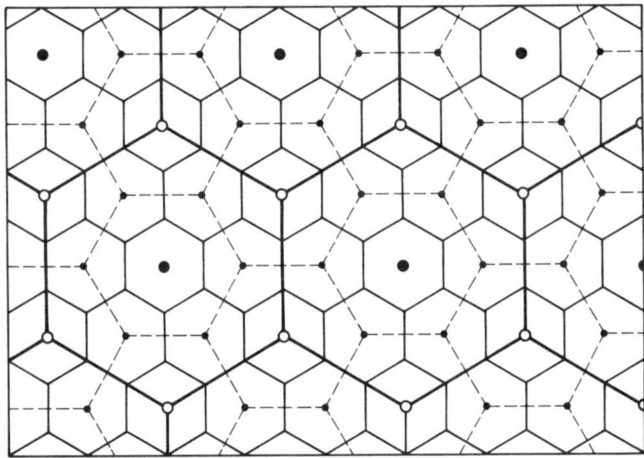

● Regional shopping center
○ Community shopping center
• Neighborhood shopping center
—— Boundary of regional trade area
---- Boundary of community trade area
—— Boundary of neighborhood trade area

Figure 4.7 The pattern of shopping centers according to central place theory. (Adapted from Fig. 7.27 (p. 203) from *The North American City*, First Edition by Maurice H. Yeates and Barry J. Garner. Copyright © 1971 by Maurice H. Yeates and Barry J. Garner. Reprinted by permission of Harper & Row, Publishers, Inc.)

centers, and their associated market areas, to be as represented in Figure 4.7. The market, or trade areas form hexagons, as circular trade areas would either overlap or leave parts of the city unserved. These hexagonal trade areas do, however, preserve the assumption that each consumer patronizes the closest store offering the desired good or service.

There are three major properties associated with this abstract pattern of shopping centers. First, the frequency of occurrence of the different levels of shopping centers follows the progression, from large to small, 1, 2, 6. One can verify this property by examining the number of shopping centers dominated by each highest-order center. There is a community center at each corner of the regional center market area, and as each of these community centers is equidistant from three regional centers, we can say that the community centers are shared three ways. Because there are six such community centers on each regional center's trade area there are six complete neighborhood centers, hence the progression 1, 2, 6.

Second, the progression of trade areas from largest to smallest is 1, 3, 9. This property can be verified by examining the number of trade areas dominated by each regional center. Each regional center dominates one regional trade area, and within that regional trade area there is one complete community trade area and portions of six others. Each of these portions represents a third of a community trade area, thus giving us one complete trade area plus six-thirds, or the equivalent of three. Finally, within each regional trade area there are seven complete neighborhood trade areas, plus portions of six others. These portions again represent thirds, thus giving us seven complete trade areas plus six-thirds, or the equivalent of nine: hence the progression 1, 3, 9.

Third, each shopping center is surrounded by a ring of six centers of the next lower level in the hierarchy, which are located at each corner of its hexagonal trade area. As a result, each lower-level center is equidistant between three centers of the next higher level in the hierarchy. This situation gives rise to a uniform spatial pattern in which shopping centers are distributed in the form of a triangular lattice.

Of course, this very regular pattern of shopping centers and associated market areas will become increasingly distorted as we *relax each of the initial simplifying assumptions.* First, it was assumed that population and income are uniformly distributed throughout the urban area. If population density is kept the same everywhere, but at a higher level than previously, the market areas will become smaller, as they need not be so large in order to capture the same threshold population. Conversely, if the population density is less everywhere, the market areas will become larger, and the shopping centers will be spaced farther apart. Similarly, if income remains constant, but at a higher level, the market areas will become smaller, as they require fewer people to reach the same threshold sales volume, because each consumer will be spending more than previously. If income is reduced everywhere, the market areas will increase, and the shopping centers will be spaced farther apart.

Now, so far we have considered the consequences of changing the levels of population density and income, but we have still kept them constant throughout the city. If we allow population density and income to vary in magnitude, the trade area size, at any given level within the hierarchy, will also vary. In the more densely populated parts of the city the trade areas will be small and the shopping centers close together, whereas in the less densely populated areas the reverse will be true. Similarly, in those areas of the city characterized by high incomes, we would expect small trade areas and closely spaced shopping centers, whereas in the poorer areas we would expect large trade areas and widely spaced shopping centers.

Second, it was assumed that our hypothetical city has an isotropic transportation surface. If this assumption is relaxed, it means that accessibility is not the same in all directions, due to freeways, physical barriers, and the like. In any event, whatever the causes of variation in accessibility, the trade areas will respond by becoming elongated in those directions of greatest accessibility, and vice versa. In other words, the previously hexagonal trade areas will be distorted into a variety of different shapes.

Third, it was assumed that consumers always minimize travel distance by going to the nearest store offering the desired good. If consumers no longer merely minimize distance, but also take into account other variables, such as the price of goods and services, the previously mutually exclusive trade areas will now overlap. For example, someone who lives very close to a particular neighborhood shopping center may travel across the city to another such center to take advantage of lower prices.

Finally, if the assumption that no excess profits are earned is relaxed, the threshold and range associated with each shopping center will no longer coincide. This situation indicates that the system is dynamic, because in those areas where the thresholds lie inside the ranges, and thus excess profits are being earned, new shopping centers will be developed. Conversely, in those areas where the thresholds lie outside the ranges, we would expect one or more shopping centers to go out of business in the long run.

In summary, the initial postulation of simplifying assumptions allows the spatial pattern of shopping centers to be understood more clearly. It is only when these assumptions are successively relaxed, however, that we move closer and closer to the actual pattern of shopping centers and trade areas in any given city. In particular, (1) relaxation of the uniform population and income assumption allows the trade areas to vary in size, (2) relaxation of the isotropic transportation surface assumption allows the trade areas to vary in shape, (3) relaxation of the distance minimization assumption allows the trade areas to overlap, and (4) relaxation of the excess profits assumption allows shopping centers to both enter and leave the system.

Empirical Testing

When applied to the intraurban retail structure, central place theory contains two major components that are amenable to empirical testing. First, data can be obtained to check the empirical validity of the suggested hierarchy of shopping centers. Second, one can investigate the spatial distributions associated with different kinds of retail establishments.

Berry and his associates (Berry et al., 1963), working in Chicago, suggested a four-tier *hierarchy* (Table 4.3). They identified major regional centers, shopping goods centers, community centers, and neighborhood centers, and the general attributes of this hierarchy are consistent with the predictions of central place theory. First, the larger centers contain more ground-floor establishments and business types. Second, there are more low-level centers than high-level centers, although this generalization breaks down at the lower end of the hierarchy, where there are fewer neighborhood centers than community centers. The main reason for the latter situation is that many of the smaller neighborhood centers were omitted from the analysis.

We also noted, when relaxing the assumptions of central place theory, that low-income areas should contain fewer shopping centers than high-income areas. This

TABLE 4.3 HIERARCHY OF SHOPPING CENTERS IN CHICAGO

Level of center	Number	Number of ground-floor establishments	Number of business types
Major regional	4	196	60
Shopping goods	14	114	43
Community	25	73	37
Neighborhood	21	41	25

Source: B. J. L. Berry, *Commercial Structure and Commercial Blight: Retail Patterns and Processes in the city of Chicago*, Department of Geography Research Paper 85, University of Chicago (Illinois), 1963, Table 6, pp. 36–43.

TABLE 4.4 REGIONAL VARIATIONS IN THE CHICAGO HIERARCHY OF SHOPPING CENTERS

	Area served	
Level of center	High income	Low income
Major regional	4	0
Shopping goods	5	9
Community	22	3
Neighborhood	7	14

Source: B. J. L. Berry, *Commercial Structure and Commercial Blight: Retail Patterns and Processes in the City of Chicago*, Department of Geography Research Paper 85, University of Chicago (Illinois), 1963, Table Bl, p. 228.

theoretical prediction is again borne out by the city of Chicago (Table 4.4). In particular, the low-income neighborhoods tend to have shopping goods centers rather than major regional centers, and neighborhood centers rather than community centers. Thus there is less variety of goods, and fewer specialized stores, in the poorer neighborhoods.

As expected, the *spatial distribution* of shopping centers in Chicago, at each level in the retail hierarchy, is fairly dispersed, with the various low-level centers filling in between the more widely spaced high-level centers (Berry et al., 1963, p. 32). A more quantitative description of the degree of dispersion associated with retail establishments, however, can be achieved via the statistical technique known as *quadrat analysis* (Rogers, 1974). Quadrat analysis is intended specifically for the investigation of point patterns, as it allows one to compare an observed point pattern with a theoretically expected point pattern, in order to calibrate the goodness of fit. For our purposes, a useful theoretical point pattern is a random pattern, as we can then judge whether the observed patterns are more dispersed than random, or more clustered than random.

In the spatial context, a Poisson probability distribution will generate a random point pattern. Moreover, the mean of a Poisson distribution is equal to its variance, so a quick check for randomness in an observed point pattern merely involves comparing the mean and variance. If, for the purpose of this comparison, we divide the variance by the mean, a value close to 1 implies that the pattern is approximately random, a value greater than 1 indicates that the pattern is more clustered than random, and a value less than 1 indicates that the pattern is more dispersed than random.

Using this technique to analyze the distribution of various kinds of stores in Stockholm, Sweden, Artle (1965) produced the results reported in Table 4.5. The more specialized stores, such as antique stores and women's clothing stores, are especially clustered, often within major regional shopping centers. The less specialized stores, however, such as grocery stores and tobacconists, are more ubiquitous, although the overall pattern is still slightly more clustered than random.

TABLE 4.5 DISTRIBUTION OF DIFFERENT KINDS OF RETAIL STORES IN STOCKHOLM, SWEDEN

Antique stores	2.48
Women's clothing stores	2.27
Furniture stores	1.87
Grocery stores	1.43
Tobacconists	1.32
Liquor stores	0.95

Source: R. Artle, *The Structure of the Stockholm Economy; Toward a Framework for Projecting Metropolitan Community Development.* Copyright © 1965 by Cornell University. Used by permission of the publisher, Cornell University Press.

4.3 COMMERCIAL BLIGHT AND DOWNTOWN REDEVELOPMENT

So far we have considered the urban retail structure within a predominantly static framework. In the present section we consider recent changes in the pattern of retailing, and how these changes have led to areas of commercial blight and the subsequent investment in a variety of downtown redevelopment schemes.

The Changing Pattern of Retailing

One of the major changes in the pattern of retailing since World War II has been the suburbanization of shopping centers, and in particular, the emergence of large, *planned shopping centers.* At first these planned centers tended to be smaller than their unplanned counterparts, as developers tried to restrict competition between stores by controlling the level of functional duplication. More recently, however, the planned shopping centers have become increasingly larger, and have also incorporated other services besides retailing, such as movie theaters and skating rinks.

A second change in the pattern of retailing, somewhat related to the first, is that the planned, regional-level shopping centers have now become the catalysts for the overall suburbanization process rather than merely the followers of that process. In other words, regional shopping centers often act as local *growth poles.* Cheap land is purchased at the periphery of the city, and the shopping center later becomes the focus for new apartment buildings, industrial parks, and so on. This kind of large-scale development will be less conspicuous in the future, however, if rising energy costs begin to seriously restrict consumer mobility. Also, local planning boards have become increasingly disenchanted with both the various forms of pollution created by these large centers and their contribution to urban sprawl.

Changes in the scale of retailing have not only led to much larger shopping centers, but also to *larger individual stores*. These larger stores draw consumers from much wider trade areas, and are therefore heavily dependent on automobile transportation. Associated with this change in scale has been the increasing importance of more specialized, high-order goods. As a result, many of the individual stores and small neighborhood shopping centers that emphasize convenience goods have been losing trade, and sometimes closing down.

Commercial Blight

A major consequence of the general changes in the pattern of retailing has been the occurrence of commercial blight. Commercial blight can take a variety of forms (Berry et al., 1963, pp. 179–182). First, *economic blight* occurs in those situations where there is a decrease in consumer demand. This decreased demand might be due to a reduction in the local population, a reduction in the income of that local population, or the development of new sources of competition. This kind of blight is often manifested by a larger than usual number of store vacancies, a decrease in the variety and quality of goods sold by the remaining stores, and an increase in the number of convenience goods stores as opposed to specialized stores.

Second, *physical blight* is characterized by the increasing deterioration of buildings. Such blight generally occurs in the older parts of the city, and reflects the overall age of the buildings. In those neighborhoods in which consumer demand is falling, entrepreneurs will be less willing to invest money in building maintenance or improvement.

Third, *functional blight*, or technological obsolescence, is a response to changes in both the supply and demand sides of retailing activity. In terms of the supply side, increased economies of scale have resulted in a greater need for large buildings, often leading to the abandonment of small street-corner stores that used to have "ma and pa" groceries. On the demand side, greater consumer mobility has had the same effect. Many of the older locations are now less viable, as retail outlets built to service streetcar passengers, for example, are often unable to provide sufficient parking for automobiles.

Fourth, *frictional blight*, or environmental blight, is due to the relationship between a business establishment and its surrounding area. A particular business may have an undesirable effect on the surrounding area because it generates traffic congestion, litter, or attracts undesirable patrons. Conversely, changes in the surrounding land use might have a deleterious effect on the retailing outlet, such as when an industrial park is located nearby.

It has been suggested that there are three major stages in the process of commercial blight (Berry, 1967, p. 123). Initially, the anticipation of neighborhood transition is associated with increasing vacancies and lack of maintenance. The second stage is characterized by diminished consumer demand and the demise of specialty stores. Finally, the system reaches a new equilibrium in which vacancies are high and profits are low.

Downtown Redevelopment

The process of commercial blight, and overall neighborhood deterioration, is often associated with the downtown area of cities. Many downtown areas have suffered significant declines in retailing activity, although this has sometimes coincided with a boom in office activity, as manifested by the increase in multistoried office buildings. Downtown retailing has adjusted to its diminished role by concentrating on very specialized goods, such as art galleries, antique stores, and fashionable clothing and furniture stores. These stores often cater to a clientele that has been attracted to the central business district by other cultural and business activities.

Entrepreneurs with business investments in the downtown area have long argued that a strong central business district is vital for the economic health of the overall city, and a variety of federal programs have been used to help finance redevelopment projects. One of the earliest large-scale projects involved redevelopment of the Golden Triangle in downtown Pittsburgh. This area of Pittsburgh suffered from air pollution, flooding, and extremely high vacancy rates. Beginning in the 1950s, however, much of the CBD was rebuilt, and it has since beome an extremely viable and attractive commercial center.

One of the major elements of downtown renewal projects has been the construction of pedestrian malls. Such malls often involve the elimination of all vehicular traffic, except for mass transit and emergency vehicles. One of the most famous of these malls is Nicollet Mall in Minneapolis, where the sidewalks have been extensively widened and lined with trees. The main retail district in downtown Minneapolis is integrated by a pedestrian walkway system that links several blocks by second-story skyways over the streets.

One of the major obstacles associated with downtown redevelopment, however, has been the problem of providing sufficient parking. Multistoried parking facilities have been constructed, while at the same time many cities have tried to encourage the use of mass transit systems rather than private automobiles. Toward this end, the cost of parking has greatly increased, and more frequent bus services have been provided in many cities.

4.4 THE PATTERN OF POPULATION DENSITY

Like the urban retail structure, the pattern of population density in cities is very closely related to the underlying land value surface. In this section we consider some of the major population density models, the reason for the relationship between land value and population density, and how the pattern of population density has changed over time.

Population Density Models

Although a variety of population density functions have since been tested (McDonald and Bowman, 1976; Zielinski, 1980), Clark (1951) first provided convincing empirical evidence to suggest that population density tends to decline in an exponential fashion with increasing distance from the CBD. That is, if population density is plotted against distance from the CBD, the resulting curve drops quite steeply at first, and then more gradually (Figure 4.8a). This relationship is expressed symbolically as follows:

$$D_d = D_0 e^{-bd} \tag{4.1}$$

where D_d is the population density at a given distance from the city center, D_0 is the density at the city center, e is the base of natural, or naperian, logarithms, b is the rate of change of density with distance, and d is distance. We have encountered a negative exponential function earlier in the book, represented by equation (2.8), and, as was the case then, the function can be linearly transformed by simply taking the natural logarithm of population density (Figure 4.8a). The equation corresponding

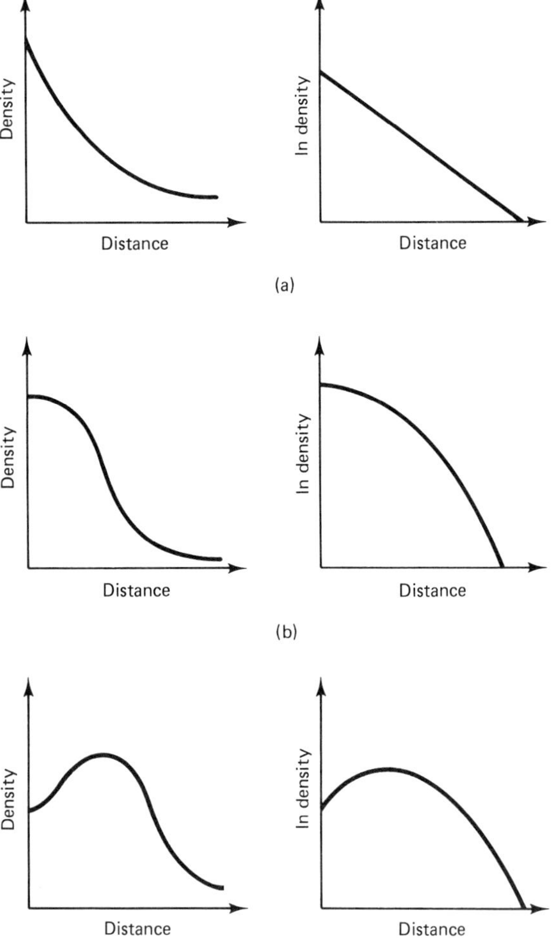

Figure 4.8 Population density models: (a) Clark; (b) Tanner and Sherratt; (c) Newling.

to the linear form of the relationship is as follows:

$$\ln D_d = \ln D_0 - bd \tag{4.2}$$

where ln is the natural logarithm and the remaining notation is the same as in equation (4.1).

The first major revision of Clark's model was independently suggested by Tanner (1961) and Sherratt (1960). They proposed that density declines exponentially with the square of distance (Figure 4.8b), as represented by the following equation:

$$D_d = d_0 e^{-bd^2} \tag{4.3}$$

where the notation is the same as in equation (4.1). Again, this equation can be put in linear form by taking the natural logarithm of population density:

$$\ln D_d = \ln D_0 - bd^2 \tag{4.4}$$

where the notation is the same as in equation (4.2).

Finally, Newling (1969) has since suggested a quadratic exponential model (Figure 4.8c), which is represented as follows:

$$D_d = D_0 e^{bd-cd^2} \tag{4.5}$$

where the notation is the same as in equation (4.1), except that we now have two parameters to be estimated, b and c. The b term is especially significant in Newling's model, as it measures the instantaneous rate of change of density with distance at the center of the city. In those situations where b is positive, it represents a density crater surrounding the CBD, where population density is comparatively low due to the presence of other kinds of land uses, especially those associated with commercial and retailing activity. Like the previous models, Newling's model can be linearly transformed by taking the natural logarithm of density, thus producing the following equation:

$$\ln D_d = \ln D_0 + bd - cd^2 \tag{4.6}$$

where the notation is the same as in equation (4.2).

Newling's model is important for two reasons. First, it incorporates the previous models of Clark and of Tanner and Sherratt. This particular property can be appreciated by considering equation (4.5). If c is zero, and b is negative, Newling's model is the same as Clark's. On the other hand, if b is zero, Newling's model is the same as that proposed by Tanner and Sherratt.

The second major contribution of Newling's model is that it can be placed within a dynamic framework that allows for the emergence of a density crater in the CBD. Newling suggsts that the density profile of a city evolves from the pattern suggested by Clark, through that suggested by Tanner and Sherratt, until a density crater emerges as in the Newling model. In other words, Clark's model is synonymous with a youthful stage, Tanner and Sherratt's model is synonymous with a mature stage, and Newling's model represents old age. When population density is in logarithmic form, this evolutionary sequence is expressed by Figure 4.9, where $t, t + 1, \ldots, t + 4$, indicate the different time periods. This diagram represents the "tidal wave of metro-

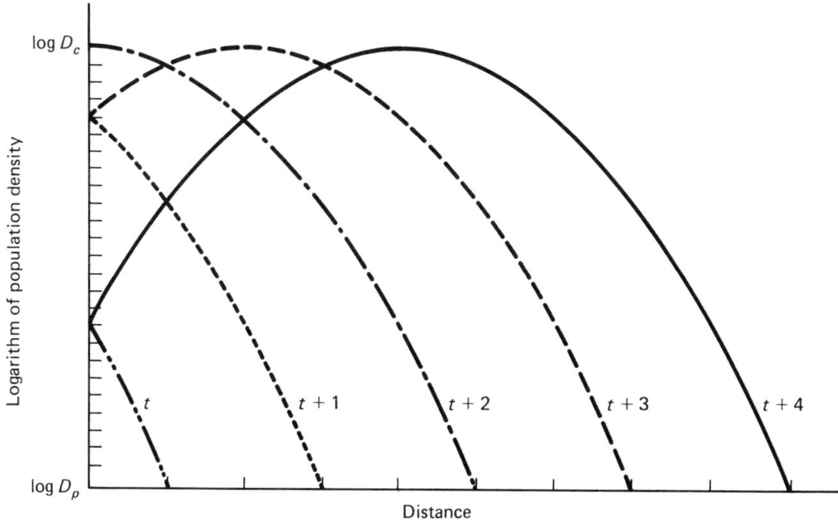

Figure 4.9 Population density curves over time. (From B. E. Newling, "The spatial variation of urban population densities," *Geographical Review*, 59, 1969, Fig. 6, p. 249, with the permission of the American Geographical Society.)

politan expansion," and contains three major elements. First, the central density gets less over time. Second, the peak density is displaced outward. Third, the overall density gradient decreases.

Some empirical validity for Newling's evolutionary schema has been provided by Latham and Yeates (1970) in a study of population density change in Metropolitan Toronto. The linear form of Newling's model, equation (4.6), was calibrated and tested for a number of different time periods (Table 4.6). The first thing to note about the results is that the coefficient of multiple determination (R^2) is very stable across the different time periods, and indicates that over 65 percent of the variation in population density within Toronto is accounted for by Newling's model. Of greater importance, however, than the overall goodness of fit is the behavior of the individual parameters. For 1956 b is negative and c is close to zero, indicating that Clark's model is appropriate for this particular time period. In the following two time periods, how-

TABLE 4.6 POPULATION DENSITY CURVES FOR METROPOLITAN TORONTO

Year	Model form	
1956	$\log D_d = 4.79 - 0.170d - 0.001d^2$	$R^2 = 67.12$
1961	$\log D_d = 4.45 - 0.052d - 0.006d^2$	$R^2 = 66.45$
1963	$\log D_d = 4.32 - 0.002d - 0.009d^2$	$R^2 = 68.43$

Source: Reprinted by permission from Robert F. Latham and Maurice H. Yeates, "Population density growth in Metropolitan Toronto," *Geographical Analysis*, 2 (April 1970), pp. 177–85. Copyright © 1970 by the Ohio State University Press.

ever, b moves toward zero, and c becomes increasingly negative, indicating a gradual shift from Clark's model toward the Tanner and Sherratt formulation. Over time, if b moves through zero to become positive, the full evolutionary cycle will be completed. In this context, it should be noted that the identification of a density crater, as implied by a positive value for b, is partly dependent on the kind of data being used. The density crater will emerge somewhat earlier if the population density values are for blocks rather than census tracts.

The Relationship between Land Values and Population Density

In Chapter 2 it was demonstrated, via the use of bid-rent curves, why land value tends to decrease in a curvilinear fashion with increasing distance from the city center. In the present chapter we have argued that population density behaves in a similar fashion. The reason for this close association between land value and population density is not hard to find (Berry and Kasarda, 1977, pp. 95–97).

Quite simply, because the price of land decreases with increasing distance from the city center, regardless of other changes, land inputs will be substituted for other inputs, such as capital. Because the intensity of land use diminishes in this fashion, declining residential densities should also be expected. Note that this statement is consistent with the fact that high-intensity, multistory apartment buildings are usually found on high-valued land near the city center, while low-density single-family dwelling units are usually found in more peripheral locations.

More precise empirical evidence for the relationship between land value and population density is presented in Figure 4.10. The points on this diagram represent

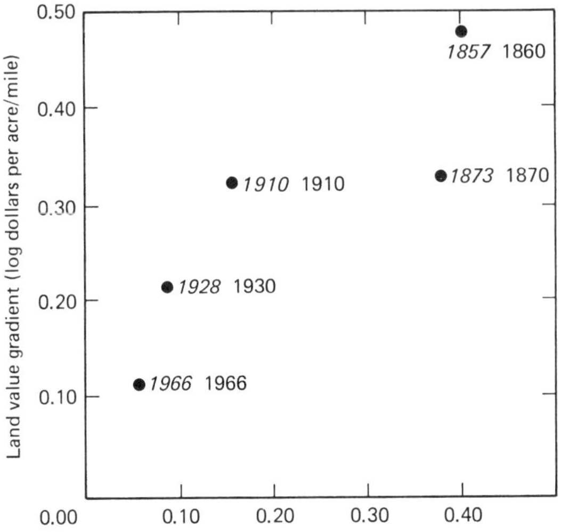

Figure 4.10 Relationship between land value and population density for Chicago. (From B. J. L. Berry and F. E. Horton, Eds., *Geographical Perspectives on Urban Systems*, Prentice-Hall, Englewood Cliffs, N.J., 1970, Fig. 9.18, p. 300. Reprinted by permission of Prentice-Hall, Inc., Englewood Cliffs, N.J.)

the land value and density gradients, for Chicago, for five different time periods. The parallel decline in these two gradients between approximately 1860 and 1960 lends support to the contention that the two phenomena are related.

Change over Time

When analyzing change over time in the pattern of population density, there are two attributes of that pattern that are usually monitored. First, we can examine changes in population density at the city center, or the central density. Second, we can examine changes in the density gradient, or the rate at which density decreases with increasing distance from the city center. These two attributes correspond to the two parameters, D_0 and b, in Clark's original model.

In terms of central density, most U.S. cities have first experienced an increase, and later a decrease. Table 4.7 illustrates this phenomenon for Denver and Milwaukee, and in this case the peak central density for both cities was reached in 1930. While the overall experience has been very similar for most cities, however, the timing of the peak central density does exhibit some variation. By contrast, the density gradient in most cities has been progressively declining over time (Edmonston, 1975, p. 65). This situation is again exemplified by Denver and Milwaukee (Table 4.7). Note also that for every year the b value, or density gradient, is negative, indicating that the density is higher in the center than at the edge of the city.

These two general changes in the overall population density pattern are summarized in Figure 4.11. The vertical axis, representing density, is in logarithmic form, so that the relationship between density and distance is linear for all three time periods. The density at the city center increases from (1) to (2), and then decreases from (2) to (3). On the other hand, the density gradient, or slope of the line, decreases from (1) to (2), and then decreases again, from (2) to (3).

TABLE 4.7 CHANGES IN THE CENTRAL DENSITY AND DENSITY GRADIENT FOR DENVER AND MILWAUKEE

	Denver		Milwaukee	
Year	Central density	Density gradient	Central density	Density gradient
1920	34,870	−0.87	68,304	−0.61
1930	36,265	−0.83	74,209	−0.56
1940	35,334	−0.76	65,434	−0.51
1948	27,779	−0.59	58,318	−0.47
1954	22,884	−0.45	44,262	−0.37
1958	19,678	−0.38	37,823	−0.32
1963	18,008	−0.33	31,123	−0.27

Source: E. S. Mills, *Studies in the Structure of the Urban Economy*, Johns Hopkins University Press, Baltimore, 1972, Table 13, pp. 45–46. Published for Resources for the Future by The Johns Hopkins University Press.

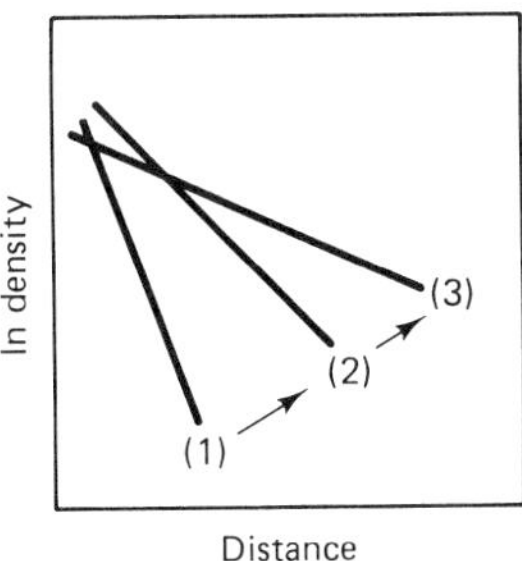

Figure 4.11 Change over time in the pattern of population density. (Adapted from B. J. L. Berry, J. W. Simmons, and R. J. Tennant, "Urban population densities: Structure and change," *Geographical Review*, 53, 1963, Fig. 10, p. 403, with the permission of the American Geographical Society.)

4.5 POPULATION DENSITY SURFACES

It is also instructive to investigate the pattern of population density in terms of a three-dimensional surface. Thus far, by simply considering how density varies with distance from the city center, we have averaged out the directional variation. Although representing the density pattern in two dimensions is useful initially, especially since it facilitates comparison with our previous discussion of land values, less information is discarded if the pattern is analyzed in three dimensions. Within this context, we will first consider the statistical technique of trend surface analysis, and then discuss some of the results of this analysis as applied to population density surfaces.

Trend Surface Analysis

Trend surface analysis is essentially a multiple regression technique, whereby the general trend in a mapped variable, such as population density, can be identified (Chorley and Haggett, 1965). As discussed in Chapter 1, a surface is created by drawing a series of isolines that join up points of equal value (Figure 4.12a). The most common type of isoline is a contour, which connects points of equal elevation, but we can also conceptualize land value surfaces, income surfaces, and so on. In the present instance, of course, the isolines connect points of equal population density, thus creating a population density surface.

Such surfaces can be expressed symbolically as follows:

$$Z = f(X, Y) \tag{4.7}$$

where Z is the mapped variable, in this case population density; X is latitude; and Y is longitude. The trend surface analysis assumes that the mapped variable can be decomposed into two components. First, there is a trend component, representing the large-scale systematic changes that extend across the map. Second, there is a local component, representing local fluctuations around the general trend.

So, for any particular location on the map, say i (Figure 4.12a), the observed height of the surface is made up of the trend component at that point, plus the local

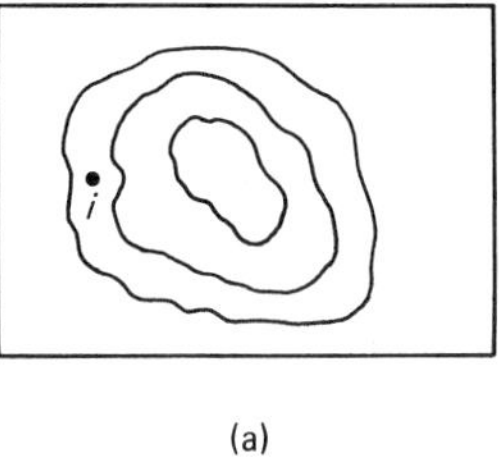

(a)

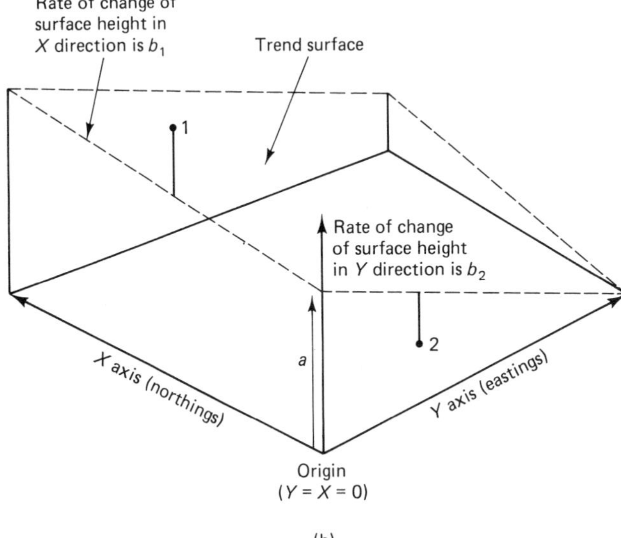

(b)

Figure 4.12 Trend surface analysis.

component, or residual. This statement can be expressed as follows:

$$Z_i = f(X_i,\ Y_i) \pm e_i \tag{4.8}$$

where Z_i is the height of the surface at location i, X_i and Y_i are the latitude and longitude associated with location i, and e_i is the local component, or residual, associated with location i.

The simplest form of surface is a linear trend, or inclined plane (Figure 4.12b). This surface can be described symbolically, for any particular location, as follows:

$$Z_1 = a + b_1 X_1 - b_2 Y_1 + e_1 \tag{4.9}$$

where Z_1 is the height of the surface at location 1; a is the height of the surface at the map origin, where X and Y are zero; b_1 is the rate of change of the surface height along the X axis; b_2 is the rate of change of the surface height along the Y axis; X and Y are latitude and longitude; and e_1 is the residual associated with location 1. Note that b_1 is positive, as the surface increases along the X axis, and b_2 is negative, as the surface decreases along the Y axis. Also, e_1 is positive, as the height of the surface at location 1 is above the general trend. Similarly, the surface can be expressed as follows for location 2 (Figure 4.12b):

$$Z_2 = a + b_1 X_2 - b_2 Y_2 - e_2 \tag{4.10}$$

where the notation is the same as in equation (4.9). The major difference is that the residual term is now negative, because the height of the surface at location 2 is beneath the general trend.

More complex surfaces can also be conceived of, generating a series of successively higher-order polynomials of the following form:

$$Z = a + b_1 X + b_2 Y \tag{4.11}$$

$$Z = a + b_1 X + b_2 Y + b_3 X^2 + b_4 XY + b_5 Y^2 \tag{4.12}$$

$$Z = a + b_1 X + b_2 Y + b_3 X^2 + b_4 XY + b_5 Y^2 + b_6 X^3 + b_7 X^2 Y + b_8 XY^2 + b_9 Y^3 \tag{4.13}$$

where the notation is the same as in equation (4.9), and equations (4.11), (4.12), and (4.13), represent linear, quadratic, and cubic surfaces, respectively. A quadratic surface contains one inflection point, while a cubic surface contains two inflection points, and so on.

How well each of these surfaces fits an actual surface can be determined using the same kind of multiple correlation and regression analysis described in Chapter 3. In other words, each of the equations above can be treated as a multiple regression equation, like the general case represented by equation (3.1). The overall goodness of fit is measured by the coefficient of multiple determination (R^2), and each of the individual regression coefficients can be estimated via least-squares analysis.

Results

Haggett and Bassett (1970) have used trend surface analysis to describe and compare the population density surfaces of 15 U.S. cities. They calculated the residential densities for equally sized subareas, and locational coordinates were defined for the midpoints of those subareas. Linear, quadratic, and cubic surfaces were tested for each of the 15 cities, and the coefficients of multiple determination are reported in Table 4.8.

Note that, for all cities, the coefficients of multiple determination increase as one moves from the simple linear surface to progressively higher-order surfaces. This situation is to be expected, of course, as the higher-order surfaces contain more terms, and thus account for more of the local variation in population density. Some cities are approximated quite well by even the linear surface, as in the case of Milwaukee, Los Angeles, and New York, while other cities have such convoluted population density surfaces that they are not even approximated by a cubic surface. Perhaps the extreme example, in this context, is San Francisco, where the coefficient of multiple determination associated with the cubic surface is only .467.

It is also of interest to examine how population density surfaces have changed over time, and Hill's (1973) study of Toronto provides an interesting, and probably representative, example. Hill tested up to a fifth-order surface for five different time

TABLE 4.8 COEFFICIENTS OF MULTIPLE DETERMINATION FOR THE TREND SURFACE ANALYSIS OF AMERICAN CITIES

	Linear	Quadratic	Cubic
Atlanta	.246	.337	.580
Cincinnati	.097	.661	.857
Cleveland	.329	.689	.996
Denver	.386	.788	.831
Los Angeles	.677	.838	.869
Miami	.529	.609	.748
Milwaukee	.719	.944	.961
Minneapolis–St. Paul	.462	.721	.913
New Orleans	.500	.666	.871
New York	.629	.795	.875
Philadelphia	.255	.519	.676
Pittsburgh	.040	.535	.749
San Francisco	.211	.341	.467
Seattle	.207	.558	.651
St. Louis	.002	.591	.688

Source: P. Haggett and K. A. Bassett, "The use of trend-surface parameters in inter-urban comparisons," *Environment and Planning*, 2 (1970), Table 1, p. 229.

periods, with the first-, second-, and third-order surfaces representing linear, quadratic, and cubic surfaces, respectively (Table 4.9). As with Haggett and Bassett's results, for any given time period the higher-order surfaces always account for more variation than their lower-order counterparts.

Hill's major finding was that for each order surface the coefficient of multiple determination tends to get less over time. This phenomenon indicates that the population density surface is becoming less regular or, in other words, there are increasingly more inflection points in the surface. It is also noteworthy that Newling's model,

TABLE 4.9 COEFFICIENTS OF MULTIPLE DETERMINATION FOR POPULATION DENSITY TREND SURFACES, METROPOLITAN TORONTO, 1941–1966

	Order of surface				
Year	1	2	3	4	5
1941	.228	.355	.486	.540	.597
1951	.229	.351	.466	.516	.561
1956	.245	.379	.486	.522	.567
1961	.211	.334	.433	.469	.517
1966	.180	.298	.373	.403	.462

Source: F. I. Hill, "Spatio-temporal trends in urban population density: A trend surface analysis," in L. S. Bourne, R. D. Mackinnon, and J. W. Simmons, Eds., *The Form of Cities in Central Canada: Selected Papers*, Department of Geography Research Publication 11, University of Toronto, Toronto, 1973. Table 7.1, p. 110.

when applied to Toronto (Table 4.6), accounted for approximately 67 percent of the variation in population density, thus emphasizing that curve fitting in a two-dimensional context smooths out the directional variation. Finally, the coefficients of multiple determination for Toronto are less than for most of the cities tested by Haggett and Bassett, partly because the latter used relatively large spatial data units, and thus filtered out more of the original variation.

This last point serves as a reminder that the results of trend surface analysis should be interpreted with some caution. First, it is desirable to have a fairly uniform distribution of data points. A clustering of data points tends to inflate the R^2 value, and the area containing the cluster of points will have an undue influence on the shape of the surface. Second, higher-order surfaces are very demanding in terms of data. A perfect fit will always be obtained in those instances where the number of terms in the trend function equals the number of data points.

4.6 POPULATION DENSITY AND SOCIAL PATHOLOGY

A variety of studies have suggested that high population densities in animal populations frequently produce pathological behavior. These suggestions have lead researchers to suspect similar relationships between population density and pathological behavior in human populations. The present section summarizes the results of some of the major studies in this area, and draws some conclusions concerning their implications for human behavior.

Perhaps the most influential study of animal behavior, in this context, is Calhoun's (1962) examination of how overcrowding influences the behavior of rats. In a series of experiments, rats were provided with sufficient food and water, but the population density was much greater than in the rats' natural habitat. Under these conditions, Calhoun observed that a variety of pathological behaviors developed. In particular, fertility rates dropped, mortality rates increased, the young were neglected by their mothers, and some of the rats became overly aggressive, while others withdrew from the community. These results, and similar findings for other animal species, led social scientists to speculate that high-density living might also have adverse consequences for human beings.

One major study investigated the relationships between population density and various kinds of pathological behavior in Chicago (Galle et al., 1972). As Calhoun's research was used as a starting point, the following five pathologies were examined: (1) fertility rates, (2) mortality rates, (3) ineffectual care of the young, (4) asocial, aggressive behavior, and (5) psychiatric disorder. The first two pathologies are distinctly biological in nature, and were measured by standardized fertility and mortality rates. The number of recipients of public assistance under 18, per 100 persons under 18, was used as a measure of ineffectual parental care of the young, while the juvenile delinquency rate was used to measure asocial, aggressive behavior. Finally, mental hospital admission rates were used to measure psychiatric disorder. Data for each of these variables were obtained for each of the 75 community areas in

Chicago, and were compared to the population densities of those same areas, as measured by the number of persons per acre.

Preliminary results suggested small, but statistically significant relationships between population density and each social pathology. The researchers noted, however, that social class and ethnic status are also related to population density, and that these two variables might account for the variations in both density and pathology, implying that there is no direct causal link between density and pathology. The use of partial correlation coefficients confirmed this line of reasoning because, when class and ethnicity were controlled for, the correlations between density and the various pathologies were not significantly different from zero. In other words, the original relationships between density and social pathology appear to have been spurious.

Still undeterred, however, the researchers felt that their measure of density might be inappropriate. In particular, they noted that overall density, or persons per acre, can be decomposed into four major components: (1) the number of persons per room, (2) the number of rooms per housing unit, (3) the number of housing units per structure, and (4) the number of residential structures per acre. The results of analyses using these four components were strikingly different from those using the overall measure of density. Even when controlling for class and ethnicity, density was now significantly related to each of the pathologies. Moreover, the analyses indicated that for mortality, fertility, ineffectual parental care, and juvenile delinquency, the most important component of density was persons per room. Of considerably less importance was the number of housing units per structure, while rooms per housing unit and structures per acre were relatively unimportant. The results for psychiatric disorder were somewhat different, as this variable was most strongly related to rooms per housing unit.

In general, then, it appears that various kinds of social pathology are at least statistically related to the number of persons per room. In other words, it seems that overcrowding, rather than population density per se, is the operative concept. However, although these results are similar to those obtained in some other investigations, they are completely at odds with a whole series of studies in which only weak relationships were found between overcrowding and various forms of social pathology, especially when socioeconomic factors were controlled for (LaGory and Pipkin, 1981, p. 224). This disconcerting incompatibility of research findings may be due to the aggregated nature of the data used.

Extreme carc is required when interpreting the results obtained from aggregated, or ecological data that has been collected from subareas within a city. For example, although delinquency rates might be statistically related to overcrowding at the aggregate level, it does not necessarily mean that it is the juveniles living in overcrowded conditions who are the delinquents. It simply means that those areas of the city characterized by overcrowding also tend to be characterized by high delinquency rates. In sum, relationships that appear at the ecological level of analysis may not appear at the individual level.

To circumvent this thorny problem of ecological interpretation, a number of studies have been undertaken at the individual level of analysis, and the majority of these studies suggest that high population density has only limited behavioral consequences. For example, Mitchell (1971), using data on Hong Kong, found that although nearly a third of the people sampled reported sleeping three or more to a bed, only very general measures of stress, such as unhappiness and worry, showed any relationship to density once the socioeconomic status of the family had been controlled for. More acute psychological problems, such as mental illness and depression, were unrelated to the household's density.

In summary, it appears that the evidence relating overcrowding and various kinds of social pathology is rather unconvincing (Fischer, 1976, p. 162). Human beings appear to be capable of adjusting to overcrowded conditions, often by imposing an existing social order on a potentially stressful situation. For example, age stratification is a basic ingredient of social order, and in overcrowded situations this mechanism is exaggerated by the increased use of parental punishment. In other words, overcrowding does not usually generate pathological behavior, but it might intensify previously established role behavior (LaGory and Pipkin, 1981, p. 228).

Stokols (1972) has attempted to synthesize some of the effects of crowding in his equilibrium model of crowding. He suggests that there are two categories of variables that influence a person's perception of and response to crowding. First, the attributes of the physical and social environments, and second, attributes of the person. Important features of the physical environment include the amount and arrangement of available space, plus potential stressors such as noise, pollution, and temperature levels. The social environment represents the influence of other people in a given situation, including the allocation of status, group size, and competition of various kinds. Finally, the important individual attributes involve momentary physiological states, such as hunger and fatigue, intelligence, and different types of personality traits.

These environmental and personal factors combine to induce psychological or physiological stress. Psychological stress occurs because the person recognizes an inconsistency between the availability of space and his or her own space requirements, thus generating feelings of infringement, lack of privacy, and general alienation. The physiological stress is manifested by an alteration of internal states, such as a rise in blood pressure or an increase in adrenalin secretion. The precise form of stress that occurs, however, depends on the particular interaction between the previously described environmental and personal factors.

People can respond to these feelings of stress in a variety of ways. For example, a reduction in stress can be achieved by leaving a crowded situation, or at least refraining from social interaction. In other words, the attributes of the physical and social environments can be adjusted somehow. Alternatively, a person might choose to respond by altering his or her perception of the situation. For example, a change in aspiration levels might increase the desirability of staying and decrease the desirability of leaving. The overall model can be usefully thought of in the context of a social gathering, or party, where one can think of the various environmental factors, such as the size of the room and the type of people present, through to the ultimate response of either staying or leaving.

5

Urban Social Areas

5.1 RESIDENTIAL SEGREGATION

Having discussed the pattern of population density in cities, it is now of interest to examine the spatial distribution of different kinds of people. In particular, we wish to know the degree to which different kinds of people live in different parts of the city. That is, what is the extent of residential segregation in North American cities? After establishing the extent of segregation, it will be instructive to investigate whether this segregation has any particular spatial manifestation, thus leading to a discussion of the zonal and sector models. The general issue of social areas in cities will then be pursued via the topics of social area analysis and factorial ecology. Finally, the relationship between social areas and crime will be explored.

Index of Segregation

The extent of residential segregation associated with a particular subgroup, in a particular city, can be measured by the index of segregation (Peach et al., 1981). This index is expressed as follows:

$$S = \frac{\sum_{i=1}^{N} |X_i - Y_i|}{2} \tag{5.1}$$

where S is the index of segregation, X_i is the percentage of a particular subgroup living in areal unit i, and Y_i is the percentage of the rest of the population living in areal unit i. The areal units are usually either blocks or census tracts.

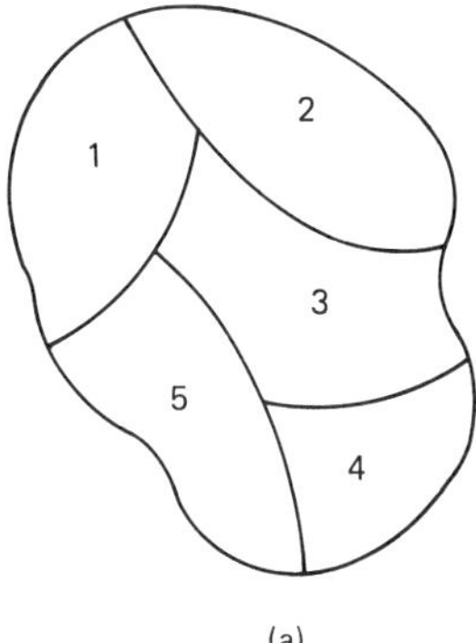

(a)

Area	Percent students	Percent rest of population	Absolute difference
1	70	30	40
2	10	20	10
3	5	20	15
4	5	20	15
5	10	10	0

(b)

Figure 5.1 Index of segregation.

A hypothetical example will clarify the use of this index. Imagine a city that is divided into five areal units (Figure 5.1a), and we wish to calculate the index of segregation associated with the distribution of students. Having listed the percentage of students and the percentage of the rest of the population in each subarea (Fig. 5.1b), we then calculate the absolute differences. These differences are summed and divided by 2, yielding a segregation index of 40. The two extremes of the index are 0 and 100. If the students were distributed in exactly the same pattern as the rest of the population, all the absolute differences would be zero. If, on the other hand, all the students were in one areal unit, and the rest of the population was in the other areal units, the absolute differences would sum to 200, yielding an index of 100. Therefore, the closer the index is to 100, the more segregated is the particular subgroup under investigation.

Segregation According to Occupation, Ethnicity, and Race

The index of segregation associated with different *occupational groups* in Chicago has been computed by Duncan and Duncan (1955). The analysis was based on census tract data for 1950, using employed males 14 years old and over, classified into eight major occupational groups (Table 5.1). When the occupational groups are ranked according to socioeconomic status, it is clear that residential segregation is associated primarily with the highest and lowest classes. The highest values are obtained for professionals and laborers, while clerical workers display the least segregation.

If the index of segregation is computed between pairs of occupational groups

TABLE 5.1 INDEX OF RESIDENTIAL SEGREGATION FOR OCCUPATION GROUPS, CHICAGO, 1950

Occupation group	Index of segregation
Professional	30
Managerial	29
Sales workers	29
Clerical	13
Craftsmen	19
Operatives	22
Service workers	24
Laborers	35

Source: Reprinted from O. D. Duncan and B. Duncan, "Residential distribution and occupational stratification," *American Journal of Sociology*, 60 (1955), Table 2, p. 497, by permission of The University of Chicago Press. Copyright © 1955 by the University of Chicago.

rather than between one occupational group and all the others combined, it is known as the *index of dissimilarity*. The values for this index, for each possible pair of occupations, is provided in Table 5.2. Note that the values increase as one moves away from the diagonal, indicating a relationship between social distance and the spatial separation of occupational groups. The least dissimilarity is observed between professional, managerial, and sales workers, while the greatest values occur between these three groups and laborers.

A more recent study by Simkus (1978) has essentially corroborated the Duncans's findings. Simkus averaged indices of residential dissimilarity, according to occupation, across 10 urbanized areas using 1970 census tract data (Table 5.3). He concluded that the degree of residential segregation associated with service workers

TABLE 5.2 INDEX OF RESIDENTIAL DISSIMILARITY FOR OCCUPATION GROUPS, CHICAGO, 1950

Occupation group	1	2	3	4	5	6	7	8
Professional	—							
Managerial	13	—						
Sales workers	15	13	—					
Clerical	28	28	27	—				
Craftsmen	35	33	35	16	—			
Operatives	44	41	42	21	17	—		
Service workers	41	40	38	24	35	26	—	
Laborers	54	52	54	38	35	25	28	—

Source: Reprinted from O. D. Duncan and B. Duncan, "Residential distribution and occupational stratification," *American Journal of Sociology*, 60 (1955), Table 3, p. 498, by permission of The University of Chicago Press. Copyright © 1955 by the University of Chicago.

TABLE 5.3 INDEX OF RESIDENTIAL DISSIMILARITY FOR OCCUPATION GROUPS, AVERAGED ACROSS TEN URBANIZED AREAS, 1970

Occupation group	1	2	3	4	5	6	7	8
Professional	—							
Managerial	16	—						
Sales workers	16	14	—					
Clerical	28	30	27	—				
Craftsmen	36	36	34	20	—			
Operatives	45	46	44	25	20	—		
Service workers	40	42	39	22	25	19	—	
Laborers	46	48	45	29	29	19	19	—

Source: A. A. Simkus,"Residential segregation by occupation and race in ten urbanized areas, 1950–1970," *American Sociological Review*, 43 (1978), Table 2, p. 84.

and laborers, vis-à-vis those in the highest occupational categories, decreased slightly during the 1960s, while segregation between persons in the higher categories remained about the same.

Indices of residential segregation have also been calculated for various *ethnic groups* in Chicago (Duncan and Lieberson, 1959). Prior to 1880, most of the European immigrants came from northwest Europe, whereas after 1880 there was an increase in the number of immigrants from eastern and southern European countries (Ward, 1971, p. 54). With the exception of Austrians, the "newer" immigrants, or more recent arrivals, from eastern and southern Europe, are considerably more segregated than the "older" immigrants, from northwest Europe (Table 5.4). Also, in general, second-generation settlers are less segregated than their foreign-born parents.

TABLE 5.4 INDEX OF RESIDENTIAL SEGREGATION FOR SELECTED ETHNIC GROUPS, CHICAGO, 1950

Country of origin	Index of segregation
England and Wales	18.9
Eire	31.8
Sweden	33.2
Germany	27.2
Poland	45.2
Czechoslovakia	48.8
Austria	18.1
USSR	44.0
Lithuania	51.5
Italy	40.5

Source: Reprinted from O. D. Duncan and S. Lieberson, "Ethnic segregation and assimilation," *American Journal of Sociology*, 64 (1959), Table 1, p. 366, by permission of The University of Chicago Press. Copyright © 1959 by the University of Chicago.

TABLE 5.5 INDEX OF RESIDENTIAL SEGREGATION BETWEEN WHITES AND NONWHITES, AVERAGED BY REGION, 1940–1970

	Mean index of residential segregation			
Year	South	Northeast	North central	West
1940	84.9	83.2	88.4	82.7
1950	88.5	83.6	89.9	83.0
1960	90.8	78.9	88.4	76.4
1970	88.0	74.3	82.6	67.9
Number of cities	45	25	29	10

Source: A. Sørensen, K. E. Taeuber, and L. J. Hollingsworth, Jr., "Indexes of racial residential segregation for 109 cities in the United States, 1940 to 1970," *Sociological Focus*, 8 (1975), Table 3, p. 132.

As one might expect, the largest values for the index of segregation tend to be associated with *race*, specifically black versus white, rather than occupation or ethnicity. Within this context, Van Valey et al. (1977) calculated the index of segregation for each of the 237 metropolitan areas in the coterminus United States that were fully tracted in 1970. The average index score was approximately 70 percent. When the authors compared these results with those for 1960, they concluded that the data indicate a general decline in the average level of racial residential segregation between 1960 and 1970. They note, however, that the greatest decreases occurred in the West, followed, in order, by the North, East, North Central, and the South.

A similar pattern of change over time has been noted by Sørensen et al. (1975), although in this instance the areal units were blocks rather than census tracts, so the values tend to be somewhat higher (Table 5.5). The northern and western cities, which typically had slight increases in segregation during the 1940s, experienced significant decreases in the following decades. Southern cities, on the other hand, became increasingly segregated during both the 1940s and 1950s, and displayed only a fairly small decline during the 1960s.

The Process of Assimilation

The degree to which an ethnic or racial group remains a distinctive social and spatial entity depends on the process of assimilation. Assimilation is generally decomposed into behavioral assimilation, or acculturation, and structural assimilation. Behavioral assimilation occurs when members of the minority group acquire the sentiments and attitudes of other groups in the society, and thus become involved in a common cultural life. Structural assimilation, on the other hand, refers to the distribution of minority members through the social systems of the society, especially its system of occupational stratification. Those ethnic groups that maintain a strong identity have usually created a set of ethnic institutions, relating to religion, education, politics, and business.

Boal (1976) has suggested that ethnic and racial residential clusters within cities serve four main functions. First, such clusters play a defensive role, whereby members of a particular minority can reduce their isolation and vulnerability. Second, ethnic and racial residential concentrations serve an avoidance function, and are often "ports of entry" before individual members are assimilated into the larger society. Third, these residential clusters allow ethnic and racial groups to preserve their own cultural heritage. Fourth, such clustering can also serve as the basis for "attack" functions against society in general, as spatial concentration may allow the group to elect its own political representatives.

Boal (1976) has also suggested a set of relationships between ethnic group distinctiveness, degree of assimilation, and the associated spatial pattern (Figure 5.2). If the entering group is very similar to the host society, rapid assimilation and few signs of spatial concentration can be expected. In those cases where the ethnic group is very different from the host society, however, the assimilation process will take longer and residential clustering will occur.

Where such residential clustering is only a temporary stage in the assimilation process, the concentration is called a *colony*. A colony is normally short-lived, and primarily serves as a port of entry for a particular ethnic group. Once the influx of new ethnic group members begins to decline, such colonies tend to disappear. In other situations the residential clustering is long term, due to a desire for cultural

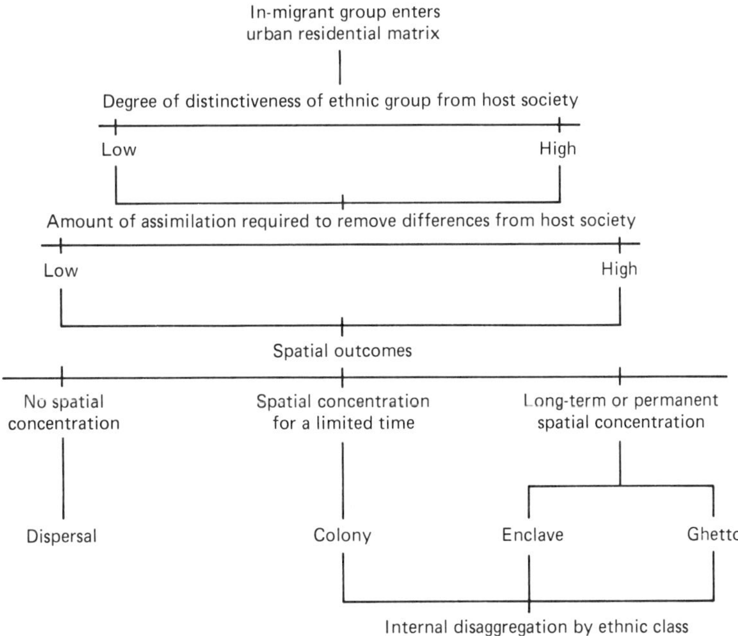

Figure 5.2 Ethnic groups, assimilation, and residential spatial outcomes. (From F. W. Boal, "Ethnic residential segregation," in D. T. Herbert and R. J. Johnston, Eds., *Social Areas in Cities*, Vol. 1: *Spatial Processes and Forms*, Wiley, New York, 1976, Fig. 2.1, p. 57. Copyright © 1976 by John Wiley & Sons, Ltd. Reprinted by permission of John Wiley & Sons, Ltd.)

preservation on the part of the ethnic group, and external pressure from the host society. Where the ethnic cluster represents a primarily voluntary phenomenon, it is called an *enclave*, as exemplified by Jewish communities in many cities. Those clusters that are more determined by external pressure, and may be involuntary in nature, are termed *ghettos*. Ghettos are often maintained by ethnic or racial prejudices within the local housing market.

5.2 THE CLASSICAL MODELS

Having shown that U.S. cities are indeed segregated according to such attributes as occupation, ethnicity, and race, it is important to consider whether this segregation is manifested in terms of particular spatial patterns. Within this context, two very influential students of urban structure have suggested that intraurban residential variation can be conceptualized in terms of zones and sectors. It is to these models of Burgess and Hoyt, respectively, that we now turn our attention.

The Concentric Zone Model

The concentric zone model was formulated by Burgess (1925), a sociologist at the University of Chicago. After studying the land use and social characteristics of Chicago in the early 1920s, Burgess suggested that the urban pattern could be summarized in terms of five concentric land use zones (Figure 5.3). These land use zones not only described the pattern at a particular point in time, but also represented the successive zones of urban expansion.

The first, or innermost zone, was the *central business district*. This zone contained the downtown retailing district, plus major office buildings and banks. It was also a major recreational center, with theaters, museums, and social clubs. Surrounding this area was the wholesale business district, with its associated warehouses. Burgess called the second zone the *zone in transition*. This zone was characterized by an inner factory belt and an outer ring of deteriorating residential neighborhoods. The residential deterioration was caused by the encroachment of business and industry from the CBD, and these transitional neighborhoods were often the first homes of immigrants from Europe, or black Americans from the rural South. The third zone was labeled the *zone of independent workingmen's homes*. Residents of this area had been able to move out of the second zone, although they still typically worked in the CBD. Many residents of these neighborhoods were second-generation immigrants. Burgess's fourth zone was entitled the *zone of better residences*. It was here that the great mass of middle-class native-born Americans lived. Most of the housing consisted of single-family dwelling units with spacious yards. The fifth, and outermost zone was the *commuter's zone*. This zone lay outside the legal boundary of the city, and consisted of a ring of small towns and villages. These settlements were mainly dormitory suburbs, with very little industry or employment of their own.

Burgess took care to emphasize that the zones should not be taken too literally, but rather that they represent an idealized pattern for the purposes of comparing

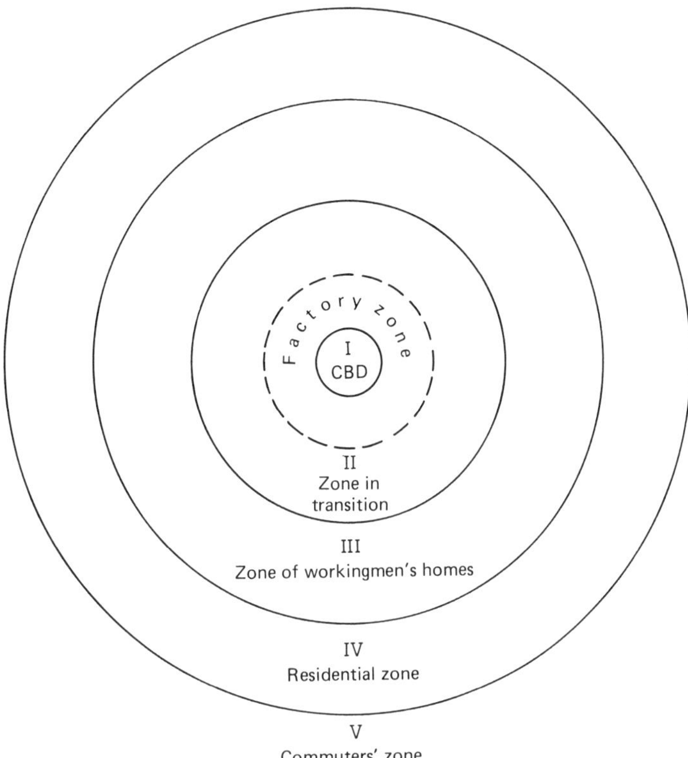

Figure 5.3 Concentric zone model. (Based on R. E. Park, E. W. Burgess, and R. D. McKenzie, *The City*, University of Chicago Press, Chicago, 1925, Fig. 1, p. 51. Copyright 1925 by the University of Chicago.)

deviations. The underlying mechanism that generated these distinctive zones was called the *process of invasion and succession*. Thus the prime characteristic of the classical ecological approach to urban structure, as represented by Burgess and his colleagues, was the utilization of a biological analogy, whereby different social groups, analogous to plant species, compete for space in the city (Timms, 1971, p. 86). Different social groups came to dominate different parts of the city, and form "natural areas." These natural areas, and their associated pathologies, were then subjected to further detailed examination (Zorbaugh, 1929).

The actual process of invasion and succession, by which a natural area came to be dominated by a new group, was divided into a series of stages (Johnston, 1971 p. 253). First, a small number of in-migrants from a different social group would penetrate a neighborhood. These in-migrants were usually upwardly mobile, and sometimes even had higher incomes than the established population. Second, this initial penetration was followed by an invasion stage, in which large numbers of the new group replaced members of the old group. Third, there was a succession, or consolidation stage, in which the original minority group became the majority group. Fourth, and finally, there was a piling-up stage, which entailed a stabilization of the area in terms of its domination by the new group. The overall process can be conveniently represented by an S-shaped curve (Figure 5.4).

In order, however, for this process of invasion and succession to create the particular spatial pattern envisioned by Burgess, certain preconditions, or assumptions about the city are necessary. First, the city needs to be growing in population and expanding at its edges. Second, there should be only one core to the city, so that the zones are concentrically arranged around a single center. Third, new housing should be built primarily for the wealthy at the edge of the city, so that the distinctive zones are created by the successive passing down of housing from the wealthy to the less wealthy. Fourth, there should be an efficient transportation system, so that the wealthy are willing to live at the edge of the city. Fifth, the city's population should be relatively heterogeneous, with a wide variety of occupational, ethnic, and racial groups, so that different kinds of social areas can emerge. It is noteworthy, therefore, that the Chicago of the 1920s contained all these necessary ingredients.

As with every model, or idealized representation of reality, the concentric zone model has not been immune from criticism. First, it has been pointed out that the biological analogy is a potentially misleading one, especially since competition in the human world, unlike that in the biological world, is restricted by conventions, laws, and institutions. Second, it has been argued that the model seriously underestimates the importance of sentimental attachments. Firey (1945) showed that the continuing attraction of Beacon Hill in Boston for high-status households was mainly due to sentimental reasons. In other words, residential neighborhoods are not merely the arenas of competition between social groups, as implied by the biological analogy, but they also represent certain symbolic qualities (Bassett and Short, 1980, p. 15).

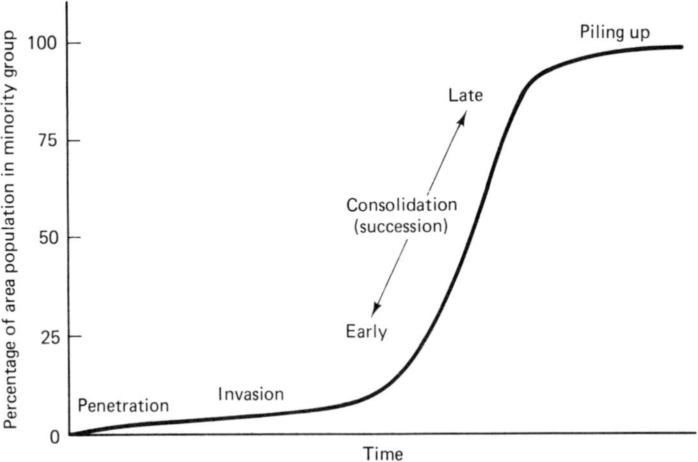

Figure 5.4 Process of invasion and succession, showing the typical stages according to the percentage of an area's population who are of the invading group. (From R. J. Johnston, *Urban Residential Patterns: An Introductory Review*, G. Bell, London, 1971, Fig. 6.3, p. 253.)

The Sector Model

Hoyt (1939) suggested that residential differentiation within cities could be summarized in terms of sectors rather than zones (Figure 5.5). Unlike Burgess, who had based his work on Chicago, Hoyt examined some 142 cities and concluded that socioeconomic status varied primarily in a sectoral fashion. On the basis of rental patterns, Hoyt made a number of general observations concerning these sectors, or pie-shaped wedges. First, the most highly valued residential areas were located in sectors on one side of the city, and sometimes extended out continuously from the city center. Second, the middle-class, or intermediate rental areas, were often found on either side of the highest-rent areas. Third, the low-rent sectors were frequently found on the opposite side of the city to the high-rent sectors.

Hoyt studied the changing distribution of high-class areas in particular, and suggested that the directional orientations and growth paths of these sectors were influenced by a variety of factors. First, the high-class areas tended to grow outward along major transportation routes. Second, they tended to grow toward high ground that was free from the risk of flooding. Third, they tended to extend toward the homes of the leaders of the community.

Like the concentric zone model, Hoyt's sector model has also been extensively criticized (Timms, 1971, pp. 227–229). One of the most ambiguous elements of the sector model is the definition of the sectors themselves. In Hoyt's original work the term "sector" is applied to areas that vary in size from single blocks to whole quadrants of the city. Also, the leaders of society are mentioned as being a major force in the expansion of high-socioeconomic-status sectors, but the identity of these leaders, and the reasons for their appeal, are never explicitly stated.

In any event, in purely geometric terms, the zonal and sector models are obviously at odds with each other, although it should be noted that Hoyt, while emphasizing the importance of sectoral differentiation, did include a zonal pattern within many of his sectors. Also, in terms of the underlying process responsible for producing these spatial patterns, Hoyt suggested a mechanism which has become known as the *filtering of housing*. The same filtering concept also played a role in the outward expansion of Burgess's zones (Berry and Horton, 1970, p. 307).

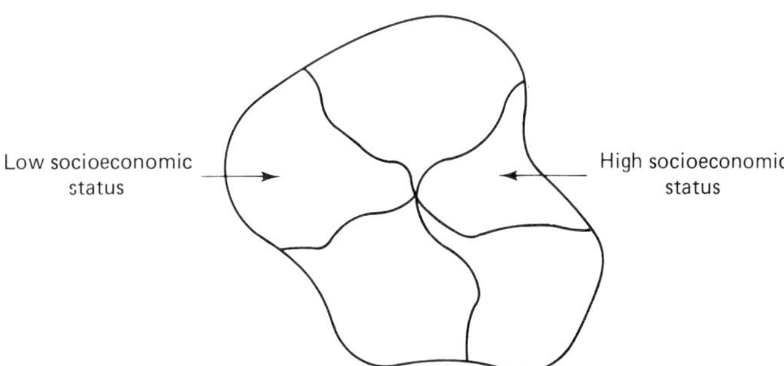

Figure 5.5 Sector model.

The Filtering of Housing

The filtering-of-housing concept suggests that as a housing unit ages and deteriorates its relative market price will decrease, and it will become available to lower-income families. As a result, it is postulated that a number of moves at the periphery of a zone, or sector, will initiate a chain reaction of vacancies that eventually extends back to the city center. Johnston (1971, p. 98) has conceptualized this chain reaction process as being composed of four stages (Figure 5.6). Thus, in terms of the classical zonal model, as the housing stock in each zone ages it is occupied by a succession of lower-income groups. That is, the housing stock in each zone is filtered down over time. The effect of an influx of poor immigrants into the city center, therefore, was much like throwing a pebble into the middle of a pond and setting up a series of waves that eventually reach the edge of that pond.

Bourne (1981, p. 149) has pointed out, however, that this argument contains a number of implicit assumptions. First, it is assumed that high-income families prefer to live in new rather than old housing. Second, these same high-income families are also assumed to prefer to live at the edge of the city rather than at the center. Third, it is assumed that housing inevitably depreciates with age, and that families prefer to move rather than rennovate their existing homes.

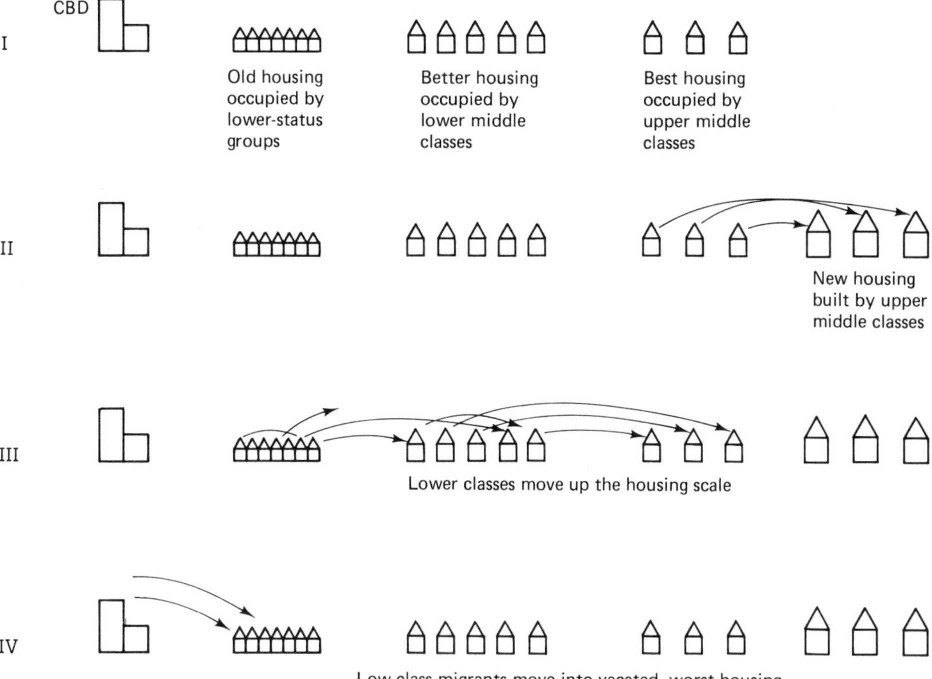

Figure 5.6 Simplified cross section through a city, from CBD to periphery, to illustrate the filtering process. (From R. J. Johnston, *Urban Residential Patterns: An Introductory Review*, G. Bell, London, 1971, Fig. 3.8, p. 98.)

The rate of filtering within a given housing market, or city, is influenced by two major factors: the rate of new housing construction and the rate of household formation. If new construction proceeds faster than the formation of new households, supply will exceed demand, and the market value of older housing will decrease quite rapidly, thus making it available to lower-income families. If, on the other hand, the rate of new construction is slow relative to the formation of new households, the rate of flitering will also be comparatively slow.

Transition probability matrices can be used to examine empirically the phenomenon of filtering (Yeates, 1974, p. 177). Table 5.6 contains data for the occupancy of 2495 homes in Kingston, Ontario, for the years 1958 and 1963. The head of household for each home is placed into one of seven occupational groupings, which have been ordered according to average income. The initial tally matrix indicates that of the 303 homes occupied by professional workers in 1958, by 1963, 6 were occupied by unskilled workers, 25 were occupied by service workers, 21 were occupied by craftsmen, and so on. In this way, the values to the left of the diagram represent homes that have filtered down to lower-socioeconomic groups, while the values to the right of the diagonal indicate homes that have filtered up to higher-socioeconomic groups.

The values in the tally matrix can be converted into transition probabilities, representing the probability that a home will be occupied by a particular type of family in 1963. These transition probabilities are obtained by calculating each entry as a proportion of the total number of homes in each row. Thus the proportion of homes

TABLE 5.6 TALLY MATRIX AND TRANSITION PROBABILITY MATRIX FOR 2495 HOMES IN KINGSTON, ONTARIO, 1958–1963

	1963 state							
1958 state	1	2	3	4	5	6	7	Total
				Tally matrix				
Unskilled	179	62	39	7	18	10	5	320
Service	116	359	103	31	32	12	18	671
Craft	64	95	337	13	22	29	8	568
Clerical	11	23	12	66	7	6	13	138
Sales	27	40	25	15	96	18	23	244
Managerial	10	24	19	12	23	146	17	251
Professional	6	25	21	9	20	15	207	303
Total	413	628	556	153	218	236	291	2495
				Transition probability matrix				
Unskilled	.559	.194	.122	.022	.056	.031	.016	1.0
Service	.173	.534	.154	.046	.048	.018	.027	1.0
Craft	.113	.167	.593	.023	.039	.051	.014	1.0
Clerical	.080	.167	.087	.478	.051	.043	.094	1.0
Sales	.111	.164	.102	.061	.394	.074	.094	1.0
Managerial	.040	.095	.076	.048	.092	.581	.068	1.0
Professional	.020	.083	.069	.030	.066	.050	.682	1.0

Source: M. H. Yeates, *An Introduction to Quantitative Analysis in Human Geography*, McGraw-Hill, New York, 1974, Tables 7-4 and 7-5, pp. 178–179. Reproduced with permission.

occupied by professionals in 1958 that are occupied by unskilled workers in 1963, is 6 divided by 303, giving a transition probability of only .02. The values along the diagonal represent homes that are still occupied by the same occupational category, and these are the largest transition probabilities. In other words, during this particular five-year period, a great many homes did not filter either up or down the socioeconomic hierarchy.

The filtering concept is of particular importance because it has become an underlying principle of *housing policy* in many countries. It is argued that an emphasis on the construction of middle- and upper-income housing will lead, as a result of the filtering process, to improved housing for all. There are a number of possible objections to this policy, however. First, rather than filtering down to lower-income families, older housing might be converted to other uses such as offices, or it might even be demolished. Second, lack of mortgage availability often restricts the movement of poorer families into available dwelling units. Third, as has already been mentioned, in order for there to be a significant amount of downward filtering, the supply of housing must exceed the demand for housing. Fourth, use of the filtering principle implies that newer housing should be for the rich, and older housing should be occupied by the poor. Fifth, even when older housing does filter down, it often burdens low-income families with prohibitive maintenance costs. In sum, it can be argued that filtering is neither an efficient nor a humane means of providing housing for low-income families (Bourne, 1981, p. 154). To maximize the benefits to the poor, a certain amount of new housing should probably be constructed specifically for that income level.

5.3 SOCIAL AREA ANALYSIS

Social area analysis attempts to provide a broader framework for the analysis of residential differentiation within cities by examining the underlying dimensions of urban society. This particular approach was first developed by Shevky and Williams (1949) in a study of Los Angeles, and was later elaborated on by Shevky and Bell (1955) in a study of San Francisco. Essentially, social area analysis classifies census tracts according to three basic constructs that supposedly summarize the important social differences between those census tracts. The three constructs are economic status, or social rank; family status, or urbanization; and ethnic status, or segregation. We will discuss the meaning of these constructs, how they were operationalized, how they were used to generate a typology of social areas, and the various ways in which social area analysis has since been criticized.

The Constructs

According to Shevky and Bell (1955, p. 3), the basic premise underlying social area analysis is that the city cannot be understood in isolation from the overall society of which it is a part. In other words, the social characteristics of urban life must be investigated within the context of the social characteristics of society at large. Thus,

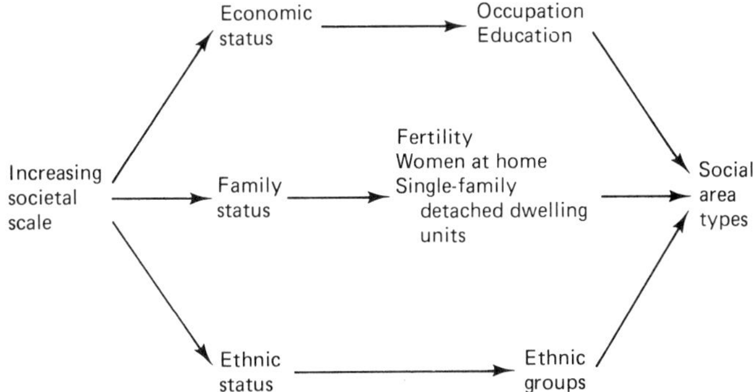

Figure 5.7 Shevky-Bell schema of social constructs and social area types. (Based on E. Shevky and W. Bell, *Social Area Analysis*, Stanford University Press, Stanford, Calif., 1955, p. 4.)

according to this thesis, residential differentiation within cities has its origins in the changing social differentiation of society.

The increasing modernization, or development of society, results in increasing *societal scale*, whereby the social and economic interchanges within the society enlarge in terms of both range and intensity (LaGory and Pipkin, 1981, p. 99). In social area analysis increasing societal scale is also held to be synonymous with the growth of an urban-industrial society (Timms, 1971, p. 127). People become more economically dependent on each other due to specialization of the labor force and improvements in transportation technology, and these changes result in new patterns of social differentiation (Figure 5.7).

First, because of the increasing division of labor, an occupational status system develops, and this system becomes the basic element of social stratification in industrial society. Second, the family becomes less important as an individual economic unit, and there is a weakening of the traditional organization of the family. Third, the improved transportation technology results in greater mobility, and the associated increased freedom of choice in terms of where to live in the city leads to a greater sorting of the population, and the segregation of various ethnic and racial groups. In summary, an increase in societal scale tends to socially differentiate people within cities according to *economic status*, *family status*, and *ethnicity*, and these three social constructs provide the criteria for differentiating social areas within cities.

Operationalization

The three constructs were originally operationalized by the use of six different variables, or indices (Figure 5.7). Economic status was measured by *occupation*, described as the total number of operatives, craftsmen and laborers, per 1000 employed persons, and by *education*, described as the number of persons who had completed no more than eight years of schooling per 1000 persons aged 25 years and over. Family status was represented by three different variables: *fertility*, the number of children four years old or less per 1000 women aged 15 to 44; *women at home*, the number of females not employed in the labor force in relation to the total number of females aged 15 years and over; and *single-family dwelling units*, the number of single-family homes as a proportion of all dwelling units. Finally, the ethnic status construct was simply measured as the number of people in specific *minority groups* as a proportion of the total population.

Data for these variables were obtained for each census tract in a city, and then combined according to the following procedure, to provide an overall value for each construct. First, the scores on the original variables were standardized, so that each variable ran between 0 and 100. For example, in there were values of 22, 62, and 72 percent for a particular variable, then 22 percent became 0, 72 percent became 100, and 62 percent became 80, as it is four-fifths of the distance between 22 and 72 percent. This transformation lent greater validity to the comparison of scores across different variables. The overall construct scores were then simply obtained by computing the average of the transformed scores for the variables associated with each of the three constructs.

Typology of Social Areas

On the basis of their scores on each of the social area constructs, the census tracts were classified into a series of social area types, and Figure 5.8 depicts the *social space* diagram for Winnipeg, Canada. The vertical and horizontal axes in the social space diagram are urbanization and economic status, respectively, where the urbanization

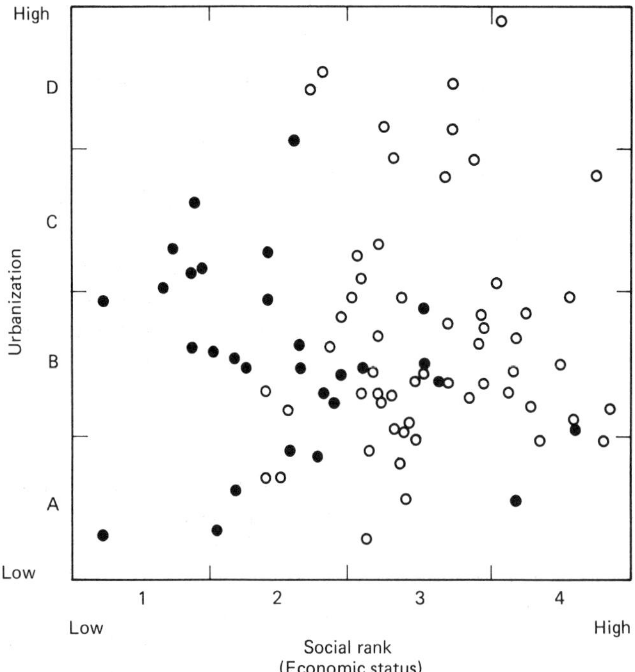

Figure 5.8 Social space diagram for Winnipeg. (From D. T. Herbert, *Urban Geography: A Social Perspective*, David & Charles, Newton Abbot, England, 1972, Fig. 40, p. 142.)

dimension is merely the reverse of the previously described family status construct, with high values for urbanization indicating low values for family status. Each census tract has a unique location within this two-dimensional space, as represented by a circle, according to its overall score on each construct.

The social space is usually partitioned into 16 cells, or social areas, by dividing the urbanization and economic status constructs into four intervals. The four intervals on each axis correspond with the ranges of 0 to 24, 25 to 50, 51 to 74, and 75 to 100 within the two major constructs. Shaded circles indicate those census tracts that have a higher-than-average percentage of some particular minority group. As one would expect, there tend to be fewer shaded circles in the right-hand cells, as these cells are associated with the highest levels of economic status.

The distance between census tracts within this abstract social space can be thought of as representing *social distance*, rather than physical distance. For example, those census tracts that fall within the upper right-hand cells, synonymous with high values for both urbanization and economic status, are obviously very similar with respect to these two dimensions, and thus separated by comparatively short social distances. Such a situation can occur even when the census tracts are located in different parts of the city, and are therefore separated by relatively large physical distances. In this respect, it is interesting to note that the term "social area" was originally used to describe a cluster of census tracts in social rather than geographical space. The later use of this term, however, implied a contiguous territorial unit (Herbert, 1972, p. 141).

Criticisms

Although it is generally accepted that social area analysis represents a promising attempt to erect a logical framework for the analysis of urban residential differentiation, it has been criticized by a number of authors. Hawley and Duncan (1957) criticized social area analysis because they believed that the theoretical framework fails to explain why residential areas should be relatively homogeneous, or why they should differ from each other. Also, the theory does not provide strong justification for using the three particular constructs of economic status, family status, and ethnic status, to differentiate between social areas (Ley, 1983, p. 76). In fact, Hawley and Duncan suggest that the theoretical framework erected by Shevky and Bell is merely an a posteriori rationalization for their choice of constructs.

Udry (1964) implies that social area analysis really involves two distinct parts, and that there is no real explanation as to how a theory of social change, on the one hand, can be translated into a static typology of residential differentiation, on the other. In other words, it requires no small inferential leap to move from a broad theory of social change to empirical regularities in the residential location of different kinds of households (Bassett and Short, 1980, p. 18). Also, in this context, the concept of increasing societal scale is probably too ambiguous to provide the key element in an overall theory of urban social structure, as it appears to be used synonymously with such general terms as industrialization, urbanization, and modernization (Timms, 1971, p. 139).

Besides being criticized on theoretical grounds, social area analysis has also been criticized for empirical reasons. In particular, the variables used to measure the three constructs are open to question (Carter, 1981, p. 258), and the methodology used for operationalizing the three constructs is statistically unsophisticated. The variables employed simply assume the constructs to be correct, without providing any tests of their empirical validity (Rees, 1970, p. 316). Such tests were later carried out using the technique known as factor analysis.

5.4 SOCIAL AREA ANALYSIS VIA FACTOR ANALYSIS

The phrase "social area analysis via factor analysis" refers to the empirical testing of the three social area constructs using the multivariate statistical technique of factor analysis. After gaining an intuitive understanding of factor analysis, we shall look at some of the results obtained when this technique is applied to U.S. cities.

Factor Analysis

Factor analysis was originally developed by psychologists as a means of reducing a large number of variables to a smaller number of underlying factors, dimensions, or components (Comrey, 1973). These underlying factors summarize the original variables, although as one moves from, say, 20 variables to only 3 factors, some of the original variation is obviously lost. Just how much of the original is lost, however, can be readily computed. It should also be noted that there are a variety of factor analysis techniques, and that, because of its widespread use in this particular context, we will be emphasizing the technique known as *principal components analysis*.

It is convenient to think of principal components analysis in terms of four matrices. The first matrix (Figure 5.9a) is simply a *data matrix* of the kind represented previously in Figure 1.2. The cases are the rows, and the variables are the columns. As we have N cases and M variables, the overall size of the matrix is $N \times M$. The data in this matrix are standardized so that each variable is expressed in terms of standard deviations from its mean, which is the same kind of standardization procedure as that discussed in Chapter 3.

The data matrix is then transformed into a *correlation matrix* (Figure 5.9b). Each variable is correlated with every other variable, using the correlation coefficient described in Chapter 2, thus creating an $M \times M$ matrix of correlation coefficients. The diagonal cells are given the value 1, as they represent the correlation of each variable with itself.

The correlation matrix is then transformed into the *components, or factor matrix* (Figure 5.9c). Each column in the matrix is a component that represents a group of interrelated variables. The variables are the rows, so if we have P components, the size of this matrix is $M \times P$. Each cell in the matrix contains a component, or factor loading, and as we shall see later, these component loadings indicate the strength of the relationships between the variables and the underlying components. Thus the

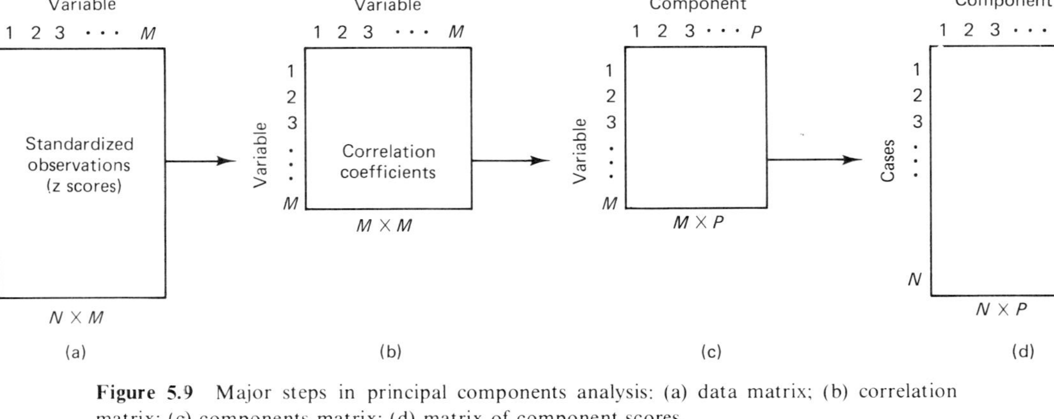

Figure 5.9 Major steps in principal components analysis: (a) data matrix; (b) correlation matrix; (c) components matrix: (d) matrix of component scores.

component loadings are used to interpret which group of variables is summarized by each particular component.

Finally, by multiplying the original data matrix by the components matrix, we obtain the *matrix of component scores* (Figure 5.9d). In this matrix the cases are once again the rows, while the components are the columns. Each cell contains a component score, and these scores indicate the value for each case on each component. In other words, after starting with values for a large number of variables, for each case, we finish with values for a smaller number of components, for each case.

This rather abstract framework will be more readily understood if we reexamine it within the specific context of social area analysis. In this situation the cases are census tracts within a city, while the variables are those used by Shevky and Bell. That is, occupation, education, fertility, women at home, single-family dwelling units, and the percentage of people in a specified minority group, such as blacks. Each cell in the data matrix contains a value for each census tract for each of these six variables.

Ideally, according to social area analysis, the resulting correlation matrix should look like the one represented in Figure 5.10a. If the crosses refer to relatively strong correlations, and the circles to relatively weak correlations, it can be seen that three groups of variables emerge: first, education and occupation are highly inter-

	(1)	(2)	(3)	(4)	(5)	(6)
Occupation (1)	—					
Education (2)	X	—				
Fertility (3)	O	O	—			
Women at home (4)	O	O	X	—		
SFDU (5)	O	O	X	X	—	
Percent black (6)	O	O	O	O	O	—

(a)

	Economic status	Family status	Ethnic status
Occupation	X	O	O
Education	X	O	O
Fertility	O	X	O
Women at home	O	X	O
SFDU	O	X	O
Percent black	O	O	X

(b)

Figure 5.10 Idealized (a) correlation and (b) components matrices associated with social area analysis.

correlated; second, fertility, women at home, and single-family dwelling units are highly intercorrelated; and third, the percent black variable is relatively independent of the other five.

These three groups of variables will then form three distinct components in the components matrix (Figure 5.10b), where the crosses represent relatively high component loadings, while the circles represent relatively low component loadings. Occupation and education both have high loadings on the first component, so this is labeled "economic status." Fertility, women at home, and single-family dwelling units all have high loadings on the second component, so this is labeled "family status," while percent black comprises the "ethnic status" component. The final matrix, containing the component scores, simply indicates the value for each census tract for each of these three components.

Before testing the empirical validity of social area analysis by examining whether these three components really do emerge from a principal components analysis of particular cities, it is helpful to visualize the statistical procedure in geometric terms (Rummel, 1970). First, imagine that we have two census tracts and six variables (Figure 5.11a), although in reality we would need many more census tracts for this type of analysis. Both census tracts have above average values on the first three variables, while census tract 1 is below average and census tract 2 is above average on the remaining three variables.

If lines are drawn from the origin to each of the six points in this two-dimensional census tract space, we obtain six vectors, one for each variable (Figure 5.11b). The cosine of the angle between each pair of vectors, or variables, denotes the *correlation coefficient* between those variables. An angle between 0 and 90 degrees indicates a positive correlation, with 0 representing a perfect linear relationship, and 90 degrees representing the complete absence of a linear relationship. Negative correlations are indicated by angles between 90 and 180 degrees. If the vectors are of unit length, the same information is represented by the projection of one vector on another. The longer the projection, the greater the correlation coefficient. In other words, the closer together the vectors in this two-dimensional space, the more strongly are the variables related.

Having discussed correlation coefficients in geometric terms, we can now consider a geometrical representation of the *component loadings* (Figure 5.11c). The first component is placed through the six vectors, or variables, in such a fashion that it maximizes the sum of the squared component loadings. The component loadings are analogous to the correlation coefficients in Figure 5.11b, but in this case each vector is projected onto the components. In other words, variable 3 is quite closely related to the first component, and thus has a relatively high component loading, while variable 1 has a relatively low component loading. If the loadings for all six variables are squared and summed, the location of the first component maximizes that sum. In technical terms, this sum of the squared component loadings is called an *eigenvalue*, and is used to determine the proportion of the total variation that is summarized by each component. The second component is introduced at right angles to the first, meaning that the two components are statistically independent of each other. The projections of each variable on this second axis provide the loadings for component

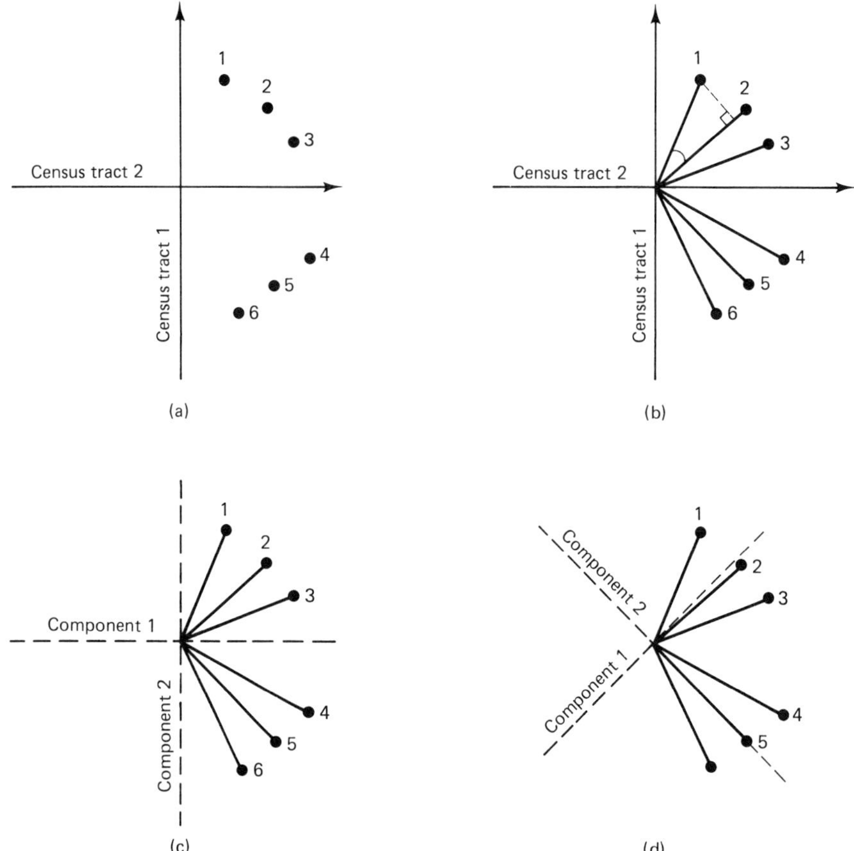

Figure 5.11 Geometric interpretation of principal components analysis; (a) location of variables in census tract space; (b) variables represented as vectors; (c) location of the principal axes; (d) location of the principal axes of rotation.

two. Further axes, or components, can be introduced at right angles to each other, although these axes cannot be represented in a two-dimensional diagram. In fact, as many axes can be fitted as there are variables, in this case six.

In order to interpret and label the different components, it is obviously advantageous to have some very high loadings, while the rest are very low, as in Figure 5.10b. The situation represented in Figure 5.11c is not ideal in this sense, as the loadings associated with the first component are neither exceptionally high nor exceptionally low. In other words, the component is not easily interpreted, or labeled, as a simple structure has not been achieved. This simple structure can often be obtained, however, by *rotating the axes* (Figure 5.11d). Now component 1 goes through the middle of the first three variables, while component 2 goes through the middle of the other three variables. As a result, both components have three high loadings and three low loadings, and thus each component summarizes three variables. If the axes, or components, are rotated while maintaining a right angle between them, the rotation is termed an *orthogonal rotation*. If, on the other hand, a right angle is not maintained, we have an *oblique rotation*, in which the components are no longer statistically independent of each other.

Empirical Tests

A major test of the empirical validity of the three constructs hypothesized by Shevky and Bell has been carried out by Van Arsdol et al. (1958). Using 1950 census tract data, they undertook factor analyses of several large U.S. cities. We will concentrate on the results they obtained for Minneapolis and Seattle.

The factor loadings for Minneapolis and Seattle, which are analogous to the previously described component loadings, are provided in Table 5.7. As expected, three main factors emerge for both cities. The first factor represents economic status, labeled "social rank" by Van Arsdol et al., and is composed of occupation and education, as the highest factor loadings for these two variables are in the social rank column. The second factor represents family status, labeled "urbanization" by Van Arsdol et al., and is composed of fertility, women in the labor force, and single-family dwelling units. The third factor represents ethnic status, here labeled "segregation," and is made up of percent Negro. Note that ordinarily one would expect women in the labor force to have a negative factor loading due to its inverse correlation

TABLE 5.7 FACTOR MATRICES FOR MINNEAPOLIS AND SEATTLE

	Social rank	Urbanization	Segregation
		Minneapolis	
Occupation	.762	.112	.121
Education	.670	−.094	−.026
Fertility	.152	.698	−.205
WLF	−.050	.913	−.061
SFDU	−.084	.757	.224
Negro	.103	−.050	.423
		Seattle	
Occupation	.848	.110	.213
Education	.631	−.181	−.257
Fertility	.030	.859	−.159
WLF	.040	.907	−.085
SFDU	−.132	.743	.162
Negro	−.039	−.080	.592

Note: Underscores indicate highest factor loading for each variable. WLF, women in the labor force; SFDU, single-family dwelling units.

Source: M. D. Van Arsdol, Jr., S. F. Camilleri, and C. F. Schmid, "The generality of urban social area indexes," *American Sociological Review*, 23 (1958), Table 2, p. 281.

TABLE 5.8 CORRELATIONS BETWEEN THE THREE FACTORS FOR MINNEAPOLIS AND SEATTLE

	SR-U	SR-Seg.	U-Seg.
Minneapolis	.002	−.675	.047
Seattle	.122	−.454	.237

Note: SR, social rank; U, urbanization; Seg., segregation.

Source: M. D. Van Arsdol, Jr., S. F. Camilleri, and C. F. Schmid, "The generality of urban social area indexes," *American Sociological Review*, 23 (1958), Table 5, p. 283.

with fertility and single-family dwelling units. In this particular instance, however, the values for the latter two variables have been subtracted from 1000.

Oblique rotations were used to obtain these factor loadings, so the factors are not necessarily orthogonal, or statistically independent of each other. The correlations between the three possible pairs of factors are reported in Table 5.8, where SR denotes social rank, or economic status; U denotes urbanization, or family status; and Seg. denotes segregation, or ethnic status. For both cities the correlations between social rank and urbanization, and between urbanization and segregation, are comparatively small. There are, however, fairly strong relationships between the social rank and segregation factors. More specifically, these relationships are negative, indicating that those census tracts with high scores for social rank tend to have low scores for segregation, and vice versa.

In summary, the factor analyses for Minneapolis and Seattle suggest that the three constructs derived from social area analysis are indeed empirically valid. This is not to say, however, that all cities exhibit exactly the same social structure. In fact, some of the other cities investigated by Van Arsdol et al., have slightly different factors, although the modifications are only minor.

5.5 FACTORIAL ECOLOGY

The more recent factorial ecological approach to studying the residential structure of cities became popular during the 1960s. This approach differs from social area analysis via factor analysis in two important ways. First, a larger number of variables are used in the factor analysis, in order to test the robustness of the three major underlying dimensions of residential differentiation. Second, factorial ecology also places much greater emphasis on the spatial patterns associated with those dimensions. This focus on spatial patterns necessitates an interest in the component scores, as well as the component loadings.

In this section we consider first the underlying dimensions of residential differentiation uncovered by a factorial ecology of Chicago. Then the spatial patterns associated with those dimensions, the ecological structures of four medium-sized U.S. cities, and various criticisms of the factorial ecological approach to understanding residential differentiation are considered.

A Factorial Ecology of Chicago

The geographer Rees (1970) has undertaken an exhaustive study of the factorial ecology of Chicago. We will focus on the results he obtained from a factor analysis of 12 variables across 1324 census tracts in the Chicago metropolitan area. These 12 variables include one measure of education, two measures of occupation, three measures of income, two measures of age, and one measure each of family size, race, housing age, and housing quality.

Three factors were extracted, and the highest factor loading for each variable has been underlined (Table 5.9). Based on the pattern of factor, or component loadings, the three factors have been labeled "socioeconomic status," "stage in the life cycle," and "race and resources," and it is immediately apparent that these three factors are very similar to the social area constructs described previously. *Socio-*

TABLE 5.9. FACTOR STRUCTURE OF THE CHICAGO METROPOLITAN AREA

	Socioeconomic status	Stage in the life cycle	Race and resources	Communality
Median school years completed	.920	−.011	−.048	.850
Percent white-collar workers	.846	−.220	−.203	.805
Percent families with incomes over $10,000	.771	−.096	−.484	.837
Median annual income	.746	−.059	−.510	.820
Percent housing built after 1950	.697	.434	−.168	.702
Percent families with incomes under $3000	−.646	−.167	.597	.802
Percent substandard housing	−.627	−.197	.488	.670
Percent unemployed workers	−.618	.035	.566	.705
Population per household	.032	.928	−.045	.864
Percent population under 18	−.133	.867	−.064	.733
Percent population over 65	−.102	−.847	−.241	.786
Percent population Negro	−.277	.172	.876	.848
Explained variance	37.3	22.3	19.3	

Note: Underscores indicate highest factor for each variable.

Source: P. H. Rees, "Concepts of social space: Toward an urban social geography," in B. J. L. Berry and F. E. Horton, Eds., *Geographic Perspectives on Urban Systems*, Prentice-Hall, Englewood Cliffs, N.J., 1970, Table 10.16, p. 356.

economic status contains the education, income, employment, and housing variables. As one would expect, percent families with annual incomes under $3000, percent substandard housing, and percent unemployed workers all have negative loadings, as they are inversely related to socioeconomic status. *Stage in the life cycle* is composed of family size and age variables. Note that percent population over 65 has a negative loading, as this variable is inversely related to population per household and percent population under 18. Finally, the *race and resources* factor is dominated by percent population Negro, although it also has some fairly high positive loadings on low-income families, substandard housing, and unemployment.

The row labeled "explained variance," in Table 5.9 indicates the percentage of the total variation that is accounted for by each factor. Recall that the sum of the squared factor loadings in each column gives us the eigenvalue associated with each factor. Using this information, the percent explained variance is simply computed by dividing the respective eigenvalues by the total number of variables, and multiplying by 100. In this particular instance, the three factors together account for 78.9 percent of the original variation. In other words, the 12 variables can be conveniently summarized by just three factors, as only 20 percent of the original variation has been lost.

The communalities indicate from which particular variables this information has been lost. A communality represents the sum of the squared factor loadings for an individual variable, so the communality for median school years completed is .85. This value tells us that 85 percent of the original variation in this variable has been preserved by the three factors, with only 15 percent being lost. By contrast, over 30 percent of the variation in percent substandard housing has been lost by reducing 12 variables to three factors.

In summary, the results for Chicago, as for many other major cities, suggest that the three basic social area constructs still emerge even when many more variables are utilized. That is, the three constructs that were deductively derived by Shevky and Bell have also been inductively derived from the analysis of a much larger set of variables. We next look at the spatial patterns associated with these constructs.

Spatial Patterns

The spatial patterns are generated by mapping the factor, or component scores, for each of the three major factors or components. A variety of studies have shown that significant regularities occur in these patterns across a large number of cities, including Chicago (Murdie, 1969). First, the *socioeconomic status* factor tends to form sectors (Figure 5.12a). The high-status sectors contain census tracts with high values for variables such as income and education, while the reverse is true of the low-status sectors.

Second, the *family-status* factor tends to be distributed according to zones rather than sectors (Figure 5.12b). The zones toward the center of the city are dominated by census tracts containing small families, often single-person families, where the head of households tends to be either very young or very old. As one moves out

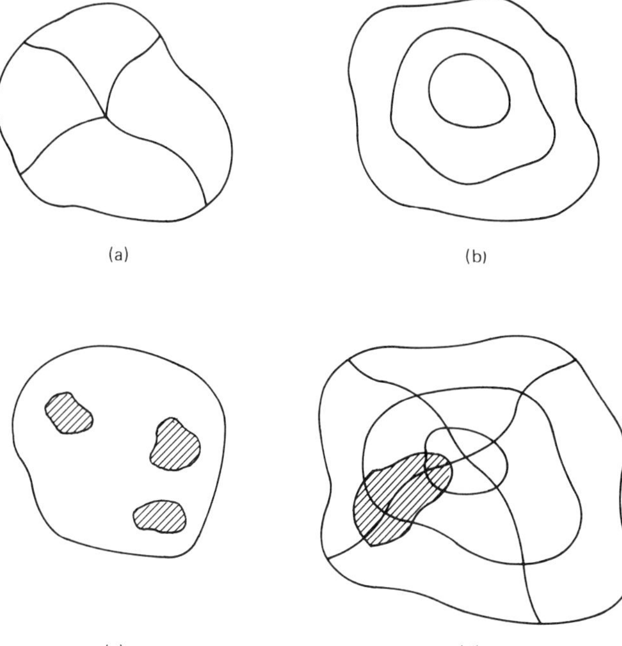

Figure 5.12 Idealized spatial patterns: (a) socioeconomic status; (b) family status; (c) ethnic status; (d) the urban mosaic.

toward the peripheral zone the factor scores for family status increase, indicating a greater preponderance of large families with middle-aged heads of household.

Third, the *ethnic status* factor tends to form clusters (Figure 5.12c). Each of these clusters represents a group of census tracts that is dominated by a particular racial or ethnic group, such as blacks, Italians, or Chinese. Such areas are known as black ghettos, Little Italy, or Chinatown, and they often represent a microcosm of the whole city, with their own internal differentiation according to economic status and family status (Rees, 1970, p. 311).

Finally, each of these three spatial patterns can be superimposed to create the *urban mosaic*. Each segment, or areal unit, in Figure 5.12d represents a region that is characterized by particular kinds of households, and these internally homogeneous social areas are differentiated according to economic status, family status, and ethnic status. Of course, social area boundaries are more convoluted than those depicted in Figure 5.12d, and it is helpful to think of the social areas as forming the individual pieces of a large-scale jigsaw puzzle.

From this spatial perspective it becomes clear that the classical models of Burgess and Hoyt are complementary rather than competitive. The spatial structure of cities is both zonal and sectoral, with family status being primarily zonal and economic status primarily sectoral. Analysis of variance is the statistical technique most often used empirically to validate this last statement, as it allows one to compare, for example, the variation between the zones with the variation within those zones. If the variation between the zones is significantly greater than the variation within the zones for a particular factor, we can conclude that the factor is distributed zonally. As we shall see in the next section, however, the spatial patterns can also be tested by multiple correlation and regression analysis using dummy variables.

In summary, factorial ecological studies have produced two major sets of conclusions. First, as predicted by social area analysis, residential differentiation can be summarized in terms of economic status, family status, and ethnicity. Second, these three dimensions of residential differentiation are spatially distributed in terms of sectors, zones, and clusters, respectively.

The Factorial Ecology of Medium-Sized Cities

As most factorial ecological studies have focused on large cities, it is of interest to see if the results obtained at that level also hold for smaller cities. With this in mind, and as part of a larger study concerned with residential mobility, the present author (Cadwallader, 1981b) chose four U.S. cities: Canton (Ohio), Des Moines (Iowa), Knoxville (Tennessee), and Portland (Oregon). These particular cities were chosen because of their intermediate size, although Portland is somewhat larger than the other three, and because they are located in different parts of the country.

Census tract data from the 1970 U.S. Census were used, and the choice of variables was circumscribed by the desire to maintain comparability with the classic social area studies (Van Arsdol et al., 1958), although it was decided not to include the ethnic status variables, as their role in determining patterns of social variation is less important in smaller cities. Six variables were chosen to represent the two factors, socioeconomic status and family status. The socioeconomic status variables consisted of median income, median school years completed by persons 25 years or over, and the number of professional, technical, and kindred workers, as a percentage of the total employed. The family status variables were persons per household, percentage of females 16 years old and over in the labor force, and persons under 18 as a percentage of the total population.

The underlying dimensions produced by these six variables were identified, as in most factorial ecological studies, by the use of principal components analysis, with an orthogonal rotation. The resulting two dimensions, or components, correspond closely to the economic status and family status dimensions found in previous studies (Table 5.10). The only variable that is inadequately represented in this structure is the percentage of females 16 years old and over in the labor force, which has communalities ranging from 0.59 in the case of Canton, to only 0.09 in the case of Knoxville. Despite these low communalities, however, the variable behaves as expected in that it is always negatively associated with the family status component. Its declining importance as an indicator of social differentiation, since the pioneering studies of the 1950s, is undoubtedly due to the increased labor force participation of females from all levels of the socioeconomic hierarchy.

To verify the apparent similarity between the components obtained for the four cities, coefficients of congruence were calculated for each pair of cities (Harman, 1967, p. 270). The coefficient of congruence is a measure of similarity between component loadings, which ranges in value from +1 for perfect agreement, through

TABLE 5.10 FACTOR MATRICES FOR CANTON, DES MOINES, KNOXVILLE, AND PORTLAND

	SES	FS	Comm.	SES	FS	Comm.
		Canton			Des Moines	
Education	.95	−.08	.91	.96	−.03	.92
Income	.94	.07	.89	.91	.34	.94
Occupation	.94	−.07	.89	.88	−.27	.85
Persons per household	.21	.95	.95	.05	.95	.91
Percent under 18	−.04	.93	.87	−.01	.95	.90
Women in labor force	.20	−.74	.59	.03	−.61	.37
Percent total variance	46.0	38.8		42.2	39.5	
		Knoxville			Portland	
Education	.94	−.14	.91	.95	.04	.90
Income	.91	.21	.86	.90	.33	.92
Occupation	.87	−.09	.76	.91	−.06	.83
Persons per household	.02	.97	.93	.12	.95	.92
Percent under 18	−.17	.95	.93	−.05	.95	.91
Women in labor force	−.03	−.29	.09	−.10	−.58	.35
Percent total variance	41.7	33.3		42.8	37.6	

Note: SES, socioeconomic status; FS, family status; Comm., communality.

Source: M. T. Cadwallader, "A unified model of urban housing patterns, social patterns, and residential mobility," *Urban Geography*, 2 (1981), Table 1, p. 122.

0 for no agreement, to −1 for perfect inverse agreement. In the present instance the coefficients for both socioeconomic status and family status are all extremely high, indicating that the components are almost identical for all four cities (Table 5.11). For example, the coefficients of congruence for Canton and Des Moines are .99 in the case of the socioeconomic status component, and .97 in the case of the family status component.

Multiple correlation and regression analysis was used to test for the zones and sectors that are supposedly associated with family status and socioeconomic status, respectively. For this purpose, each city was partitioned into six sectors and six zones, and the extent to which these sectors or zones account for the spatial variation in either of the two dimensions, as measured by their component scores, was determined by calculating the multiple correlation coefficient for the following equation:

$$Y_i = b_1X_{i1} + b_2X_{i2} + b_3X_{i3} + b_4X_{i4} + b_5X_{i5} \tag{5.2}$$

where Y_i is the value for census tract i of the component being tested, and $X_{i1}, \ldots, X_{i5}$ are dummy variables denoting the zone or sector in which any census tract i

TABLE 5.11 COEFFICIENTS OF CONGRUENCE

	(1)	(2)	(3)	(4)
Canton (1)	—	.97	.95	.98
Des Moines (2)	.99	—	.96	.99
Knoxville (3)	.98	.99	—	.97
Portland (4)	.98	.99	.99	—

Note: Coefficients for family status above the diagonal; coefficients for socioeconomic status below the diagonal.

Source: M. T. Cadwallader, "A unified model of urban housing patterns, social patterns, and residential mobility," *Urban Geography*, 2 (1981), Table 2, p. 122.

is located. This procedure is slightly different from analysis of variance, which is normally used when searching for zonal or sectoral variation, and it is important to note that when using dummy variables, there should be one term fewer than there are zones or sectors; otherwise, one is faced with singularity problems (Kmenta, 1971, p. 413). Also, the multiple correlation coefficients derived in this manner should be made directly comparable by using exactly the same number of zones and sectors for each city.

In general, the multiple correlation coefficients indicate that the variation in both socioeconomic status and family status can be equally well accounted for by either zones or sectors (Table 5.12). For example, in the case of Canton, approximately 45 percent of the variation in the socioeconomic status dimension is accounted for by the zones, and approximately 53 percent is accounted for by the sectors. An important exception to this rule, however, is Portland, where, as postulated by other factorial ecological studies, the variation in socioeconomic status is primarily sectoral, while the variation in family status is primarily zonal. This finding suggests that the degree of spatial sorting associated with residential structure might be related to spatial scale, with larger cities being likely to exhibit higher degrees of spatial sorting than their smaller counterparts.

To verify further these results concerning the spatial patterns, the same regression equations were calibrated using the original variables, rather than the

TABLE 5.12 MULTIPLE CORRELATION COEFFICIENTS FOR THE ZONES AND SECTORS

	Zones	Sectors	Zones	Sectors
	Canton		Des Moines	
Socioeconomic status	.669	.730	.629	.581
Family status	.537	.577	.522	.705
	Knoxville		Portland	
Socioeconomic status	.605	.536	.214	.734
Family status	.556	.292	.737	.230

components, as the dependent variables. This second test was performed as a response to the argument that component scores might be misleading as indicators of spatial pattern in that their values depend, to a certain extent at least, on variables that are associated only slightly with the particular component under investigation. This problem is especially apparent when there are a large number of variables involved in the study, in which case the minor variables, in concert, can have a major influence on the component scores. The multiple correlation coefficients for the variables used here, however, indicated conclusions similar to those arrived at by using the component scores themselves.

Criticisms

Criticisms of the factorial ecological approach to understanding residential differentiation within cities can be grouped into three main categories. First, it is unclear to what extent the results are dependent on the particular *research design* employed. It is possible, for example, that the underlying factors, and their associated spatial patterns, would be somewhat different if blocks were used rather than census tracts. Similarly, the results tend to vary according to the type of factor analysis performed, and the various kinds of orthogonal and oblique rotations (Davies, 1978). Even within a given type of factor analysis various problems are associated with the interpretation and labeling of those factors (Palm and Caruso,1972).

Second, it can be argued that factorial ecology is a purely *descriptive* form of analysis, as it fails to identify the processes that result in the urban mosaic. Attempts to address these processes generally involve investigating residential mobility. At the aggregate, or macro level, the classical ecologists invoked such concepts as invasion and succession to help understand residential mobility (Section 5.2). At the individual, or micro level, on the other hand, attempts have been made to model residential mobility within the framework of individual choice behavior (Chapter 9). In addition, the operation of the urban housing market has been scrutinized, with particular emphasis being given to the role of intermediaries in the housing market, such as real estate agents and financial institutions (Chapter 3). Although residential differentiation in urban areas has traditionally been explained in terms of social ecological processes and individual consumer preferences, research on the city of Baltimore (Harvey, 1974) has explicated the pivotal role played by financial and governmental institutions.

Finally, the social areas identified by factorial ecology do not always constitute cohesive *communities*. Using the terminology discussed in Chapter 1, these social areas are uniform regions, but not necessarily functional regions. That is, they are relatively homogeneous with respect to certain specified variables, such as income, education, and family size, but they might not be characterized by a high degree of internal interaction. Attempts to measure the amount of internal interaction have focused on activity patterns associated with the workplace, friends, and clubs (Everitt, 1976). Within this context, factorial ecological classifications of the Minneapolis metropolitan area have suggested that the derived regions are not always related to behavioral and attitudinal characteristics. For example, an examination of the flows of telephone calls between exchange districts in Minneapolis showed little relationship between the pattern of calls and the underlying social areas (Palm, 1973a). Similarly, a study concerning readership preferences for particular magazines and newspapers exhibited no significant differences in reading habits across the various types of social areas (Palm, 1973b).

Despite such criticisms, however, there is no doubt that these socially uniform residential neighborhoods have a distinctive role to play in urban society (Scott, 1980, pp. 124–127). First, by creating an environment that reinforces the ideological orientations of the dominant neighborhood group, they help to socialize the children in mutually acceptable ways. Second, they help sustain cultural homogeneity, as exemplified by certain ethnic neighborhoods. Third, they symbolize the social status of their inhabitants.

5.6 URBAN SOCIAL AREAS AND CRIME

The classical ecological approach to understanding residential structure, discussed earlier in this chapter, had three major goals (Berry and Kasarda, 1977, pp. 5–6): first, to apply concepts derived from plant ecology, such as competition, invasion, and succession, to the analysis of urban neighborhoods; second, to provide detailed descriptions of "natural areas," or social areas within cities (Zorbaugh, 1929); and third, to investigate the relationships between these social areas and various kinds of social pathology. It is to this third type of study that we now turn, using criminal behavior as our example of social pathology.

One of the most exhaustive studies of urban crime has been undertaken by Schmid, for the city of Seattle. In particular, he documented the relationship between certain crime variables and the previously described *social area constructs* (Schmid, 1960). As one might expect, most of the crime indicators were negatively related to social rank and family status, and positively related to the segregation construct (Table 5.13). In a similar study, Willie (1967) used a modified form of social area

TABLE 5.13 CORRELATIONS BETWEEN CRIME VARIABLES AND SOCIAL CONSTRUCTS FOR SEATTLE

	Social constructs		
Crime variables	Social rank	Family status	Segregation
Attempted suicide	−.295	−.460	.304
Fighting	−.342	−.256	.499
Vagrancy	−.319	−.225	.395
Indecent exposure	−.035	−.405	−.065
Petty larceny	−.331	−.257	.421
Shoplifting	−.189	−.373	.330
Automobile theft	−.219	−.535	.136
Burglary	−.232	−.286	.258

Source: C. F. Schmid, "Urban crime areas: Part II," *American Sociological Review*, 25 (1960), Table 5, p. 673.

analysis and found fairly strong relationships between delinquency and economic status and family status, thus concluding that delinquency is associated with harsh economic environments and unstable family life. Johnstone (1978) studied juvenile delinquency in Chicago within a social area analysis framework and also stressed the importance of "social location."

The systematic nature of the relationships suggest that social area analysis is a useful tool for understanding the spatial pattern of crime within cities, despite the suggestion that the role of single diagnostic variables might be more easily interpreted than that of social area constructs (Baldwin, 1974). Three methodological issues should be borne in mind when interpreting these results, however. First, one must remember the "ecological fallacy" involved in inferring patterns of individual behavior from results obtained at an aggregate level of analysis. More specifically, Schmid's results imply that areas with low values for social rank and family status have high crime rates, but they cannot be used to infer that it is the low-income persons from broken homes who actually commit the crimes.

Second, simple correlation techniques may be inappropriate for studying even the ecological, or aggregate-level relationships between neighborhood characteristics and crime. Using data from Portland, Oregon, Polk (1967) demonstrated that although each of the classical social area constructs contributes a unique effect to the distribution of delinquency, there are also important interaction effects which cannot be captured by simple correlation analysis. For example, in Portland, delinquency tends to be lowest where high social status and high family status occur together, and highest where low social status and low family status are combined. Nevertheless, although delinquency generally decreases with increasing social and family status, at the very lowest levels of family status, delinquency tends to increase with increasing social status.

Third, it is important to recognize the weaknesses in all forms of crime statistics (Herbert, 1982). For example, some crimes are not reported at all, creating a bias that may vary systematically from area to area. Similarly, police policy in making arrests, and assigning disproportionate numbers of officers to different areas, may also bias recorded statistics.

Despite these methodological problems, however, a variety of ecologically based theories of criminal behavior have been developed (Herbert, 1976), of which perhaps the two most important have been labeled "social disorganization" and "differential association." The *social disorganization* theory stresses the relationship between crime and various neighborhood characteristics, especially residential mobility, or turnover rates. It is argued that neighborhoods with high turnover rates tend to lack social cohesion, and thus become breeding grounds for deviant behavior, although there is often a highly developed social structure within the deviant groups themselves.

A related viewpoint is represented by *differential association* theory, which argues that criminal behavior is the product of a socialization process whereby adolescents become delinquent because of their interaction with criminal groups. Such behavior is reinforced by the fact that these adolescents also tend to be isloated from anticriminal ideals. This notion of deviant subcultures within cities, dominated by unconventional norms, implies that adolescents become criminals because of the social context in which they grow up, rather than because of underlying personal inclinations.

Note that both these theories, as with the ecological approach in general, stress the significance of the social context when analyzing individual behavior. Such theories, however, are unable to account for individual differences, and more recent studies of urban crime emphasize the importance of obtaining individual-level data (Herbert, 1979b). Also, in those situations where reference is made to some broader societal structure, the local environment, or social area, is often felt to be too specific. Radical critiques of criminological theory argue that the underlying causes of lower-class crime cannot be found at the neighborhood level, as criminal behavior is partly a response to the social inequalities within the society in general (Hamnett, 1979).

6

Urban Industrial Structure

6.1 THE PRINCIPLES OF INDUSTRIAL LOCATION

When deciding where to locate their factories, industrialists consider a variety of factors (Smith, 1981). We first examine these factors in general, and then assess how they influence the spatial distribution of industrial activity within cities, commenting especially on the suburbanization of industry and the associated phenomenon of planned industrial parks. The economic base concept is then introduced as a technique for describing an individual city's economy, and also for explaining urban growth. Finally, input–output analysis is discussed, to provide a more detailed accounting of the flows within an economic system, and to derive the multiplier effect for individual sectors of the economy.

Attributes of the Raw Materials

If the raw materials used by a particular industry lose a great deal of *weight* during the manufacturing process, that industry tends to be located close to its raw materials, as it is cheaper to transport the finished product. The amount of weight loss is measured by the material index, which is calculated by dividing the weight of the raw materials by the weight of the finished product. If the index is greater than 1, it is best to locate near the raw materials, and this general tendency is reflected by the locational behavior of the 65 British industries represented in Table 6.1. The iron and steel industry is a good example of an industry that has traditionally been raw materal oriented, due to the weight loss involved in the production of pig iron.

Perishable raw materials also encourage the associated industry to be raw

TABLE 6.1 OBSERVED RELATIONSHIP BETWEEN THE MATERIAL INDEX AND INDUSTRIAL LOCATION

	Material index			
Location	Greater than 5	2–5	1–2	Less than 1
At materials	2	4	16	0
Partly at materials	0	4	5	3
Not at materials	0	8	12	11

Source: Based on W. Smith, "The location of industry," *Transactions of the Institute of British Geographers,* 21 (1955), Table 1, p. 7.

material oriented, in terms of location. For example, the fruit canning and preserving industry is located where the fruit is grown, in Florida and California, while the milk products industry tends to be located in those states where dairy farming is important, such as Wisconsin. In general, however, the improvement of refrigeration techniques has made the perishability factor increasingly less significant.

The *value per unit weight* of the raw materials is also an important determinant of industrial location. A raw material that has a comparatively high value per unit weight can bear the cost of transportation much better than can a raw material that has a comparatively low value per unit weight. As a result, those industries that are dependent on raw materials with low values per unit weight tend to locate near those raw materials.

Finally, the *substitutability* and *number* of raw materials must be considered. The locational pull of any particular raw material is less in those situations where the industry can substitute one raw material for another. Similarly, the more raw materials an industry uses, the less the locational influence of any one of those raw materials.

Attributes of the Finished Product

Some products undergo a *weight* gain during the manufacturing process, as reflected by a material index of less than 1. The soft-drink industry provides an excellent example of this phenomenon, as the flavors are transported in liquid, or syrup form to local bottlers, who add water and bottle. As the weight of the final product is largely composed of the water and bottle, transportation costs are minimized by locating near the products' market. Consequently, the soft-drink industry tends to be concentrated in large cities.

A second consideration, in terms of the attributes of the finished product, is the perishability of that product. A *perishable* product tends to make an industry market oriented. The bakery industry is a good example here, as it requires the prompt delivery of fresh goods.

The *value per unit weight* is a third important attribute of the finished product. These industries with high-valued products per unit weight, such as watches, are more able to absorb transportation costs and are less tied to a market location. On the other hand, those industries with low-valued products per unit weight, such as cement, are less able to absorb transportation costs, and tend to be more market oriented in terms of location.

Finally, a *bulky* finished product also encourages an industry to be market oriented. For example, the furniture industry tends to be located near the major markets for its products because of the transportation costs associated with moving such bulky items as tables and sofas. Automobile assembly plants provide a similar example. Although many of the parts are produced in Detroit, the automobiles themselves are assembled in plants that are dispersed throughout the United States.

Transportation Costs

Transportation costs are perhaps the single most important determinant of plant location. In general, transportation costs increase with increasing *distance,* although in a curvilinear fashion (Figure 6.1a). The cost per mile tends to decrease with increasing distance because the same fixed costs, associated primarily with loading and unloading, have to be paid regardless of distance. More specifically, freight costs are often stepped, with the steps being superimposed on the general curvilinear relationship (Figure 6.1b). These steps indicate that the same rate is charged for a given range of distances, thus obviating the necessity to compute a separate rate for each individual journey. If there is a break of bulk point, or discontinuity, the freight rate will increase at that distance, before beginning to taper off again (Figure 6.1c). Such break of bulk points occur, for example, when transferring from land to water, thus creating a new set of fixed costs.

Transportation costs are also influenced by factors other than distance. First, the form of the relationship between transportation costs and distance tends to vary according to the *mode of transportation* (Figure 6.2), with road transportation being cheapest for short distances, rail being cheapest for intermediate distances, and water being cheapest for long distances. Second, transportation costs will vary according to the *size of shipment,* because large shipments permit economies in terms of both administrative and terminal costs. Third, the *perishability* of the product makes a difference, with such goods as fruits and vegetables generating higher charges because of the special handling involved with refrigeration or rapid transportation. Fourth, it is usually cheaper to transport *lower-valued products,* because of the special packing and insurance costs associated with high-valued products. Finally, transportation rates will be cheaper in those situations where there is active *competition* between the various modes of transportation.

The Factors of Production

The factors of production—land, labor, and capital—are the three essential elements of the manufacturing process once all the raw materials have been assembled. These factors are combined in a variety of ways by different firms and industries, creating labor-intensive industries, where labor is a major input; captial-intensive industries,

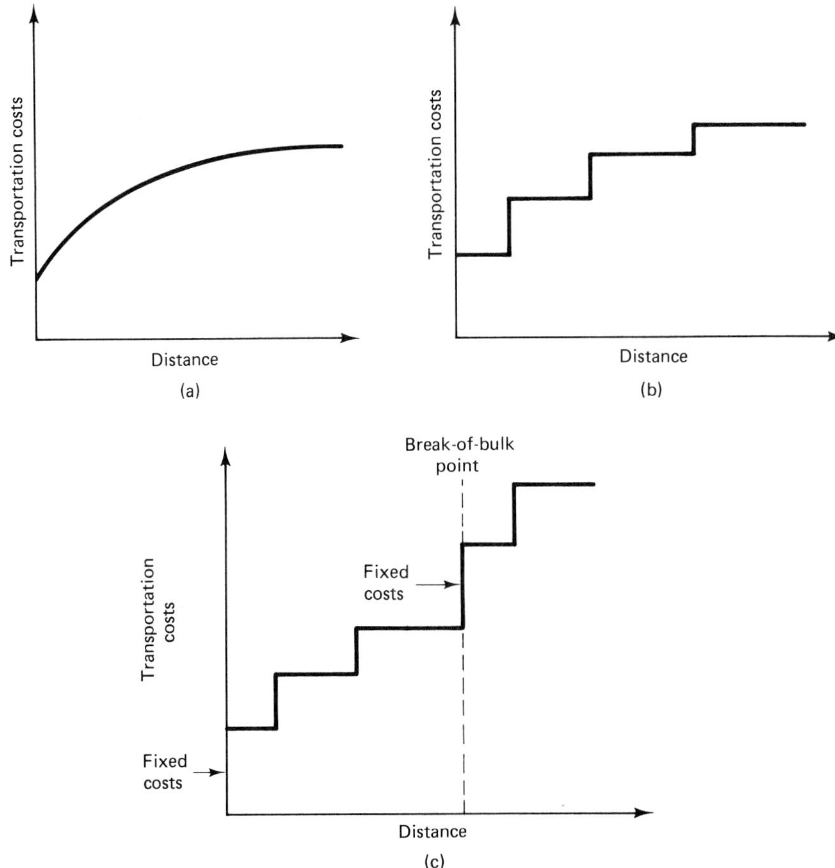

Figure 6.1 Relationship between transportation costs and distance: (a) general relationship; (b) stepped transportation costs; (c) discontinuity in transportation costs.

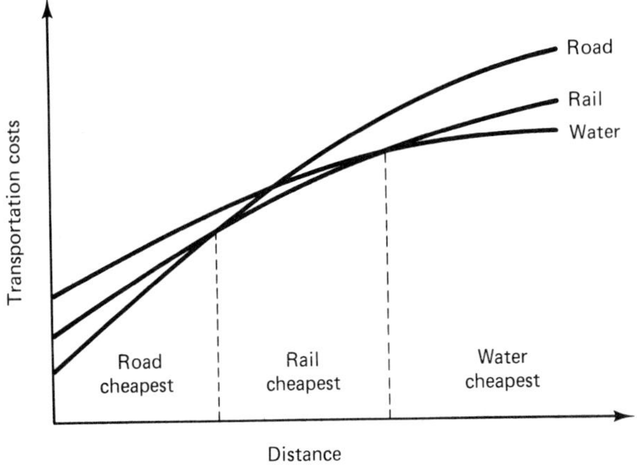

Figure 6.2 Variation in transportation costs for different modes of transportation.

where capital is a major input; and so on. In recent years, there has been a move toward more capital-intensive industries, which are highly mechanized and require relatively little labor.

All industries need a certain amount of *land* on which to locate their factories. Some firms, however, have special requirements concerning the physical attributes of the site. Many firms, for example, use large volumes of water in the manufacturing process, or require rivers or lakes into which effluence can be deposited. Other firms might require an extensive area underlain by solid bedrock, to support special equipment. As discussed in Chapter 2, the cost of land in cities varies quite systematically. In general, land values decline with increasing distance from the city center, although ridges of higher-valued land also extend along the major traffic arteries, and certain sites might be unavailable because of zoning ordinances prohibiting industrial activity in that part of the city. Overall, however, the cost of land is probably less important in the long run, when considering potential locations, than are labor and capital costs. The cost of land is a major expenditure when starting a factory, but it becomes far less significant when costed over a long period, or when rent is computed as a proportion of the total production costs.

Firms consider two major characteristics of the *labor* supply when deciding where to locate. First, the quality of labor, in terms of certain specialized skills, might be important. Some industries, such as the aerospace industry, need a large pool of highly skilled technical labor, and so tend to be attracted to regions like southern California. The other main consideration is the cost of that labor. This factor is especially important for those industries that are comparatively labor intensive, such as the clothing industry. Berry et al. (1976, p. 149) have identified four major kinds of regions in which labor costs tend to be low: first, where the supply of labor is increasing at a faster rate than the demand for labor; second, where economic opportunities are decreasing relative to a large local labor force; third, where employment opportunities are available only for a subset of the population, such as males; and fourth, where the cost of living is exceptionally low, so that real wages are high relative to money wages. However, although these regional differences in labor costs are undoubtedly important in the short run, in the long run such differences tend to be equalized by labor migration. Also, the spread of unionism has tended to decrease the regional variation in labor costs.

Finally, *capital* costs can be divided into those associated with financial captial on the one hand, and fixed capital equipment on the other. "Financial capital" refers to the money required to start up a firm, and although financial captial is generally quite mobile, it is easier to secure loans in rich areas such as southern California than in poor areas such as Appalachia. Also, especially for small firms, loans are more easily obtained from local banks and credit institutions, where the entrepreneur is well known. Fixed capital equipment is much less mobile than financial capital, and is thus similar to land as a factor of production, as buildings and machinery are comparatively fixed in space. This situation leads to industrual inertia, as it is usually cheaper to occupy existing industrial facilities than it is to construct a new factory. When a completely new factory is contemplated, however, industries consider the regional variation in construction costs. The costs of machinery, and its repair, are also subject to a certain amount of regional variation.

Economies of Scale

Production costs may also differ according to various economies of scale. These economies are usually divided into two types: those that are internal to the individual firm and those that are external to it. Internal economies of scale imply that, up to a certain point, the cost of producing a unit of output decreases with increasing plant size. Our major interest, however, is in the external economies of scale, as these are an important component of the overall location decision (Scott, 1983).

External economies of scale can be subdivided into urbanization economies and localization economies. *Urbanization economies* refer to the benefits that accrue to industries by locating in large cities, where there are already a large number of other industries. First, a large city can provide a varied labor force, with a whole range of specialized skills. Second, large cities tend to minimize transportation costs because they provide a local market and superior transportation facilities. Third, the larger the city, the greater the number of ancillary services that it can supply, such as fire protection, police protection, gas, electricity, and waste disposal. Often, however, some of these same economies of scale became diseconomies of scale if the city grows too large. Transportation facilities become overloaded and congested, pollution and crime become major problems, and competition for space increases the cost of land.

Localization economies occur when the firms in the same industry, or closely related industries, cluster in the same location. First, a pool of skilled labor becomes available to the industrial firms. Second, local services tend to adapt to the needs of a particular type of industry. Third, research facilities and marketing organizations can be shared by a group of similar industries. Fourth, similar industries can also share parts suppliers and machine repairers. Often, these localization economies result in cities that are dominated by a particular industry, or group of industries.

Other Factors

Energy considerations also influence the location of industry. Most modern industries use some form of powered machinery, so fuel costs may contribute significantly to the overall production costs. There are large regional variations in the cost of fuel, with coal being comparatively cheaper in the North and East, and oil being less expensive in the South and West.

Most firms are subject to some form of *taxes* on their revenue. These taxes may be paid to a local authority, such as the city or county, to the state, and to the federal government. As local taxes can vary considerably from place to place, industries consider this factor when choosing a suitable location (Charney, 1983). In particular, tax rates appear to be highest toward the city center, and then decrease as one moves toward the suburbs.

The *government* itself can also profoundly influence the spatial distribution of industrial activity. First, direct expenditures by the federal government, such as defense spending, are not evenly distributed throughout the country. Second, government land use zoning ordinances prohibit industrial activity in certain areas. Third, the government uses financial inducements, such as low-interest loans, to attract industry to economically depressed regions such as Appalachia.

Finally, *historical accidents* have influenced the location of industry. For example, some cities have certain industries simply because the founder of that industry happened to be born there. Also, the local invention of new machinery has often resulted in the growth of a particular industry in a particular city.

6.2 THE LOCATION OF INDUSTRY WITHIN CITIES

Having examined the factors that influence industrial location in general, we can now turn our attention to the locational pattern of industries within cities. In particular, we will discuss industrial types, the suburbanization of industry, and the development of industrial parks.

Industrial Types

In a classic study of industrial location within cities, Pred (1964) identified seven types of industry. First, *ubiquitous industries,* whose markets comprise the entire metropolitan area, tend to concentrate toward the edge of the central business district. Food processing, such as bread and cake plants, is illustrative of this type of industry, especially since the basic raw materials are nonlocal in origin. There is often a strong link with wholesaling activity, and the many warehouses and multistory buildings near the central business district are attractive to large-scale food manufacturers.

The second type of industry is the *centrally located communication economy industry,* in which face-to-face contact between buyer and seller is a distinct advantage and so a central location is highly desirable. Job printing is a good example of this kind of industry, because a downtown location maximizes accessibility to such consumers of printed material as lawyers, theaters, and advertising agencies. A second example is provided by the fashion clothing industry in New York's garment district. Note that both job printing and the garment industry tend to be characterized by small plants, so the high rents associated with central locations are not a major problem.

The third type of industry involves *local market industries with local raw material sources.* That is, those industries which use locally produced raw materials to manufacture goods that are also sold within the same urban area. Ice manufacturing plants are a good example of this type of industry, as are industries using raw materials that are by-products of local firms involved in iron and steel production. These industries are essentially randomly distributed throughout the city, although there is often some concentration toward the central business district.

Nonlocal market industries with high-value products comprise Pred's fourth type of industry. As transportation costs are relatively insignificant to these industries, because of the high value per unit weight of the products, they are not constrained to locate near transportation arteries or railroad terminals. As a result, the spatial distribution of firms is generally random, although again, there is sometimes a tendency to cluster in downtown locations. The manufacture of computer equipment is an excellent example of this kind of industry.

The fifth type of industry involves *noncentrally located communication economy industries.* These industries also have high-value products and serve national markets, but they realize communication economies by clustering together. Good examples of these industries are electronics and the aerospace industry, which locate together partly to keep abreast of the latest innovations. Unlike other industries to whom communication economies are important, however, these industries are not usually located downtown, as they are independent of the various kinds of services associated with the central business district.

The sixth type of industry is the *nonlocal market industry on the waterfront.* This industry is highly dependent on adequate transportation facilities, and often involves foreign materials and markets. These industries are usually heavy industries, such as petroleum refining and ship building, whose raw materials and finished products are most easily moved via water transportation.

Finally, there are those *industries oriented toward national markets.* These industries have bulky finished products, with relatively low value per unit weight, so they are strongly influenced by transportation considerations. Such industries include the iron and steel industry and motor vehicle assembly plants.

Northam (1979, pp. 413–417) has suggested an alternative classificatory schema that focuses on the identification of manufacturing zones within cities. He suggests that there are generally three major zones. The *central zone,* surrounding the central business district, is dominated by industries that have relatively low space needs per worker, but relatively high-value raw materials and finished products. In other words, land is used intensively in order to offset the high cost of land and taxes. Food products, the garment industry, and printing are the type of industries in this central zone. It is also in this zone, however, that the best examples of industrial blight are found. Many of the older firms and buildings are located here, often intermixed with nonindustrial land use, and there is a high incidence of dilapidation and abandonment. Congestion is also a problem, as most of the industries are labor intensive, but lack adequate parking facilities.

The next zone, or *intermediate zone,* as one moves away from the central business district, is characterized by industries engaged in the production of household appliances, automobiles, and various kinds of machinery. Such industries often require large amounts of storage space, extensive horizontal assembly lines, and considerable parking space for employees. Usually, there are a number of informal industrial districts within this zone, dominated by firms engaged in similar activities, as exemplified by the food-processing firms in the stockyards district of Chicago.

Beyond this intermediate zone is an *outer zone,* which also has a number of clustered industrial districts. The firms occupy large sites, and are attracted by the lower land costs in suburban areas. Industries involved with national rather than local markets tend to predominate, and the industrial districts are usually located close to major traffic arteries, such as interstate highways. The number of industries in this zone has been steadily growing in recent years, and in the following section we consider some of the factors responsible for the suburbanization of industry.

The Suburbanization of Industry

Since World War II industrial activity within U.S. cities has become increasingly decentralized (Struyk and James, 1975; Erickson, 1983), and the factors that have contributed to this situation are often categorized into two groups (Scott, 1982). On the one hand, there are a series of factors that have made the central city increasingly unattractive for industry. First, especially in the older cities, many of the industrial plants have become obsolete, and new industries have constructed modern facilities in the suburbs rather than renovate old buildings in the city center. Second, planning restrictions on industry, and urban renewal in central areas, have often combined to reduce the amount of land available for industrial use. Third, traffic congestion has contributed to the decreasing attractiveness of the central city. Fourth, the high price of land in central cities, combined with the high tax rates on industry, have encouraged centrally located firms to vacate their present locations in order to capitalize site values. Fifth, the interaction of labor shortages, high levels of unionization, and comparatively high wages has helped detract from the attractiveness of central-city locations.

On the other hand, there are a variety of reasons why peripheral locations have become more attractive. First, the development of modern freeway systems has made the suburbs accessible for the movement of raw materials and finished products. Second, the development of horizontal plant layouts has drawn industry toward the comparatively cheap land to be found in the suburbs. Third, the decentralization of the labor force, and the fact that the managerial staff in particular reside in the suburbs, has added to the attractiveness of peripheral locations. Fourth, most major airports are located in the suburbs.

Such a listing of often disparate factors, however, does not necessarily lead to the development of broader, integrative theories that can address the process of industrial decentralization (Brown, 1979). An attempt to develop a more cohesive perspective can be conveniently labeled the *incubation, product cycle, and hierarchical filtering theory* (Scott, 1982). As the name implies, this theory has three major parts to it, involving the locational requirements of small firms entering the industrial system, the changing pattern as these firms grow and mature, and finally, the filtering of firms down through an urban hierarchy.

Small, new firms tend to be attracted to the center of the city, where they can participate in economics of scale. In this sense the central city acts as an incubator for immature firms (Leone and Struyk, 1976). Those firms that remain in business will eventually grow and expand, and ultimately begin to generate their own internal economies of scale. It is at this stage that they will move to the suburbs, to take advantage of the cheaper land and lower taxes on the periphery. The incubator thesis complements the idea of a product cycle in that as the market for a new product begins to expand, the production process is standardized, firms grow larger, and peripheral locations become increasingly attractive (Norton and Rees, 1979). Finally, with respect to the hierarchical filtering process, the largest firms tend to establish branch plants, often using the cheaper and relatively unskilled labor found in smaller towns. So as a particular industrial process develops and matures it often leaves the largest metropolitan areas and is filtered down through the urban hierarchy (Leinbach, 1978).

Scott (1982) has sketched out an even broader theoretical perspective, emphasizing the essentially interdependent nature of locational choice and choice of production technique. He argues that, within the context of the capitalist commodity producing process, the locational patterns of urban industry can be divided into two main categories. First, labor-intensive firms tend to locate toward the center of the urban labor market. Second, capital-intensive firms are attracted by the relatively cheap land inputs at the peripheral locations. Historically, the manufacturing industry has increasingly substituted capital for labor, thus generating a more decentralized locational pattern.

Whatever the explanation, the various components of this *shift in industrial activity* have been well documented for Vancouver, Canada (Steed, 1973). Steed used the following accounting equation to measure the elements of industrial change:

$$X = b - d + m - e \tag{6.1}$$

where X is the net change in the number of industrial plants in any particular area of the city; b is the number of new plants, or births within the area; d is the number of plants closing down, or deaths within the area; m is the number of plants moving, or migrating into the area; and e is the number of plants leaving, or emigrating from the area.

This equation was calibrated for 13 subareas within Vancouver. Between 1955 and 1965 by far the greatest decrease in the number of industrial plants was experienced by the most central area, while the greatest increases were experienced in the more peripheral locations. Steed's equation indicates that the declining importance of the downtown area was due primarily to the out-migration of plants. On the other hand, the peripheral areas grew mainly because of the generation of new plants, or births, and only secondarily because of plant immigration.

This suburbanization of industry has had a number of serious *consequences for central cities*. Perhaps the most important of these, as discussed in Chapter 1, has been the reduction in the central city's tax base. Also, however, as identified by De Vise (1976) for Chicago, there have been wide-ranging repercussions in terms of the spatial distribution of employment opportunities, and the associated length of the journey to work. Between 1960 and 1970 Chicago lost 211,000 jobs, while its suburbs gained 548,000 jobs. Moreover, employment opportunities suburbanized twice as fast as the labor force. De Vise (1976) suggests that blacks have been especially hurt by this shift of employment opportunities. First, a disproportionate number of blacks are in the suburbanizing blue-color occupations. Second, blacks often cannot afford suburban housing, and are sometimes excluded on racial as well as economic grounds. The suburbanization of jobs has also increased the length of the journey to work. De Vise (1976) indicates that in the Chicago metropolitan area the average work trip was $5\frac{1}{2}$ miles in 1960, compared to 7 miles in 1970. Finally, as a corollary of the locational shift in jobs, there has been increased freeway congestion, and a general underutilization of public transportation facilities.

Yeates and Garner (1980, pp. 371–375) have suggested three possible *policy responses* for alleviating the problems generated by the changing distribution of industry within cities. First, a conservative philosophy would simply let the problems be solved by forces operating in the marketplace. The vacated properties in the central city will be taken over by other types of land use that are more capable of earning a profit in that particular location. Meanwhile, the increased demand for labor in the suburbs will have a tendency to raise wages, while the labor surplus in the inner city will tend to reduce wages. In the long run, industry will return to the inner city to take advantage of these lower wages, thus increasing employment opportunities. In other words, it is contended that "natural market forces" will always act to remove any short-term disequilibrium in the distribution of industrial employment.

A second way to reduce industrial unemployment in the inner city would be to encourage the return of industrial plants to that part of the city. This approach exemplifies the liberal interventionist perspective, which argues that market forces are insufficient to redress the balance, and that they should be augmented by various kinds of government programs. Such programs might include labor retraining, to upgrade certain specialized skills, and low-interest loans for firms willing to locate in the central city. More radical interventionists would advocate the state ownership of industry, so that its location would be simply a matter of government policy.

A third major approach involves moving potential employees closer to the jobs rather than trying to move the jobs back to the employees. This approach also represents a liberal interventionist perspective, as it would require programs to help relocate the inner-city poor, who would ordinarily be unable to rent or own homes in the suburbs. These programs might include direct housing supplements for low-income families, mortgage schemes to encourage the construction of low-cost housing in the suburbs, and government construction of low-income apartment buildings in the suburbs.

Planned Industrial Parks

The increasing suburbanization of industry has been paralleled by the emergence of planned industrial parks, which are usually located toward the edge of the city. These industrial parks have been developed according to comprehensive plans that include the provision of streets, warehouses, sewers, utilities, and other ancillary services. The aim has been to generate a community of industries that are compatible, and often functionally linked. As such, planned industrial parks are very different from informal concentrations of industrial activity, where such factors as the overall spatial organization of the area and the compatibility of individual industries are given little explicit consideration.

Although the first planned industrial parks were developed during the early part of the twentieth centry, it was not until after World War II that the concept became really popular. During the period 1940–1959, over 1000 planned industrial districts were developed in the United States, whereas only 33 had been developed prior to that time (Buck, 1980). Most of the industrial parks in the United States have been developed by private corporations, such as railroads, industrial firms, and real estate brokers. Some industrial parks, however, were originated by nonprofit organizations, such as chambers of commerce and development commissions, while a few have been developed by local government, port, and airport authorities.

Public ownership is generally at the municipal level, and reflects an effort to attract industry in those situations where private initiative is lacking. The local government receives direct benefits in terms of increased tax revenue, and indirect benefits through increased employment, which enlarges the payroll of the community and thus leads to a greater demand for various goods and services. Public ownership can be a disadvantage if frequent administrative and political changes hamper the process of long-term development management, however, and often the most successful parks are those owned and managed by industrial developers. Such developers tend to retain ownership of many of the buildings, and the park is well maintained in order to attract tenants.

There are a variety of reasons why these planned industrial parks have become so popular. First, the lack of industrially zoned land in central cities has forced firms to pursue alternative locations. Second, the newer single-story plants, which facilitate horizontally organized production lines, require more space than is easily acquired in the central city. Third, the new industrial parks are generally free of traffic congestion and provide ample parking space for employees. Fourth, many industrial entrepreneurs appreciate the administrative help provided by the park management organizations. Fifth, as discussed previously, certain important economies of scale are derived when industries cluster together. Sixth, most industrial parks maximize accessibility considerations by being located near major highways, railroads, or airports. Seventh, services such as police and fire protection tend to be much more efficient in planned industrial parks.

Although all planned industrial parks have many characteristics in common, Hartshorn (1980, pp. 392–397) has identified three major types of industrial park. The first he calls *fabrication, distribution, and warehouse parks*. These parks are the most numerous, and they involve mainly light manufacturing and market-oriented industries. The individual firms are often quite small, and although peripheral locations are the most popular, some of these parks have been developed in downtown areas as part of urban renewal projects. When the overall development becomes very large, hotel complexes, shopping centers, and even golf courses are included in these predominantly industrial facilities, and great care is taken to create a pleasing landscape.

Hartshorn's second category involves *research and science parks*, which are often located next to major universities. An excellent example of this type of park is the Research Triangle Park, which is located toward the center of a triangle formed by Duke University in Durham, North Carolina State University in Raleigh, and the

University of North Carolina at Chapel Hill. These universities provide a pool of research consultants, and also ancillary services such as computers, libraries, and research laboratories. Purely research parks are fairly rare, however; science parks, incorporating various kinds of light manufacturing, are more common. The electronics and aerospace industries are especially attracted to these parks, as their products involve large inputs of research and development.

The third, and most recent kind of industrial park, is the *business park.* These parks, although dominated by office buildings, often contain some light manufacturing, hotels, restaurants, and professional services, including doctors and lawyers. In fact, this variety of functionally compatible activities is perhaps the major characteristic of business parks, and even residential functions are sometimes successfully integrated into the overall development scheme.

6.3 THE ECONOMIC BASE CONCEPT

The economic base concept has been a very popular technique for describing an individual city's economy and for explaining differential urban growth rates. In this section we examine the basic/nonbasic ratio, the economic multiplier, and a model of urban growth that is based on the economic multiplier.

The Basic/Nonbasic Ratio

The economic activity in any city can be divided into two sectors: basic and nonbasic. *Basic activity,* or the basic sector, refers to those goods and services that are produced within a settlement but sold outside that settlement. In contrast, *nonbasic activity,* or the nonbasic sector, refers to goods and services that are produced within a settlement and sold within that settlement. The basic sector has been variously described as the export, surplus, or city-forming sector, while the nonbasic sector has been referred to as the local, residentiary, or city-serving sector. According to export, or staple theory, the basic sector is the most important sector in terms of influencing urban growth, especially in the short run. Fluctuations in exports are of paramount importance to any urban area, as it is these exports that generate money for the community. As a result, forecasts of economic activity in cities are often based on the relationships between basic and nonbasic activity.

Symbolically, the total economic activity in a given city can be represented as follows:

$$TA = BA + NBA \tag{6.2}$$

where TA is total activity, BA is basic activity, and NBA is nonbasic activity. The basic/nonbasic ratio is then simply expressed as the ratio of the number of employees in the basic sector to the number of employees in the nonbasic sector. If the labor force is equally divided between the two sectors, the basic/nonbasic ratio is 1:1. For every

TABLE 6.2 BASIC/NONBASIC RATIO FOR SELECTED CITIES IN THE UNITED STATES

City	Population	Basic/nonbasic ratio
New York (New York)	12,500,000	1/2.2
Detroit (Michigan)	2,900,000	1/1.2
Cincinnati (Ohio)	907,000	1/1.7
Brockton (Massachusetts)	119,000	1/0.8
Albuquerque (New Mexico)	116,000	1/1.0
Madison (Wisconsin)	110,000	1/0.8
Oshkosh (Wisconsin)	42,000	1/0.6

Source: J. W. Alexander, "The basic–nonbasic concept of urban economic functions," *Economic Geography,* 30 (1954), p. 259.

person employed in basic activity there is also one person employed in nonbasic activity. If, on the other hand, 25 percent of the labor force is in the basic sector, leaving 75 percent in the nonbasic sector, the ratio is 1 : 3. For every person involved in basic activity there are three people involved in nonbasic activity. In this situation, assuming that the ratio is stable, an increase of 20 new employees in basic activity will be matched by an increase of 60 new employees in nonbasic activity, resulting in an overall increase of 80 employees.

Table 6.2 gives the basic/nonbasic ratios for a number of cities in the United States, together with their populations at the time of the study. Obviously, there is some variation in the basic/nonbasic ratio across different cities, but this variation appears to be primarily related to size. Such a relationship is to be expected, as large cities perform many specialized functions for themselves that are not found in smaller cities.

In addition to population size, two other factors help explain the variation in basic/nonbasic ratios. First, a city's location can make a difference. If a city is located next to a much larger metropolis, its nonbasic sector might be comparatively undeveloped, as many of the goods and services usually provided by that sector will be provided by the larger metropolis. On the other hand, a city of similar size that is relatively isolated has to be more self-sufficient, and thus generates a larger nonbasic sector. Second, variation in the basic/nonbasic ratio is sometimes attributable to the population characteristics of cities. For example, cities with a small proportion of younger people will require fewer schools, thus diminishing nonbasic activity. Similar kinds of differences can be related to income variation.

The Economic Multiplier

Consideration of the basic/nonbasic ratio leads quite naturally to an examination of the economic multiplier. In essence, the economic multiplier relates growth in basic activity to growth in total activity. Consequently, given estimates of the future magnitude of basic, or export activity, the economic multiplier allows us to forecast changes in total activity.

If the level of nonbasic activity is assumed to be a constant proportion of total activity, then

$$NBA = kTA \tag{6.3}$$

where k represents the proportion of activity that is nonbasic and the remaining terms are the same as in equation (6.2). Equation (6.3) can be rewritten as follows:

$$TA = \frac{1}{k} NBA \tag{6.4}$$

simply by dividing both sides by k. Therefore,

$$TA = \frac{1}{1 - k} BA \tag{6.5}$$

where the terms are the same as in equations (6.2) and (6.3). For example, if the proportion of activity in the nonbasic sector is three-fifths, the proportion in the basic sector must be two-fifths. Finally, equation (6.5) can be rewritten as follows:

$$TA = mBA \tag{6.6}$$

where m is the economic multiplier relating total activity to basic activity.

In summary, the economic structure of any city can be characterized by three terms, all derived from simply dividing the economy into two sectors, as represented by equation (6.2). First, the basic/nonbasic ratio relates basic activity to nonbasic activity. Second, the constant k relates nonbasic activity to total activity. Third, the economic multiplier, m, relates basic activity to total activity.

An arithmetic example will help to clarify these relationships. If we return to our previous example of an increase in 20 employees in basic activity being matched by 60 new employees in nonbasic activity, for an overall increase of 80 new employees in total activity, the following values are generated. First, the basic/nonbasic ratio is 20:60, or 1:3. Second, rewriting equation (6.3) to solve for k, we get

$$k = \frac{NBA}{TA} \tag{6.7}$$

which in this example is 60 divided by 80, or three-fourths. Third, rewriting equation (6.6) to solve for m, we get

$$m = \frac{TA}{BA} \tag{6.8}$$

which in this example is 80 divided by 20, or an economic multiplier of 4. In other words, each new job in the basic sector generates four new jobs overall.

Despite its computational simplicity, however, the economic base concept suffers from a number of *methodological and philosophical problems*. First, there is the problem of choosing an appropriate unit of measurement to determine the relative magnitudes of the basic and nonbasic sectors. Employment figures are usually used, both because these data are comparatively easy to obtain and because the multiplier is often used to predict population changes. A more sensitive measure, however, might be wage rates, as changes in nonbasic employment are not always simply a function of changes in basic employment. For example, just a salary increase in basic activity leads to increased demand for nonbasic activity, thus increasing jobs in the nonbasic sector.

Second, it is often difficult to decide whether an establishment's function is basic or nonbasic. In many cases part of a firm's product is exported outside the city, while the rest is sold locally. In such situations it is necessary to determine the proportion of the firm's labor force that is associated with its basic activity, and the proportion that is associated with its nonbasic activity. Similar problems arise with respect to service functions. For example, in the context of hotels, some guests come from outside the city, and are therefore part of the basic sector, whereas other guests come from within the city, and so contribute to the nonbasic sector.

Third, the values obtained for the basic/nonbasic ratio depend partially on how the spatial extent of the city is defined. The size of the base area determines what activities are treated as basic, because it determines which transactions involve exports. All other things being equal, the larger the base area, the greater the number of activities that are nonbasic, as reflected in Table 6.2. For example, if only the central city is included in the basic area, goods and services sold to the suburbs are regarded as exports. If, however, the suburbs are included in the base area, those same goods and services now represent nonbasic activity.

Fourth, in a more philosophical context, it is not clear that the basic, or export sector, is the only determinant of growth in a city. It has sometimes been argued that the nonbasic sector is equally important in determining urban growth. For example, in the southwest United States much of the recent urban growth appears to have been generated by the increasing importance of service activity.

Fifth, it should be noted that values for the economic multiplier are obtained by averaging over the whole city. In reality, however, the economic multiplier varies from industry to industry, reflecting the fact that some industries have greater growth-generating potential than do others. A more detailed analysis of the urban economy, at the level of individual industries, is provided by input–output analysis, which will be discussed shortly. First, however, we will consider a more detailed conceptualization of how the economic multiplier, or multiplier effect, is actually related to urban economic growth.

Urban Economic Growth

The relationship between the multiplier and urban economic growth has been discussed at some length by Pred (1977, pp. 88–93). His conceptual framework involved a simple causal chain (Figure 6.3). Imagine an isolated city in which a new industry is located, or an existing industry is enlarged. This new industry will initiate a chain reaction effect. Purchasing power in the city will rise, due to the increased number of jobs, thus increasing the local demand for goods and services, such as housing, shops, restaurants, and banks. This increased demand will in turn create

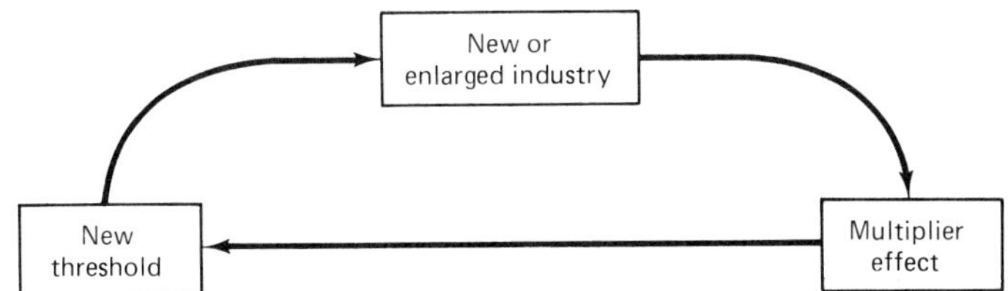

Figure 6.3 Economic multiplier and urban growth. (Based on Allan R. Pred, "Industrialization, initial advantage, and American metropolitan growth," *Geographical Review*, 55, 1965, Fig. 1, p. 165.)

more jobs in the construction industry, the retailing industry, and so on. Thus, for every new job in the factory, a number of other jobs are created in the local economy. Exactly how many more jobs are created is measured by the economic multiplier. Finally, the city eventually reaches a new threshold population and is large enough to support another new industry, thus initiating another round of growth.

The different effects that the introduction of a new industry will have on a city's economy are summarized by the following equation:

$$M_i = E_i + \sum_{j=1}^{N} E_{ij} + \sum_{k=1}^{M} E_{ik} \tag{6.9}$$

where M_i is the total employment generated by the new industry i, E_i is the employment *directly* created by industry i, E_{ij} is the employment *indirectly* created by the demands of industry i on other industries ($j = 1$ through N), and E_{ik} is the *induced* employment created by the impact of industry i on other sectors of the economy ($k = 1$ through M). In this schema, the employment directly created by the new industry refers to the new employees actually working in that industry. The employment indirectly created by the new industry refers to the jobs that are created by industry i demanding certain inputs from other industries. These inputs are summed over the N other industries involved. Finally, the induced employment created by the new industry refers to the jobs that are generated by the increased local demand for housing, banks, doctors, and so on.

Of course, this scenario assumes that there are no major leakages in terms of the multiplier effect. Such leakages can occur in two ways. First, the new industry might buy some of its materials from outside the local area, thus reducing its indirect effect. Second, the new employees of that industry might travel outside the local area to buy certain goods and services, thus reducing the induced effect.

This particular chain reaction process described by Pred is one example of a more general process that Myrdal (1957) has called the principle of *circular and cumulative causation,* whereby any change in a social system tends to set up forces which both increase and reinforce that change. In other words, within the urban context, growth tends to breed more growth. The process of circular and cumulative causation can also work in reverse, however, with a contraction in industrial activity leading to further contractions, via the same multiplier effect. In this case, when an industry leaves a city, the labor force and overall purchasing power of that city declines accordingly. As a result, there is less demand for local goods and services, thus decreasing still further the number of jobs in the city. Eventually, the urban population will fall below a certain threshold size, and another industry will leave.

It is of interest, within this context, to examine why for some cities the principle of circular and cumulative causation leads to increasing growth, whereas for other cities it results in decline. Thompson (1965, p. 22) investigated the growth rates of different-sized cities and suggested the concept of an *urban size ratchet*. By this concept he meant that once a city reaches a certain size, a kind of ratchet mechanism comes into effect, locking in past growth and preventing future contraction.

There are a number of reasons why such a ratchet effect might operate. First, as cities grow, their industrial structure tends to become more diversified. This notion of industrial diversification can be visualized in terms of a Lorenz curve (Figure 6.4). The various industries in a particular city are placed along the horizontal axis, from largest to smallest in terms of the number of employees, while the vertical axis represents the cumulative percentage of the total labor force. Curve A indicates a completely diversified economy, where each industry has an equal share of the total labor force, whereas curve B indicates a city that has an overwhelming majority of its labor force employed in its largest industry. Those cities that are closer to the situation represented by curve A, usually the larger ones, tend to be less vulnerable to economic depressions than those represented by curve B. In the latter case, a decline in demand associated with the major industry could be devastating, as other industries would be unable to pick up the slack. Second, large cities can generate more political support, and therefore more federal and state assistance, than can their smaller counterparts. Third, large cities tend to generate more economies of scale, as discussed in Section 6.1. Fourth, as industry becomes increasingly consumer oriented, big cities provide immediate access to a large potential market.

Despite these apparent advantages, however, a number of large U.S. cities have

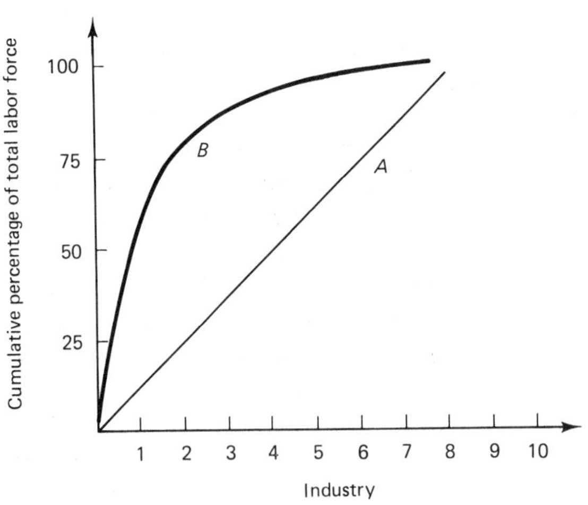

Figure 6.4 Lorenz curves showing different degrees of industrial diversification.

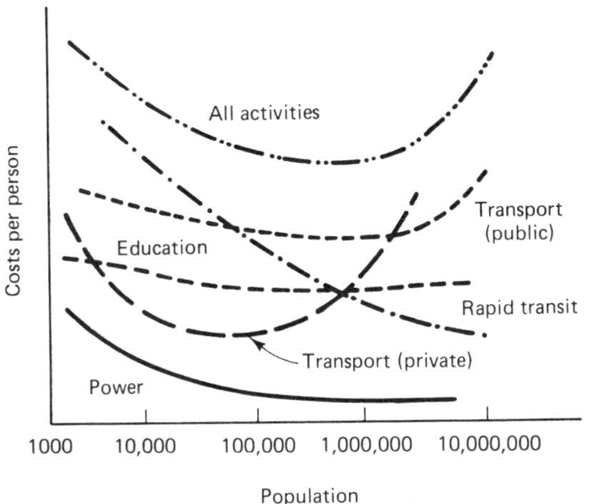

Figure 6.5. Economies and diseconomies of scale. (From *The Spatial Organization of Society* by Richard L. Morrill, © 1970 by Wadsworth Publishing Company, Inc., Belmont, California 94002. Reprinted by permission of the publisher.)

recently begun to decline in population. This decline is due at least partially to the onset of diseconomies of scale. Such diseconomies are represented hypothetically in Figure 6.5, which suggests how the cost per person for various kinds of services varies with city size. The cost curve for all services combined suggests that medium-sized cities are more efficient than either very small or very large cities, but there is remarkably little agreement with respect to what constitutes an optimal city size. One of the problems, as the individual cost curves indicate, is that diseconomies of scale emerge at different city sizes, depending on the particular service that is being considered.

6.4 INPUT-OUTPUT ANALYSIS

Input-output analysis is a more detailed technique than the economic base concept for characterizing the economic structure of cities (Isard, 1975). Unlike the economic base concept, multiplier effects are not averaged for the whole city, but are computed for each individual sector of the economy. As a result, input-output analysis allows us to trace the effects of an increase, or decrease, in production in one sector of the economy on all the other sectors. The input-output approach was pioneered by Leontief (1951) and has since become a major ingredient of economic planning in the industrially developed nations of the world (Morrison and Smith, 1977).

Input-Output Coefficients

We will discuss input-output analysis using an example adapted from Abler et al. (1971). Suppose we have a simple urban economy that is composed of two major industries, automobile manufacturing and the iron and steel industry. The money flows in this two-industry economy, during a given time period, can be represented in

TABLE 6.3 FLOW MATRIX FOR INPUT–OUTPUT ANALYSIS

Producing industry	Purchasing industry: Automobile	Purchasing industry: Iron and steel	Final demand	Total output
Automobile	$0	$5	$15	$20
Iron and steel	8	0	2	10
		Total output for the economy = $30		

terms of a flow matrix (Table 6.3). This flow matrix indicates that, of the $20 worth of total output produced by the automobile industry, $5 worth is purchased by the iron and steel industry, while $15 worth goes to final demand, or individual consumers. Similarly, of the $10 worth of total output produced by the iron and steel industry, $8 worth is purchased by the automobile industry, and $2 worth goes to consumers. The output for the city as a whole, during this time period, is $30.

As the name implies, the flow matrix simply summarizes the flow of money within an urban economy, and so highlights the interconnections, or linkages, between the different sectors of that economy. The exact nature of these linkages is specified by the *input–output coefficient,* which is measured as follows:

$$a_{ij} = \frac{x_{ij}}{X_j} \tag{6.10}$$

where a_{ij} is the input–output coefficient expressing the input from industry i required to produce a unit of output in industry j, x_{ij} is the input, or amount of goods, flowing from industry i to industry j, and X_j is the total output of industry j.

The input–output coefficients for our particular example are represented in Table 6.4. First, we can consider the case where automobile manufacturing is the input, or producing sector, and the iron and steel industry is the output, or purchasing sector. In this situation, substituting in equation (6.10), we have

$$a_{AI} = \frac{x_{AI}}{X_I} \tag{6.11}$$

where A represents the automobile industry and I, the iron and steel industry. Using the values given in the flow matrix (Table 6.3), we get the following:

$$a_{AI} = \frac{\$5}{\$10} = \$0.5 \tag{6.12}$$

This input–output coefficient indicates that in order to produce each dollar's worth of output, the iron and steel industry must purchase one half-dollar, or 50 cents worth of input from the automobile industry.

Similarly, we can consider the case where the iron and steel industry is the input sector, and automobile manufacturing is the output sector. Again substituting in

TABLE 6.4 INPUT–OUTPUT COEFFICIENTS

Producing industry (input)	Purchasing industry (output)	
	Automobile	Iron and steel
Automobile	—	\$0.5
Iron and steel	\$0.4	—

equation (6.10), we have

$$a_{IA} = \frac{x_{IA}}{X_A} \tag{6.13}$$

where the notation is the same as in equation (6.11). Using the values given in the flow matrix (Table 6.3), we get the following:

$$a_{IA} = \frac{\$8}{\$20} = \$0.4 \tag{6.14}$$

In other words, in order to produce each dollars worth of output, the automobile industry must purchase 40 cents worth of input from the iron and steel industry.

Once the input–output coefficients have been obtained, the information contained in the original flow matrix can be specified by two simple equations, as follows:

$$X_A = 0.5X_I + 15 \tag{6.15}$$

and

$$X_I = 0.4X_A + 2 \tag{6.16}$$

where the notation is the same as in equation (6.11). Equation (6.15) indicates that the total output of the automobile industry equals half the total output of the iron and steel industry, because for every dollar's worth of output by the iron and steel industry 50 cents' worth must be purchased from the automobile industry, plus \$15 of final demand. Similarly, equation (6.16) indicates that the total output of the iron and steel industry equals four-tenths the total output of the automobile industry, plus the final demand of \$2.

Equations (6.15) and (6.16) are simultaneous equations that can be solved to find the total output for each industry, as we have two equations and two unknowns, X_A and X_I. First, to find X_A, we can take equation (6.15) and multiply both sides by 2, giving

$$2X_A = X_I + 30 \tag{6.17}$$

Then, subtracting 30 from both sides, we have

$$X_I = 2X_A - 30 \tag{6.18}$$

Therefore, from equations (6.16) and (6.18),

$$0.4X_A + 2 = 2X_A - 30 \tag{6.19}$$

We now have one equation with one unknown, and so can easily solve for X_A. If both sides of equation (6.19) are multiplied by 5, we obtain

$$2X_A + 10 = 10X_A - 150 \tag{6.20}$$

Then, subtracting $2X_A$ from both sides and adding 150 to both sides, we have

$$8X_A = 160 \tag{6.21}$$

Therefore,

$$X_A = 20 \tag{6.22}$$

Then, substituting the value for X_A in equation (6.16), we have

$$X_I = 0.4\ (20) + 2 \tag{6.23}$$

so

$$X_I = 10 \tag{6.24}$$

Note that these two values, $X_A = 20$ and $X_I = 10$, match the total outputs in the original flow matrix, so the two simultaneous equations, equations (6.15) and (6.16), are an accurate reflection of the flows, or interactions, within the economy.

Measuring the Impact of Change

One of the great advantages of calculating input–output coefficients, and being able to represent the economy in terms of equations, is that it becomes relatively easy to measure the overall impact of a change in any particular sector of that economy. For example, suppose that the final demand associated with the iron and steel industry increases from \$2 to \$6, so that we now have the following pair of simultaneous equations:

$$X_A = 0.5X_I + 15 \tag{6.25}$$

and

$$X_I = 0.4X_A + 6 \tag{6.26}$$

Equation (6.25) is exactly the same as the original equation (6.15), while equation (6.26) is the same as equation (6.16), except that the final demand has been changed from 2 to 6.

By solving equations (6.25) and (6.26) in the same way that we solved equations (6.15) and (6.16), we can measure the overall impact of changing the final demand for the iron and steel industry. As before, both sides of equation (6.25) are multiplied by 2, giving

$$2X_A = X_I + 30 \tag{6.27}$$

and 30 is subtracted from both sides, to give

$$X_I = 2X_A - 30 \tag{6.28}$$

Therefore, from equations (6.26) and (6.28),

$$0.4X_A + 6 = 2X_A - 30 \tag{6.29}$$

If both sides of equation (6.29) are multiplied by 5, we obtain

$$2X_A + 30 = 10X_A - 150 \tag{6.30}$$

Then, subtracting $2X_A$ from both sides and adding 150 to both sides, we have

$$8X_A = 180 \tag{6.31}$$

Therefore,

$$X_A = 22.5 \tag{6.32}$$

Then, substituting the value for X_A in equation (6.26), we have

$$X_I = 0.4\,(22.5) + 6 \tag{6.33}$$

so

$$X_I = 15 \tag{6.34}$$

Thus the new output for the automobile industry is \$22.5, while that for the iron and steel industry is \$15.

By inspecting the revised flow matrix (Table 6.5) we can see that a fairly minor change in the final demand for the iron and steel industry has had widespread repercussions for the whole economy. Because the total output of the iron and steel industry has increased by \$5, another \$2.50 worth of input must be purchased from the automobile industry, thus giving the automobile industry a new total output of \$22.5. This same increase of \$2.50 in the total output of the automobile industry, however, means that another \$1 worth of input must be purchased from the iron and steel industry, as for each dollar's worth of output in the automobile industry 40 cents' worth of input has to be purchased from the iron and steel industry. So, because of the interrelationships between the two industries, as measured by the input-output coefficients, an increase of \$4 in the final demand for the iron and steel industry has

TABLE 6.5 REVISED FLOW MATRIX FOR INPUT-OUTPUT ANALYSIS

	Purchasing industry			
Producing industry	Automobile	Iron and steel	Final demand	Total output
Automobile	\$0	\$7.5	\$15	\$22.5
Iron and steel	9	0	6	15
			Total output for the economy = \$37.5	

TABLE 6.6 INPUT–OUTPUT COEFFICIENTS FOR THE PHILADELPHIA REGION, 1968

Producing sector \ Purchasing sector	1. Agriculture, fisheries	2. Food processing / kindred products	3. Textile mill products	4. Apparel	5. Lumber and wood products	6. Furniture and fixtures	7. Paper and allied products	8. Printing and publishing	9. Chemicals and chemical products	10. Petroleum refining and products	11. Rubber and misc. plastic products	12. Leather and leather products	13. Stone, clay, and glass products	14. Primary metals	15. Fabricated metal products	16. Machinery (excl. electric)	17. Electric machinery	18. Motor vehicles
1. Agriculture, fisheries	.301	.148	.034	.001	.003	—	—	—	*	—	.061	*	*	*	—	—	—	—
2. Food processing and kindred products	.067	.258	*	*	—	—	.001	—	.010	*	—	.158	*	—	—	*	—	—
3. Textile mill products	.001	*	.285	.296	—	.011	.003	.001	.006	—	.027	.019	.004	*	*	*	*	*
4. Lumber and wood products	.002	*	—	.048	—	—	*	—	—	—	—	.005	.002	—	—	—	*	*
5. Furniture and fixture	.004	.001	*	*	.290	.052	*	*	—	—	*	.001	.006	.002	.004	.002	.002	.008
6. Furniture and fixtures	—	—	—	—	.002	.024	—	—	—	—	—	—	—	—	—	*	.018	.001
7. Paper and allied products	.002	.041	.009	.008	.038	.021	.277	.203	.189	.009	.013	.009	.021	.001	.013	.002	.010	.003
8. Printing and publishing	*	.004	.001	.001	.022	.002	.003	.059	.008	.001	.003	.001	.002	.001	.001	.004	.002	.010
9. Chemical and chemical products	.016	.004	.027	.001	.033	.021	.029	.015	.181	.035	.108	.028	.028	.007	.028	.002	.008	.004
10. Petroleum refining and products	.037	.004	.004	.001	.002	.003	.007	.001	.017	.072	.002	.003	.016	.016	.005	.006	.002	.002
11. Rubber and misc. plastic products	.002	*	*	.001	*	.010	.014	*	.002	.001	.007	.009	.004	*	.008	.004	.010	.009
12. Leather and leather products	—	—	.001	.001	—	*	—	*	—	—	*	.137	—	—	—	*	—	—
13. Stone, clay, and glass products	.002	.007	.003	—	.019	.004	—	—	.010	.004	*	—	.110	.016	.004	.003	.012	.004
14. Primary metals	—	*	*	*	.002	.144	.001	.005	.002	.004	.006	.004	.020	.132	.299	.182	.069	.146
15. Fabricated metal products	.003	.018	*	.001	.106	.049	*	.001	.008	.032	.002	.009	.011	.001	.017	.048	.028	.036
16. Machinery (excl. electric)	.003	*	*	*	*	.002	*	.009	.001	*	.002	*	.001	.014	.007	.059	.011	.080
17. Electric machinery	—	—	—	—	.008	—	*	—	*	—	—	—	*	*	*	.056	.210	.033
18. Motor vehicles	.001	—	—	—	—	—	—	—	.002	—	—	—	—	—	—	*	*	.087

Note: Asterisks indicate coefficients less than .0005. Figures have been rounded to nearest .001.

Source: Walter Isard, *Introduction to Regional Science,* © 1975, pp. 122–123. Reprinted by permission of Prentice-Hall, Inc., Englewood Cliffs, N.J.

increased the total output of the overall economy from \$30 to \$37.5. In other words, the multiplier effect associated with the iron and steel industry is \$7.5 divided by \$4, or approximately 1.8.

We have only, of course, been considering a two-industry economy, but it is a fairly simple matter to add other industries. For example, the equations for a three-industry economy would be as follows:

$$X_1 = a_{11}X_1 + a_{12}X_2 + a_{13}X_3 + d_1 \tag{6.35}$$

$$X_2 = a_{21}X_1 + a_{22}X_2 + a_{23}X_3 + d_2 \tag{6.36}$$

$$X_3 = a_{31}X_1 + a_{32}X_2 + a_{33}X_3 + d_3 \tag{6.37}$$

where X is the total output for industries 1, 2, and 3; a is the input–output coefficient representing the interrelationship between each pair of industries; and d is the final demand for each industry. Four industries would generate four equations, five industries would generate five equations, and so on. Such equations can be used to measure the overall impact of a change in consumer demand associated with one or more of the individual industries. Also, the input-output coefficients can be expected to change over time, due to technological innovations that allow alternative inputs to be substituted in the production process. For example, if the automobile industry begins to build cars out of wood rather than metal, the flow of inputs from the iron and steel industry to the automobile industry will obviously decrease, resulting in a lower input–output coefficient.

The input–output coefficients for the Philadelphia region in 1968 are reported in Table 6.6. It is of special interest to note some of the higher input–output coefficients, such as those relating paper and allied products to printing and publishing, and primary metals to fabricated metal products. High input–output coefficients reflect strongly linked pairs of industries, whereas low input–output coefficients reflect those industries that are only marginally linked within the economic marketplace.

In summary, input–output analysis records a great deal of information about the economy in the form of flows between individual industries, or sectors. Moreover, the calculation of input–output coefficients allows us to predict the impact of an increase, or decrease, in activity in any one industry on the economy as a whole. The higher the input–output coefficients, the greater that impact, while if all the input–output coefficients are zero, the individual industries are independent of each other. In the latter situation, the economic health of one sector of the economy would not influence the economic health of any other sector of that economy, as there would be no multiplier effects.

In practice, of course, input–output analysis does involve certain problems. First, it is often extremely difficult to obtain all the necessary flow data to undertake a very disaggregated examination of a city's economy. Second, the input–output coefficients are partly dependent on how the industries, or economic sectors, are classified in the first place. Nevertheless, despite these problems, input–output analysis provides great insight into the economic structure of urban areas, and is an extremely important tool of urban and regional planning.

7

The City of the Mind

7.1 THE BEHAVIORAL ENVIRONMENT

The *city of the mind* refers to the structure of the city as it is perceived by individual residents. People can call forth mental, or cognitive maps of the cities in which they live, and these cognitive maps influence their behavior within those cities. We begin our discussion by considering the concept of a behavioral environment, as this concept underlies the behavioral approach to urban geography. Spatial representations of the behavioral environment, as expressed in cognitive maps, are then considered, followed by a discussion of the geometric and appraisive information contained within such maps.

Kirk (1963) has made an important distinction between what he labeled the "phenomenal" and the "behavioral" environments. The *phenomenal environment* refers to the objective, physical environment in which behavior takes place, whereas the *behavioral environment* is the subjective, psychological environment in which decisions are made that are then translated into overt action in the phenomenal environment. A fundamental axiom of the behavioral approach is that decision making has its roots in the behavioral environment rather than in the phenomenal environment. In other words, a person's behavior is based on his or her perception of the environment, not on the environment as it actually exists.

Social and physical "facts" of the phenomenal environment are incorporated into the behavioral environment, and two major processes are at work in this transformation of information: selectivity and distortion. The notion of *selectivity* indicates that each of us selects certain items of information to be incorporated into our behavioral environment, as it would be impossible to maintain complete information. Even the information selected, however, tends to be *distorted* in various ways, so that the behavioral environment is both an incomplete and an inaccurate representation of its phenomenal counterpart. As we shall discuss later, variables such as socioeconomic status and length of residence help to explain the various kinds of selectivity and distortion that take place.

While the spatial structure of the phenomenal environment is portrayed in traditional maps, based on longitude and latitude, the the behavioral environment is represented in terms of a cognitive, or mental map. Similarly, physical, or objective distance has as its counterpart cognitive, or subjective distance. Before discussing the concepts of cognitive maps and cognitive distance more fully, however, we consider first two studies that verify the previously mentioned axiom that spatial behavior can best be understood within the context of the behavioral environment.

In a study based on a sample of households located in West Los Angeles, the present author (Cadwallader, 1975) investigated the spatial rationality of *consumer behavior,* in order to demonstrate that more consumers think they patronize the closest supermarket than actually do. In other words, the hypothesis was that consumers are more rational with respect to cognitive distance than they are with respect to physical distance. To test this hypothesis, the sampled group of consumers all lived within three blocks of each other, and so possessed almost identical opportunity sets in terms of the available supermarkets. Each consumer was asked to estimate the distance from his or her home to each of five local supermarkets. Time estimates were used to provide a measure of cognitive time distance, and the method of direct magnitude estimation, which will be described later, was used to obtain a measure of cognitive mileage distance. The shortest road distances to the supermarkets varied between 0.43 mile and 1.75 miles.

The data were analyzed to determine the proportion of consumers who thought they were using the closest supermarket, as opposed to the proportion of consumers who were actually using the closest supermarket. To accomplish this comparison, the consumers were also asked to indicate which supermarkets they patronized most often. Note that they were not asked to identify which one they had used on their last shopping expedition, as that might have represented only a minor fluctuation in their overall shopping strategy. The results indicate that the hypothesis was well founded (Table 7.1). That is, for this particular group of consumers, more people thought they

TABLE 7.1 SPATIAL RATIONALITY OF CONSUMER BEHAVIOR

Patronizing closest in terms of:	Percent
Physical distance	53
Cognitive mileage distance	70
Cognitive time distance	72

Source: M. T. Cadwallader, "A behavioral model of consumer spatial decision making," *Economic Geography,* 51 (1975), Table 2, p. 342.

went to the nearest supermarket than actually did. The evidence suggests that the consumers are at least intendedly rational with respect to distance, and that cognitive distance, or distance as it occurs in the behavioral environment, is a better predictor of consumer behavior than is physical distance, distance as it occurs in the phenomenal environment.

On a more general level, these results pose an interesting problem of interpretation. Consumers might choose between supermarkets partly on the basis of a priori distance estimates. Alternatively, the distance distortions might be attributable to some kind of cognitive dissonance process that occurs after a store has been chosen. In general, cognitive dissonance takes place after any decision in which a person has chosen between two fairly attractive alternatives. The person tends to reduce the dissonance by exaggerating the attractive features of the chosen alternative and the unattractive features of the rejected alternative (Festinger, 1964). In the context of cognitive distance and consumer behavior, this argument would suggest that, after patronizing a particular supermarket, the consumer will begin to rationalize his or her decision, and imagine that the chosen supermarket is relatively closer than the alternatives.

An examination of *pedestrian behavior* in the "Monroe" district of Philadelphia (Ley, 1974, pp. 219–226) also testifies to the importance of the behavioral environment as a means of understanding spatial behavior. A sample of residents were asked to specify what routes they would take when walking from their home, at night, to particular locations within Monroe. Only 27 percent of the responses represented a direct route between the origin and destination, while the largest group of responses indicated an indirect route, adding a fourth, or even a half or more to the length of the journey.

To explain this apparently irrational behavior, Ley computed a stress surface, based on answers to the question "Are there any blocks around here which have a bad reputation?" Such a stress surface can be represented by isolines joining points of equal perceived stress (Figure 7.1), and in the case of Monroe there were two notable peaks of higher-than-average stress, associated with the turfs of local gangs. When considered in the light of this perceived stress surface, the pedestrian behavior appeared to be much more rational. The area was traversed by following the valleys in the stress surface, just as a hiker might traverse a mountainous area by following the river valleys and avoiding the higher elevations. In other words, pedestrian behavior is governed by a kind of "invisible landscape," which is incorporated within the behavioral environment but is not a part of the phenomenal environment.

7.2 COGNITIVE MAPS

Early in the present century, Trowbridge (1913), in a paper concerned with the perception of direction, used the term *imaginary map*. This paper specifically addressed the cognitive representation of large-scale environments, and implied that people possess spatial images of those environments. Trowbridge investigated these

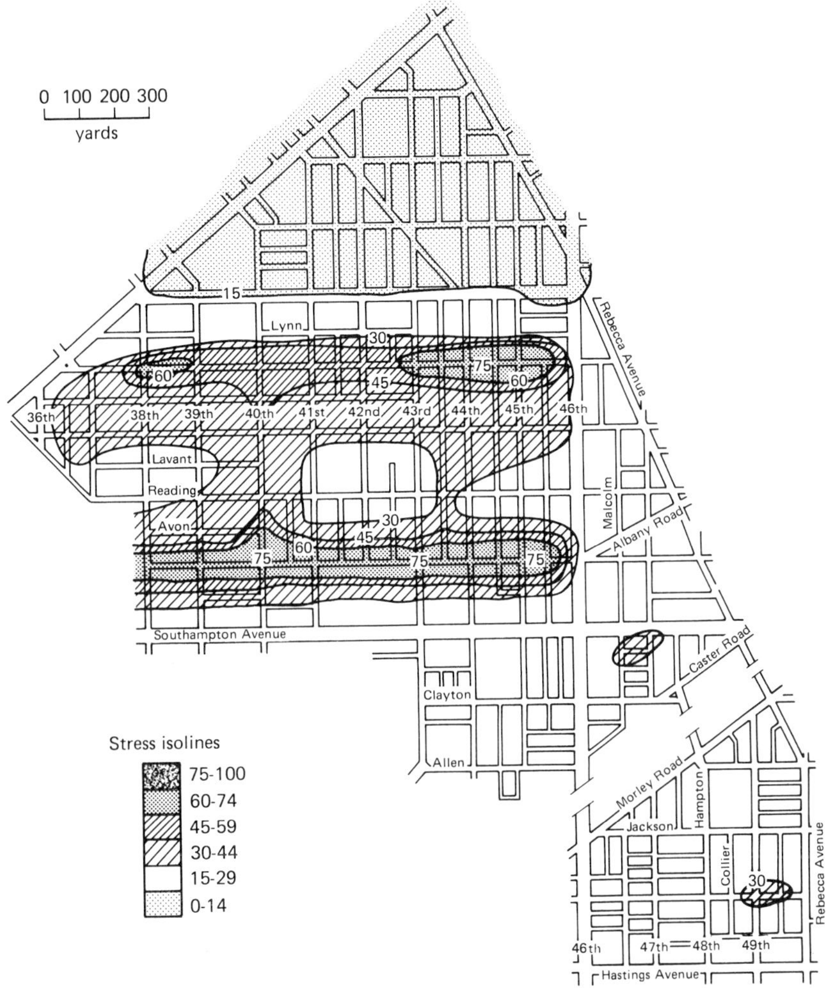

Figure 7.1 Monroe stress surface. (From D. Ley, *The Black Inner City as Frontier Outpost: Images and Behavior of a Philadelphia Neighborhood*, Monograph #7, Association of American Geographers, Washington, D.C., 1974, Fig. 36, p. 221.)

spatial images by asking subjects to indicate the directions of such cities as New York, London, and San Francisco on a circular piece of paper. Although he did not indicate the scoring procedure, he concluded that more than half the subjects revealed adequate imaginary maps.

The term *cognitive map* was apparently coined by Tolman (1948). His experimental data consisted of observations on rat behavior, but he believed that the results had significance for human bahavior. In general, Tolman contended that during the learning process something akin to a field map of routes and paths becomes established in the rat's brain, and that it is this map which ultimately determines the rat's behavior.

Both these terms, imaginary map and cognitive map, together with the more recent label *mental map* (Gould and White, 1974), tend to imply that our internal representations of the physical world are in map form. This is not ncessarily the case, however. In the present context, the term "map" is being used to indicate a functional analog, as we are interested in a cognitive representation that has the functions of a cartographic map, but not necessarily the physical properties of such a map (Downs, 1981). In this respect, *cognitive mapping* refers to the process by which information about the spatial environment is organized, stored, recalled, and manipulated, while a *cognitive map* is simply the product of this process at any particular point in time (Downs and Stea, 1977, p. 6).

The Image of the City

One of the first, and certainly most influential investigations of cognitive maps was undertaken by Lynch (1960). He selected a small sample of residents from three U.S. cities and analyzed their perception of the downtown area of those cities. A variety of methodologies were used, such as verbal lists of distinctive features and detailed descriptions of trips through the city, but the most important technique involved the use of sketch maps, where subjects were asked to make a quick map of the central city, covering all the main features.

Five major features, or elements as Lynch called them, were abstracted from these maps (Lynch, 1960, pp. 47–48). First, *paths* represented linear features in the city along which movement occurred. These paths were generally major highways, and they served to connect the different elements on the map. Second, *edges* represented linear features that were not necessarily used for movement. Primarily, these edges were the boundaries between different parts of the landscape, closing one region off from another. Third, *districts* were distinctive areas of urban space which had certain unifying characteristics. Subjects could conceptualize being either "inside" or "outside" such districts. Fourth, *nodes* were strategic points or intensive foci within the city, usually associated with the intersection of major paths. Fifth, *landmarks* were another type of point reference, which often served to orient the observer when traveling through the city. Most maps contained these five elements, although different examples of each, and they provided Lunch with a vocabulary for examining urban form.

Using as an example a person's cognitive map of Madison, Wisconsin, we can see how the elements are combined to create an overall image (Figure 7.2). The major highways are denoted as paths, including the beltline that circles much of the city. The shores of Lakes Mendota and Monona represent the major edges of the map, and Capitol Square is the major node, or focus of the city. Two districts are represented by the villages of Shorewood Hills and Maple Bluff, and the Capitol Building and Camp Randall, where the University of Wisconsin football team plays, are major landmarks.

For anybody familiar with Madison, it is obvious that this sketch map is not a

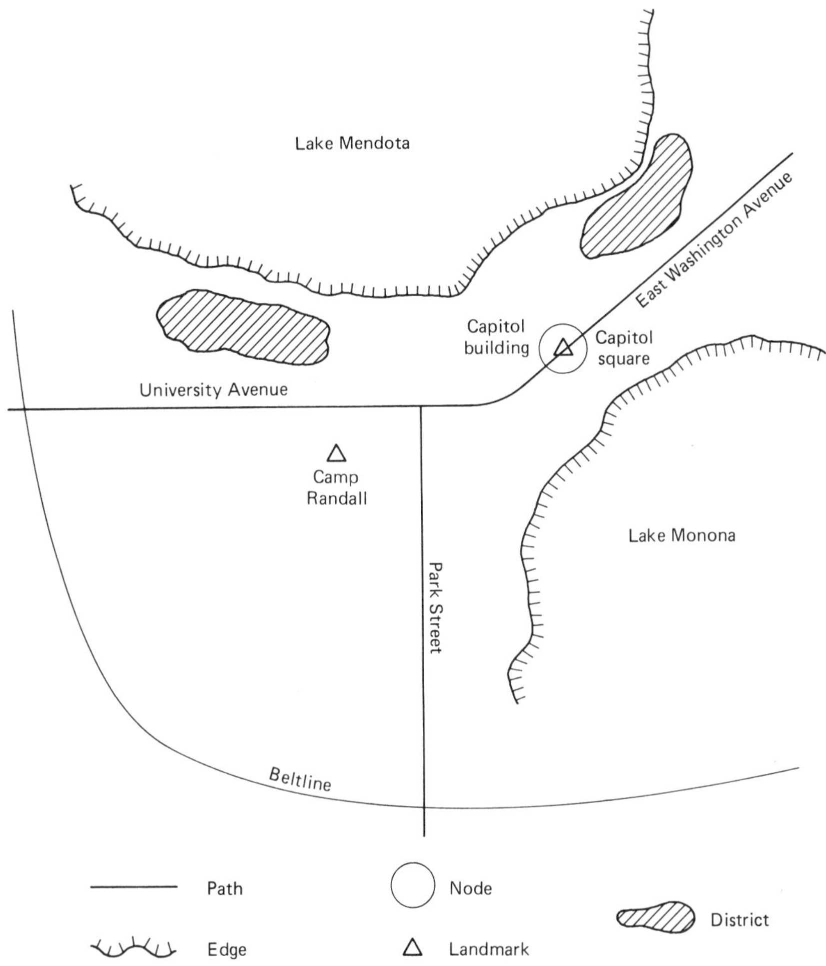

Figure 7.2 Cognitive map of Madison, Wisconsin.

completely accurate representation of the city. In particular, as we discussed when considering the relationship between the phenomenal and behavioral environments, it reflects a certain amount of selectivity and distortion. In terms of selectivity, for example, only the major highways and lakes have been portrayed. Also, only those districts, or neighborhoods, that are particularly distinctive have been shown. In terms of distortion, there are four major categories: first, there is distance distortion, as the elements on the map are not the correct distance apart; second, there is directional distortion, as the elements are not correctly oriented with respect to each other; third, there is size, or areal distortion; and fourth, the shapes of the elements have been changed. Later in this chapter we consider in some detail the characteristics of distance and directional distortion.

In research of this nature there is always some question concerning the degree to which the results are independent of methodology. Does, for example, a person's sketch map tell us more about cartographic ability than about urban images? In this respect, it is significant that Lynch used a variety of methodologies, in order to compare the different results. He found that the relationship between the cognitive map derived from a person's sketch map on the one hand, and his or her interview, on the other, was in some cases rather weak. However, when the data from all the interviews were combined to form a composite map and this was compared with a composite map derived from the individual sketches, the two maps were remarkably similar.

Some significant differences did remain, however (Lynch, 1960, pp. 144–145). The sketch maps tended to emphasize paths, and excluded those elements that were especially difficult to draw. The sketch maps also tended to have a higher "threshold," meaning that those elements that were least frequently mentioned in the interviews did not appear at all in the sketches. Finally, the sketch maps were unduly fragmented in terms of connections and overall organization, reflecting the difficulty of fitting everything together simultaneously.

In general, the methodologies employed by Lynch have all the advantages and disadvantages of the clinical approach in psychology (Lee, 1976). The information is gently teased out of the subject's consciousness and is not unduly constrained by a rigid framework of imposed instructions. The resulting maps reflect the schematic nature of imagery, including the selectivity and distortion that takes place during the process of perception and memory. As with the clinical approach in psychology, however, the open-ended nature of the research design makes it difficult to quantify and generalize the kinds of selectivity and distortion that are represented.

In a practical context, one of Lynch's major concerns was to address the issue of urban design. To this end, a central concept of his work was the idea of *imageability,* or legibility. Cities were imageable if they could be comprehended as coherent patterns with interconnected parts, and imageable cities were desirable for a number of reasons. First, clarity is generally regarded as being esthetically attractive, whereas cluttered images are regarded as ugly. Second, an imageable city is easy to use and find one's way around in. Third, an imageable city provides an excellent framework for helping a person to incorporate new items of information. Fourth, clarity of image enhances the ability of politicians, planners, and residents to communicate ideas about their city.

Socioeconomic Status

Much of the work on cognitive maps, since Lynch's original pioneering effort, has focused on variations related to differences in socioeconomic status. As different socioeconomic groups live in different parts of the city, they tend to form different images of that city. In particular, sketch maps drawn by higher-status socioeconomic groups are far more extensive, detailed, and interconnected than those drawn by lower-status groups. Also, performance in terms of accuracy tends to improve with increasing socioeconomic status.

One reason for these differences is that high socioeconomic status is often associated with more developed cartographic and verbal skills. A second, and probably more important difference, however, is that the lower classes have more restricted activity spaces. They generally travel shorter distances to work or recreation, and are more likely to use public transportation than private automobiles. The latter point is significant, as the flexibility of private transportation encourages the formulation of more detailed and extensive images.

One study, in particular, has empirically verified these socioeconomic differences. In an investigation carried out by the Los Angeles City Planning Commission and reported by Orleans (1973), a series of five composite maps of Los Angleles were constructed from sketch maps drawn by distinctive samples of residents, in five different locations. Subjects in the primarily black, lower-socioeconomic-status sample, located in a southeastern neighborhood of Los Angeles known as Avalon, near Watts, had a rather restricted spatial image of the city (Figure 7.3). Most of the

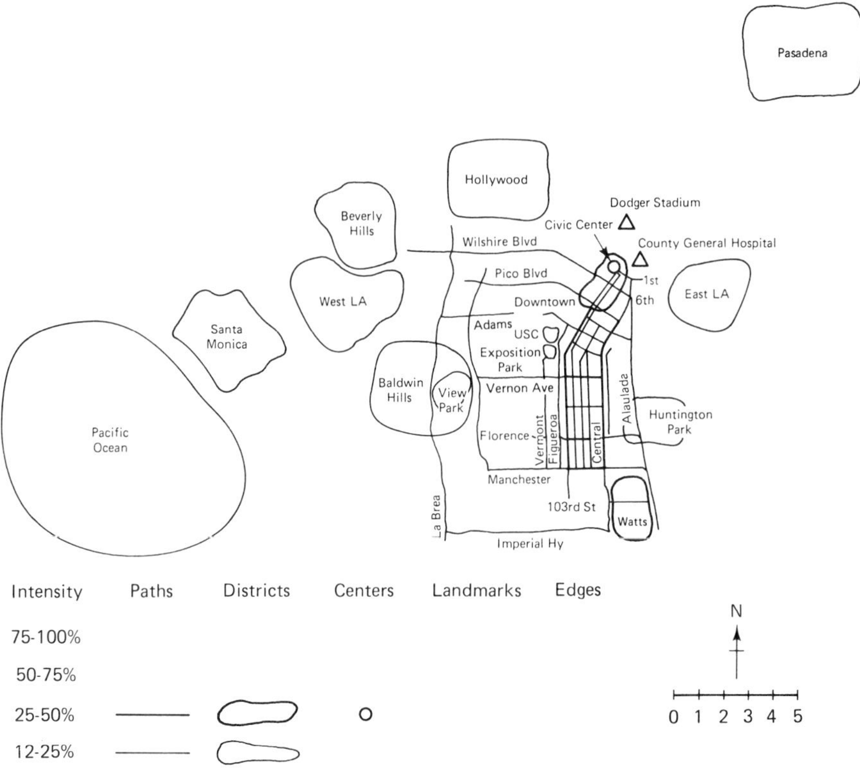

Figure 7.3 Avalon composite city image. (From P. Orleans, "Differential cognition of urban residents: Effects of social scale on mapping," in R. M. Downs and D. Stea, Eds., *Image and Environment: Cognitive Mapping and Spatial Behavior,* Aldine, Chicago, 1973, Fig. 7.2, p. 120.)

north-south roads linking Avalon and the city center were noted, but surprisingly few subjects mentioned such major edges as the Pacific Ocean and the Santa Monica Mountains. Much of the information was represented in the form of districts, but these were not well connected, and there was remarkably little interstitial material.

By contrast, the composite map produced by the upper-class sample from Westwood, near the UCLA campus in West Los Angeles, was much more detailed and extensive (Figure 7.4). In fact, most subjects had a fairly detailed image of the entire Los Angeles basin. A wide variety of paths, edges, nodes, districts, and landmarks were included, and these were well integrated into an overall conceptual schema that linked the different elements of the spatial image.

Similar variations in cognitive maps are also related to sex differences, as a result of the different roles played by husbands and wives. These variations due to role differences have been demonstrated using the concept of *home area analysis* (Everitt and Cadwallader, 1981), which involves asking subjects to mark on a map "the boundaries of your home area," where home area is described as being "the area in which you feel at home." The study was conducted in the Mar Vista area of West Los Angeles, using a sample of 65 couples, and it was assumed that people think in terms of contiguous home areas rather than a system of individual pathways. This assumption proved reasonable, as all but one subject was able to define such an area. The one exception did not drive, but took buses, so her home area map consisted of a set of bus routes.

The results of the analysis supported the hypothesis that the wives would demonstrate greater attachment to the local neighborhood by designating a larger home area (Figures 7.5 and 7.6). First, the average home area size was 3.4 square kilometers for wives and only 1.8 square kilometers for husbands. Second, 28 percent of the wives, as against 20 percent of the husbands, drew at least one of their boundaries outside the base map. Third, 56 percent of the wives' maps were larger than their respective husbands' map, as against 41 percent of the cases where the reverse was true.

The difference in home area size between husbands and wives was related to role differences, as 94 percent of the husbands went out to work, whereas only one-third of the wives did so. This relationship was reinforced by the fact that the workplace significantly influenced other major behavior patterns. For example, the development of friendships and club memberships often directly resulted from the workplace, and this was also true for some forms of recreation. By contrast, the wives tended to have greater social interaction within the local neighborhood.

Spatial Learning

Obviously, the structure of a person's cognitive map of a city develops over time, and Golledge (1978) has argued that this development is associated with the relative connectivity of points, lines, and areas within the cognitive map. When a person first moves into a new city, he or she initially identifies a home, a place of employment, and

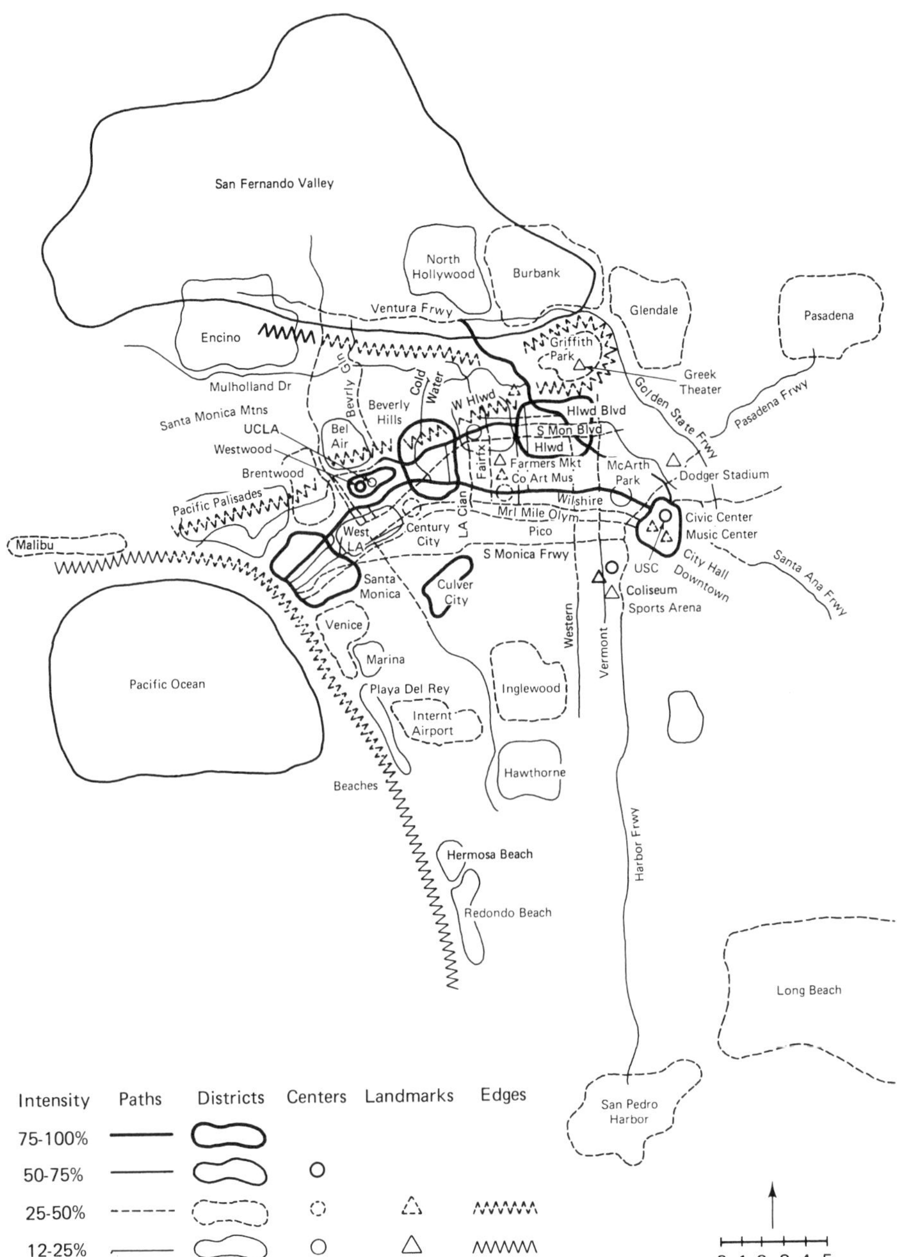

Figure 7.4 Westwood composite city image. (From P. Orleans, "Differential cognition of urban residents: Effects of social scale on mapping," in R. M. Downs and D. Stea, Eds., *Image and Environment: Cognitive Mapping and Spatial Behavior,* Aldine, Chicago, 1973, Fig. 7.4, p. 122.)

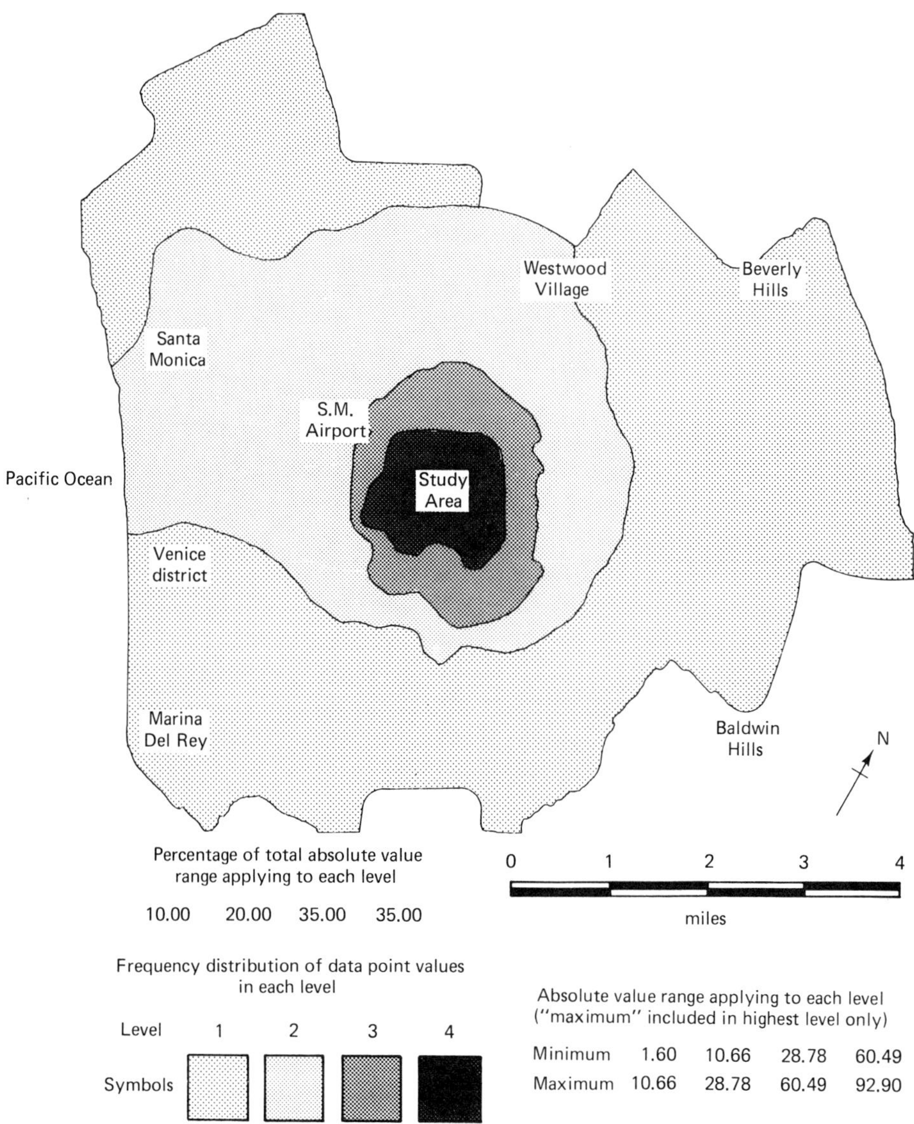

Figure 7.5 Wives' composite map of their home area. (From J. C. Everitt and M. T. Cadwallader, "Husband-wife role variation as a factor in home area definition," *Geografiska Annaler,* 63 B, 1981, Fig. 2, p. 29.)

the location of various food sources (Figure 7.7a). The home and workplace are very quickly established as dominant nodes in the emerging cognitive map, whereas shopping involves a trial-and-error process, and is more subject to change.

Once the dominant nodes have been established, together with the major links connecting them, there is a spread effect on the areas surrounding these nodes. Minor

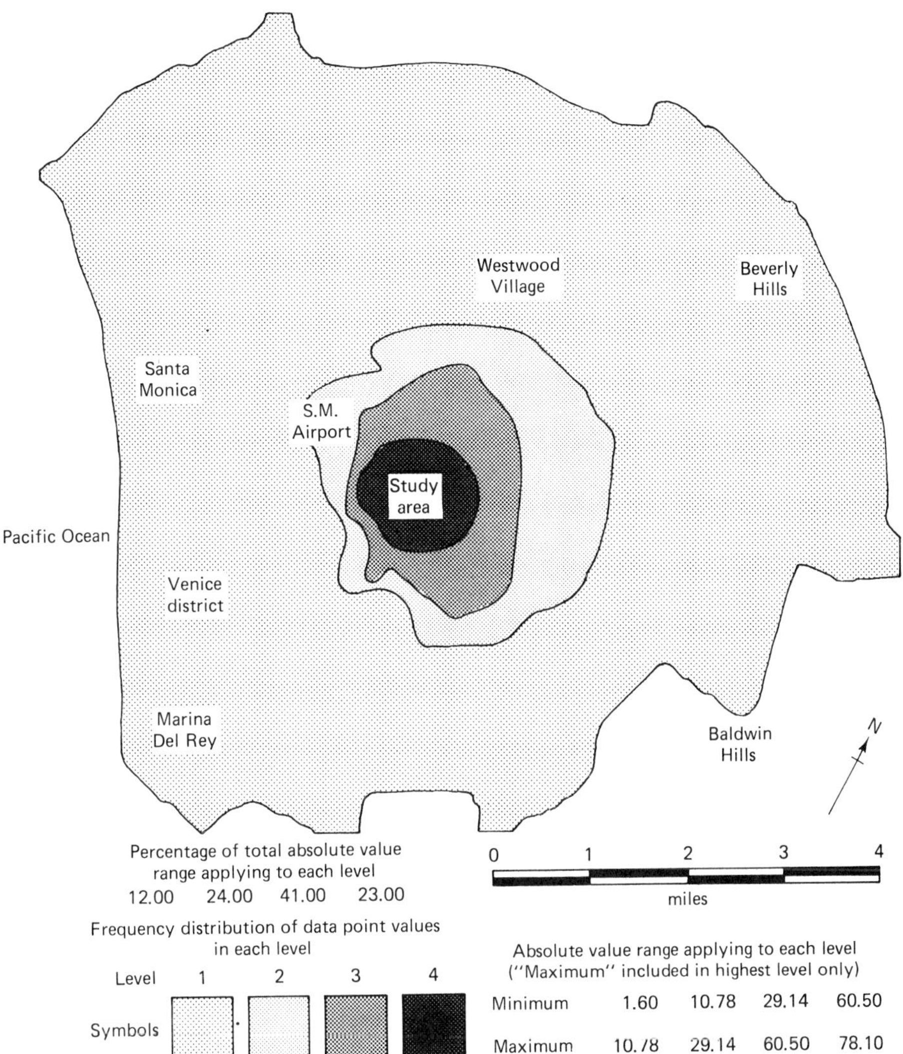

Figure 7.6 Husbands' composite map of their home area. (From J. C. Everitt and M. T. Cadwallader, "Husband-wife role variation as a factor in home area definition." *Geografiska Annaler*, 63 B, 1981, Fig. 3, p. 30.)

nodes are established within the vicinity of the major nodes, joined by a set of minor links. Eventually, the patterns of shopping and recreational behavior lead to consolidated areas, or districts, of detailed information (Figure 7.7b), involving an articulated network of primary, secondary, and minor nodes. This hierarchical development of nodes and links is based on the reasonable supposition that people learn about the urban environment primarily by interacting with it.

The learning process is not necessarily a continuous one, although the cognitive

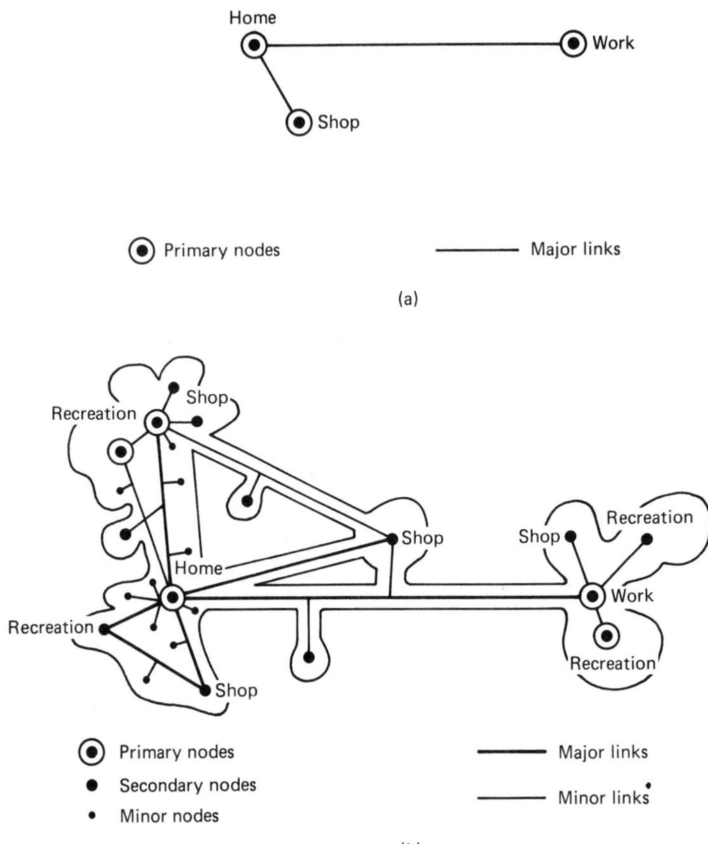

Figure 7.7 Length of residence and the changing cognitive map: (a) skeletal node-path relations; (b) nodes, paths, and neighborhoods. (From R. G. Golledge, "Learning about urban environments," in T. Carlstein, D. Parkes, and N. Thrift, Eds., *Making Sense of Time,* Edward Arnold, London, 1978, Fig. 1, p. 78, and Fig. 3, p. 80.)

map tends to emerge quite gradually and smoothly as more information is gathered about the local area. Sudden increases in information can occur when a trip is made to a previously unfamiliar part of town, and a whole new area of the cognitive map begins to be sketched in. The locations of the minor nodes and links, and even some of the major ones, are relatively flexible in the early stages of cognitive map development, but as time passes the cognitive representation tends to become increasingly stable, and new information results in only minor adjustments to the basic structure of the map.

Golledge's suggestion that initial knowledge about nodes and links eventually leads to more detailed information about districts or neighborhoods implies partially that people develop from a route-mapping stage, involving a network of major nodes and links, to a survey-mapping stage, involving a knowledge of both areas and the interconnections between them. This conceptualization is somewhat similar to Appleyard's (1969) attempt to derive a taxonomy for sketch maps. In particular, he distinguished between maps that emphasize sequential elements, such as paths, and maps that emphasize spatial elements, such as districts (Figure 7.8). In sequential maps the constituent parts are relatively connected, whereas in spatial maps the constituent parts are more disconnected and scattered.

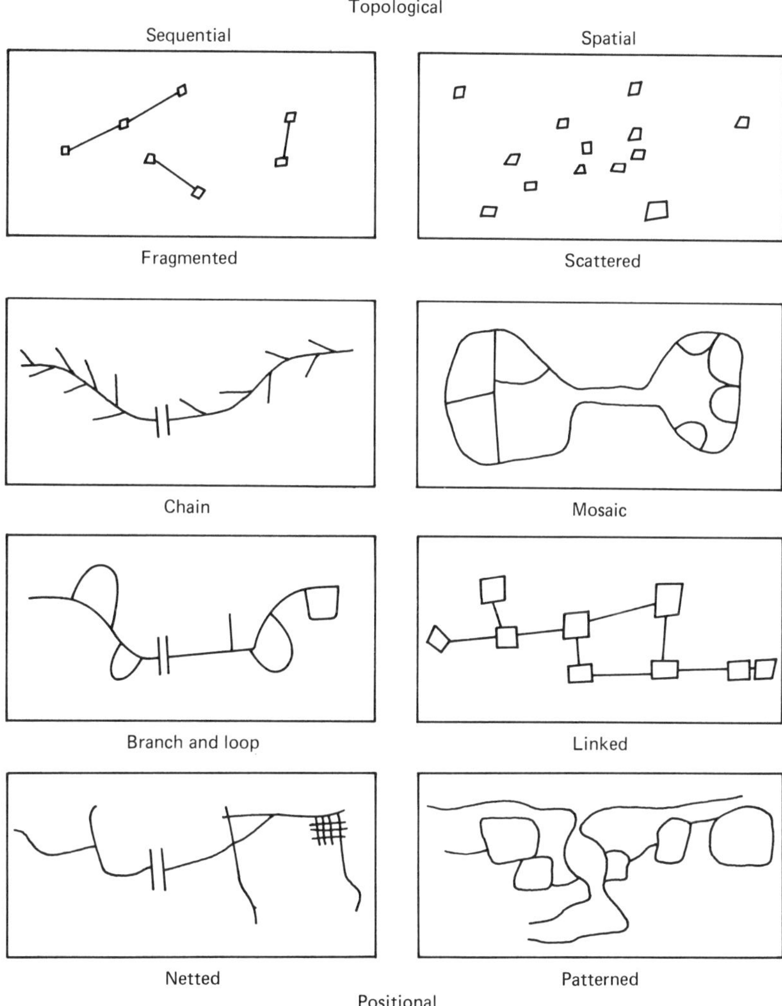

Figure 7.8 Types of sketch maps. (From D. Appleyard, "City designers and the pluralistic society," in L. Rodwin, Ed., *Planning Urban Growth and Regional Development: The Experience of the Guayana Program of Venezuela,* MIT Press, Cambridge, Mass., 1969, Fig. 23.2, p. 437. Copyright © 1969 by The Massachusetts Institute of Technology.)

According to Appleyard, the most primitive kind of *sequential map* is a fragmented map, which consists of fragmented paths. A chain map is equally simple, but tends to be more schematic, with impressionistic bends. Branch and loop maps contain branches and loops as outcrops from the basically linear system, while a netted map is the most complete in terms of its representation of the major paths, or links.

The simplest form of *spatial map* is a scattered map, containing such elements as individual buildings, without any drawn connections. A mosaic map is characterized by the enclosure of districts using schematic boundaries, and looks something like a neighborhood map. A linked map consists of places, or districts, connected by schematic linkages, and a patterned map represents the most complete and accurate form of spatial map.

In a study of Ciudad Guayana, in Venezuela, Appleyard (1970) found that sequential maps were the dominant form of representation, although this result might be due partially to two factors peculiar to his particular study. First, Ciudad Guayana is described as being a generally linear city with no dominant center, thus increasing the potential for sequential, or path-oriented sketch maps. Second, the subjects were instructed to draw a map of the city between the steel mill and San Felix. The wording of this instruction tends to emphasize the linearity of the city, and if the subjects had simply been asked to draw a map of Ciudad Guayana, a rather different set of sketches might have emerged. Finally, in this context, recent work suggests that it is only in those situations where the task is relatively complex that people move from a sequential map to a more developed spatial map; otherwise, there appear to be strong and consistent individual preferences for mapping style that persist throughout the learning process (Spencer and Weetman, 1981).

7.3 DESIGNATIVE PERCEPTIONS

The information contained within cognitive maps can be categorized as being either designative or appraisive (Cox and Zannaras, 1973). Purely *designative perceptions* of places involve such attributes as distance, direction, size, and shape, and are devoid of evaluative content. *Appraisive perceptions,* on the other hand, involve the value judgments that we have of different places. The present section focuses on the designative information contained within cognitive maps, especially as it pertains to the cognition of distance and direction; in the next section we consider the appraisive information contained within cognitive maps.

Cognitive Distance

At this point in the discussion it is important to note the difference between cognitive distance and perceived distance. The notion of perceived distance has attracted the attention of psychologists for a number of years (Baird, 1970), but what we are concerned with here are those physical distances that are too large to be perceived in a single glance. When working at the urban scale, it is assumed that people can think about distances in the abstract, without actually "seeing" them. The term "cognitive distance" is more appropriate for these "unseen" distances. Our cognitions include not only that information gathered from direct experience, as in perceived distance, but also information gathered from various other sources, such as road maps (Thorndyke, 1981). In this way people are able to estimate the distances to places they may never have actually visited.

Cognitive distance is likely to be a factor in at least three major types of decisions concerning spatial interaction: (1) it affects the decision to stay or go, (2) it affects the decision of where to go, and (3) it affects the decision of which route to take. Given the influential role of cognitive distance in spatial decision making, it is important to understand the nature of the relationship between physical distance and cognitive distance, as this will help us to transform physical space into the relevant cognitive space.

Most of the research on cognitive distance indicates that the relationship between physical distance and cognitive distance can be satisfactorily approximated by either a linear function, or the following power function (Cadwallader, 1976):

$$CD = a(PD)^b \tag{7.1}$$

where CD is cognitive distance, PD is physical distance, and a and b are constants. The dashed line in Figure 7.9 represents the situation where there is no difference between physical and cognitive distance, so the power function indicates that whereas short distances are overestimated, longer distances tend to be underestimated. The point of changeover in this relationship varies, with a distance of between 6 and 7 miles being

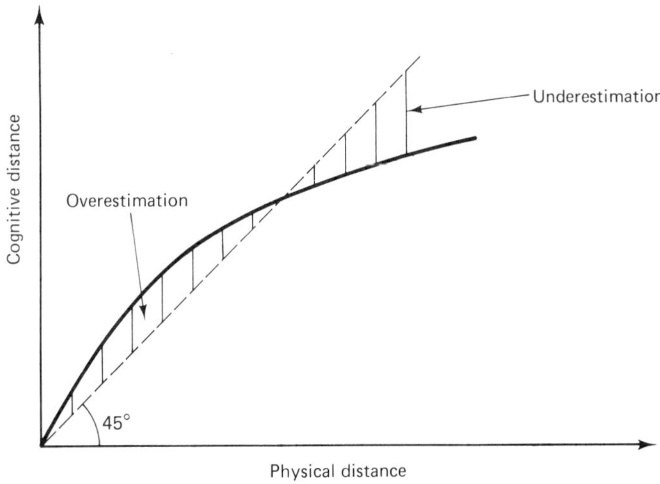

Figure 7.9 Relationship between cognitive distance and physical distance.

suggested as the breakpoint for London, and only about 3 miles for Dundee (Pocock and Hudson, 1978, p. 53).

A variety of reasons have been advanced to explain the discrepancies between cognitive and physical distances, although the empirical evidence for them has often been less than impressive. The explanatory variables can be categorized as representing the attributes of the stimuli, or locations, the attributes of the subjects, and the attributes of the routes. In terms of the *characteristics of the stimuli,* it has been suggested that cognitive distance is influenced by the direction of the stimulus from the subject, although there is some confusion as to the precise nature of this relationship. Lee (1970) compared the cognitive distances involved in journeys toward downtown and journeys away from downtown, and concluded that there was a much greater overestimation of outward journeys. Experiments conducted by Golledge et al. (1969), however, yielded results that directly contradict this finding. Although noting that cognitive distance does vary with direction, they found that distances away from the central business district tend to be underestimated, whereas those toward the central business district tend to be overestimated. Similarly, the relative attractiveness of the stimuli, or destination, has also been found to account for some of the deviations between physical and cognitive distance. Thompson (1963) presented evidence for this phenomenon when he found that, within the context of consumer behavior, the relative attractiveness of the retailing outlet influences consumer evaluations of time and distance to that outlet.

Characteristics of the subjects are also significant in terms of explaining distance judgments. A person's familiarity with a particular city will obviously influence his or her distance estimates within that city. As one might expect, it has been shown that an effective learning process enables long-term residents to estimate distances more accurately than do recent arrivals (Golledge et al., 1969).

Finally, the *characteristics of the route,* and the mode of transportation, tend to influence distance judgments. Generally, the greater the number of turns or intersections in a journey, the greater the imagined length of that journey. In terms of mode of transportation, Canter (1977, p. 99) reports that bus travelers in London tend to relatively underestimate distances. In a wider context, Canter and Tagg (1975) suggest that the general layout, or imageability of a city is related to the pattern of distance distortion. A city with a confusing image, like Tokyo, often leads to the overestimation of distances, whereas a more legible city, like Glasgow, may lead to underestimation.

Any overall summary of the work on cognitive distance is exceedingly difficult, however, as a number of *methodological differences* preclude the direct comparison of results (Cadwallader, 1973). First, there have been differences of opinion as to whether subjects should be asked to estimate route distances or straight-line distances. For example, Lee (1970) used estimates of the shortest walking distance, whereas Canter and Tagg (1975) used straight-line, or "crow-flight" estimates. It seems that straight-line distances are more appropriate, however, because if it is maintained that subjects possess some kind of spatial representation of the physical environment, straight-line distances can be drawn fairly easily from this abstract representation, whereas a knowledge of route distances might require direct experience with those routes. This argument follows from the theoretical assumption that people tend to work from some kind of cognitive map, rather than retracing in their mind specific trips that they might have taken in the past. Although it is unclear what actually transpires inside the "black box" of the human brain, most researchers assume that some form of externalized map can be drawn from the spatial relations held in the mind.

Second, there has been considerable variation with respect to the spatial scale involved in cognitive distance studies. For example, Lundberg (1973) asked his subjects to estimate the distances between 13 cities located in different parts of the world, whereas others have focused on distances within individual cities (Briggs, 1973). These differences make it difficult to compare results, because the threshold distance at which overestimation changes to underestimation is partly a function of spatial scale.

Third, most studies have aggregated the individual estimates, consequently masking the possibility that a variety of relationships exist at the individual level. For example, some subjects might exhibit linear relationships between physical and cognitive distance, whereas for others the relationship might be curvilinear. In addition, it has been shown that aggregated data significantly exaggerate the strength of the relationship between physical and cognitive distance (Cadwallader, 1973).

Finally, the method of obtaining distance estimates has varied from study to study, as there are a variety of ways in which subjects can be asked to scale physical distances subjectively. For example, they can be asked to draw maps, from which the experimenter can extract the appropriate cognitive distance information, or they can be asked to arrange scale models into their real-world pattern, again allowing the experimenter to measure cognitive distance. The most popular methodology, however, has involved a number of scaling techniques, such as ratio estimation and direct magnitude estimation (Phipps, 1979).

Research has indicated that the precise form of the relationship between cognitive distance and physical distance is not independent of methodology (Baird et al., 1982). For example, Day (1976) compared distance estimates derived in four different ways. The subjects were asked to draw maps, provide verbal estimates, mark scales of a specified length, and use a ratio scaling method. Although the relationship between physical and cognitive distance was approximately linear when using all four estimation techniques, the slope of the least-squares line varied.

The present author (Cadwallader, 1979a) addressed this problem of methodological inconsistency by comparing results obtained at the individual level, to see whether subjects give different distance estimates according to the form in which they are asked to provide those estimates. The subjects were asked to estimate the distances between pairs of cities using both the method of direct magnitude estimation and category rating scales. *Direct magnitude estimation* is a technique used by psychologists to measure such sensory magnitudes as loudness (Stevens, 1956), and it has already been mentioned in the context of the consumer behavior study reported in Section 7.1. The experimenter usually selects a particular single stimulus on a given physical continuum, such as distance, and assigns a number to its subjective magnitude. The subject is then presented with a set of variable stimuli and is instructed to assign to each stimulus a number which is proportional to its subjective magnitude as compared to the standard stimulus. In the present experiment the stimuli were the pairs of cities which the subjects were asked to estimate the distance between, while the standard stimulus was the particular pair of cities chosen by the experimenter.

A brief example will clarify the use of this technique. Assume that there are 10 physical distances (*A*, . . . , *J*) for which estimates are needed. The distance *E* can be assigned the standard value of 100, and then the subjects are asked to rate the other distances accordingly. It is advisable to select the standard stimulus so that it is in the middle range of the variable stimuli, and to assign it a number like 100, as this is easy to divide into simple ratios and allows the subjects to think in terms of percentages. If a person thinks that distance *I* is twice as long as distance *E*, he or she will assign *I* the value 200; if he or she thinks that *I* is only half as long as *E*, then *I* will be assigned the value 50, and so on, until all the distances have been estimated.

A *category rating scale,* on the other hand, is produced when a subject judges a set of stimuli, in this case physical distances, in terms of a set of categories, distinguished by either numbers or adjectives. The subject is requested to assign the smallest stimulus to the first category, the largest to the last category, and to use the other categories in such a way that they are equally spaced subjectively (Luce and Galanter, 1963). An odd number of categories are normally used, and the stimuli are chosen so that the subjects tend to choose the various categories equally often.

The consistency of the estimates across these two methodologies was assessed by correlating the two sets of responses for each person, with a strong positive correlation indicating a high degree of similarity between the estimates. It should be noted, however, that for most variables the relationship between a magnitude scale and a category scale lies somewhere between a linear and a logarithmic function (Shinn, 1974). The category widths seem to increase as one moves up the category scale, meaning that two stimuli close together on the low end of the scale are more easily discriminated between than those close together on the high end of the scale. In other words, it becomes increasingly difficult to distinguish between two stimuli as their magnitudes increase.

Following this reasoning, the two sets of distance estimates for each person were correlated in two different ways. First, the magnitude scale was correlated with the category scale, and second, the logarithm of the magnitude scale was correlated with the category scale (Table 7.2). In both cases the majority of correlations fell within the range .61 to .80, indicating that the individual estimates were not completely consistent across the two measurement techniques. That is, the distance estimates provided by an individual subject were not always independent of the way in which he or she was asked to provide those estimates, thus reflecting one of the major difficulties involved in attempting to calibrate the relationship between physical and cognitive distance.

TABLE 7.2 COMPARISON OF DIFFERENT METHODOLOGIES FOR MEASURING COGNITIVE DISTANCES

Pearson correlation coefficients for the relationship between magnitude scales and category scales:

Coefficients	Frequency
.40 or less	0
.41 to .60	7
.61 to .80	32
.81 to 1.00	26

Pearson correlation coefficients for the relationship between the logarithm of magnitude scales and category scales:

Coefficients	Frequency
.40 or less	0
.41 to .60	7
.61 to .80	35
.81 to 1.00	23

Source: M. T. Cadwallader, "Problems in cognitive distance: Implications for cognitive mapping," *Environment and Behavior,* 11 (1979), Tables 1 and 2, p. 568.

Intransitivity and Noncommutativity in Cognitive Distance

Efforts to calibrate the relationship between physical and cognitive distance have also been thwarted by the problems of intransitivity and noncommutativity. *Intransitivity* occurs if the following conditions hold: A is estimated to be greater than B, B is estimated to be greater than C, but C is estimated to be greater than A, where A, B, and C are interpoint distances. The degree of intransitivity in different kinds of judgmental behavior is an empirical question, and it is important to know to what extent distance estimates are intransitive, as any inherent intransitivity means that cognitive distance, and therefore cognitive maps, cannot be represented in terms of Euclidean geometry.

In an experiment designed to address this problem of intransitivity (Cadwallader, 1979a), 56 subjects made a series of paired comparison judgments, in which they were required to estimate which one of two intercity distances was longer. In all, there were six intercity distances, so each subject made 15 paired comparison judgments. The data from the experiment were first analyzed at the aggregate level, in order to determine the relative amounts of strong, moderate, and weak stochastic transitivity (Coombs, 1964, p. 106). Strong stochastic transitivity asserts that if the probabilities of estimating A greater than B and B greater than C are both equal to or greater than 0.5, then the probability of estimating A greater than C is equal to or greater than the larger of the other two probabilities. Moderate stochastic transitivity asserts that if the probabilities of estimating A greater than B and B greater than C are both equal to or greater than 0.5, then the probability of estimating A greater than C is equal to or greater than the smaller of the other two probabilities. While weak stochastic transitivity simply asserts that if the probabilities of estimating *A* greater than *B* and *B* greater than *C* are both equal to or greater than 0.5, then the probability of estimating *A* greater than *C* is also equal to or greater than 0.5. The six intercity distances used in the experiment created 20 different distance triads, or combinations of three distances, of which 17 met the conditions of strong stochastic transitivity, while the other three met conditions of moderate stochastic transitivity.

A different picture emerged, however, when intransitivity was investigated at the level of individual subjects. As there were 56 subjects, and 20 triads per subject, there were 1120 triads in the complete experiment. Of these, 92 triads, or 8 percent, were intransitive. This represents quite a large percentage, as within each triad of distances there are six possible transitive orderings and only two possible intransitive orderings (David, 1963, p. 11). Table 7.3 is a frequency table, indicating the number of intransitive triads for each subject. Of the 56 subjects, 29 had at least one intransitive triad, and of the 27 subjects who had no intransitive triads, not one of them had all six stimuli, or intercity distances, in the correct order. Indeed, of 1028 triads that were transitive, only 339, or 33 percent, contained the correct ordering of the three stimuli. An extreme example of this phenomenon was the subject who exhibited complete transitivity but had the stimuli within every triad in an incorrect order.

In summary, then, research on cognitive distance, and ultimately cognitive maps, is faced with the problem that distance estimates are sometimes intransitive. This intransitivity means that the subjects are unable to order the stimuli on a single continuum. As a result, it appears that efforts to uncover a simple linear or curvilinear relationship between cognitive distance and physical distance are oversimplifying a complex situation.

The second major problem in analyzing cognitive distance is the issue of *noncommutativity* (Burroughs and Sadalla, 1979). Cognitive distance is noncommuta-

TABLE 7.3 COGNITIVE DISTANCE AND INTRANSITIVITY

Number of intransitive triads	Frequency
0	27
1	6
2	6
3	6
4	6
5	0
6	3
7	2

Source: M. T. Cadwallader, "Problems in cognitive distance: Implications for cognitive mapping," *Environment and Behavior,* 11 (1979), Table 4, p. 572.

TABLE 7.4 COGNITIVE DISTANCE AND NONCOMMUTATIVITY

Percentage difference	Frequency
0	259
0.1 to 9.9	255
10.1 to 19.9	358
20.0 to 29.9	301
30.0 to 39.9	158
40.0 to 49.9	97
50.0 or more	72

Source: M. T. Cadwallader, "Problems in cognitive distance: Implications for cognitive mapping," *Environment and Behavior,* 11 (1979), Table 5, p. 574.

tive if the following condition holds:

$$CD(A, B) \neq CD(B, A) \tag{7.2}$$

where A and B are point locations, and CD is cognitive distance. Thus noncommutativity means that the estimated distance from A to B does not equal the estimated distance from B to A. An example of such a situation would be the often-felt experience that the journey to work seems shorter than the journey home from work.

In order to investigate the degree to which distance estimates are noncommutative, an experiment was conducted in which subjects were asked to estimate the distances between 30 pairs of cities in the United States (Cadwallader, 1979a). Later, as part of the same experiment, they were asked to repeat this task, but this time the order of each pair of cities had been reversed. The difference between each pair of estimates was calculated as a percentage of the largest estimate. In 259 instances, both estimates were exactly the same (Table 7.4). Most pairs of estimates, however, revealed a difference of somewhere between 10 and 40 percent.

These results indicate that distance estimates are often noncommutative, suggesting that people do not possess internal spatial representations of the environment that can be portrayed in terms of Euclidean geometry (Golledge and Hubert, 1982). The only other conclusion is to speculate that noncommutativity merely represents some form of measurement error. On the basis of present evidence, however, it seems dangerous not to at least entertain the idea that noncommutativity is a genuine property of cognitive maps.

Frame Dependency in Cognitive Maps

Less attention has been given to the directional component of cognitive maps, although the locational information contained in such maps is a composite of both distance and directional distortions. It has been argued that the directional distortions can be analyzed in terms of the frame-of-reference concept employed in psychological investigations of the perception of verticality (Cadwallader, 1977). Psychologists have long been concerned with the distortion of the vertical within visible frames of reference, but far less consideration has been given to frame dependency in the horizontal plane (Howard and Templeton, 1966). Also, when discussing cognitive maps, it should be remembered that we are involved with the influence of "unseen" frames of reference, that is, frames of reference that exist in physical space but whose size prevents them from being encompassed in a single glance. These frames of reference are represented in the cognitive map, and any displacement of their orientation from the true orientation can result in a corresponding displacement of all the directional information contained within that map.

Various typologies for *frames of reference* have been developed, and using the terminology of Downs and Stea (1973, p. 291), what we are concerned with here are those reference systems that are based in the environment. In such systems, various elements of the social or physical environment may act as the frame of reference. For example, Trowbridge (1913), in a pioneering investigation of directional orientation in Manhattan, suggested that the differences between the true directions and the estimated directions were due to the belief among his subjects that the longitudinal streets of Manhattan are isomorphic with a north-south axis. He argued that the subjects were using the street system as their frame of reference, and, as they believed that the street system corresponded to a north-south and east-west grid system, their directional estimates were displaced from the true directions in direct association with this inaccurate frame of reference.

A similar study was undertaken by the present author (Cadwallader, 1977), to determine the extent to which a group of residents located in West Los Angeles orient themselves according to major features of the physical landscape. More specifically, it was hypothesized that the edge of the Pacific Ocean would provide the major frame of reference for their cognitive maps. The experimental design was similar to that used by Trowbridge (1913), and required each subject to estimate the direction to 30 cities in the Los Angeles basin. The resulting data were analyzed by means of directional statistics, as we are dealing with circular rather than linear distributions.

The mean estimated direction to each city was determined, and these directions were compared to the real directions. On the average, the estimated directions were 18.57 degrees less than the real directions. This difference suggests that the coastline was being used as a frame of reference, as its orientation is northwest to southeast. In other words, the subjects appeared to think that the coastline runs north-south, although it is actually displaced from this orientation, with the result that the estimated directions were similarly displaced. An analysis of the difference between the estimated direction and the real direction, for each of the 30 cities, indicated that 27 of those cities had a mean estimated direction that was less than their real direction, thus reflecting a displacement toward the frame of reference. Moreover, the difference between the estimated direction and the real direction appeared to be greatest for those cities closest to the coastline. That is, the degree of frame dependency varied according to the distance of the stimuli from the frame of reference.

Although this experiment provided some evidence that cognitive maps are frame dependent, there are still a number of unanswered questions. For example, it is unclear whether one frame of reference is usually applied to the whole map, or whether different frames of reference are utilized for different parts of the map. Also, we as yet know very little about why particular elements in the environment are chosen as a frame of reference, or whether the chosen frame of reference changes over time.

7.4 APPRAISIVE PERCEPTIONS

Having discussed the designative component of cognitive maps, we now turn our attention to the appraisive information contained within such maps. In particular, we will focus on the amount of information and the perceived attractiveness associated with different parts of the cognitive map. Much of the pioneering work in this area was carried out by Gould (Gould and White, 1974), who investigated the perceived residential desirability of different regions within the United States.

Residential Preference Patterns

If the residential desirability of each state, as rated by a group of subjects, is measured on a scale from 0 to 100, these values can be used to construct a residential preference surface. Isolines connect the points of equal value, thus creating a surface that reflects the hills and valleys of desirability for a particular group of people. For example, Figure 7.10 shows the residential desirability surface for a group of subjects located in

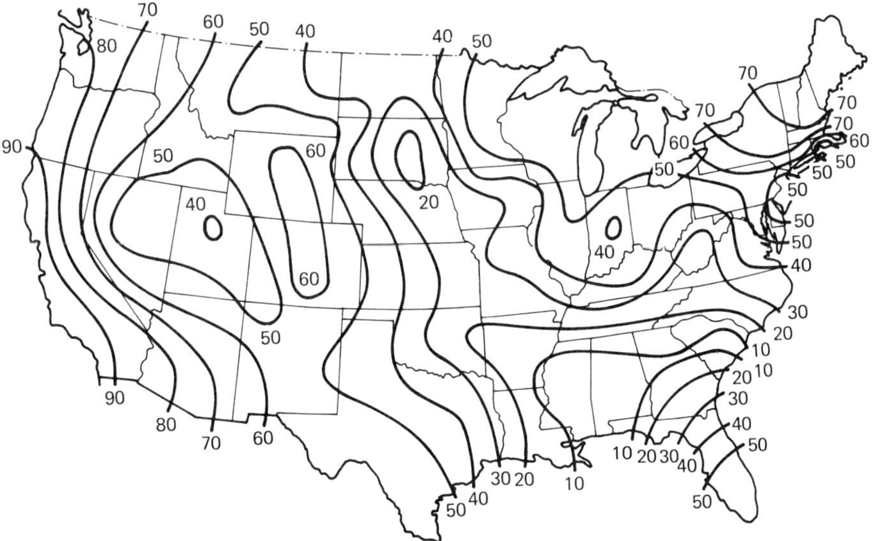

Figure 7.10 Residential desirability surface from California. (From R. Abler, J. S. Adams, and P. R. Gould, *Spatial Organization: The Geographer's View of the World,* Prentice-Hall, Englewood Cliffs, N.J., 1971, Fig. 13.31, p. 520.)

California. Where the isolines are far apart it means that the perceived residential desirability changes quite slowly, while closely spaced isolines indicate more dramatic changes in the preference surface.

Similar surfaces have also been constructed for individual cities, and they have implications for the issue of neighborhood revitalization (Day and Walmsley, 1981). Clark and Cadwallader (1973b) analyzed a series of residential preference maps of Los Angeles. The sample consisted of 1024 persons spread throughout the metropolitan area. Each subject was shown a map of Los Angeles which included the freeway system and the Santa Monica mountains. In addition, approximately 180 neighborhoods were indicated by name on the map, although their boundaries were not given. After looking at the map, each subject was asked to do the following: "Taking your family income into consideration, please show me on this map the three neighborhoods where you would most like to live, starting with the one you would like to live in most." The income constraint was used so that people would not automatically choose such obviously attractive, but realistically unattainable communities as Beverly Hills, Bel Air, or Palos Verdes.

The first choice preferences of the subjects are shown in Figure 7.11. The neighborhoods are mapped with an intensity according to the number of times they were chosen by the 1024 subjects, so that the most heavily shaded areas represent

Figure 7.11 First-choice preferences of sample respondents in the Los Angeles metropolitan area. (From W. A. V. Clark and M. T. Cadwallader, "Residential preferences: An alternate view of intraurban space," *Environment and Planning*, 5, 1973, Fig. 3, p. 697.)

communities that were chosen by the greatest number of people. A minimum of six subjects was used as the cutoff point for the highest preference category, as this was the number of choices that every community would receive if they were all perceived as being equally attractive. The preference map contains four distinctive regions of highly preferred neighborhoods. First, there is a ridge extending from Santa Monica in the west to Hollywood in the east, reflecting the physically attractive nature of this area and its relatively good access to the ocean and mountains. Second, the beach communities, such as Malibu and Redondo Beach are also highly preferred. Third, there is a highly preferred region in the eastern portion of the Los Angeles basin, including such communities as Arcadia and Pasadena, where Arcadia represents newer housing opportunities and Pasadena represents a very established residential community. Finally, the belt of highly preferred communities from Long Beach to Downey reflects the residential preferences of lower-income whites, blacks, and Mexican Americans.

Urban Information and Preference Surfaces

A more detailed investigation of urban and information preference surfaces in the Los Angeles basin was undertaken by the present author (Cadwallader, 1978b) in order to look backward from these "invisible landscapes" to some of the casual influences that form them. Whereas a *preference surface* reflects the varying attractiveness that people assign to different locations or places, an *information surface* reflects the varying amount of information that people possess about those same locations or places. In this particular instance, the aim was to account for any regularities in these surfaces, and also to examine their underlying structures, in the hope of identifying variables involved in the evaluation process. To this end, trend surface analysis was used to generate the explanatory hypotheses, which were then tested by means of correlation and regression analysis. The underlying structures were examined by means of principal components analysis.

The data for the research were collected from residents of West Los Angeles, and the subjects all lived within three blocks of each other. In this way individual differences in the information and preference patterns could be compared while holding location constant. Both the information and preference data were obtained by the previously described method of direct magnitude estimation, with each subject being asked to rate his or her familiarity with, and preference for, 30 cities in the Los Angeles basin (Figure 7.12), using Culver City and Hollywood as the standard stimuli.

Trend surface analysis (see Section 4.5) was used to fit linear, quadratic, and cubic surfaces to the information and preference data (Table 7.5). The best fit for both the information and preference surfaces was provided by a cubic surface, although even the cubic surfaces only accounted for just over half the total variation in the data. The comparatively small coefficients of determination indicate that the surfaces were extremely convoluted. Of greater interest, however, is the fact that the trend surface analysis successfully identified a number of important explanatory variables.

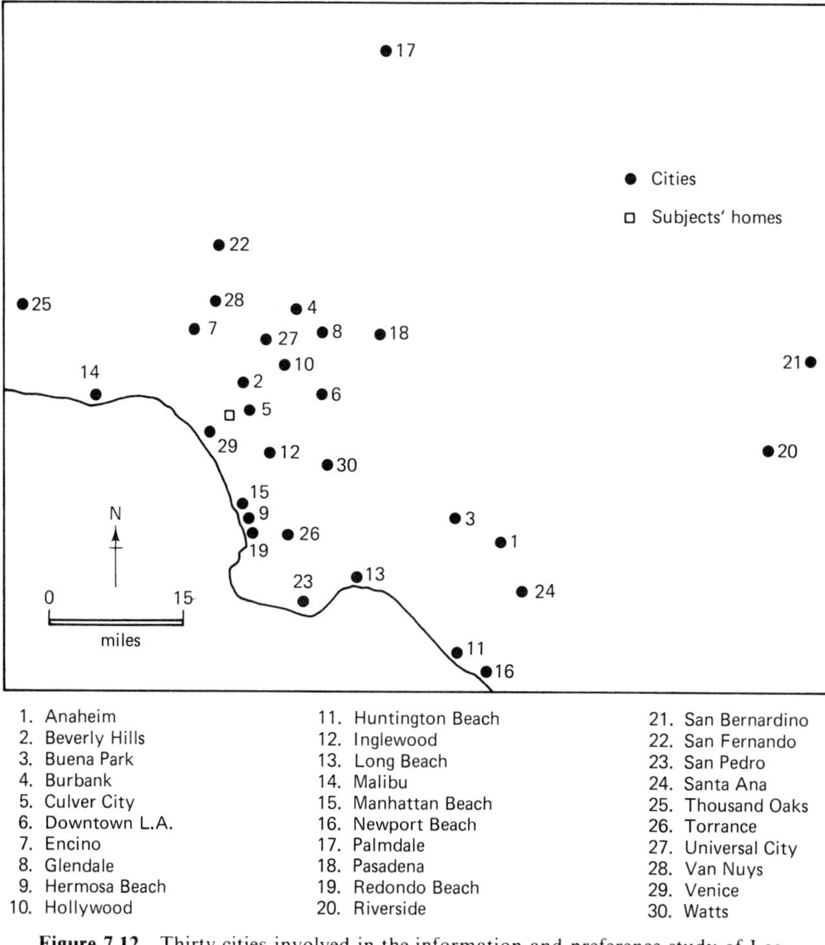

Figure 7.12 Thirty cities involved in the information and preference study of Los Angeles. (From M. T. Cadwallader, "Urban information and preference surfaces: Their patterns, structures, and interrelationships," *Geografiska Annaler,* 60 B, 1978, Fig. 1, p. 99.)

Inspection of the preference surfaces, and their residuals, suggested the significance of distance from the Pacific Ocean as a determinant of residential desirability. Also, some measure of affluence appeared to be important, as cities such as Beverly Hills and Malibu were constantly given high ratings. In terms of the information surfaces, distance again appeared to be a prominent factor, although in this case it was distance from the subjects' homes that was important rather than distance from the ocean. City size emerged as a second variable influencing information levels, suggesting that the larger cities tended to be more familiar than the smaller ones.

TABLE 7.5 TREND SURFACE ANALYSIS OF THE INFORMATION AND PREFERENCE SURFACES FOR LOS ANGELES

	Information surface (R^2)	Preference surface (R^2)
Linear	.13	.15
Quadratic	.24	.34
Cubic	.53	.60

Source: M. T. Cadwallader, "Urban information and preference surfaces: Their patterns, structures, and interrelationships," *Geografiska Annaler,* 60 B (1978), Table 1, p. 101.

The extent to which these four variables accounted for the variation in the information and preference surfaces was investigated by means of multiple correlation and regression analysis (see Section 3.1). For the preference surface, the multiple regression model was as follows:

$$Y_i = a - b_1X_{i1} + b_2X_{i2} \tag{7.3}$$

where Y_i is the attractiveness of city i, X_{i1} is the distance of city i from the Pacific Ocean, X_{i2} is the average income of city i, and a, b_1, and b_2 are constants. The multiple correlation coefficient for this equation was .85, and the partial correlation coefficients suggest that average income was more important than distance from the ocean (Table 7.6). Note that the coefficient for average income was positive, indicating that the affluent cities were more highly preferred, whereas the coefficient for distance from the ocean was negative, indicating that residential desirability decreased with increasing distance from the ocean.

The variation in information levels was analyzed using the following multiple

TABLE 7.6 PARTIAL CORRELATION COEFFICIENTS ASSOCIATED WITH THE INFORMATION AND PREFERENCE SURFACES FOR LOS ANGELES

Information surface	
Distance from the subjects' homes	−.54
City size	.15
Preference surface	
Distance from the ocean	−.44
Average income for city	.80

Source: M. T. Cadwallader, "Urban information and preference surfaces: Their patterns, structures, and interrelationships," *Geografiska Annaler,* 60 B (1978), Table 2, p. 101.

regression model:

$$Y_i = a - b_1X_{i1} + b_2X_{i2} \tag{7.4}$$

where Y_i is the information level for city *i*, X_{i1} is the distance of city *i* from the subjects' homes, X_{i2} is the population of city *i*, and a, b_1, and b_2 are constants. The multiple correlation coefficient for this equation was .58, with distance from the subjects' homes being more important than population size (Table 7.6). Again, note that information levels decreased with increasing distance, but increased with increasing population size.

The latter results correspond closely with those obtained by Gould (1975) when investigating information surfaces at a national scale. Using data from Swedish schoolchildren, Gould found that the configuration of the information surfaces could be satisfactorily accounted for by population and distance variables. Similar results have also been reported when measurements are made concerning the accuracy of information rather than just the quantity (Webber et al., 1975).

A principal components analysis (see Section 5.4) was also undertaken, to uncover the underlying structures associated with the information and preference patterns. With the subjects as cases and the cities as variables, an orthogonal rotation was performed, in order to emphasize most clearly the groupings of cities. Those cities with highly correlated familiarity, or preference ratings, would be associated with the same components, and it was hoped that the interpretation of these components would suggest the underlying dimensions which the subjects had used to evaluate the cities.

The underlying structure of the preference surface is represented in Table 7.7, and the highest loading for each city, on any of the four components, was used to interpret those components. The four components describing the preference pattern accounted for approximately 87 percent of the total variance, while the first two components alone accounted for over 65 percent. The first component was associated with interior cities such as San Bernardino, Thousand Oaks, and Riverside, whereas the second component was associated with cities on, or close to, the coastline (Figure 7.12). The latter cities included Hermosa Beach, Redondo Beach, San Pedro, and Long Beach. The only exception to this general rule was Malibu, which loaded more heavily on the first component. The overwhelming importance of the first two components in terms of variance accounted for, and their easy interpretation, is significant. It suggests that the subjects, when asked to evaluate the cities according to their relative attractiveness, simply thought in terms of two dimensions: coastal cities and interior cities. As a result, the coastal cities all received similar ratings, as did the interior cities. However, the relative attractiveness of coastal cities in general, as opposed to interior cities in general, varied across individuals.

The results of the principal components analysis of the information surface were less easily interpreted. It required six components to account for 76 percent of the total variance, and no single component accounted for more than approximately 17 percent (Table 7.8). It is noteworthy, however, that cities grouped together in information

TABLE 7.7 PREFERENCE STRUCTURE OF CITIES IN THE LOS ANGELES BASIN

City	Components I	II	III	IV
Anaheim	.808	.383	.289	−.066
Beverly Hills	.656	.715	−.090	−.093
Buena Park	.778	.562	.153	−.120
Burbank	.890	.369	.140	−.034
Downtown L.A.	−.031	−.005	.816	.260
Encino	.724	.603	.070	−.153
Glendale	.855	.317	.215	.223
Hermosa Beach	.481	.817	.094	.174
Huntington Beach	.415	.766	−.001	.269
Inglewood	.660	.681	.062	.018
Long Beach	.442	.780	.323	−.227
Malibu	.786	.549	−.100	.023
Manhattan Beach	.442	.834	.061	.193
Newport Beach	.370	.770	−.053	.006
Palmdale	.253	−.120	.768	.115
Pasadena	.844	.293	.213	.217
Redondo Beach	.491	.786	.096	.203
Riverside	.830	.380	.326	.008
San Bernardino	.723	.570	.290	−.041
San Fernando	.502	.075	.736	−.072
San Pedro	.014	.624	.632	.071
Santa Ana	.857	.350	.328	−.023
Thousand Oaks	.864	.449	−.029	−.060
Torrance	.345	.780	.357	−.208
Universal City	.519	.249	.623	−.149
Van Nuys	.328	.185	.719	−.347
Venice	.064	.153	.334	.817
Watts	−.122	.096	.810	.278
Percent of total variance:	36.4	29.0	16.7	5.0

Note: Underscores indicate highest factor loading for each variable.

Source: M. T. Cadwallader, "Urban information and preference surfaces: Their patterns, structures, and interrelationships," *Geografiska Annaler,* 60 B (1978), Table 3, p. 102.

space also tended to be grouped together in physical space (Figure 7.12). For example, San Bernardino and Riverside were associated with the same component, as were Long Beach and San Pedro, and Hermosa Beach, Manhattan Beach, and Redondo Beach. This finding was not unexpected, as it means that if a person possesses a great deal of information about a city in one particular part of the Los Angeles basin, he or she is also likely to be very familiar with other cities in the same area. As with the preference structure, however, the relative amount of information associated with each group of cities varied from person to person.

TABLE 7.8 INFORMATION STRUCTURE OF CITIES IN THE LOS ANGELES BASIN

	Components					
Cities	I	II	III	IV	V	VI
Anaheim	.333	<u>.611</u>	.261	.141	.504	.234
Beverly Hills	<u>.624</u>	.268	.153	.425	−.145	.000
Buena Park	<u>.792</u>	.103	.253	.030	.363	.214
Burbank	.232	<u>.566</u>	−.024	.031	.493	−.008
Downtown L.A.	.324	−.017	.105	<u>.749</u>	.206	.188
Encino	<u>.644</u>	.041	.566	.115	−.141	.154
Glendale	.071	.131	.183	.193	<u>.789</u>	.119
Hermosa Beach	.358	−.069	.116	.015	.285	<u>.779</u>
Huntington Beach	<u>.750</u>	.036	.006	.390	.246	.272
Inglewood	<u>.605</u>	.113	.037	−.017	.139	.040
Long Beach	.281	.124	<u>.571</u>	.215	.507	.297
Malibu	<u>.672</u>	.423	.046	.376	−.114	.236
Manhattan Beach	.132	.234	.123	.038	.026	<u>.905</u>
Newport Beach	.112	.205	.068	.365	.067	<u>.657</u>
Palmdale	.143	.259	<u>.568</u>	.073	.427	.152
Pasadena	.196	.044	.425	<u>.642</u>	.132	.237
Redondo Beach	.132	−.001	.303	.502	.150	<u>.581</u>
Riverside	.438	<u>.588</u>	.263	.022	.436	.288
San Bernardino	.064	<u>.936</u>	.094	.177	.077	.058
San Fernando	.155	<u>.879</u>	.183	−.082	.009	.055
San Pedro	.296	.140	<u>.512</u>	.258	.506	.175
Santa Ana	<u>.616</u>	.155	.280	.176	.522	.206
Thousand Oaks	<u>.801</u>	.063	.356	.053	.205	.163
Torrance	−.048	−.036	−.285	<u>.862</u>	.040	.007
Universal City	.029	<u>.897</u>	.168	−.027	.127	.118
Van Nuys	.088	.399	<u>.777</u>	−.025	.001	.125
Venice	.203	.204	.324	<u>.473</u>	.326	.125
Watts	.254	.073	<u>.638</u>	−.036	.322	.034
Percent of total variance:	17.3	15.1	11.7	11.0	10.7	10.4

Note: Underscores indicate highest factor loading for each variable.

Source: M.T. Cadwallader, "Urban information and preference surfaces: Their patterns, structures, and interrelationships," *Geografiska Annaler,* 60 B (1978), Table 4, p. 103.

In summary, then, having distinguished between the behavioral and phenomenal environments, we explored in some detail the concept of cognitive maps. More specifically, we discussed how such maps might be elicited from a set of subjects, how they vary according to socioeconomic status, and how they change over time. We concluded by distinguishing between the designative information contained in cognitive maps, especially with respect to distance and direction, and the appraisive information, which invovles the value judgments that we have of different places.

8

Movement Patterns within Cities

8.1 TRAFFIC FORECASTING MODELS

Movement patterns within cities can be categorized as being of either short-term or long-term duration. Short-term, or daily movement, consists of trips involving such activities as work, shopping, and recreation, whereas long-term, or more permanent movement, involves changing residence. In the present chapter we focus on daily movement patterns, especially the journey to shop; residential mobility is considered in Chapter 9. After first considering the nature of traffic forecasting models in general, we then consider the trip distribution component of such models in more detail. Within the context of the journey to shop, we discuss the traditional gravity model approach, the revealed preference approach, the behavioral approach, and a dynamic, or learning-based approach. The exploration of movement patterns is vital for a true understanding of urban areas. Movement both creates, and reflects the spatial structure of cities described in the earlier chapters of this book. For example, the hierarchy of shopping centers in any city is partially a response to consumer preferences with respect to travel behavior, but also a determinant of that travel behavior. Similarly, social neighborhoods within cities are simultaneously created by movement patterns, while also helping to mold those patterns.

Attempts to forecast daily movement patterns involve the construction of four interrelated submodels: trip generation and attraction, trip distribution, modal choice, and trip assignment (Stopher and Meyburg, 1975). These submodels are usually used to forecast traffic flows between regions known as traffic zones and they parallel the kinds of decisions facing the intending traveler. First, there is the initial decision to make a trip, thus contributing to the overall trip generation associated with a particular traffic zone. Second, a destination must be selected, thus contributing to the overall distribution of trips between various pairs of traffic zones. Third, a particular form of transportation must be chosen. Fourth, a particular route must be selected.

Trip Generation and Attraction

There are a variety of variables that influence the amount of *traffic that is generated* by individual traffic zones (Daniels and Warnes, 1980). In particular, the number of automobile trips per family is inversely related to population density. This relationship is partly due to the negative correlation between population density and income, but it also reflects the fact that high-density zones are characterized by a large proportion of walking trips, which are usually excluded from trip generation equations. In addition, the number of automobile trips per family is related to car ownership rates. All other things being equal, as the number of cars owned by a household increases, the daily trips per household also tends to increase. The relationship between car ownership rates and family income also implies that high-income regions within a city tend to generate more than their share of automobile traffic.

Each of the trip generation variables is usually combined within a multiple regression model in order to predict the overall amount of traffic that will be generated by any individual traffic zone. Some of these regression models are very satisfactory, in terms of the associated coefficients of multiple determination (Lane et al., 1973, p. 72), but certain important methodological problems detract from their reliability. For example, the explanatory, or independent variables, are often quite highly intercorrelated. As suggested previously, there is usually a positive relationship between car ownership and income, whereas population density and income tend to be negatively correlated. Where possible, it is desirable to purge the multiple regression model of highly correlated independent variables.

Trip attraction rates for individual traffic zones are related primarily to type of land use. Residential, manufacturing, and public lands appear to generate about the same number of person trip destinations per square mile, but the number associated with commercial land use is often considerably higher. As one would expect, the higher the land use density, the greater the trip attraction rate.

Trip Distribution

Having forecast the number of trips that will be generated by, and attracted to, each individual traffic zone, the next step is to forecast the distribution of trips between pairs of traffic zones. This problem can be conceptualized in terms of an interaction matrix (Fig. 8.1). There are N traffic zones in this hypothetical example. The rows are the origins, representing the traffic generated by each zone, and the columns are the destinations, representing the traffic attracted to each zone. The purpose of any trip distribution model is to forecast the number of trips in each cell of the interaction matrix, such as t_{32}, which indicates the number of trips beginning in zone 3 and ending in zone 2.

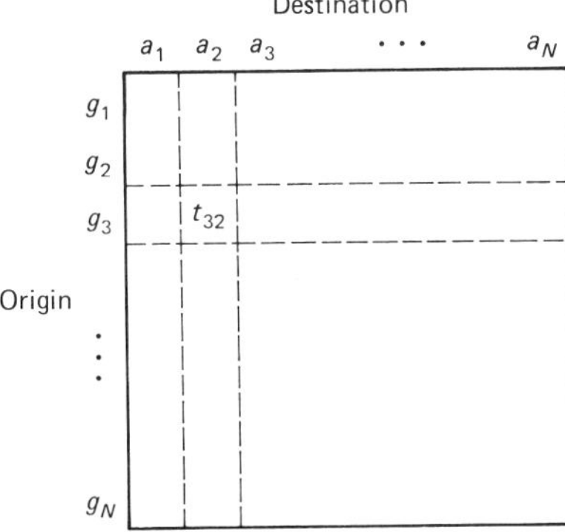

Figure 8.1 Interaction matrix.

Two types of models, or equations, are generally used to predict the distribution of trips within a city. The simplest of these is an equation designed to capture the *friction-of-distance* effect, which reflects the fact that trip numbers are inversely related to increasing distance (Taylor, 1971). More specifically, a curvilinear relationship is usually observed, with the number of trips decreasing quite rapidly at first, and then more gradually (Figure 8.2). Such a relationship is conveniently expressed by a power function, discussed in Chapter 2:

$$T_{ij} = aD_{ij}^{-b} \tag{8.1}$$

where T_{ij} is the number of trips between traffic zones i and j, D_{ij} is the distance between traffic zones i and j, and a and b are constants. Recall that the constants can be estimated by least-squares analysis if the equation is transformed into the following linear function:

$$\log T_{ij} = \log a - b(\log D_{ij}) \tag{8.2}$$

where log refers to common logarithms to the base 10 and the remaining notation is the same as in equation (8.1). The value of b represents the slope of the line and provides a

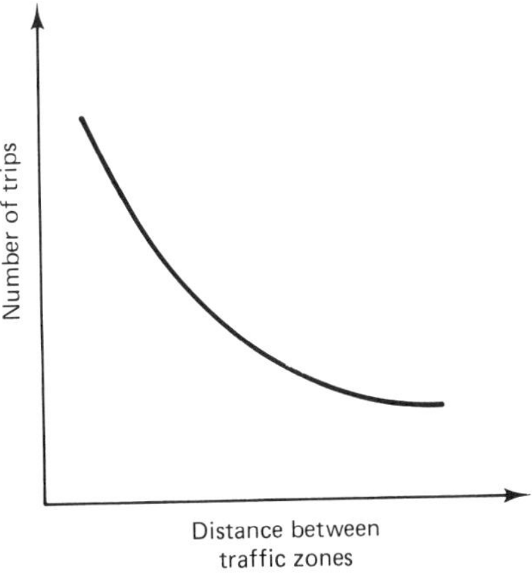

Figure 8.2 Friction-of-distance effect.

TABLE 8.1 FRICTION-OF-DISTANCE EFFECT FOR WALKING TRIPS VERSUS AUTOMOBILE TRIPS

	r	b
Walking trips	−0.986	−2.022
Automobile trips	−0.941	−0.885

Source: R. S. Yuill, "Spatial behavior of retail customers: Some empirical measurements," *Geografiska Annaler*, 49 B (1967), Table 6, p. 111.

numerical value for the frictional effect of distance. In those situations where b has a relatively high value, indicating a steep slope, it means that the number of trips decline very rapidly with increasing distance.

As one might expect, it has been demonstrated that the value of b is at least partially dependent on the mode of transportation involved. For example, in a study of consumer behavior in Ann Arbor, Michigan, Yuill (1967) compared the friction-of-distance curves for automobile and walking trips. As reflected by the correlation coefficients (Table 8.1), both curves were fit very well by a power function, but the frictional effect of distance was much greater for walking trips than for automobile trips.

The *gravity model,* however, is the most popular trip distribution forecasting tool (Tocalis, 1978). In its simplest form it is represented as follows:

$$T_{ij} \propto \frac{P_i P_j}{D_{ij}} \tag{8.3}$$

where P_i is the population of zone i, P_j is the population of zone j, $\propto$ means "proportional to," and the remaining notation is the same as in equation (8.1). A simple example will help to clarify how it is used for traffic forecasting.

Imagine that we have just three traffic zones, labeled A, B, and C, with populations and distances as represented in Figure 8.3. Substituting in equation (8.3), we can predict the proportion of traffic that will flow between each pair of traffic zones. Starting with zones A and B, we obtain:

$$T_{AB} \propto \frac{P_A P_B}{D_{AB}} = \frac{(50)(20)}{10} = \frac{1000}{10} = 100 \tag{8.4}$$

Then, for zones A and C,

$$T_{AC} \propto \frac{P_A P_C}{D_{AC}} = \frac{(50)(40)}{10} = \frac{2000}{10} = 200 \tag{8.5}$$

Finally, for zones B and C,

$$T_{BC} \propto \frac{P_B P_C}{D_{BC}} = \frac{(20)(40)}{5} = \frac{800}{5} = 160 \tag{8.6}$$

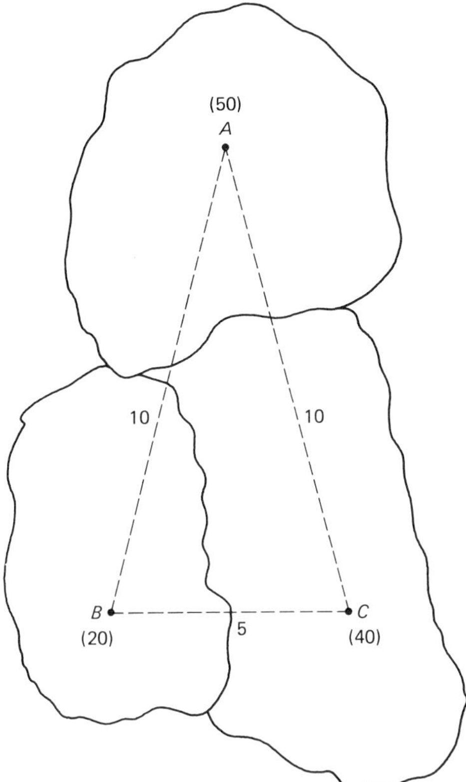

Figure 8.3 Hypothetical gravity model example.

Therefore, if for any given day there are 1000 trips within this hypothetical city, then using equations (8.4), (8.5), and (8.6), we would predict that

$$T_{AB} = \frac{100}{460}(1000) = 217 \tag{8.7}$$

$$T_{AC} = \frac{200}{460}(1000) = 435 \tag{8.8}$$

and

$$T_{BC} = \frac{160}{460}(1000) = 348 \tag{8.9}$$

This general model can be adapted to predict specific types of trips. For example, when considering the journey to work, the gravity model is often rewritten as follows:

$$T_{ij} = a\frac{P_i E_j}{D_{ij}^b} \tag{8.10}$$

where E_j is the number of employment opportunities in zone j, a and b are constants, and the rest of the notation is the same as in equations (8.1) and (8.3). Note that trip generation is measured by population, as it refers to the home end of the work trip, trip attraction is measured by employment opportunities, and the friction of distance effect is included as the denominator.

Modal Choice

Modal choice models attempt to predict which mode of transportation will be chosen for particular journeys. For example, Daniels and Warnes (1980, p. 199) identified five sets of variables that influence the choice of travel mode for the journey to work (Figure 8.4). First, the *location* of the person with respect to his or her workplace will

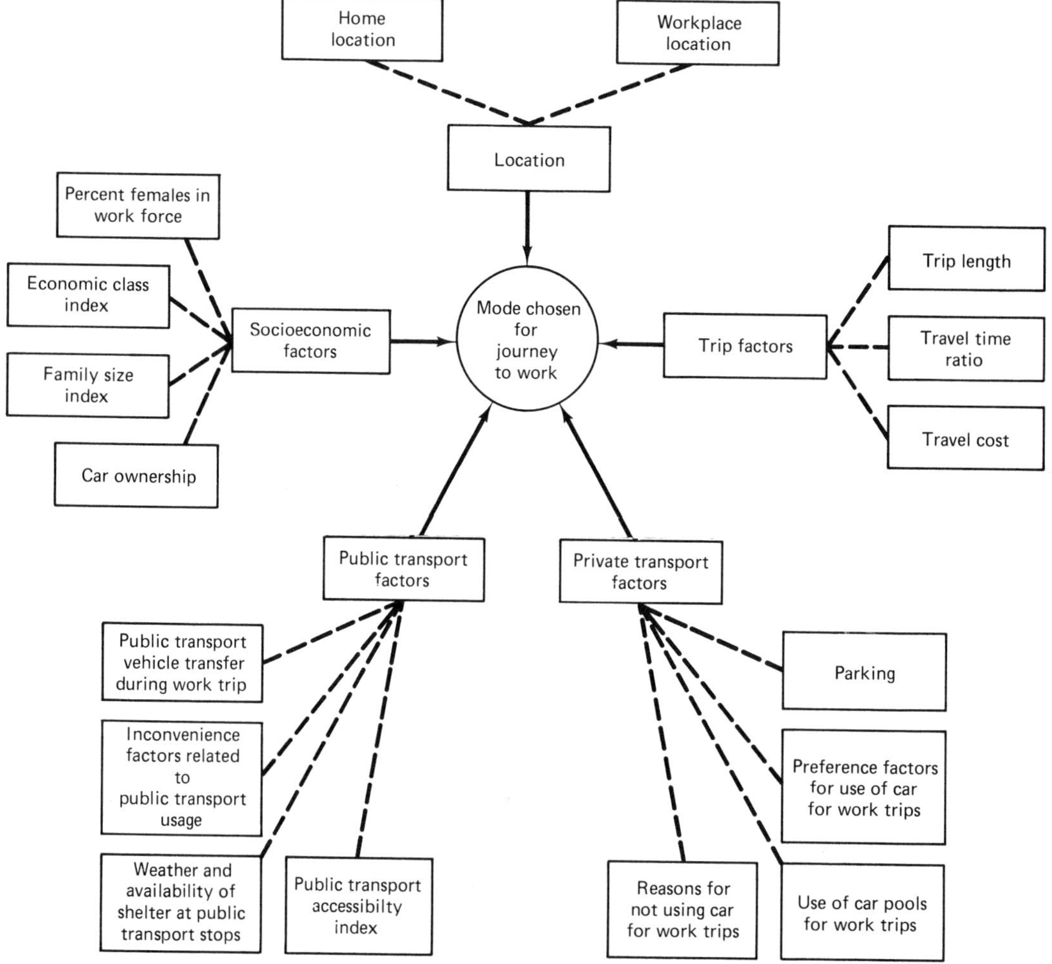

Figure 8.4 Some factors affecting the choice of transportation mode for the journey to work. (From P. W. Daniels and A. M. Warnes, *Movement in Cities: Spatial Perspectives on Urban Transport and Travel,* Methuen, New York, 1980, Fig. 7.4, p. 198.)

obviously make a difference. If the person lives only a few blocks away from work, he or she might well walk or ride a bicycle.

Second, and related to the location factor, are a set of *trip factors.* These factors include the trip length, the travel cost, and the travel-time ratio. The travel-time ratio is often particularly significant, as it compares the travel times associated with different modes of transportation.

Third, there are a number of *private transportation factors.* Parking facilities near the workplace, and the cost of parking, are of primary concern. Also, the availability of suitable car pools will influence the decision of whether to use private transportation.

Fourth, a set of *public transportation factors* are involved. These factors include the accessibility of the person to public transportation facilities, such as buses and trains, and the inconveniences associated with using public transportation. For example, during cold weather the decision to use mass transit systems is often dependent on the availability of bus shelters, and the like.

Fifth, and finally, modal choice is influenced by a set of *socioeconomic factors.* In particular, automobile ownership rates and economic status are important. Areas characterized by high economic status tend to be less dependent on public transportation than are areas characterized by low economic status.

Trip Assignment

The final task, in terms of forecasting traffic flows, is to assign trips to particular roads, or routes, within the city. In other words, trip assignment involves models of route choice. The simplest such model, when predicting flows between traffic zones, postulates that everybody will choose the route with the shortest travel time. This approach is termed an *all-or-nothing assignment,* as one route is assumed to carry all the traffic.

A variety of problems occur when using all-or-nothing assignments (Lane et al., 1973, pp. 102–103). First, as with modal choice, people not only consider travel time when selecting a route, but also travel cost. Second, individual perceptions of travel time will vary. Third, traffic conditions, and therefore travel time, will also vary according to the time of day. Fourth, and most important, when two or more routes are close together, one route has to be only marginally quicker than the others for it to be assigned all of the trips.

In an effort to address this last problem, many transportation models use *proportional assignment* rather than all-or-nothing assignment. Basically, proportional assignment involves assigning proportions of traffic among a number of alternative routes, as a function of the time differences between those routes. Thus, although this approach is more realistic in terms of producing a multipath solution, it remains rather simplistic, as travel time is still the only determinant of route choice.

A more sophisticated, but somewhat cumbersome model of route choice might include variables that attempt to capture travel time in terms of the number of traffic lights, or expected congestion. Similarly, the perceived attractiveness of different routes might be included in the model. In the latter context, the desire to avoid dangerous areas of the city would need to be calibrated in some way.

8.2 THE GRAVITY MODEL APPROACH

In the present section and the following three, we focus our attention on the trip-distribution component of the traffic forecasting model. In particular, we explore the traditional gravity model approach, the revealed preference approach, the behavioral approach, and a dynamic, or learning-based approach. Each of these approaches will be examined within the context of a particular kind of spatial interaction, that of shopping behavior, to facilitate comparisons. In this sense, the problem becomes one of describing and explaining how consumers choose between various kinds of spatial alternatives, as represented by individual supermarkets or shopping centers. At the same time, however, it should be remembered that these same approaches can be applied to a variety of other kinds of movement patterns.

Reilly's Law of Retail Gravitation

Reilly (1931) presented one of the first mathematical formulations of a gravity concept of human interaction in his study of the retail trade areas associated with cities in Texas. He postulated that two cities would attract consumers from some smaller, intermediate city in direct proportion to their population sizes, and in inverse proportion to the square of their distances from the intermediate city. More formally, he expressed these relationships as follows:

$$\frac{B_a}{B_b} = \frac{P_a}{P_b}\left(\frac{D_b}{D_a}\right)^2 \tag{8.11}$$

where B represents the proportion of retail business from the intermediate city attracted to city a and city b, P is population, and D is distance from the intermediate city.

This same model can be applied just as easily to shopping behavior within a particular city by imagining that a and b represent supermarkets, or shopping centers, and that there is some neighborhood, or census tract, located between them. In this context, the model predicts the proportion of households from the intermediate neighborhood that patronize each of the two supermarkets. The population size variable can be replaced by retail floor space in the case of supermarkets, and by number of individual establishments in the case of shopping centers.

A simple, hypothetical example will serve to clarify the use of equation (8.11). Figure 8.5 depicts a situation in which there are two supermarkets, a and b, that draw consumers from some intermediate neighborhood, X. The sizes and distances are represented, and the symbol S, for supermarket size, has replaced the population term in Reilly's original formulation. By substituting the appropriate values in the equation, it

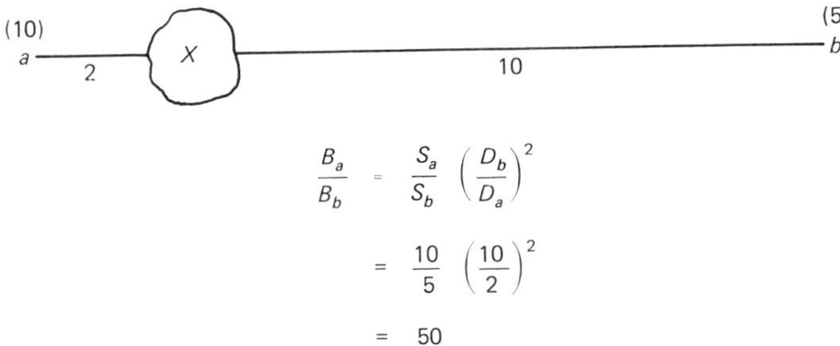

Figure 8.5 Reilly's law of retail gravitation.

can be calculated that supermarket a should receive 50 times as much trade from the intermediate neighborhood as does supermarket b.

Reilly's law of retail gravitation is representative of what is known as the *social physics approach* to understanding human behavior, as an effort is made to construct a theory of interaction based on an analogy with Newtonian physics (Tocalis, 1978). In this respect, Reilly suggested that interaction can be understood in terms of a mass-divided-by-distance formulation, and to maintain the analogy with Newton's laws of motion, the distance term was squared. The use of the distance variable is comparable to the friction-of-distance concept described earlier, except that in the latter context the exponent associated with distance is not determined a priori, but is empirically estimated for a particular set of data.

Reilly's law of retail gravitation was later modified by Converse (1949) to create the *breaking-point formula*. This modification makes it possible to predict the point between two competing supermarkets or shopping centers where the trading influence of each is equal. The breaking-point formula is expressed as follows:

$$D_a = \frac{D_{ab}}{1 + \sqrt{S_b / S_a}} \tag{8.12}$$

where D_a is the breaking point between supermarkets a and b measured in miles from supermarket a, S is supermarket size, and D_{ab} is the distance separating the two supermarkets. Using the values in Figure 8.5, and substituting them in equation (8.12), we obtain the following:

$$D_a = \frac{12}{1 + \sqrt{5/10}} = 7.03 \tag{8.13}$$

Thus the breaking point is approximately 7 miles from supermarket a. Note that if we wish to calculate the distance of the breaking point from supermarket b, we simply divide the size of a by the size of b in the denominator of equation (8.12).

In the presence of a set of competing supermarkets, or shopping centers, the breaking-point formula can be used to predict the retail trade area associated with any individual supermarket or shopping center. Figure 8.6 illustrates the situation where

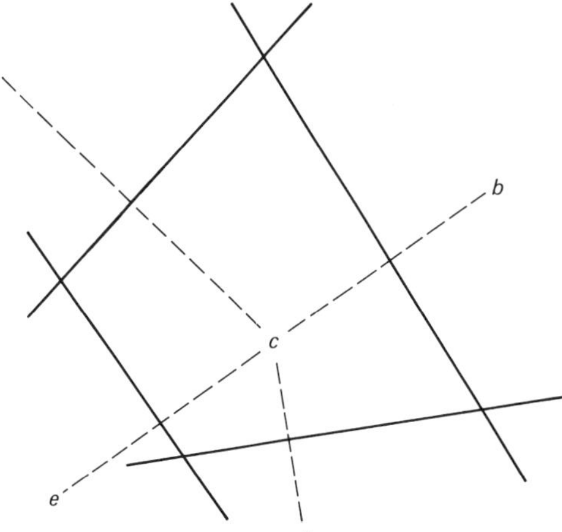

Figure 8.6 Estimating a retail trade area using the breaking-point formula.

there are five competing supermarkets, of various sizes, and depicts supermarket *c*'s trade area by lines drawn through the breaking points associated with supermarket *c* and each of the other four supermarkets. As can be judged from the regular geometrical shape of this trade area, however, the delimitation of trade areas using the breaking-point formula can be regarded only as a highly generalized representation of reality. Actual trade areas will be far more irregularly shaped, as discussed in Section 4.2.

A Probabilistic Model

Huff (1964) has suggested an alternative model for delimiting retail trade areas in which the trade area is represented in terms of probability contours (Figure 8.7a). A person located at *X* has a probability between 0.9 and 1.0 of patronizing supermarket *a*, while a person located at *Y* has a probability of 0.8. The probability contours for competing supermarkets within a given area can be superimposed on each other, so that a person located at *X* in Figure 8.7b has a 0.75 probability of going to supermarket *a* and a 0.25 probability of going to supermarket *b*. Note that the probabilities associated with the alternative opportunities, or supermarkets, sum to 1.

Huff suggested that the necessary probabilities, to create the probability contours, can be estimated by calculating the ratio of the utility, or attractiveness, of a particular supermarket to the total utility of all the supermarkets. Symbolically, this ratio can be expressed as follows:

$$P_{ij} = \frac{U_j}{\sum_{j=1}^{M} U_j} \tag{8.14}$$

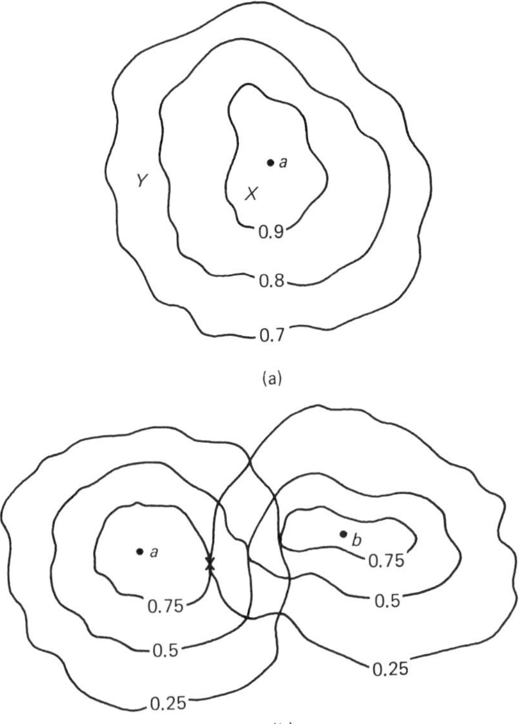

Figure 8.7 Retail trade areas represented by probability contours.

where P_{ij} is the probability of a consumer at location i traveling to supermarket j, U is the utility value associated with each supermarket, and M is the number of supermarkets. Huff postulated that the utility value of any supermarket, for any particular consumer, is directly proportional to the size of that supermarket, and inversely proportional to its distance from the consumer. Thus the utility associated with supermarket j can be expressed as follows:

$$U_{ij} = \frac{S_j}{T_{ij}^b} \tag{8.15}$$

where U_{ij} is the utility value of supermarket j for consumer i, S_j is the size of supermarket j as measured by retail floor space, T_{ij} is the travel time involved in getting from i to j, and b is an exponent reflecting the frictional effect of distance, as discussed in Section 8.1. By substituting the size and distance terms from equation (8.15) in equation (8.14), we get the following expression:

$$P_{ij} = \frac{S_j / T_{ij}^b}{\sum_{j=1}^{M} S_j / T_{ij}^b} \tag{8.16}$$

where the notation is the same as in equations (8.14) and (8.15).

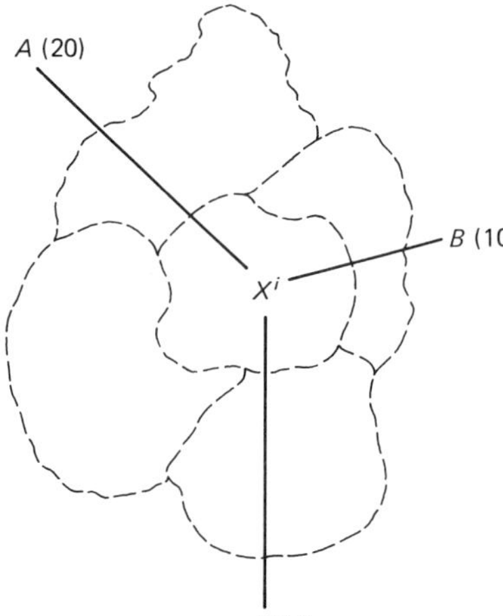

Figure 8.8 Hypothetical example to illustrate Huff's probability model.

A hypothetical example will help to clarify how equation (8.16) is used to obtain the required probabilities. Imagine that we have an individual consumer located at *i*, who has to choose between three supermarkets, labeled *A*, *B*, and *C* (Figure 8.8). For computational ease we will assume that *b*, representing the frictional effect of distance, is 1. Then, substituting in equation (8.16), we can calculate the probability associated with supermarket *A* as follows:

$$P_{iA} = \frac{20/5}{20/5 + 10/2 + 5/5} = 0.4 \tag{8.17}$$

Similarly, the probabilities associated with supermarkets *B* and *C* turn out to be 0.5 and 0.1, respectively.

This model can also be used at an aggregate, as well as an individual level of analysis. Suppose that we are dealing with census tracts rather than individual consumers, as represented by the dashed lines in Figure 8.8. Then the expected number of consumers within a given census tract *i* that will patronize a particular supermarket *j* is equal to the number of consumers within *i* multiplied by the probability that any one of them will select supermarket *j*. That is,

$$E_{ij} = P_{ij} C_i \tag{8.18}$$

where E_{ij} is the expected number of consumers within census tract *i* who will patronize supermarket *j*, P_{ij} is the probability that any given consumer within census tract *i* will patronize supermarket *j*, and C_i is the total number of consumers within census tract *i*. Similarly, we can estimate the total demand for any particular supermarket by simply adding up the number of expected consumers from each census tract, as follows:

$$TD_j = \sum_{i=1}^{N} P_{ij} C_i \tag{8.19}$$

where TD_j is the total number of consumers expected to patronize supermarket j, N is the number of census tracts, and the remaining notation is the same as in equation (8.18).

Despite its probabilistic nature, Huff's model is very similar to Reilly's law of retail gravitation, as the utilities associated with the different supermarkets are simply a function of size and distance. Huff's formulation does have certain distinct advantages, however. First, it allows the retail trade areas to be graduated in terms of probabilities. Second, as reflected by the denominator in equation (8.16), the attractiveness of any individual supermarket takes into account the attractiveness of all other supermarkets. Third, the exponent reflecting the frictional effect of distance is free to vary, rather than being arbitrarily set at 2.

However, although it has been demonstrated that the gravity model is a useful predictor of aggregate consumer behavior, it has often been argued that such an approach is incapable of articulating an explanation of that behavior in terms of the underlying decision-making process. Although efforts have been made to erect a theoretical foundation for the gravity model, especially within the contexts of utility theory (Sheppard, 1978) and statistical mechanics (Wilson, 1971), in many ways it is still little more than a crude physical analogy of the individual choice strategy. For example, it is probably naive to presume that people choose stores to patronize by simply making a psychological trade-off between size and distance. In other words, the gravity model can be regarded as a kind of black box which provides useful information about aggregate consumer behavior for reasons which are not altogether clear at the level of individual consumers (Bucklin, 1971), although it is worthwhile remembering that the original gravity model was not intended to be a model of micro-level behavior. Attempts to probe inside this black box, in order to understand something about the decision-making process itself, have led to an interest in the revealed preference approach, and it is to this particular approach to understanding consumer spatial behavior that we now turn our attention.

8.3 THE REVEALED PREFERENCE APPROACH

The revealed preference approach involves the examination of observed behavior in order to uncover the underlying preference structure, and so establish rules of spatial behavior (Pipkin, 1979). In this respect, the use of revealed preferences can be viewed as a reaction to the gravity type of models, where the exponents are dependent on the spatial structure of the area within which the model is calibrated, and so provide only descriptions of behavior in space, rather than fundamental parameters of some spatial choice theory (Timmermans and Rushton, 1979). The concept of revealed preferences has been extensively utilized within the theory of consumer demand, where it has been argued that it is possible to obtain a unique ranking of objects from any consistent statement of preferences derived from the paired comparisons of those objects (Samuelson, 1948). Such a ranking can be graphically portrayed in terms of an *indifference surface,* which shows different combinations of goods between which the consumer is indifferent. In the present context, the objects to be ranked are supermarkets, or shopping centers, and we have already come across the notion of an indifference curve when discussing the concept of bid-rents (see Section 2.1).

The gravity model can be explored via the revealed preference approach, as it implies that consumers make a trade-off between the size of a supermarket or shopping center, and the distance to that supermarket or shopping center (Rushton, 1969). Figure 8.9a illustrates such a trade-off, where the indifference lines join equal values of size divided by distance, and thus represent various combinations of size and distance that consumers rank equally attractive. Consumers would prefer to be on the highest indifference line, as this line indicates those supermarkets or shopping centers that are among the largest and closest. Reilly's particular formulation of the gravity model, in which distance is squared, would imply the series of indifference curves shown in Figure 8.9b. The use of an exponent greater than 1 indicates that longer distances play a proportionately more important role than do shorter distances in terms of establishing the underlying preference structure.

Similarly, central place theory (see Section 4.2) implies the set of indifference

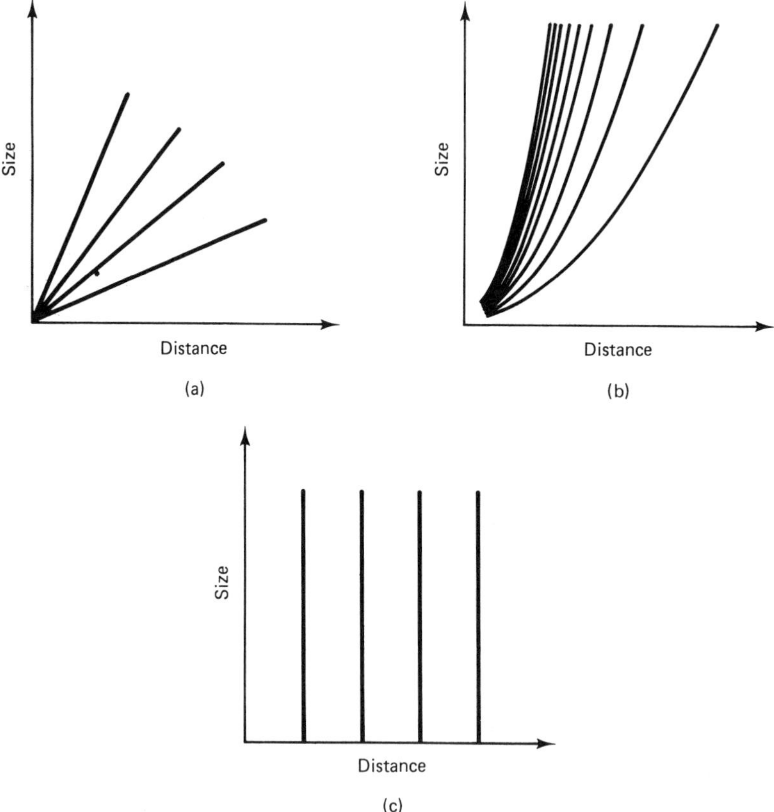

Figure 8.9 Examples of indifference curves.

lines shown in Figure 8.9c. Recall that one of the fundamental assumptions of central place theory is that consumers will patronize the nearest store offering the desired good. This assumption results in a set of vertical indifference lines, as it means that consumers care only about distance and are completely indifferent to variations in size. All consumers are assumed to prefer the left-hand indifference lines, because these are associated with the shortest distances. The greater the degree of substitution between the variables, in this case size and distance, the more the indifference curves will depart from the vertical, or the horizontal.

The aim of the revealed preference approach is to derive the form of the indifference curves empirically from an analysis of overt, or observed behavior. In this way, the actual trade-offs between various combinations of variables, in any given situation, can be identified (Rushton, 1981). A hypothetical example will help to clarify the underlying methodology. Assume that we ask a person to rank order the five available supermarkets in a particular city, according to how often he or she uses them. Such a task might generate the data shown in Figure 8.10a, where the distance and size associated with each supermarket are also represented. From these data the indifference curves can be mapped (Figure 8.10b), noting that the tied ranks for

Supermarket	Rank	Size (square feet)	Distance (miles)
A	3	4,000	20
B	2	4,000	15
C	1	5,000	8
D	3	3,000	10
E	5	2,000	20

(a)

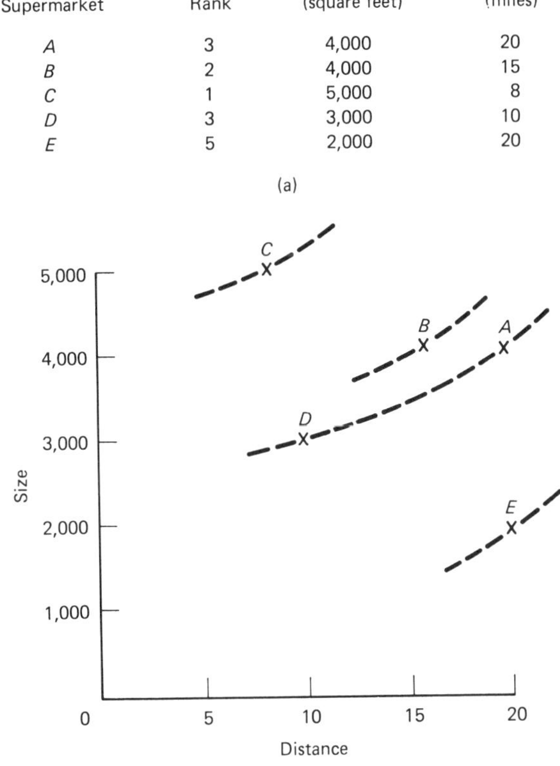

(b)

Figure 8.10 Deriving a person's indifference curves.

supermarkets A and D indicate that they both lie on the same curve. The consumer prefers to be on the uppermost curve, as this represents the most attractive combination of size and distance. In general, however, we wish to generate the indifference curves for a group of consumers, rather than a single consumer, in order to filter out the effect of individual idiosyncracies. The next section describes some of the results obtained from one such aggregate study.

An Empirical Example

The data used in the analysis were obtained, via questionnaires, from 521 households in the city of Christchurch, New Zealand (Clark and Rushton, 1970). Each household was requested to identify its major supply center for six commodities, including groceries, and data were collected regarding the size of these supply centers, and their distance from the household. It was argued that if a particular spatial opportunity was chosen whenever it was present, that opportunity is the most preferred one in the consumer's mental ranking of alternatives. On the other hand, a spatial opportunity that was never chosen, even when available, must occupy the lowest rank in the consumer's evaluation of alternatives.

With this argument in mind, the following index was constructed to reflect the mental ordering of spatial alternatives:

$$I_{ij} \frac{A_{ij}}{P_{ij}} \tag{8.20}$$

where I_{ij} is the index value for center size class i and distance class j, A_{ij} is the number of households that chose to patronize a center in the ith center size class and the jth distance class, and P_{ij} is the total number of households that could have chosen a center in the ith center size class and the jth distance class. So the index represents the ratio of the number of times a spatial opportunity was chosen to the number of times it was available to be chosen.

Table 8.2 contains the values for this index, in the context of grocery shopping, for 10 center size and distance classes. For example, the values in the top left-hand cell indicate that out of a possible number of 87 households, 36 actually chose this particular combination combination of size and distance, giving an index value of 41.38 percent. A pictorial representation of the index values is provided in Figure 8.11. The lines are indifference curves, implying that a household is indifferent between all the spatial opportunities represented on any one indifference curve. Also, each household should prefer any alternative on a higher curve to one on a lower curve.

These indifference curves, then, represent the actual trade-off between size and distance in the context of grocery shopping. The behavior with respect to a number of different kinds of commodities can be compared, using these indifference curves, as long as the size and distance scales are kept the same. Relatively speaking, the steeper the slope, the greater the influence of distance, and we might expect the slope to vary according to the type of good. In general, convenience goods are characterized by

TABLE 8.2 GROCERY PURCHASES IN CHRISTCHURCH, NEW ZEALAND: THE RANKING OF SPATIAL ALTERNATIVES

	Distance to center of major grocery purchases (hundredths of a mile)									
Center size (functions)	0–13	13–26	26–38	38–51	51–76	76–101	101–201	201–301	301–401	401–9000
0–2	87	255	362	516	1370	1781	9974	13755	14822	35763
	36	30	11	8	9	1	1	1	1	0
	41.38	11.76	3.04	1.55	0.66	0.01	0.01	0.01	0.01	0.00
3	17	37	73	106	252	361	2175	2915	3277	8607
	7	6	5	1	3	1	1	0	0	0
	41.18	16.22	6.85	0.94	1.19	0.28	0.05	0.00	0.00	0.00
4	10	27	40	42	157	206	1230	1946	1985	5742
	3	8	2	1	2	1	0	0	0	0
	30.00	29.63	5.00	2.38	1.27	0.49	0.00	0.00	0.00	0.00
5–6	12	33	45	72	203	272	1448	1900	2139	5756
	6	11	4	4	6	2	1	2	0	1
	50.00	33.33	8.89	5.56	2.96	0.74	0.07	0.11	0.00	0.00
7–8	11	19	35	37	94	158	927	1186	1400	6528
	8	6	8	1	0	1	1	0	0	0
	72.73	31.58	22.86	2.70	0.00	0.63	0.11	0.00	0.00	0.00
9–10	10	23	34	51	105	149	868	1171	1462	4542
	9	12	6	4	4	1	0	0	1	0
	90.00	52.17	17.65	7.84	3.81	0.67	0.00	0.00	0.07	0.00
11–13	3	12	18	23	102	114	662	991	1045	2970
	3	3	4	2	3	0	3	0	0	0
	100.00	25.00	22.22	8.70	2.94	0.00	0.45	0.00	0.00	0.00
14–15	7	18	23	49	112	137	926	1205	1419	3529
	2	8	3	5	3	2	3	0	0	0
	28.57	44.44	13.04	10.20	2.86	1.46	0.32	0.00	0.00	0.00
16–27	12	32	43	67	147	193	1052	1366	1554	3949
	8	20	13	7	11	8	5	1	1	1
	66.67	62.50	30.23	10.45	7.48	4.15	0.48	0.07	0.06	0.03
28	2	22	20	47	112	148	991	1420	1427	2741
	2	18	8	18	19	10	23	18	7	8
	100.00	81.32	40.00	38.30	16.96	6.76	2.32	1.27	0.49	0.29

Note: For each group of three values, the first is the possible; the second, the actual; and the third, the percent actual to possible.

Source: W. A. V. Clark and G. Rushton, "Models of intra-urban consumer behavior and their implications for central place theory," *Economic Geography*, 46 (1970), Table 2, p. 494.

steeper slopes than are luxury items, as consumers are prepared to travel much farther to purchase a car than to purchase a loaf of bread.

The revealed preference approach has been subjected to a certain amount of criticism, because it has been argued that only purely discretionary behavior can be analyzed meaningfully in terms of revealed preferences (Pirie, 1976). In those situations

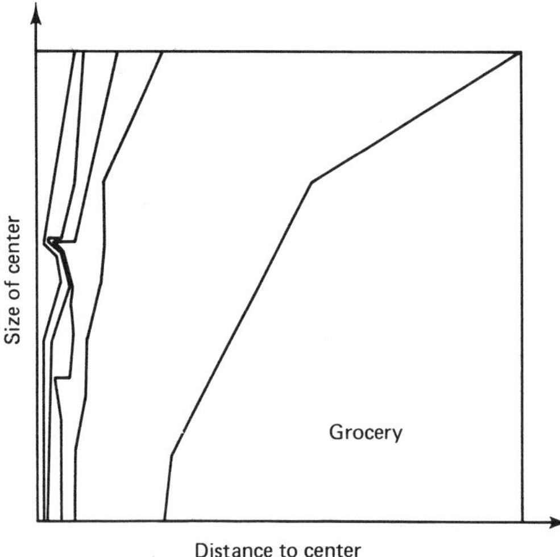

Figure 8.11 Indifference curves for grocery purchases. (From W. A. V. Clark and G. Rushton, "Models of intra-urban consumer behavior and their implications for central place theory," *Economic Geography* 46, 1970, Fig. 6, p. 495.)

where the choice is constrained in some way, such as when the shopping trip must be combined with the journey to work, it is the study of the constraints themselves that may prove to be the most rewarding. Furthermore, it has also been argued that as space itself is a constraint on choice, because of imperfect information and awareness spaces, as well as being a dimension of choice, as represented by distance, we cannot assume that preferences are independent of the environment in which they are studied (MacLennan and Williams, 1979). Thus Timmerman's (1979) suggested incorporation of discontinuous consumer awareness spaces into the basic preference model is of prime importance. Until the extent of various information constraints on decision making can be identified, we cannot truly know the degree to which observed behavior reflects underlying preferences.

Since the revealed preference approach enables one only to deduce a preferential ordering for the range of spatial opportunities that are available in the study area, some researchers have attempted to develop experimental designs that allow attribute values to be manipulated such that a variety of abstract combinations can be produced, thus creating a set of hypothetical alternatives that is independent of any particular spatial structure. Perhaps the most popular approaches, in this context, have been information integration theory and the conjoint measurement model. *Information integration theory*, and its associated method of "functional measurement," has been applied to a wide variety of behaviors (Louviere and Norman, 1977; Louviere and Henley, 1977). The procedure essentially involves constructing an algebraic model of human information processing, and then testing that model by means of analysis of variance. One of the major disadvantages of the technique, however, is that the experimental levels associated with each of the attributes have to be predetermined by the experimenter, and these levels will not necessarily coincide with the internalized thresholds for these attributes held by the subjects themselves.

The *conjoint measurement model,* like information integration theory, is also used in an experimental context, and provides a method for defining a utility value for each alternative as a joint effect of its constituent attributes (Odland and Jakubs, 1977). The coefficients associated with these attributes indicate their individual contributions to the overall utility value. Studies of supermarket choice and migration (Lieber, 1979; Schuler, 1979) have successfully utilized the conjoint measurement technique, and its main advantage over the revealed preference approach is that subjects are directly evaluating the attributes assumed to underlie supermarket or shopping center preferences, rather than the alternatives themselves (Prosperi and Schuler, 1976). It is in this respect that the derived rules of spatial choice are considered to be independent of the particular opportunity set being considered. As in information integration theory, however, the subject is presented with combinations of hypothetical levels of different attributes, and it is the necessary prior selection of these levels that constitutes one of the weaknesses of this approach.

In the next section we consider an approach that is rather different from the revealed preference approach, although the overall aims are very similar. In the behavioral approach, the underlying rules or preferences associated with spatial behavior are not deduced from the analysis of observed behavior. Rather, they are hypothesized in an a priori fashion by constructing a decision-making model, and then are tested by comparing the predictions derived from the model with actual behavior.

8.4 THE BEHAVIORAL APPROACH

Like the revealed preference approach, the behavioral approach is based on the premise that there are regularities in spatial behavior, and that these regularities are invariant across different spatial structures. That is, it is assumed that there are some innate rules of spatial behavior, regardless of structure. Consequently, it is argued, we need to identify these basic behavioral postulates, in contrast to the strategy of merely explaining behavior in terms of the structure in which it is operating.

In general, behavioral geographers have attempted to replace the behaviorally unsatisfactory concept of "economic man," and its attendant assumptions of profit maximization and perfect information, with a more realistic counterpart (Pipkin, 1981). Following Simon (1957), it has been suggested that a more realistic model of human beings would combine the principles of *satisficing* behavior and bounded rationality. In other words, it is assumed that people are sometimes satisfied with less than optimal profit levels, and decisions are often made in a context of incomplete knowledge and uncertainty. The rejection of "economic man" as a workable descriptive model of human beings appears eminently reasonable, as complete rationality with respect to the real world is but one of a range of possible behaviors. However, as Harvey (1981) has pointed out, care must be taken to replace it with something that is amenable to operationalization and is theoretically useful. As yet, due to the difficulties involved in determining aspiration levels, the satisficer concept has proven very difficult to operationalize.

By comparison to the satisficing concept, the *principle of bounded rationality* appears to be more promising. It takes into account our simplified and distorted view of reality, thus attempting to explain behavior in space in terms of the individual's perception of that space. In this sense, the principle of bounded rationality is very similar to the concept of a behavioral environment that was discussed in Section 7.1. This line of reasoning does not deny that "economic man" is a very powerful tool in a normative context, but simply emphasizes that the behavioral approach is concerned with identifying regularities in actual, not optimal behavior.

A Behavioral Model of Consumer Spatial Decision Making

The present author (Cadwallader, 1975) has constructed and tested a decision-making model that conveniently illustrates the behavioral approach to understanding consumer spatial behavior. For our purposes *decision making* is defined as the cognitive process of selecting from among alternatives, and in this particular example the alternatives are represented by five different supermarkets. The general form of the model has already been discussed within the context of the model building process (see Section 1.4).

Around every household, or group of households, there exists an objectively defined *opportunity set*. That is, within a certain radius around every household, there is a finite number of supermarkets. The problem then becomes one of analyzing how the household chooses among the alternatives presented by the opportunity set. In the present instance the aim is to construct a model that is capable of predicting the proportion of consumers who will choose each of the five different supermarkets. If this is successfully accomplished, it suggests that some of the major variables involved in the decision-making process have been identified.

The *conceptual form* of the model postulates that a prospective consumer sorts his or her information about each store, in order to form judgments about their relative attractiveness and accessibility. The interplay between these two factors, attractiveness and distance, is then translated into an overt response. After a store has been patronized, there will be a feedback effect as regards the amount, and nature, of the information that the consumer possesses concerning his or her opportunities. This new information will cause the consumer to reassess his or her judgments regarding the relative merits of each store. In this way the decision-making process keeps repeating itself, and the stores are continually reevaluated in the light of new information. The model can be regarded as a dynamic process–response model. Initially, in the search stage, there will be major fluctuations in the response pattern, as consumers try to acquaint themselves with the system of opportunities. Eventually, however, a more consistent response pattern will develop (Golledge and Brown, 1967). Any changes in the system of opportunities, such as the appearance of a new store, are likely to result in renewed search behavior.

The *model* suggests that the proportion of consumers patronizing a particular store will depend on the interplay among attractiveness, distance, and information. Symbolically these relationships can be expressed as follows:

$$P_i = f(A_i, D_i, I_i) \tag{8.21}$$

where P_i is the proportion of consumers patronizing supermarket i, A_i is some measure of the attractiveness of supermarket i, D_i is some measure of the distance to supermarket i from the consumers' homes, and I_i is some measure of the amount of information generated by supermarket i. More specifically, it is postulated that the proportion of consumers patronizing any particular store increases with increasing attractiveness, and decreases with increasing distance. This trade-off between distance and attractiveness operates in conjunction with an information variable. The stores that are known to exist by more consumers will tend to attract more trade; a consumer cannot patronize a store that is outside his or her field of information. These particular relationships can be expressed as follows:

$$P_i = \frac{A_i}{D_i} I_i \tag{8.22}$$

where the notation is the same as in equation (8.21).

It is noteworthy that this kind of formulation is very different from that contained in central place theory, where it is assumed that consumer behavior is solely distance minimizing, and that the attributes of the stores are identical. It is, however, similar to a gravity model formulation, with the addition of the information variable. The major difference between this model and the conventional gravity model lies in the specification of the mass and distance variables. In the present model these variables are measured subjectively by the consumers, whereas in the more conventional forms of the gravity model the mass is measured according to some objective criterion, such as retail floor space, and distance is measured in terms of physical distance. Also, the conventional models generally specify the distance variable in exponential form. This is not done in the present model, however, as the intention is to show how the distance variable may be most suitably defined, rather than to search for the best exponent. In this context it should be noted that the exponent attached to the distance variable may well vary according to the particular pattern of spatial alternatives under investigation. However, the most appropriate definition of distance, either cognitive time distance, cognitive distance, or physical distance, is likely to remain the same, irrespective of any particular configuration of spatial opportunities.

The following paragraphs describe how each part of the model can be *operationalized,* and then the output from the model is compared with observed behavior. This comparison provides an indication of the predictive capacity of the model. The data for this research were collected, by questionnaires, from 53 households located in west Los Angeles. The questions were answered by the member of the family who was normally responsible for the grocery shopping. Only the static form of the model is tested, as the data collected preclude analysis of the feedback effect.

In accordance with the behavioral approach, *supermarket attractiveness* is evaluated by the consumers themselves. In the present instance supermarket attractiveness is measured across four variables: (1) speed of checkout service, (2) range of goods sold, (3) quantity of goods sold, and (4) prices. These variables were chosen on

TABLE 8.3 ATTRACTIVENESS MATRIX

	Supermarkets				
	A	*B*	*C*	*D*	*E*
Checkout service	4.62	5.39	5.13	5.71	4.78
Price	3.34	6.00	5.33	6.00	3.82
Quality of goods	6.57	5.24	5.33	5.86	5.33
Range of goods	6.74	5.16	5.40	5.29	4.77

Source: M. T. Cadwallader, "A behavioral model of consumer spatial decision making," *Economic Geography,* 51 (1975), Table 3, p. 343.

the basis of a pilot study, in which consumers were asked to list those factors which they considered most important when selecting a supermarket. The items mentioned most often were included in the final questionnaire.

Each supermarket was rated by the consumers with respect to each of the four variables. This was accomplished by using a seven-point rating scale going from very unsatisfactory to very satisfactory. The resulting scale values for each store on each variable were then aggregated, using the median scale values, into a 4 by 5 attractiveness matrix (Table 8.3). This matrix indicates, for example, that the average level of satisfaction with supermarket *B*, with respect to prices, is 6.0. It is noteworthy that in some cases there are relatively small disparities between the stores with respect to a particular variable. For example, the highest value for the checkout service is 5.71 and the lowest value is 4.62. There are two possible reasons for this. First, it could be that the differences between the supermarkets as regards the checkout service are not sufficiently large to warrant significant differentiation. Second, it could be related to the methodology. As already noted, the subjects were provided with a seven-point scale, and the tendency is to choose the middle points on the scale. The effect of this is magnified when the median values are used, as is the case here.

The consumers were also asked to rank the variables in order of their importance in selecting a supermarket. This ranking produced a row weighting vector, the values of which have been standardized so that they add to 1 (Table 8.4). This vector shows, for example, that the prices and quality of goods sold are judged to be of equal importance. The attractiveness matrix was then premultiplied by this row weighting vector. In effect, this means that the scores on each variable, and the resulting

TABLE 8.4 WEIGHTING VECTOR

Checkout service	0.13
Price	0.32
Quality of goods	0.32
Range of goods	0.23

Source: M. T. Cadwallader, "A behavioral model of consumer spatial decision making," *Economic Geography,* 51 (1975), Table 4. p. 343.

TABLE 8.5 ATTRACTIVENESS VECTOR

Supermarket *A*	5.322
Supermarket *B*	5.485
Supermarket *C*	5.321
Supermarket *D*	5.754
Supermarket *E*	4.646

Source: M. T. Cadwallader, "A behavioral model of consumer spatial decision making," *Economic Geography,* 51 (1975), Table 5, p. 344.

aggregate attractiveness of each store, are adjusted by the importance consumers attach to each variable. The resulting row vector describes the relative attractiveness of each supermarket (Table 8.5). This vector indicates that supermarket *D* is perceived to be the most attractive supermarket. It is significant that, in order for the variables to be additive, they are assumed to be independent. In general, this seems to be reasonable. For example, there is no reason to suppose that the range of goods sold is related to the quality of goods sold. The only exceptions to this assumption might be the quality of goods sold and prices, where one might expect some interdependence.

The construction of this attractiveness index is similar to the work of Kotler (1968), who was concerned with the problem of brand loyalties. Kotler developed what he called a competitive marketing mix matrix, which summarized the average market perception of three different brands across eight different dimensions of competition. Golledge (1970) later applied Kotler's model to shopping centers, but the distance variable was not separated out from the other variables, such as prices and product quality.

The next step in the model construction is to operationalize the concept of *distance.* This is accomplished by using three different measures of distance: cognitive distance, cognitive time distance, and physical distance. This means that the trade-off between store attractiveness and distance can be expressed in the following three ways:

$$A_i/CD_i \tag{8.23}$$

$$A_i/CTD_i \tag{8.24}$$

$$A_i/PD_i \tag{8.25}$$

where A_i is the attractiveness of store i, CD_i is the cognitive distance to store i as measured by the method of direct magnitude estimation (see Section 7.3), CTD_i is the cognitive time distance to store i, and PD_i is the physical distance to store i. The median value for each distance measure, to each supermarket, was computed (Table 8.6). It is evident that there is some variation in the distance measures as regards the ordering of alternatives. For example, supermarket *D* is perceived to be closer than supermarket *C* in terms of cognitive time distance, but farther away in terms of cognitive distance. This difference is not surprising, as the two variables are measuring two different kinds of cognitive distances. In this situation the aim is to identify which of these distance measures should be inserted in models of consumer behavior.

TABLE 8.6 COGNITIVE AND PHYSICAL DISTANCES TO EACH SUPERMARKET

Supermarket	*CD*	*CTD* (minutes)	*PD* (miles)
A	100	5.18	0.55
B	100	5.26	0.43
C	258	10.48	1.60
D	289	10.22	1.75
E	192	7.42	0.80

Source: M. T. Cadwallader, "A behavioral model of consumer spatial decision making," *Economic Geography,* 51 (1975), Table 6, p. 345.

Having operationalized the concepts of attractiveness and distance, all that remains is to specify how the level of *information* is measured. In the present study this is accomplished very simply. Information is regarded as a dichotomous variable; a consumer is either aware of a particular store or is unaware of that store. Following from this, the level of information associated with each store is measured by the proportion of consumers who are aware of that store (Table 8.7). This vector indicates, for example, that whereas all the consumers are aware of supermarket A, only 60 percent are aware of supermarket D. It is obvious that these disparities in levels of information must be incorporated within any worthwhile model, as without this constraint the attractiveness matrix is grossly misleading.

The final step is to combine the measures of attractiveness, distance, and information into the *complete model.* Because of the three different distance measures, we obtain the following three formulations:

$$P_i = \frac{A_i}{CD_i} I_i \tag{8.26}$$

$$P_i = \frac{A_i}{CTD_i} I_i \tag{8.27}$$

$$P_i = \frac{A_i}{PD_i} I_i \tag{8.28}$$

TABLE 8.7 INFORMATION VECTOR

Supermarket *A*	1.00
Supermarket *B*	0.97
Supermarket *C*	0.68
Supermarket *D*	0.60
Supermarket *E*	0.74

Source: M. T. Cadwallader, "A behavioral model of consumer spatial decision making," *Economic Geography,* 51 (1975), Table 7, p. 345.

where the notation is the same as in equations (8.21) through (8.25). The results obtained from equations (8.26), (8.27), and (8.28) can be compared with the actual proportion of consumers patronizing each supermarket by using the index of dissimilarity, which is constructed in a fashion similar to the index of segregation described in Section 5.1. These results can also be compared with the predicted proportion of consumers patronizing each supermarket as calculated from a classical gravity model formulation, in which the variables are measured in objective terms. For this purpose the following equation was used:

$$P_i = \frac{OA_i}{PD_i} \tag{8.29}$$

where OA_i is the objective attractiveness of supermarket i, as measured by retail floor space, and the remaining notation is the same as in equation (8.28).

From the results it is evident that the predictive capacity of the model is very high (Table 8.8). When using equation (8.26), three of the five predicted values are exactly equal to their observed counterparts. Also, the use of the cognitive distance measures gives better results than when using physical distance. When using cognitive distance the index of dissimilarity is 3, whereas when using physical distance it is 8. It can also be seen that the purely objective measures, equation (8.29), provide the least satisfactory predictions.

All the equations have comparatively small values for the index of dissimilarity, given that the index has a range of from 0 to 100. At first glance this would suggest that all four formulations work almost equally well. However, if we know nothing about the underlying decision-making process, our best prediction would be that an equal proportion of consumers will patronize each supermarket. That is, 20 percent of the consumers will patronize each of the five supermarkets. If this prediction is compared to the observed behavior, the index of dissimilarity is 27. Thus 27 is a more plausible extreme value for the index, in this particular context, than is 100. Viewed in this light,

TABLE 8.8 OBSERVED VERSUS PREDICTED BEHAVIOR (PERCENT)

		Predicted by equation			
Supermarket	Observed	(8.26)	(8.27)	(8.28)	(8.29)
A	32	35	32	32	40
B	35	35	32	41	31
C	13	10	11	7	9
D	8	8	11	6	7
E	12	12	14	14	13
		$D = 3$	$D = 5$	$D = 8$	$D = 9$

Note: D refers to the index of dissimilarity.

Source: M. T. Cadwallader, "A behavioral model of consumer spatial decision making," *Economic Geography*, 51 (1975), Table 8, p. 346.

the results suggest that the predictive power of equations (8.26) and (8.27) is genuinely superior to that of equations (8.28) and (8.29).

In general, then, these results substantiate the claim that consumer spatial behavior can be better understood in terms of subjectively measured variables than in terms of their more objective counterparts. It is pertinent to bear in mind, however, that, although the model shows an encouraging predictive capacity, full explanation has yet to be reached. The model is based on the premise that the subjectively distorted environment is a better predicter of human behavior than is the objective environment. However, it does not go so far as to explain why the environment is subjectively distorted in the way that it is.

Further Modifications

The behavioral model described above is an example of what are generally known as multi-attribute attitude models. Such models use a compositional approach, in that the utility of some object is postulated to be a weighted sum of that objects perceived attribute levels. In other words, a particular spatial alternative, such as a supermarket, can be viewed as a bundle of attributes, and the overall attitude toward that alternative is presumed to reflect the net resolution of a person's cognitions as to the degree to which it possesses those attributes, weighted by the importance of each attribute to the person (Wilkie and Pessemier, 1973). These weighted additive models are also compensatory in the sense that low ratings on one attribute can be compensated for by high ratings on another attribute.

The traditional weighted additive model can be modified in at least two major ways, however. First, the *differential weighting* of the items is usually represented by simple numbers, but the weighting function can also be calibrated by incorporating some kind of sliding scale, to reflect the widespread phenomenon of decreasing marginal utilities associated with higher attainment levels. Second, multiplicative versions of the model can also be formulated, to reflect the fact that subjective judgments often conform to a multiplying rule between factors (Louviere and Norman, 1977). A major characteristic of the multiplicative model is that if any attribute is at a near-zero psychological value, the overall attractiveness value will be very low irrespective of how high the other attributes might be rated. Recent research on consumer behavior suggests that the additive and multiplicative functions often perform equally well (Cadwallader, 1981a), and additive models appear to provide satisfactory predictions whenever the predictor variables are monotonically related to the dependent variable (Dawes and Corrigan, 1974).

The same basic model presented above has also been tested for *different income groups* (Lloyd and Jennings, 1978). Predictions of the proportion of consumers patronizing each of five stores were computed for a high-income sample and a low-income sample. The model worked well for the low-income sample, but was less successful in terms of predicting the behavior of the high-income sample (Table 8.9). In the latter case, the proportion patronizing store *A* was seriously overestimated.

TABLE 8.9 OBSERVED AND PREDICTED PERCENTAGES OF CONSUMERS PATRONIZING FIVE COMMON GROCERY STORES

	High-income sample		Low-income sample	
Store	Observed	Predicted	Observed	Predicted
A	22	70	73	78
B	37	14	0	6
C	37	15	17	12
D	4	1	7	3
E	0	0	3	1

Note: Predicted values are based on Cadwallader's model.

Source: R. Lloyd and D. Jennings, "Shopping behavior and income: Comparisons in an urban environment," *Economic Geography*, 54 (1978), Table 4, p. 163.

8.5 DYNAMIC MODELS OF CONSUMER BEHAVIOR

The models of consumer behavior discussed thus far have been static in nature. That is, they have not involved a sequence of decisions, and have therefore not considered the kind of learning process that is involved in consumer behavior. In the present section we explore the use of Markov chain analysis in the context of consumer behavior, and then discuss a simple learning model.

Markov Chain Models

Markov chain analysis is a useful technique for modeling sequences of decisions, as any individual choice is assumed to be dependent on some preceding choice (Golledge and Brown, 1967). For example, imagine that we have two supermarkets, *A* and *B*, in a particular area, and that an individual consumer makes the following sequence of decisions regarding these two stores: *AABABAABAA*. In other words, *A* is chosen, then *A* again, then *B*, and so on. This sequence can be expressed in terms of probabilities: (1) the probability of *B* following *A* is 0.5, (2) the probability of *A* following *A* is 0.5, (3) the probability of *A* following *B* is 1.0, and (4) the probability of *B* following *B* is 0.0.

These same probabilities can also be expressed in terms of a *transition probability matrix* (Figure 8.12a), where stores *A* and *B* represent states that the system can be in at any particular point in time. The value 0.5 in the upper right-hand cell of this matrix is the probability of moving, or making the transition from state *A* to state *B*. Note that each event in the sequence of decisions depends on the event immediately prior to it. In general, the one-step transition probabilities for a set of states S_1, S_2, S_3 are expressed as in Figure 8.12b, where P_{13} represents the probability of making the transition from S_1 to S_3.

$$\begin{array}{c} \\ A \\ B \end{array} \begin{array}{c} \begin{array}{cc} A & B \end{array} \\ \begin{bmatrix} 0.5 & 0.5 \\ 1.0 & 0 \end{bmatrix} \end{array}$$

(a)

$$t \begin{array}{c} \\ S_1 \\ S_2 \\ S_3 \end{array} \begin{array}{c} t+1 \\ \begin{array}{ccc} S_1 & S_2 & S_3 \end{array} \\ \begin{bmatrix} P_{11} & P_{12} & P_{13} \\ P_{21} & P_{22} & P_{23} \\ P_{31} & P_{32} & P_{33} \end{bmatrix} \end{array}$$

(b)

$$\begin{array}{c} \\ A \\ B \\ C \end{array} \begin{array}{c} \begin{array}{ccc} A & B & C \end{array} \\ \begin{bmatrix} 0.4 & 0.2 & 0.4 \\ 0 & 1 & 0 \\ 0.3 & 0.3 & 0.4 \end{bmatrix} \end{array}$$

(c)

$$\begin{array}{c} \\ A \\ B \\ C \end{array} \begin{array}{c} \begin{array}{ccc} A & B & C \end{array} \\ \begin{bmatrix} 0.4 & 0 & 0.6 \\ 0.7 & 0 & 0.3 \\ 0.8 & 0 & 0.2 \end{bmatrix} \end{array}$$

(d)

Figure 8.12 Transition probability matrices.

There are certain rules associated with such transition probability matrices. First, an item can only be in one of the states at any given time. Second, the sum of the elements in any row must equal unity, meaning that all possible alternatives have been specified. Third, an item moves successively within a state, or from one state to another, in constant intervals, and each of these moves is referred to as a *step*.

Two special situations can occur with respect to transition probability matrices. First, if an element on the diagonal of such a matrix has a value of unity, the state to which it pertains is called an *absorbing state,* as it would be impossible to leave that state. Figure 8.12c illustrates an absorbing state, as once the item is in state *B*, in other words, store *B* has been chosen, it is impossible to get out of that state. Second, an *inaccessible state* is one where all the elements of the associated column are zero. For example, in Figure 8.12d it is impossible to enter state *B*, or choose store *B*.

The transition probabilities can be obtained either empirically or theoretically. If they are to be empirically derived one starts with a tally matrix, which is then converted into a transition probability matrix. We discussed this procedure when describing the filtering-of-housing concept in Section 5.2. In that example the transition probabilities represented the probability that a home will be occupied by a particular type of family

(Table 5.6). The transition probabilities can also be derived from some theory, such as the gravity model, in which case the probabilities would reflect the sizes and distances to the various states, or supermarkets.

Besides the transition probabilities, we also need to know the values in the *starting vector* before we can analyze a Markov chain model. The starting vector summarizes the distribution of the item, or items, among the various states at the beginning of the time period under investigation. For example, the following starting vector illustrates the situation where we have just one consumer who is patronizing store number 2 at the beginning of the time period:

$$[S_1 \quad S_2 \quad S_3] = [0 \quad 1 \quad 0] \tag{8.30}$$

Similarly, the following starting vector illustrates the situation where we are monitoring the behavior of a number of consumers, so the distribution is depicted in terms of the proportion of consumers initially patronizing each of the three stores:

$$[S_1 \quad S_2 \quad S_3] = [0.12 \quad 0.53 \quad 0.35] \tag{8.31}$$

Abler et al. (1971, pp. 506–508) have developed a simple example to illustrate the use of Markov chain analysis in the context of consumer behavior. Imagine that we have an individual consumer who is faced with choosing between three supermarkets, A, B, and C. If the starting vector at time t_0 is multiplied by the transition probability matrix, we obtain the state vector for time t_1, as follows:

$$\begin{matrix} A & B & C \\ [0 & 1 & 0] \end{matrix} \quad \begin{matrix} \\ A \\ B \\ C \end{matrix}\begin{bmatrix} \overset{A}{0.72} & \overset{B}{0.20} & \overset{C}{0.08} \\ 0.49 & 0.35 & 0.16 \\ 0.47 & 0.29 & 0.24 \end{bmatrix} = \begin{matrix} A & B & C \\ [0.49 & 0.35 & 0.16] \end{matrix} \tag{8.32}$$

Note that after initially choosing supermarket B, at time t_0, there is an approximately 50 percent chance that the consumer will switch to supermarket A at time t_1, a 0.35 probability that he or she will again patronize supermarket B, and a 0.16 probability that he or she will switch to supermarket C.

If we continue to multiply each new state vector for the succeeding time periods by the transition probability matrix, the state vector eventually converges on the following values:

$$\begin{matrix} A & B & C \\ [0.633 & 0.248 & 0.119] \end{matrix}$$

In other words, our consumer eventually learns to choose supermarket A about two-thirds of the time, supermarket B about one-fourth of the time, and supermarket C for the remaining 12 percent. In this sense, he or she progresses from a search stage, in which all three supermarkets are used quite frequently, to a much more predictable pattern of behavior that is focused on supermarket A.

Of course, this model is very simplistic, as it assumes that the transition probabilities remain constant. In reality the transition probabilities will tend to change over time, as a result of the consumer's experiences of success or failure with each supermarket. In any event, the amount of time it takes the consumer to move from the search stage to a more stereotyped pattern of response, or habitual stage, is a reflection of the rate of learning, which can be explored by a variety of learning models.

Learning Models

Golledge (1981a) has suggested a number of learning models that might be profitably used in the context of consumer behavior. Perhaps the simplest of these is a *single-operator linear model,* which can be described by a first-order difference equation of the following form:

$$P_{t+1} = P_t + (1 - X)(1 - P_t) \tag{8.33}$$

where P_{t+1} is the probability of selecting a particular alternative on trial $t + 1$; P_t is the probability of selecting that alternative on the previous trial, t; and X is a fraction representing the probability of making an error on successive trials. In other words, the model assumes that the probability of choosing a particular alternative on trial $t + 1$ is the sum of the probability of choosing that alternative on trial t, and an increment that is a proportion of the maximum possible increase, $1 - P_t$ (Golledge, 1970).

A hypothetical example will help to clarify the use of this model. Suppose that, for a given person, P_t is 0.5 and X is 0.8; then, using equation (8.33), we have

$$P_{t+1} = 0.5 + (1 - 0.8)(1 - 0.5) = 0.6 \tag{8.34}$$

Using the calculated value of P_{t+1} to calculate P_{t+2}, we obtain

$$P_{t+2} = 0.6 + (1 - 0.8)(1 - 0.6) = 0.68 \tag{8.35}$$

Then, continuing to P_{t+3}, we obtain

$$P_{t+3} = 0.68 + (1 - 0.8)(1 - 0.68) = 0.744 \tag{8.36}$$

and so on. Thus, the probability of choosing a new alternative, or store, on the next trial, decreases at a decreasing rate (Figure 8.13a). Note that the learning curve will not intersect the horizontal axis, as the learning parameter X generates an asymptotic relationship.

A second hypothetical example will provide a useful comparison with the first. Imagine that this time P_t is 0.5 and X is 0.2; then, using equation (8.33), we have

$$P_{t+1} = 0.5 + (1 - 0.2)(1 - 0.5) = 0.9 \tag{8.37}$$

and

$$P_{t+2} = 0.9 + (1 - 0.2)(1 - 0.9) = 0.98 \tag{8.38}$$

In this case, where the probability of making an error has been reduced from 0.8 to 0.2, habitual behavior is approached more rapidly (Figure 8.13b).

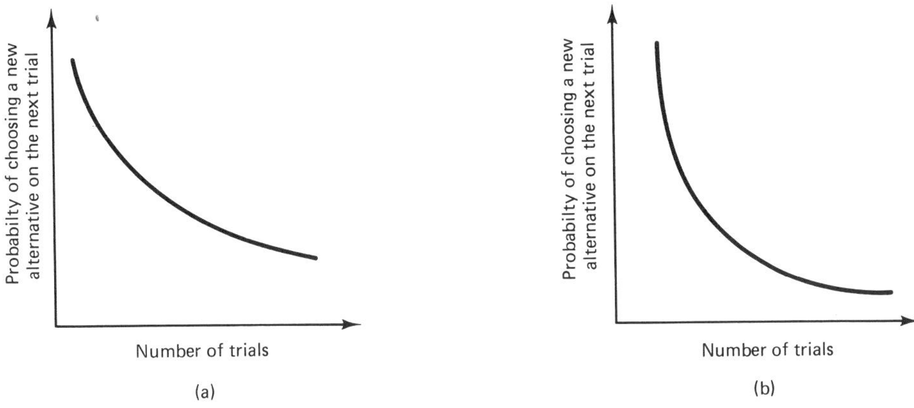

Figure 8.13 Learning curves.

Social scientists are interested in how and why the learning parameter, X, varies across subgroups and different kinds of behavior. As we have noted, the magnitude of this learning parameter influences the rate of approach toward habitual behavior. A large value for the learning parameter indicates that the decision maker quickly terminates search activity and assumes a stable behavioral pattern in which he or she regularly patronizes one particular alternative. Such a situation may occur where previous experience, latent learning, or urgency of action are factors that influence the decisions made on each trial (Amedeo and Golledge, 1975, p. 376). A small value for the learning parameter indicates that the habitual stage is preceded by a long period of search behavior, such as might occur in those situations where there are an especially large number of alternatives to choose among.

In summary, we have explored the traditional gravity model approach, the revealed preference approach, the behavioral approach, and a learning-based approach for analyzing the trip-distribution component of the traffic forecasting model. The gravity model is generally a useful predictor of aggregate behavior, but is less successful in explaining that behavior in terms of the underlying decision-making process. As a reaction to the gravity model, revealed preferences have been used to analyze observed behavior, in order to uncover the underlying preference structure. Although providing descriptive insights into the various trade-offs involved in the decision-making process, however, it is often difficult to distinguish true preferences from underlying constraints. As a result, in the behavioral approach the preferences associated with spatial behavior are not deduced from an analysis of observed behavior, but are hypothesized in an a priori fashion, and then compared with actual behavior. Finally, the learning approach attempts to address the processes involved in making a sequence of decisions.

9

Residential Mobility

9.1 PATTERNS OF MOBILITY

With approximately 20 percent of the U.S. population changing residence every year, residential mobility is a characteristic, to varying degrees, of all urban neighborhoods. Indeed, it is this mobility which is largely responsible for the changing socioeconomic structure of neighborhoods, and is generally associated with the deterioration and decline of particular regions within cities. Almost half of the U.S. population made at least one residential move during the five-year period from 1970 to 1975, and 45 percent of those moves represented changes of residence within the same metropolitan area (Quigley and Weinberg, 1977). The proportion of households moving within a given time period is much smaller, however, in the northern metropolitan areas of high stability or out-migration, such as Scranton or Johnstown, than in the fast-growing cities of the Southwest, such as Reno or Colorado Springs (Adams and Gilder, 1976).

Moore (1972, p. 10) has concluded that the most frequently reported correlate of movement propensity is stage in the life cycle. This relationship between stage in the life cycle and residential mobility is primarily a response to the changing dwelling-space needs of the family (Clark and Onaka, 1983). The highest probability of moving occurs between the ages of 20 and 30, with the beginning of married life and the arrival of children. There tends to be greater stability while the children are at school and the head of household is consolidating his or her career, and then mobility often increases again when the children leave home and less living space is required.

Most descriptions of individual mobility have focused on the biases associated with distance and direction (Clark, 1982a). There is strong evidence to suggest that the distribution of distances can be adequately represented by a family of negative exponential functions (Morrill and Pitts, 1967), reflecting the greater frequency of short- as opposed to long-distance moves. Indeed, for the city of Seattle, it has been estimated that the average length of an intracity move is less than 3 miles, with 16 percent being less than ½ mile (Boyce, 1969). Similar results have also been reported for a number of other U.S. cities (Knox, 1982, p. 120).

In terms of directional biases associated with mobility patterns, it has been suggested that although central-area moves appear to be random in direction, the moves within the suburban areas of the city tend to be biased in a sectoral fashion (Clark, 1971). This sectoral bias has been related to the idea that urban residents might possess mental images of the city that are predominantly sectoral rather than zonal (Adams, 1969; R. J. Johnston, 1972) and also to the fact that the underlying socioeconomic structure of the city often has a strong sectoral component (Clark, 1972). Efforts to generalize the nature of directional biases across different cities have failed, however, largely due to the fact that the direction of moves will be as sensitive to the idiosyncratic location of new housing opportunities in a particular city as it is to the overall spatial pattern of cities in general.

Perhaps the most significant regularity in terms of mobility patterns, however, is that households seem to move between areas of similar socioeconomic status. Most moves, often up to as many as 70 percent, take place within, or between, census tracts of similar economic characteristics (Clark, 1976). This phenomenon emphasizes the considerable economic constraints provided by income and housing costs, and suggests that, at the aggregate level at least, intraurban migration flows are remarkably predictable.

The present chapter begins by focusing on the spatial distribution of mobility rates within cities, and then goes on to explore the interrelationships between mobility rates and other features of the urban environment, such as socioeconomic, demographic, and housing characteristics. A simultaneous-equations approach is then introduced to address the possibility of feedback effects, or reciprocal causation, between residential mobility and these other variables. Finally, some behavioral models of residential relocation are discussed, to provide some comparison with the aggregate models described previously. For this purpose the decision-making process is compartmentalized into the decision to move and the search for alternatives, and the evaluation of those alternatives.

The Spatial Distribution of Mobility Rates

The amount of mobility, or population turnover, within urban areas is closely associated with different types of neighborhoods, and thus varies quite substantially from one part of the city to another. The present author (Cadwallader, 1982) has analyzed the spatial pattern of mobility rates for Portland, Oregon, for three different time periods. Data for the study were derived from census tract material for Portland, using Multnomah County to identify the spatial extent of the city. The amount of residential mobility, or rather lack of it, was defined to be the number of people residing in the same house in 1970 as in 1965, as a percentage of persons 5 years old and over in 1970, for each census tract. Values for 1950 and 1960 were derived in exactly the same fashion as for 1970, except that the data for 1950 involved the number of people residing in the same house in 1950 as in 1949. Although this modification obviously changes the absolute values, the spatial patterns associated with 1950, 1960, and 1970 can still be meaningfully compared in a relative, or distributional, sense.

The initial analysis involved investigating the relationship between residential mobility and distance from the central business district, by calibrating the following three equations:

$$RM = a + bD \tag{9.1}$$

$$RM = ae^{bD} \tag{9.2}$$

$$RM = aD^{b} \tag{9.3}$$

where RM is residential mobility, as defined previously, and D is straight-line distance from the central business district. These three equations represent linear, exponential, and power functions, respectively, and the latter two can be fitted using least-squares analysis by making the following logarithmic transformations (as discussed in Section 2.4):

$$\ln RM = \ln a - bD \tag{9.4}$$

$$\log RM = \log a - b(\log D) \tag{9.5}$$

where the notation is the same as in equations (9.1), (9.2), and (9.3); ln refers to natural, or naperian, logarithms, and log refers to common logarithms to the base 10.

The results of this curve-fitting exercise (Table 9.1) are similar to those produced by Moore (1971), in that for all three time periods the amount of residential stability increases with increasing distance. The coefficients of determination indicate that the power function is the most appropriate form for specifying this relationship, although clearly, even in this case, there is still a comparatively large proportion of unexplained variation, suggesting that more complex functional relationships might be profitably explored. Trend surface analysis (see Section 4.5) was used to facilitate this exploration, as it allows the pattern of residential mobility to be conceptualized as a

TABLE 9.1 COEFFICIENTS OF DETERMINATION FOR RESIDENTIAL MOBILITY AND DISTANCE FROM THE CBD

	1950	1960	1970
Linear function	.09	.17	.17
Power function	.26	.33	.34
Exponential function	.10	.19	.18

Source: M. T. Cadwallader, "Urban residential mobility: A simultaneous equations approach," *Transactions of the Institute of British Geographers*, New Series, 7 (1982), Table I, p. 461.

TABLE 9.2 COEFFICIENTS OF DETERMINATION FOR THE TREND SURFACE ANALYSES OF THE RESIDENTIAL MOBILITY SURFACES

	1950	1960	1970
Linear surface	.24	.08	.02
Quadratic surface	.45	.40	.10
Cubic surface	.57	.52	.21

Source: M. T. Cadwallader, "Urban residential mobility: A simultaneous equations approach," *Transactions of the Institute of British Geographers*, New Series, 7 (1982), Table II, p. 462.

surface, rather than simply averaging the mobility rates across different directions from the city center.

The goodness of fit between the computed surface and the mapped variable, in this case residential mobility, is usually stated in terms of the percentage reduction in the total sum of squares attributable to the fitted surface. In this context it should be remembered that the distribution of data points in a trend surface analysis is of some importance, as a clustering of data points will tend to inflate the R^2 values. The distribution of data points is not a problem in the present study, however, as they represent the centroids of census tracts and are thus fairly evenly distributed throughout the city. What little clustering there is is associated with the smaller tracts toward the center of the city, and is not considered critical, as there is experimental evidence to suggest that trend surface analysis is fairly robust to small departures from a completely uniform distribution of data points (Unwin, 1970; Robinson, 1972).

The results of fitting linear, quadratic, and cubic surfaces are given in Table 9.2, although the significance levels associated with each surface are not reported, as these are notoriously difficult to interpret in the case of trend surface analysis (Horvath, 1967; Tinkler, 1969). More complex surfaces were not explored, as it is often extremely difficult to determine the empirical meaning of anything beyond a third-order surface. Also, degrees of freedom begin to become a problem with higher-order surfaces, as a perfect fit will result whenever the number of terms in the trend equation equals the number of data points.

For all three years the best fit is provided by the cubic surface, with between 21 and 57 percent of the variation in mobility rates being accounted for, although, in general, the comparatively small coefficients of determination indicate that the actual surfaces are extremely convoluted. Of greater interest, however, is the change over time. For all three surfaces, the linear, quadratic, and cubic, the amount of explained variation is greatest for 1950 and least for 1970. This situation, which remains the same even after calculating the corrected coefficients of determination, in order to take into account the different number of census tracts for each time period, indicates that the mobility surface has become increasingly complex over time. Significantly, in previous research, similar kinds of results have been obtained when investigating the configuration of population density surfaces over time (see Section 4.5).

9.2 THE RELATIONSHIPS AMONG HOUSING PATTERNS, SOCIAL PATTERNS, AND RESIDENTIAL MOBILITY

As suggested earlier, however, in addition to identifying the spatial pattern of mobility rates, it is also of interest to establish the interrelationships between mobility rates and other features of the urban environment, such as socioeconomic, demographic, and housing characteristics. Although the spatial distribution of housing characteristics and the nature of housing markets within cities has become one of the major research foci of urban geography (Chapter 3), there has been little effort to relate this research on housing markets to the ecological literature concerning social areas in cities (Chapter 5). In the present section the intention is to explore explicitly the interaction between the demand for housing, as expressed by different social groups, and the supply of housing, as represented by different types and quality of housing, and to identify the interrelationships between housing patterns and social patterns, on the one hand, and rates of residential mobility, on the other. These interrelationships are expressed in the form of a causal model (Figure 9.1), based on research conducted by the present author (Cadwallader, 1981b), which is analyzed by means of path analysis.

The general framework of the causal model is based on the essential interplay between *households and housing stock*. As the housing stock of an area changes, we might expect a simultaneous adjustment of the population characteristics of that area. For example, the aging and extensive subdivision of a particular neighborhood will lead to a higher proportion of multifamily dwelling units, and thus a higher proportion of small and often low-income families. In many ways, this association between housing stock and household characteristics is dynamically articulated by the filtering process, whereby housing that is occupied by one income group deteriorates over time and thus becomes available to the next lower income group (see Section 5.2). Intermediaries, such as financial institutions and real estate agents, also play an important role in this matching of demand and supply in the housing market

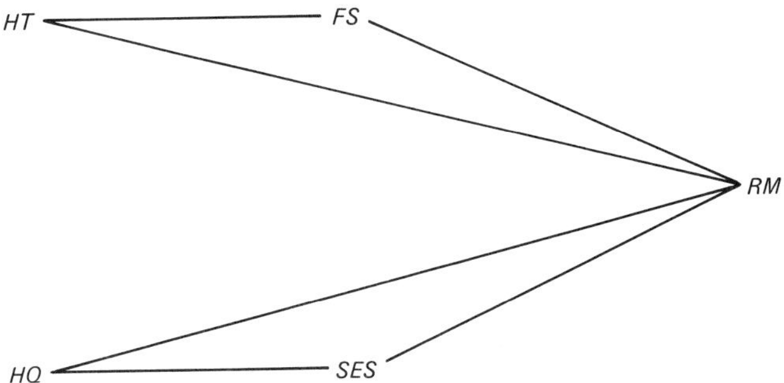

Figure 9.1 Causal model representing the interrelationships among housing patterns, social patterns, and residential mobility. *HT*, housing type; *HQ*, housing quality; *FS*, family status; *SES*, socioeconomic status; *RM*, residential mobility.

(see Section 3.2), although these social institutions are not explicitly considered in the present model.

As it can be argued that the housing stock is generally less mobile, at least in the short run, than the consumers, or occupants, it seems plausible to suggest that housing characteristics should be placed causally prior to population characteristics. In other words, the housing stock is considered to be a constraint on the pattern of housing opportunities, and thus is a major mechanism responsible for the evolution of residential differentiation in general and social areas in particular. Changes in the supply, or evolution, of the housing stock arise largely because of the aging process. Differences in the timing of housing development, due to building cycles and prevailing economic conditions, thus produces different residential patterns within cities (Adams, 1970).

Bourne (1976) suggests that housing stock can be divided according to type, ownership, and costs. For the purpose of the present model, type and ownership, or tenure status, are collapsed into one dimension and costs are reinterpreted more broadly as housing quality. As such, these two housing dimensions, representing type and quality, closely parallel the type and value and quality dimensions suggested by Rees (1970). Population characteristics are also divided into two major dimensions, socioeconomic status and family status, based on the classic social area analysis studies (see Section 5.3). Thus it is postulated that when choosing a home the prospective buyer must select in terms of the type and quality of housing, and that this decision will be influenced primarily by the buyer's stage in the life cycle and socioeconomic status. For example, those areas of the city containing spacious homes and yards will tend to be particularly attractive to large families with young children. Hence, in general, a neighborhood occupying a particular location in social space, defined in terms of socioeconomic status and family status, is liable to occupy an analogous, or equivalent, location in housing space, where the major axes represent the type and quality of housing (Rees, 1970). Also, we might expect socioeconomic status to be especially associated with quality of housing, and family status to be especially associated with type of housing. In other words, it is assumed that socioeconomic status primarily determines the quality of housing purchased, while stage in the life cycle primarily determines the type of housing purchased.

Finally, *residential mobility* is interpreted as a phenomenon of the housing market, with families changing their housing stock as they experience changes in terms of both family status and socioeconomic status. More specifically, the pattern of residential mobility, as measured by turnover rates, is expected to be related primarily to housing type and family status, rather than to housing quality and socioeconomic status, as previous research has shown stage in the life cycle to be one of the dominant forces behind the decision to move (Simmons, 1968; Webber, 1983). As Rossi (1980, p. 61) stresses, residential mobility is the proces by which families adjust their housing to meet the demands for space generated by changing family composition. In an aggregate sense, low-family-status areas are disproportionately inhabitated by young people, renters, and apartment dwellers, all of which are characteristics normally related to high mobility rates. High-family-status areas, on the other hand, are comprised mainly of families with children, homeowners, and single-family dwelling units—characteristics usually associated with high rates of stability (Speare et al., 1974, p. 100).

By contrast, the effects of socioeconomic status on residential mobility are extremely difficult to disentangle. Whereas Abu-Lughod and Foley (1960) were able to show that movers have lower incomes than nonmovers, Fredland (1974) suggests that mobility increases slightly with increasing income. Higher education levels appear to be associated with higher mobility rates (Abu-Lughod and Foley, 1960), but in some instances there is no evidence of a relationship (Speare et al., 1974). Finally, occupation of the head of the household has generally been a poor predictor of mobility (Long, 1972).

This overall conceptual schema can be formally expressed as follows:

$$H_i = f(HT_i, HQ_i) \tag{9.6}$$

$$S_i = f(SES_i, FS_i) \tag{9.7}$$

where H_i is the location of area i in housing space, HT_i is the type of housing associated with area i, HQ_i is the quality of housing associated with area i, S_i is the location of area i in social space, SES_i is the socioeconomic status associated with area i, and FS_i is the family status associated with area i. In addition,

$$S_i = f(H_i) \tag{9.8}$$

and more specifically,

$$FS_i = f(HT_i) \tag{9.9}$$

$$SES_i = f(HQ_i) \tag{9.10}$$

where the notation is the same as in equations (9.6) and (9.7). Finally,

$$RM_i = f(FS_i, HT_i) \tag{9.11}$$

where RM_i is the amount of residential mobility associated with area i. The corresponding hypothesized causal model (Figure 9.1) also shows links between housing quality and residential mobility, and between socioeconomic status and residential mobility, but these were not expected to be statistically significant.

In accordance with the proposed theoretical framework, the empirical analyses are divided into four parts: (1) the postulated major dimensions, or axes, of social space are verified via principal components analysis; (2) the major dimensions of housing space are examined in a fashion similar to the social space dimensions; (3) the hypothesized interrelationships between the social and housing patterns are tested using correlation analysis; and (4) their relationships with residential mobility, as expressed in the causal model, are explored by means of path analysis. As in the factorial ecological studies, census-tract-level information was used, with appropriate data being collected from the 1970 U.S. Census of Population and Housing for four U.S. cities: Canton (Ohio), Des Moines (Iowa), Knoxville (Tennessee), and Portland (Oregon). Four cities were chosen in order to test the robustness of the conceptual schema in different contexts, and these particular cities were chosen as they provide variation in terms of both size, with one large and three smaller, and spatial location. The data for each city included split tracts but excluded those tracts containing zero for any of the selected variables.

Social Space and Housing Space

The major dimensions of *social space* for these four cities, as identified by principal components analysis, have already been described (Table 5.10), and the coefficients of congruence, for both socioeconomic status and family status, are all extremely high, indicating that the components are almost identical for all four cities (Table 5.11). Similar analyses to those undertaken for social space were used to identify and describe the major dimensions of *housing space*. In this case, however, the previous literature was far less helpful as a guide to the selection of variables, because there has been no consistent approach to the definition of housing submarkets, especially in a spatial context (Bourne 1976). As a result, two major criteria were used when choosing the housing variables. First, they should be representative of the mix of attributes that together make up the housing "package" or "bundle," as identified in previous studies (Kain and Quigley, 1970). Second, they should have theoretical implications with respect to patterns of residential mobility (Quigley and Weinberg, 1977).

With these criteria in mind, the following six variables were chosen to represent housing space: percentage of all-year-round housing units owner-occupied; number of single-family dwelling units as a percentage of all-year-round units; median number of rooms; median housing value for owner-occupied dwelling units; percentage of all-year-round housing units with more than one bathroom; and percentage of all-year-round housing units built in 1939 or earlier. The tenure status and single-family dwelling unit variables were chosen because they have been found to be among the most powerful predictors of residential mobility (Michelson, 1977; Speare et al., 1974). Part of the reason for the stability of owner-occupiers lies in their higher moving costs, combined with a greater flexibility in terms of being able to adjust in situ by remodeling, and their greater social commitment to the local neighborhood. Dwelling unit size, especially when related to household size, is also an important determinant of mobility (Rossi, 1980). The remaining three variables—housing value, number of bathrooms, and housing age—are generally indicative of housing quality. Housing value in particular is obviously a very direct indicator of housing quality, while a number of studies have shown how housing values are associated with a variety of other housing attributes, such as age and number of bathrooms (Blumner and Johnson, 1975; Mark, 1977). Previous researchers have also used the age of the dwelling unit as a surrogate for housing quality (Quigley, 1976).

The principal components analyses of the housing variables, again using a varimax rotation, revealed two distinct dimensions, labeled "housing type" and "housing quality" (Table 9.3). Housing type consists of owner-occupancy rates, number of single-family dwelling units, and number of rooms, and housing quality is made up of housing value, number of bathrooms, and housing age. It is interesting to

TABLE 9.3 HOUSING SPACE

	HT	HQ	Comm.	HT	HQ	Comm.
	Canton			Des Moines		
Housing value	.28	.94	.96	.14	.97	.96
Number of bathrooms	.24	.94	.94	.23	.96	.97
Age of housing	−.46	−.75	.77	−.65	−.40	.58
Percent owner occupied	.90	.39	.96	.97	.20	.98
Percent single-family dwelling units	.96	.19	.96	.99	.03	.98
Number of rooms	.75	.35	.69	.70	.55	.79
Percent total variance	44.0	44.0		48.5	39.5	
	Knoxville			Portland		
Housing value	.03	.97	.94	−.02	.95	.90
Number of bathrooms	.42	.87	.93	.31	.86	.84
Age of housing	−.53	−.63	.67	−.30	−.46	.30
Percent owner occupied	.94	.29	.96	.96	.23	.97
Percent single-family dwelling units	.99	.06	.97	.98	.05	.96
Number of rooms	.82	.52	.94	.84	.43	.89
Percent total variance	49.8	40.8		46.2	34.8	

Source: M. T. Cadwallader, "A unified model of urban housing patterns, social patterns, and residential mobility," *Urban Geography*, 2 (1981), Table 3, p. 124.

note that the number of rooms loads consistently high on housing type rather than on housing quality, while housing age is associated predominantly with housing quality, although in the case of Des Moines it loads more highly on housing type. Overall, the variation in housing age is the least satisfactorily accounted for of the housing measures with communalities ranging form .77 to .30.

The congruency coefficients between the housing dimensions reveal that the cities are remarkably similar in terms of housing structure, with the coefficients for both housing type and housing quality being as high as those previously reported for the social space dimensions (Table 9.4). For example, in the case of Knoxville and

TABLE 9.4 COEFFICIENTS OF CONGRUENCE FOR HOUSING SPACE

	(1)	(2)	(3)	(4)
Canton (1)	—	.96	.99	.98
Des Moines (2)	.99	—	.99	.99
Knoxville (3)	.98	.99	—	.99
Portland (4)	.98	.97	.99	—

Note: Coefficients for housing quality are above the diagonal; coefficients for housing type are below the diagonal.

Source: M. T. Cadwallader, "A unified model of urban housing patterns, social patterns, and residential mobility," *Urban Geography*, 2 (1981), Table 4, p. 124.

TABLE 9.5 CORRELATION COEFFICIENTS BETWEEN THE SOCIAL SPACE AND HOUSING SPACE DIMENSIONS

	Canton	Des Moines	Knoxville	Portland
Socioeconomic status and housing quality	.855	.928	.910	.885
Socioeconomic status and housing type	.296	.023	.114	.044
Family status and housing quality	.015	.115	.057	.018
Family status and housing type	.685	.857	.723	.827

Source: M. T. Cadwallader, "A unified model of urban housing patterns, social patterns, and residential mobility," *Urban Geography*, 2 (1981), Table 5, p. 125.

Canton the coefficient of congruence is .99 for housing quality and .98 for housing type. The interpretability of the components, plus their obvious similarity across the four cities, suggests that an orthogonal rotation is quite capable of identifying simple structure, thus obviating the necessity for employing more complex and sophisticated oblique rotations (see Section 5.4).

Having identified two distinctive and recurring sets of dimensions associated with social space and housing space, the next step in the analysis was to investigate the interrelationships between these dimensions. These interrelationships were analyzed simply by calculating the zero-order correlation coefficients between the social and housing dimensions. The results of the zero-order correlation analysis indicate quite clearly that socioeconomic status is closely related to housing quality, and family status is equally closely related to housing type (Table 9.5). In the case of Portland, for example, socioeconomic status and housing quality have a correlation of .885, while family status and housing type have a correlation of .827. By contrast, family status and housing quality, and socioeconomic status and housing type, have correlations of only .018 and .044, respectively. The unambiguous nature of these results is especially encouraging, as they provide extremely strong evidence for the relationships postulated in equations (9.9) and (9.10).

Social Space, Housing Space, and Residential Mobility

The interrelationships among the social space and housing space dimensions and residential mobility were analyzed by means of path analysis, with the amount of residential mobility, or rather lack of it, being defined as in Section 9.1. Path analysis (see Section 3.3) allows one to estimate the magnitude of the linkages between variables, which then provide information about the underlying causal processes. In the present instance, the causal model being postulated is recursive, as the dependent variables have an unambiguous causal ordering. In this situation, ordinary least-squares regression techniques can be used to obtain the path coefficients provided, of course, that the normal regression assumptions are met. In particular, we are forced to assume that the disturbance terms in the structural equations are uncorrelated with the causal variables in those same equations (Duncan, 1975, p. 5). The path coefficient associated with the disturbance terms, incorporating the combined effect of all unspecified variables, is simply the square root of the unexplained variation in the dependent variable under consideration (Asher, 1976, p. 31).

The *causal model* to be calibrated is represented by the following set of structural equations (see also Figure 9.1):

$$FS = b_1 \mathrm{HT} \tag{9.12}$$

$$SES = b_1 HQ \tag{9.13}$$

$$RM = b_1 HT + b_2 HQ + b_3 SES + b_4 FS \tag{9.14}$$

where the notation is the same as in equations (9.6) through (9.11). There are no values for the intercepts, as the variables are all in standardized form, and the standardized regression coefficients for these equations provide the path coefficients. Note that there are no links between housing type and housing quality, and family status and socioeconomic status, as these variables represent independent components derived from the principal components analyses. Also, there are no paths between housing type and socioeconomic status, and housing quality and family status, as these interrelationships were found to be insignificant in the correlation analysis (Table 9.5).

The results of the *path analysis* (Figures 9.2 to 9.5) are strikingly similar for all four cities. In every case, the path coefficients for housing type and family status, and housing quality and socioeconomic status, are very large and in the expected positive direction. Similarly, in all cases, the path coefficient between housing type and res-

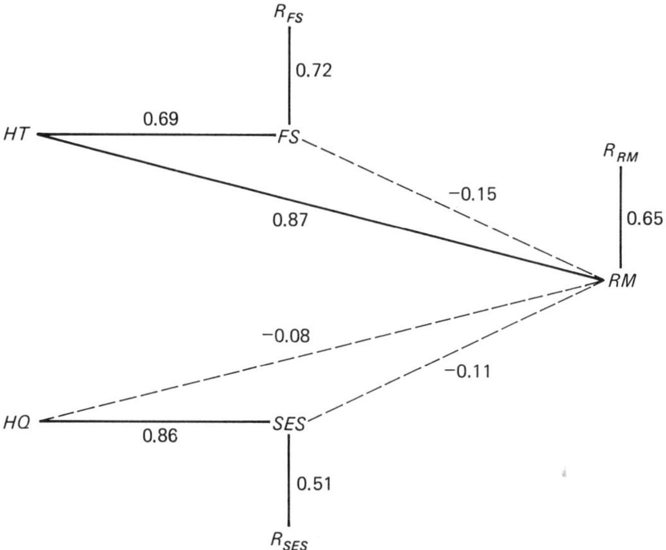

Figure 9.2 Path coefficients for Canton. *R*, residual; dashed lines represent paths that are not statistically significant at 0.05. (From M. T. Cadwallader, "A unified model of urban housing patterns, social patterns, and residential mobility," *Urban Geography*, 2, 1981, Fig. 1, p. 116.)

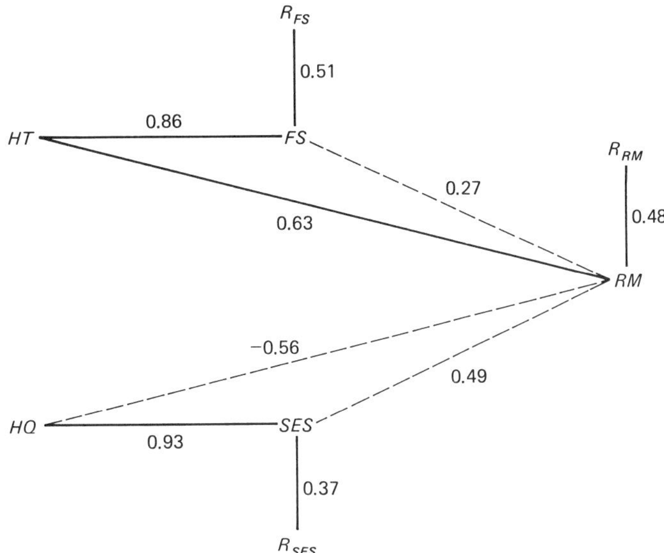

Figure 9.3 Path coefficients for Des Moines. (From M. T. Cadwallader, "A unified model of urban housing patterns, social patterns, and residential mobility," *Urban Geography,* 2, 1981, Fig. 2, p. 116.)

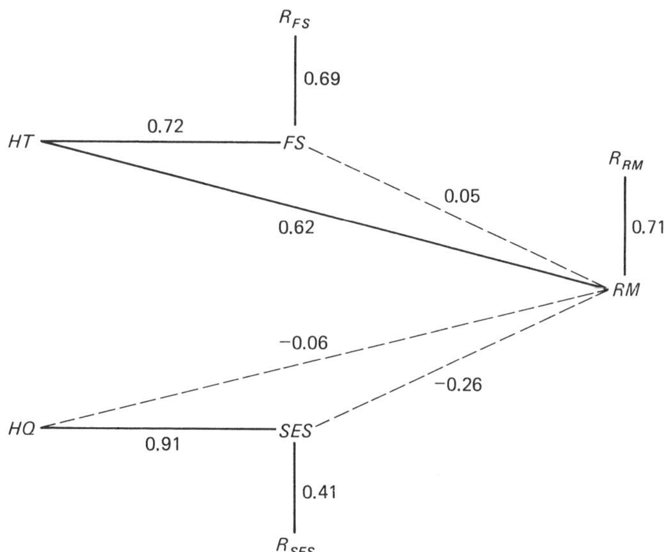

Figure 9.4 Path coefficients for Knoxville. (From M. T. Cadwallader, "A unified model of urban housing patterns, social patterns, and residential mobility," *Urban Geography,* 2, 1981, Fig. 3, p. 117.)

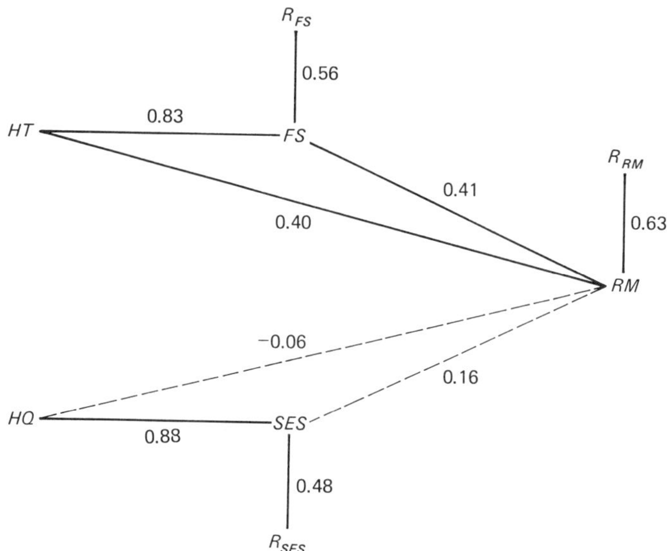

Figure 9.5 Path coefficients for Portland. (From M. T. Cadwallader, "A unified model of urban housing patterns, social patterns, and residential mobility," *Urban Geography*, 2, 1981, Fig. 4, p. 118.)

idential mobility is significant and positive, indicating that it is those census tracts with high proportions of owner-occupied and single-family dwelling units that experience the least amount of residential mobility. For three of the four cities, there are no other significant links between any of the causally prior variables and residential mobility; but in the case of Portland, housing type also has an indirect effect via family status. These results indicate that the same comparatively simple causal structure can be postulated for all four cities. Moreover, the path coefficients associated with this causal structure are strikingly similar for each city. Nevertheless, as the path coefficients connected with the disturbance terms testify, there remain other, as yet unidentified variables that should be included in the analysis.

In summary, there are three major results to this analysis. First, it has been demonstrated that the housing attributes of urban subareas can be decomposed into housing quality and housing type dimensions. Second, evidence has been presented to support the hypothesis that the social space and housing space dimensions are significantly interrelated and, more specifically, that socioeconomic status is a direct function of variation in housing quality and family status is a direct function of variation in housing type. Third, a causal model, constructed to elucidate the interrelationships between the social space and housing space dimensions and residential mobility, generated remarkably consistent results across four different cities, with the housing type dimension proving to be the single most important determinant of residential mobility.

9.3 A SIMULTANEOUS-EQUATIONS APPROACH

The path models of residential mobility described in the preceding section are recursive in nature and thus do not consider the possibility of two-way, or reciprocal causation. The exclusion of two-way causality presents a major theoretical problem, as it can be reasonably argued that although the socioeconomic characteristics of urban subareas undoubtedly influence the magnitude of residential mobility rates, the reverse is also equally true. With this problem in mind, the purpose of the present section is to introduce the idea of simultaneous equations, and to describe a simultaneous-equation model of residential mobility.

Simultaneous Equations

An introduction to causal models in general was provided in Section 3.3, but the issue of nonrecursive models, involving two-way causation, was not examined explicity. The causal structure depicted in Figure 9.6a represents a nonrecursive model, as there is a feedback relationship between variables X_1 and X_3. This causal structure can be expressed by the following three equations:

$$X_1 = a + b_3X_3 + e_1 \tag{9.15}$$

$$X_2 = a + b_1X_1 + e_1 \tag{9.16}$$

$$X_3 = a + b_1X_1 + b_2X_2 + e_3 \tag{9.17}$$

Note that there is one equation for each variable, as the values for each variable are at least partly determined by the other variables within the causal system (see Section 3.3 for a discussion of the distinction between exogenous and endogenous variables). Each equation also contains an error term, summarizing the effects of those variables that are not explicitly included within the causal system.

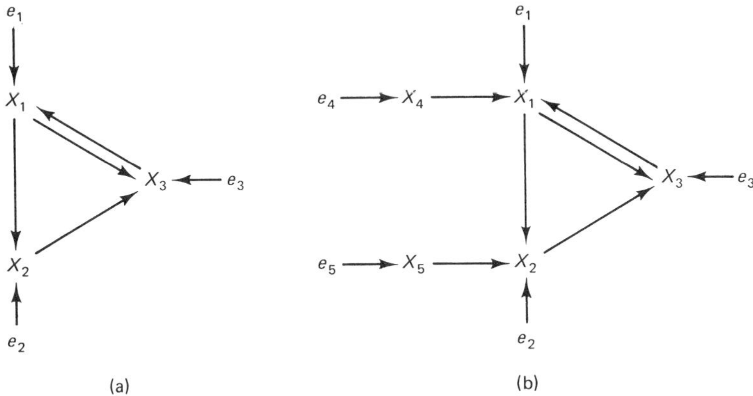

Figure 9.6 Causal models with reciprocal relationships.

There are three major issues involved when dealing with a simultaneous equation model: specification, identification, and estimation. Misspecification, or *specification error*, involves what might be more simply called using the wrong model (Duncan, 1975, p. 101). Specification error includes the omission of relevant variables in the model, and the misspecification of the correct form of the equations. In the latter context, equations (9.15), (9.16) and (9.17) assume that the relationships between the variables are both linear and additive. A linear relationship implies that a unit change in X_2 has the same effect on X_1, whatever the value of X_2, while an additive relationship implies that a unit change in X_2 has the same effect on X_1, whatever the values of the other variables in the equation (Macdonald, 1977, p. 84).

Second, in order for the unknown coefficients in equations (9.15), (9.16), and (9.17) to be estimated, the model should be appropriately *identified*. The issue of identification is a rather complex one, involving the relationship between the number of equations and the number of unknowns (Fisher, 1966). A necessary, although not sufficient condition for the identifiability of an individual equation within a given linear model is that the number of variables excluded from that equation should be at least equal to the number of equations, or in other words, endogenous variables, minus one. Thus, if there are k equations, at least $k - 1$ of the coefficients must be set equal to zero. If precisely $k - 1$ are set equal to zero, the equation is exactly identified, whereas if more than $k - 1$ are set equal to zero, the equation is overidentified (Namboodiri et al., 1975, p. 503). In those situations where the parameters cannot be identified in any given equation, and so the equation is underidentified, exogenous variables must be added to the system. With respect to the causal model represented in Figure 9.6a, all three equations (9.15), and (9.16), and (9.17) are underidentified, as none of them omit as many as two variables. However, by adding two exogenous variables, X_4 and X_5, to the causal system (Figure 9.6b), we obtain the following three equations:

$$X_1 = a + b_3X_3 + b_4X_4 + e_i \tag{9.18}$$

$$X_2 = a + b_1X_1 + b_5X_5 + e_2 \tag{9.19}$$

$$X_3 = a + b_1X_1 + b_2X_2 + e_3 \tag{9.20}$$

Note that two of the five variables are omitted from each of the equations, leaving them all exactly identified.

The coefficients in these three equations must now be *estimated*. Ordinary least-squares analysis should not be used as an estimation procedure when dealing with nonrecursive systems, as the disturbance, or error terms in each equation will ordinarily be correlated with the independent variables in that equation, thus leading to biased estimates (J. Johnston, 1972, p. 376). For example, in equations (9.18) and (9.20) e_1 influences X_1, which in turn influences X_3. Therefore, e_1 is not independent of X_3. An appropriate way to estimate the unknown coefficients, however, is to use two-stage least-squares analysis (Intriligator, 1978, p. 385). As the name implies, this procedure estimates the coefficients in two stages. First, each of the endogenous variables is regressed on the exogeneous variables, thus producing the *reduced-form-equa-*

tions. Second, the predicted values for the endogenous variables, obtained from the reduced-form equations, are substituted on the right-hand side of the original simultaneous equations, in order to estimate the coefficients. In essence, then, the general idea behind two-stage least-squares analysis is to purify the endogenous variables that appear in the equation to be estimated in such a way that they become uncorrelated with the disturbance term in that equation (Namboodiri et al., 1975, p. 514).

In particular, in the context of equations (9.18), (9.19), and (9.20), we have two exogenous variables, X_4 and X_5, and three endogenous variables, X_1, X_2, and X_3, thus producing the following three reduced-form equations:

$$\hat{X}_1 = a + b_4X_4 + b_5X_5 \tag{9.21}$$

$$\hat{X}_2 = a + b_4X_4 + b_5X_5 \tag{9.22}$$

$$\hat{X}_3 = a + b_4X_4 + b_5X_5 \tag{9.23}$$

where $\hat{X}_1$, $\hat{X}_2$, and $\hat{X}_3$ are the predicted values of X_1, X_2, and X_3, respectively, based on the use of ordinary least-squares analysis. These predicted values are than substituted into the right-hand side of the original simultaneous equations (9.18), (9.19), and (9.20), giving the following equations:

$$X_1 = a + b_3\hat{X}_3 + b_4X_4 + e_1 \tag{9.24}$$

$$X_2 = a + b_1\hat{X}_1 + b_5X_5 + e_2 \tag{9.25}$$

$$X_3 = a + b_1\hat{X}_1 + b_2\hat{X}_2 + e_3 \tag{9.26}$$

These three equations are then estimated using oridinary least-squares analysis. Thus two-stage least-squares analysis essentially involves two separate applications of oridinary least-squares analysis.

An Empirical Example

Using the data for Portland, Oregon, described previously, the present author (Cadwallader, 1982) estimated a simultaneous equation model of mobility rates (Figure 9.7) for 1950, 1960, and 1970. Housing and population dimensions, similar

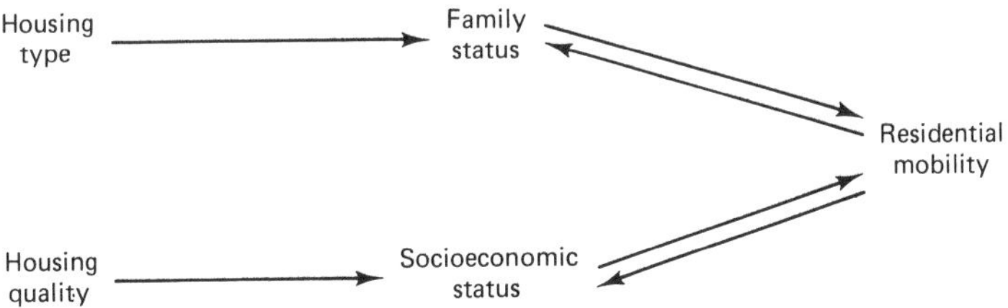

Figure 9.7 Causal structure represented by the simultaneous equation model. (From M. T. Cadwallader, "Urban residential mobility: A simultaneous equations approach," *Transactions of the Institute of British Geographers,* New Series, 7 1982, Fig. 1, p. 466.)

to those described in Tables 9.3 and 5.10, respectively, served as input for the following simultaneous equations:

$$RM = a + b_1 SES + b_2 FS \tag{9.27}$$

$$SES = a + b_1 RM + b_2 HQ \tag{9.28}$$

$$FS = a + b_1 RM + b_2 HT \tag{9.29}$$

where RM is residential mobility, SES is socioeconomic status, FS is family status, HQ is housing quality, and HT is housing type. Note that, unlike the path models described previously, residential mobility is expected to exhibit reciprocal relationships with both socioeconomic status and family status. Given the definition of residential mobility (see Section 9.1), all the relationships were expected to be positive.

TABLE 9.6 ESTIMATED REDUCED-FORM EQUATIONS

1950	
$RM = 76.05 + 4.87HT^* + 1.02HQ$	$R^2 = 0.74$
(0.41) (0.42) (0.42)	
$SES = -0.01 + 0.34HT^* + 0.82HQ^*$	$R^2 = 0.79$
(0.06) (0.06) (0.06)	
$FS = -0.01 + 0.79HT^* - 0.06HQ$	$R^2 = 0.62$
(0.09) (0.09) (0.09)	
1960	
$RM = 50.25 + 6.07HT^* - 1.19HQ$	$R^2 = 0.52$
(0.64) (0.64) (0.64)	
$SES = 0.02 + 0.22HT^* + 0.88HQ^*$	$R^2 = 0.80$
(0.05) (0.05) (0.05)	
$FS = 0.00 + 0.91HT^* - 0.09HQ$	$R^2 = 0.84$
(0.04) (0.04) (0.04)	
1970	
$RM = 50.67 + 6.99HT^* + 0.86HQ$	$R^2 = 0.55$
(0.67) (0.60) (0.68)	
$SES = -0.01 + 0.03HT + 0.89HQ^*$	$R^2 = 0.78$
(0.04) (0.04) (0.04)	
$FS = 0.05 + 0.74HT^* + 0.01HQ$	$R^2 = 0.68$
(0.05) (0.05) (0.05)	

Note: The values in parentheses are standard errors, and the asterisks indicate those coefficients that are significantly different from zero at 0.01.

Source: M. T. Cadwallader, "Urban residential mobility: A simultaneous equations approach," *Transactions of the Institute of British Geographers*, New Series, 7 (1982), Table VI, p. 467.

Reduced-form equations were calibrated to derive estimates for the three endogenous variables: residential mobility, socioeconomic status, and family status (Table 9.6). Housing quality and housing type, the two exogenous, or predetermined variables, were used to obtain these estimates. In all cases the coefficients of determination are greater than .5, and most of them are above .7. Housing type is a consistently more important predictor of residential mobility than is housing quality, and, as anticipated, the direction of the relationship is positive. Also, as expected, housing type is by far the major determinant of family status, and housing quality is the major determinant of socioeconomic status, although in this latter case housing type also plays a minor role.

The *structural equations*, using the estimated values for the endogenous variables, exhibit reassuringly high coefficients of determination (Table 9.7). For all

TABLE 9.7 ESTIMATED STRUCTURAL EQUATIONS

1950

$$RM = \underset{(0.63)}{76.11} + \underset{(0.75)}{1.65}\hat{S}ES + \underset{(0.85)}{5.47}\hat{F}S^* \qquad R^2 = 0.40$$

$$SES = \underset{(0.98)}{-5.24} + \underset{(0.01)}{0.07}\hat{R}M^* + \underset{(0.06)}{0.75}HQ^* \qquad R^2 = 0.81$$

$$FS = \underset{(6.33)}{4.56} - \underset{(0.08)}{0.06}\hat{R}M + \underset{(0.42)}{1.08}HT^* \qquad R^2 = 0.65$$

1960

$$RM = \underset{(0.77)}{50.27} - \underset{(0.86)}{0.69}\hat{S}ES + \underset{(0.85)}{6.81}\hat{F}S^* \qquad R^2 = 0.29$$

$$SES = \underset{(0.43)}{-1.79} + \underset{(0.01)}{0.04}\hat{R}M^* + \underset{(0.05)}{0.92}HQ^* \qquad R^2 = 0.78$$

$$FS = \underset{(2.94)}{-3.61} + \underset{(0.06)}{0.07}\hat{R}M + \underset{(0.36)}{0.48}HT \qquad R^2 = 0.58$$

1970

$$RM = \underset{(0.69)}{50.23} + \underset{(0.79)}{0.86}\hat{S}ES + \underset{(0.84)}{9.47}\hat{F}S^* \qquad R^2 = 0.52$$

$$SES = \underset{(0.28)}{-0.24} + \underset{(0.01)}{0.01}\hat{R}M + \underset{(0.04)}{0.89}HQ^* \qquad R^2 = 0.78$$

$$FS = \underset{(3.01)}{-0.57} + \underset{(0.06)}{0.01}\hat{R}M + \underset{(0.42)}{0.65}HT \qquad R^2 = 0.71$$

Note: $\hat{S}ES$, $\hat{F}S$, and $\hat{R}M$ refer to the estimated values derived from the reduced-form equations.

Source: M. T. Cadwallader, "Urban residential mobility: A simultaneous equations approach," *Transactions of the Institute of British Geographers*, New Series, 7 (1982), Table VII, p. 468.

three time periods, family status is significantly related to residential mobility in the hypothesized positive direction. The coefficient for socioeconomic status, however, is not significantly different from zero at the .01 significance level. The equations for socioeconomic status are generally as hypothesized, with both housing quality and residential mobility exhibiting positive coefficients that are significantly different from zero. The only exception to this pattern is the coefficient associated with the residential mobility variable for 1970, which is positive, but not significantly different from zero. In contrast, family status is somewhat less satisfactorily accounted for in all three years. Housing type has the expected positive relationship with family status in all cases, but is only significantly different from zero in 1950. Residential mobility, on the other hand, has an unexpected negative relationship for 1950, and is not significantly different from zero for any of the three time periods. In other words, the amount of residential mobility appears to primarily influence the socioeconomic status of an area rather than the family status. In terms of change over time in the structural coefficients the overall impression is one of remarkable stability. The coefficients have generally similar signs for all three years, and the pattern of statistically significant relationships is also noticeably similar. This temporal stability parallels that found for the housing and population dimensions themselves.

9.4 THE DECISION TO MOVE AND THE SEARCH FOR ALTERNATIVES

In contrast to the aggregated models described above, behavioral models of residential relocation focus on the individual decision maker, and normally conceptualize the descision-making process as being composed of three stages: the decision to move, the search for available alternatives, and the evaluation of those alternatives (Brown and Moore, 1971). Although this compartmentalization of the decision-making process obviously represents an oversimplification (Popp, 1976), it has had the advantage of allowing researchers to focus their attention on different parts of the whole. In the present section we explore some models of the decision to move and the search for alternatives; the evaluation of those alternatives will be discussed in the following section.

The Decision to Move

Investigations of the initial decision to seek a new residence have emphasized the importance of prior mobility history as a determinant, and the duration-of-residence effect, whereby the longer a household remains in a particular location the less likely it is to move, has been termed the *principle of cumulative inertia* (McGinnis, 1968). As always, however, there are exceptions to the rule, and for certain subpopulations the probability of a move appears actually to increase with increasing duration of stay (Clark and Huff, 1977).

An alternative approach to predicting the propensity to move of individual households has revolved around the concept of locational or *residential stress* (Clark and Cadwallader, 1973a; Brummell, 1981). The decision to move can be viewed as being a function both of the household's present level of satisfaction and of the level of satisfaction it believes may be attained elsewhere. The differences between these levels can then be viewed as a measure of stress created by the present residential location. The decision of the household actually to go ahead and seek a new residence can be viewed as an adjustment to that stress. The term "stress," of course, has many different meanings (Horvath, 1959), and our techniques for measuring stress and its effects are as yet rather crude compared to our ability to measure intelligence, attitude, or perceptual skills (McGrath, 1970, p. 3). Selye (1956), however, has proposed a set of terms that have been accepted by many psychologists and physiologists. He uses *stress* to refer to the state of the organism, *stressors* to refer to stress-producing agents, and *stress reactions* to refer to those responses which are characteristic of a stressed organism.

Using this terminology, we can turn our attention to identifying the stressors. The overall amount of stress experienced by an individual household can be measured across a fairly simple set of stressors. For the study being reported here (Clark and Cadwallader, 1973a) the level of stress was measured with regard to (1) the size and facilities of the dwelling unit, (2) the kind of people living in the neighborhood, (3) the proximity of the household location for interaction with friends and relatives, (4) proximity to the workplace, and (5) the amount of air pollution in the neighborhood. These stressors are representative of both the physical aspects of the dwelling and social conditions of the neighborhood, but additional and alternative stressors are not precluded in extensions of the model. An additional proximity variable, accessibility to goods and services, was considered but not included in the analysis principally because of the difficulty of aggregating all goods and services into one stressor. Other stressors used in the study involve essentially one element. It seemed that respondents might be confused and seek to understand which particular good or service they were to consider. To give them a variety of potential goods and services would have considerably enlarged the questionnaire.

The *size and facilities* of the dwelling unit were included because these, in conjunction with the household's position in the life cycle, have been found to be of great importance with regard to residential satisfaction. For example, Rossi (1980, p. 61) has indicated that the major function of mobility is to enable families to adjust their housing to the housing needs that are generated by the shifts in family composition that accompany life-cycle changes. The *kind of people* living in the neighborhood provides a measure of the relative importance of the social environment. How the household sees itself in relation to that environment is significant, as it has been suggested that residential mobility is sometimes the spatial expression of vertical mobility (Simmons, 1968). The influx of a different socioeconomic class into a neighborhood may be particularly influential in inducing the residents to move. This is especially noticeable in the case of an influx of blacks (Morrill, 1965; Rose, 1969). The *distance* variables involved are proximity to friends and relatives and distance to work. Some studies have rejected job location as an important variable (Simmons, 1968), but there is recent evidence that the journey to work is a significant factor in the relocation of households (Clark and Burt, 1980). Finally, numerous studies have found that *smog* contributes to residential dissatisfaction (Schusky, 1966), and as the study was carried out in Los Angeles, such a variable seems to be especially appropriate.

The effect of these stressors can be combined to calculate an overall measure of residential stress. The *stress value* for the individual is

$$S_i = \text{Md of } [(EOS_j - LS_j) + 7] \tag{9.30}$$

where S denotes the household's median level of stress, EOS is the household's ease of obtaining satisfaction elsewhere (another location), and LS is its present level of satisfaction. The function is calculated from the j stressors already outlined.

To measure ease of obtaining greater satisfaction elsewhere (EOS), each household was requested to consider how easy or difficult it would be to find a more desirable location elsewhere in Los Angeles. The respondent was asked to rate this on an attitude scale going from very difficult (1) to very easy (7), for each of the five characteristics. Similarly, the household was asked to evaluate its present level of satisfaction (LS) on an attitude scale going from very dissatisfied (1) to very satisfied (7), for each of the five characteristics. The greatest amount of stress is experienced when the household thinks that it is very easy to find better housing elsewhere, at the same time as being very dissatisfied with the present location. It is in this situation that the household is most likely to exhibit a strong desire to move. The problem of obtaining negative stress values, as a result of the subtraction involved in equation (9.30), is circumvented by adding 7 to each median stress level. The stress scale then varies from 1 (lowest possible stress) to 13 (highest possible stress).

A *modified stress value*, with a weighting factor, was also calculated. The magnitude of this weighting factor is based on the importance of a particular characteristic (j) to an individual household, as revealed in its ranking of these factors as regards having a satisfactory home. The weighted stress function is

$$S_i = \text{Md of } [(EOS_j - LS_j) + 7 + w_j] \tag{9.31}$$

where the notation is the same as in equation (9.30), except for the addition of the weighting factor, w_j.

The data used to calibrate equations (9.30) and (9.31) were obtained from a random sample of 169 households in the city of Santa Monica, within the Los Angeles metropolitan area. The sample was derived by first choosing a simple random sample of 40 equal-sized block units and then systematically sampling households within the block units. Of the 169 households, 39 refused to be interviewed and 21 could not be contacted after three call-backs. The results of the sampling yielded 106 usable interviews. Thirty-seven percent of the respondents lived in houses and the remainder in apartments.

First, the relationship between a household's median stress level and the household desire to move was investigated, and then the individual stressors were analyzed. The household's desire to move was measured on an attitude scale of 1 to 7, 1 denoting

TABLE 9.8 RELATIONSHIP BETWEEN THE DESIRE TO MOVE AND RESIDENTIAL STRESS

Correlation between the household's median stress level and desire to move:	
Kendall tau	.384
Correlation between the household's weighted median stress level and desire to move:	
Kendall tau	.343

Source: W. A. V. Clark and M. T. Cadwallader, "Locational stress and residential mobility," *Environment and Behavior*, 5 (1973), Table 3, p. 37.

no desire to move, and 7 denoting a very strong desire to move. According to the model, higher levels of stress should be associated with a strong desire to move. As the attitude scales provide ordinal-level data, *Kendall's tau* was utilized to examine the relationship between the desire to move and residential stress. Kendall's tau is an appropriate measure of association when both variables are measured at the ordinal level, and as with the correlation coefficient (see Section 2.4), its values range from −1.0 for a perfect negative relationship to +1.0 for a perfect positive relationship. The correlation between desire to move and residential stress is .384 (Table 9.8). As expected, then, the greater the household's level of stress, the greater the potential mobility exhibited by the household. Note, however, that the weighted stress formulation does not improve the strength of the relationship.

The different amounts of stress produced by each of the five stressors can be most conveniently compared on the basis of the median stress value generated by each stressor (Table 9.9). The differences between the median stress levels are very small, suggesting that apart from the smog stressor, each of the other four stressors is working equally in the creation of stress on the household. The small difference among the stressors may be a partial explanation for the lack of improvement in the weighted stress model. Correlations between the stressors and the desire to move give

TABLE 9.9 STRESSORS

	Median value on the:	
Stressor	Stress scale: 1 to 13	Weighted stress scale: 2 to 18
Proximity to friends and relatives	6.091	7.921
Proximity to work	5.417	8.056
Kind of people living in the neighborhood	5.231	8.038
Size and facilities of the dwelling unit	5.094	8.821
Amount of smog in the area	3.000	5.974

Source: W. A. V. Clark and M. T. Cadwallader, "Locational stress and residential mobility," *Environment and Behavior*, 5 (1973), Table 4, p. 37.

TABLE 9.10 RELATIONSHIPS BETWEEN THE INDIVIDUAL STRESSORS AND THE DESIRE TO MOVE

Correlation between the household's stress due to the size and facilities of the dwelling unit and desire to move:

	Coefficient	Significance
Tau	.352	.001

Correlation between the household's stress due to the kind of people living in the neighborhood and desire to move:

	Coefficient	Significance
Tau	.343	.001

Correlation between the household's stress due to the distance from friends and relatives and its desire to move:

	Coefficient	Significance
Tau	.253	.001

Correlation between the household's stress due to the amount of smog in the area and desire to move:

	Coefficient	Significance
Tau	.181	.005

Correlation between the household's stress due to the distance from work and desire to move:

	Coefficient	Significance
Tau	.082	.137

Source: W. A. V. Clark and M. T. Cadwallader, "Locational stress and residential mobility," *Environment and Behavior*, 5 (1973), Table 5, p. 38.

a clearer indication of the relative importance of each stressor as regards the process of residential mobility. In this case, stress due to the size and facilities of the dwelling unit appears to be the most important factor, and proximity to work seems to be somewhat less important (Table 9.10).

The Search for Alternatives

If a household is experiencing high levels of stress, and thus a strong desire to move, it must then either modify its present home, or begin an explicit search for alternative accommodation (Clark, 1982b). There are three interrelated questions that are crucial to any understanding of the residential search process (Clark, 1981). First, what are the information sources used to find vacant dwellings in the city? Second, how intense is the search activity? Third, what is the spatial pattern associated with that search activity?

By far the most important *sources of information* to prospective movers are newspaper advertisements, personal contacts, personal observation of "for sale" signs, and real estate agents. Rossi (1980, p. 209) has concluded, however, that personal contacts, while being the second most frequently used medium, after newspapers, are by far the most effective. The use of different sources of information varies, however, according to the type of dwelling unit that is desired. For example, Michelson (1977) suggests that newspaper advertisements are more often used when searching for an apartment rather than a house, and that real estate agents are an effective source for house hunters, especially in the context of out-of-town buyers (Clark and Smith, 1982). These results are generally substantiated by those of Rossi (1980, p. 209), although he emphasizes the particular significance of personal contacts and direct search when planning to rent rather than purchase.

The characteristics of the different information sources are also of some interest. Real estate agents are perhaps the most complex channel of information transmission, as they act as both recipients and transmittors of information (Palm, 1976). Prospective buyers pass messages with respect to housing preferences, while real estate agents may either intentionally, or unintentionally, transform and filter vacancy messages (see Section 3.2). Newspaper advertisements often have to omit important information, and are potentially rather ambiguous, while vacancies suggested by personal contacts tend to be rather localized. The sequential structure of information collection, via these various sources, has also been the subject of some debate (Clark and Smith, 1979).

The *intensity* of search activity has been addressed in a major empirical investigation of search behavior in Toronto. Using a sample of 380 cases, drawn from a population of 1486 movers, Barrett (1976) computed the amount of time spent searching (Table 9.11) and the number of houses searched (Table 9.12). Simply summarized, the lack of an extensive search phase was the major behavioral characteristic, as a large majority of households spent approximately one month looking at

TABLE 9.11 LENGTH OF TIME SPENT SEARCHING

Time	Frequency	Percent
Did not search	27	7.11
1 month	154	40.53
2 months	55	14.47
3 months	27	7.11
4 months	17	4.47
5 months	18	4.73
6 months to 1 year	29	7.63
1 year to 2 years	19	5.00
2 years or more	34	8.95
Total	380	100.00

Source: F. Barrett, "The search process in residential relocation," *Environment and Behavior*, 8 (No. 2, June 1976), Table 4, p. 176. Copyright © 1976 by Sage Publications, Inc. Reprinted by permission of Sage Publications, Inc.

TABLE 9.12 NUMBER OF HOUSES SEARCHED

Number of houses	Frequency	Percent
1	52	13.68
2 to 4	109	28.69
5 to 7	65	17.11
8 to 10	28	7.37
11 to 20	64	16.84
21 to 30	26	6.84
31 to 40	3	0.79
41 to 50	3	0.79
Over 50	30	7.89
Total	380	100.00

Source: F. Barrett, "The search process in residential relocation," *Environment and Behavior*, 8 (No. 2, June 1976), Table 5, p. 177. Copyright © 1976 by Sage Publications, Inc. Reprinted by permission of Sage Publications, Inc.

between two and four houses. Probability models have been constructed to devise optimal "stopping rules" for housing search activity (Flowerdew, 1976; Phipps and Laverty, 1983), but such models need to incorporate the various personality factors involved in the decision-making process. Conservative households, for example, might follow a satisficing strategy and merely choose an acceptable alternative rather than attempt to optimize their decision. Most search theories tend to incorporate the idea of a critical utility value which differentiates acceptable and unacceptable vacancies, but the search process itself often induces changes in this threshold value, due to learning and preference modification (Smith et al., 1979).

Finally, Barrett (1976) suggests that the *spatial pattern* of search is remarkably constrained. Of his sample of 380 respondents, more than 92 percent restricted themselves to average search distances of less than 3 miles. In addition, Brown and Holmes (1971) have demonstrated that the search activity of low-income, inner-city residents is more localized than that of their higher-income, suburban counterparts. In general, this restricted search space implies that households first choose an appropriate neighborhood, and then search for a suitable house within that neighborhood. It is to the process of neighborhood choice that we now turn our attention.

9.5 THE EVALUATION OF ALTERNATIVES

The third part of the residential decision-making process, the process of neighborhood evaluation and choice, involves two major questions (Hourihan, 1979a and b). First, what are the evaluative dimensions across which people assess the relative desirability of alternative neighborhoods? Second, once those evaluative dimensions have been identified, what are the appropriate rules for combining them into an overall utility value for each neighborhood?

The Evaluative Dimensions

An initial study by Johnston (1973) suggested that neighborhood preferences can be understood in terms of three underlying cognitive categories, or evaluative dimensions: (1) the impersonal environment, composed mainly of the physical attributes of the neighborhood; (2) the interpersonal environment, composed mainly of the social attributes of the neighborhood; and (3) the locational attributes of the neighborhood. Unfortunately, however, the data for Johnston's study were aggregated across different neighborhoods, thus masking the possibility that different sets of evaluative dimensions might be associated with different individual neighborhoods. With this aggregation problem in mind, the present author (Cadwallader, 1979b) examined whether the same evaluative dimensions are used for different types of neighborhoods.

The data used for the study were obtained, in questionnaire form, from 148 residents of Madison, Wisconsin. The original sample size of 255 households yielded 189 completed questionnaires. Of these completed questionnaires, however, 41 were considered unusable, mainly because of missing data. The sample design required the selection of all households within an area containing approximately 10 city blocks, as it was felt that all the subjects should be located in the same neighborhood, thus ensuring some measure of comparability when they rated other neighborhoods. The city blocks were composed of single-family dwelling units and, on average, the subjects had lived at their present addresses for approximately 12 years, although all portions of the duration-of-residence curve were well represented.

Each subject was asked to rate eight Madison neighborhoods on 11, seven-point rating scales. The neighborhoods were chosen by the experimenter with a view to maximizing ease of recognition on the part of the subjects. If a subject so desired, he or she was shown a map of Madison that outlined the eight neighborhoods. The comparatively long residency in Madison of most of the subjects ensured that there were few problems associated with neighborhood identification.

The subjects were presented with the 11 rating scales, across which the neighborhoods were to be evaluated, in the form of a semantic differential test. The *semantic differential technique* was originally developed by psychologists to investigate the meaning of words (Osgood et al., 1957), but it has also been used in the analysis of environmental images (Downs, 1970; Norcliffe, 1974). The methodological procedure involves presenting the subjects with a set of stimuli, or concepts, which they are required to evaluate across a series of scales consisting of bipolar adjectives. In the present context the neighborhoods represent the stimuli, while the 11 rating scales represent the bipolar adjectives (Table 9.13). These particular rating scales were chosen partly to maintain comparability with Johnston's study, and also to reflect the selection of attributes used in other studies involving some aspect of residential preferences (Chapin, 1974, p. 63; Ermuth, 1974, p. 62; Root, 1975). Care was taken to randomize the order of both neighborhoods and scales, and also to ensure that there was no regular sequence with respect to whether the right-hand or the left-hand member of the polar terms represented the positive one.

The data derived from the semantic differential procedure provided a 148×11

TABLE 9.13 NEIGHBORHOOD ATTRIBUTES

1	Crowded	— Spacious
2	Poorly kept yards	— Well-kept yards
3	Open	— Private
4	Poor reputation	— Good reputation
5	Poor-quality housing	— Good-quality housing
6	Noisy	— Quiet
7	People dissimilar to me	— People similar to me
8	Unsafe	— Safe
9	Inconvenient location	— Convenient location
10	Poor park facilities	— Good park facilities
11	Ordinary	— Distinctive

Source: M. T. Cadwallader, "Neighborhood evaluation in residential mobility," *Environment and Planning A*, 11 (1979), Table 1, p. 395.

data matrix for each of the eight neighborhoods. These matrices were subjected to principal components analysis (see Section 5.4) in order to identify any underlying evaluative dimensions. Components with eigenvalues greater than 1 were extracted and then rotated to a simple structure according to the varimax criterion. For each neighborhood there were three components with eigenvalues greater than 1, and the highest loading for each scale on these components is reported (Table 9.14). In almost every case the percentage of the total variance accounted for by these three components is fairly low, with the first component accounting for approximately 20 to 30 percent of the total variance. Such low levels of explained variation suggest that the 11 scales are not easily collapsed into significant underlying dimensions.

The structures of these components were analyzed, however, to determine whether they matched those postulated by Johnston (1973). For this purpose a matrix was constructed to show how many times the highest loading for each scale was associated with the same compartment as the highest loading for every other scale (Table 9.15). For example, in the case of four neighborhoods the highest loadings for quiet and privacy were on the same component, and for five of the eight neighborhoods the highest loadings for quiet and spaciousness were on the same component. The major variable groupings in this matrix were then uncovered by means of elementary linkage analysis (Yeates, 1974, p. 96). Two major groupings emerged, the first contained the scales representing spaciousness, housing quality, distinctiveness, quiet, and privacy, and the second contained the scales representing neighborhood reputation, yard upkeep, safety, type of people, and park facilities. The location variable was not included in either of these typal structures, as its highest loading was not regularly associated with the same component as the highest loading of any other variable. In general, then, these variable, or scale, groupings are of great interest, as they can be conveniently categorized as representing physical characteristics, social characteristics, and location. As such, they are encouragingly similar to the three evaluative dimensions postulated by Johnston (1973), although a more recent study has

TABLE 9.14 EVALUATIVE DIMENSIONS

Dimension	I	II	III	I	II	III	I	II	III	I	II	III
	Middleton			*Maple Bluff*			*Shorewood Hills*			*Monona*		
Spaciousness	.72			.75			.65			.75		
Yard upkeep	.66				.59		.73			.55		
Privacy	.50				.72			.41				.75
Reputation	.61				.49			.78			.75	
Housing	.60			.78			.82			.52		
Quiet	.75			.68				.70		.78		
People			.61			.78			.85		.52	
Safety	.72				.60				.41	.58		
Location		.74				.78		.77				.56
Park facilities			.84		.70			.65			.78	
Distinctiveness		.68		.86			.77					.60
Variance (% of total)	28	16	13	25	19	13	26	25	10	21	18	14
	Indian Hills			*Hilldale*			*Nakoma*			*Odana*		
Spaciousness	.71			.79			.71			.69		
Yard upkeep	.49				.60			.59			.81	
Privacy			−.70	.52					.87	.69		
Reputation	.66				.83			.79			.65	
Housing	.79			.60			.81			.62		
Quiet	.53			.77					.64			.65
People		.51			.73			.53			.76	
Safety	.62				.82		.68					.77
Location			.71			.71		.68				−.51
Park facilities		.86				.75		.74		.46		
Distinctiveness	.71			.74			.69					.50
Variance (% of total)	30	15	10	23	22	25	26	23	12	18	18	16

Source: M. T. Cadwallader, "Neighborhood evaluation in residential mobility," *Environment and Planning A*, 11 (1979), Table 2, p. 396.

TABLE 9.15 ASSOCIATIONS BETWEEN NEIGHBORHOOD ATTRIBUTES

	1	2	3	4	5	6	7	8	9	10	11
1 Spaciousness	—										
2 Yard upkeep	4	—									
3 Privacy	3	2	—								
4 Reputation	2	6	3	—							
5 Housing	8	4	3	2	—						
6 Quiet	5	3	4	3	5	—					
7 People	0	3	0	4	0	0	—				
8 Safety	4	5	2	4	4	4	2	—			
9 Location	0	1	3	2	0	2	2	1	—		
10 Park facilities	1	2	3	4	1	1	4	1	3	—	
11 Distinctiveness	5	2	2	1	5	4	0	3	3	0	—

Source: M. T. Cadwallader, "Neighborhood evaluation in residential mobility," *Environment and Planning A*, 11 (1979), Table 3, p. 397.

suggested four evaluative dimensions, representing the preponderence of residential land uses, lot size, social character, and housing quality (Preston, 1982).

Despite this general similarity, however, it is obvious that the factor structures associated with each neighborhood are far from identical (Table 9.14). For this reason, further analysis was pursued to see if there was any evidence for similar neighborhoods being cognized in terms of similar evaluative dimensions. The perceived similarity between the neighborhoods was measured by a similarity rating, which was obtained by asking the subjects to take each neighborhood in turn as an "anchor neighborhood" and to identify the three other neighborhoods which they regarded as most similar to the anchor neighborhood. The similarity rating for each pair of neighborhoods is shown by the values above the diagonal (Table 9.16), with the highest values indicating the greatest similarity.

The degree of factorial similarity across the neighborhoods was measured by the coefficient of congruence (see Section 5.5). Usually, each component from one factor structure is compared with the components from all other factor structures and is then paired with the one with which it has the highest coefficient of congruence (Harman, 1967, p. 271). In the present instance, however, only the first components from each factor structure were compared, as the eigenvalues associated with the remaining components are rather small. The congruency coefficients are shown below the diagonal (Table 9.16).

Inspection of the similarity ratings and congruency coefficients (Table 9.16) suggests that neighborhoods that are perceived to be similar are indeed cognized in terms of similar evaluative dimensions. This phenomenon is especially marked with respect to the three neighborhoods of Maple Bluff, Shorewood Hills, and Nakoma. The congruency coefficients between these three are all equal to or greater than .90, and they also have the three highest similarity ratings. In sum, although the evaluative dimensions are not exactly the same for all neighborhoods, it does appear that subjects utilize similar dimensions when evaluating similar neighborhoods.

TABLE 9.16 MATRIX OF SIMILARITY RATINGS AND CONGRUENCY COEFFICIENTS

	1	2	3	4	5	6	7	8
1 Middleton	—	.01	.18	.19	.02	.30	.02	.22
2 Maple Bluff	.77	—	.06	.02	.41	.05	.35	.02
3 Indian Hills	.91	.88	—	.16	.09	.20	.07	.23
4 Hilldale	.74	.87	.82	—	.06	.15	.09	.29
5 Shorewood Hills	.86	.91	.92	.85	—	.04	.38	.04
6 Monona	.88	.89	.86	.84	.84	—	.05	.20
7 Nakoma	.83	.94	.94	.78	.90	.92	—	.10
8 Odana	.68	.55	.67	.76	.59	.53	.58	—

Source: M. T. Cadwallader, "Neighborhood evaluation in residential mobility," *Environment and Planning A*, 11 (1979), Table 4, p. 397.

Before considering the *relative importance of the neighborhood attributes*, in terms of explaining neighborhood preferences, it is worth noting the important roles that some of them have been assigned in various theories of urban residential differentiation. Alonso (1964a), for example, has distinguished between the historic and structural theories of urban form. The *historic theory*, associated mainly with the name of Burgess, is essentially the spatial manifestation of the filtering process, whereby new houses are built for upper-income families, and in time are filtered down to lower-income families (see Section 5.2). An important element of this theory, then, is the assumption that households locate so as to maximize their satisfaction in terms of housing quality.

The *structural theory*, on the other hand, places the emphasis on the trade-off between the demand for accessibility and the demand for land (see Section 2.2). It is assumed that accessibility behaves as an "inferior good," so that as families increase their incomes they prefer to substitute land for accessibility. In other words, it is postulated that lower-income households will locate so as to maximize locational advantages, whereas upper-income households will attempt to maximize their desire for spacious lots.

A third major theory of residential differentiation can be conveniently labeled the *segregation theory*. This theory is implicit in factorial-ecological studies (see Section 5.5), which purport to demonstrate that people attempt to live apart from those unlike themselves, and thus minimize the possibility of conflict because of class, generational, racial, and religious or national differences (Rees, 1970). The segregation theory assumes therefore that when evaluating neighborhoods in terms of residential desirability, households will focus particular attention on the kind of people living in the neighborhood.

The relative importance of the neighborhood attributes was examined by analyzing how the subjects rated the attributes on a seven-point scale, going from very unimportant (1) to very important (7). The mean rating is used as the aggregate measure of importance for each attribute (Table 9.17). As expected from the preced-

TABLE 9.17 RELATIVE IMPORTANCE OF THE NEIGHBORHOOD ATTRIBUTES

Attribute	Mean	Attribute	Mean
1 Location	6.12	7 Spaciousness	5.53
2 Housing	6.06	8 Yard upkeep	5.49
3 Safety	6.02	9 Park facilities	4.87
4 Noise	5.94	10 Reputation	4.82
5 Privacy	5.67	11 Distinctiveness	4.41
6 People	5.55		

Source: M. T. Cadwallader, "Neighborhood evaluation in residential mobility," *Environment and Planning A*, 11 (1979), Table 5, p. 399.

ing theoretical discussion, the attributes of location and housing quality were both considered to be very important. The types of people living in the neighborhood were considered to be somewhat less important, although the influence of this variable might have been muted by the fact that Madison is not characterized by large ethnic or racial differences. Also considered to be of relatively minor importance was the spaciousness scale; thus there was some doubt cast on one of the major ingredients of the structural theory of urban form, although this result could be somewhat misleading, given the strong association between housing and spaciousness (Table 9.15).

Neighborhood Choice

Having identified the major evaluative dimensions involved in the residential choice process, the next step is to explore how the subjective ratings associated with these three evaluative dimensions are integrated into an overall utility value for a particular neighborhood. As location, housing, and safety, proved to be the three most important attributes, these were used to represent the locational, physical, and social characteristics dimensions, respectively. A series of *multiattribute attitude models* (see Section 8.4) were used to determine whether the attributes should be combined in an additive, multiplicative, or weighted additive form (Cadwallader, 1979c).

In particular, the following three models were tested:

$$P_i = \sum_{j=1}^{n} A_{ij} \tag{9.32}$$

$$P_i = \prod_{j=1}^{n} A_{ij} \tag{9.33}$$

$$P_i = \sum_{j=1}^{n} A_{ij} W_j \tag{9.34}$$

where P_i is the relative attractiveness of neighborhood i, A_{ij} is the attractiveness rating of neighborhood i on attribute j, and W_j is the relative importance of attribute j. These models represent additive, multiplicative, and weighted additive forms, respectively, and all the constituent variables, such as overall neighborhood preference, the attractiveness ratings on each of the three dimensions, and the relative weightings, were measured on the previously defined seven-point scales that were then averaged across subjects.

The results indicate that at least for this particular context and sample of subjects, the additive model is more appropriate than its multiplicative counterpart, but that there is no difference between the additive versions (Table 9.18). The first column shows the actual percentage of subjects who preferred each of the eight neighborhoods, while the remaining columns show the percentages predicted by each of the three models. The goodness of fit associated with each model is measured by the index of dissimilarity, which ranges from 0, indicating a perfect fit, to 100.

At first glance all three models appear to provide reasonably good fits, with the two additive formulations being only marginally superior. However, in this particular situation, the maximum possible value of 100 is a little misleading. If we knew nothing about the underlying decision-making process, our best prediction would be that an equal proportion of subjects would rate highest each of the eight neighborhoods. A comparison of this prediction and the observed behavior leads to a value of 7.5 for the index of dissimilarity. Viewed in this light, then, the results suggest that the additive models are genuinely superior to the multiplicative model.

A major reason for the excellent performance of the additive formulations in this study is the fact that whenever the predictor variables are monotonically related to the dependent variable, as in the present situation, the linear model tends to fit well (Louviere and Norman, 1977). Also, the predictor variables were genuinely independent, as they had been derived from an orthogonal factor analysis. On the other hand, one of the major problems with the multiplicative model is that if any

TABLE 9.18 COMPARISON OF NEIGHBORHOOD CHOICE MODELS

	Actual	Additive	Multiplicative	Weighted Additive
Shorewood Hills	16	14	19	14
Nakoma	16	14	16	14
Maple Bluff	13	13	13	13
Hilldale	12	14	16	14
Odana	12	13	13	13
Middleton	11	11	9	11
Indian Hills	11	11	8	11
Monona	9	10	6	10
		$D = 4$	$D = 8$	$D = 4$

Note: D refers to the index of dissimilarity.
Source: M. T. Cadwallader, "The process of neighborhood choice," paper presented at the International Conference on Environmental Psychology, University of Surrey, Guildford, England, 1979.

attribute is at a near-zero psychological value, the overall utility value will be very low, irrespective of how high the other attributes might be rated.

Nevertheless, it is somewhat surprising that the simple additive model performed as well as the weighted additive model, given the greater information content of the latter. In the present context, however, this situation is perhaps understandable, as the individual indicators for the evaluative dimensions did not vary markedly in terms of relative importance. Where a greater variance in the weightings occur, one would expect the weighted additive model to perform better than the simple additive model. This issue emphasizes the significance of distinguishing between determinant as opposed to important attributes, as attributes rated as important by subjects will not be pivotal in the decision-making process if the levels associated with such attributes are relatively invariant across the alternatives (Myers and Alpert, 1968).

Finally, the simple additive model was retested by incorporating a familiarity variable, as previously research has suggested the importance of familiarity, or information levels, in the formation of preferences (see Section 7.4). This reformulation provided the following equation:

$$P_i = \sum_{j=1}^{n} A_{ij} + F_i \tag{9.35}$$

where the notation is the same as in equations (9.32), (9.33), and (9.34), and F_i is the level of familiarity associated with neighborhood i, as measured by the previously defined seven-point rating scale. The index of dissimilarity for equation (9.35) is 3, so it is a slightly better predictor than the simple additive model.

In summary, people tend to evaluate alternative neighborhoods across three major evaluative dimensions, representing the physical, social, and locational characteristics of those neighborhoods. There is also evidence that the overall relative attractiveness of neighborhoods can be predicted using a simple additive model, although it has been suggested that the utility functions used to evaluate alternatives might change during the course of the decision-making process (Phipps, 1983). Finally, it is important to note that the overall pattern of residential mobility will reflect a combination of forces representing not only household preferences, but also such external constraints as housing market opportunities and the behavior of financial institutions.

10

Urban Planning

10.1 STATE INTERVENTION

In Chapter 1 it was suggested that one way of understanding the evolution of cities is to think of the urban future as being a response to the present pattern of socioeconomic forces plus the intervention of the state and other factors outside the urban system itself (Figure 1.1). It is now time to consider explicitly the role of state or government intervention, and the nature of urban planning. After reviewing various theories of the state, in order to appreciate fully the role of the state in planning, we consider the planning process itself. The problem of urban deprivation and the cycle of poverty is then discussed, followed by a brief overview of possible urban spatial plans.

Theories of the State

There are many theories of the state, and a variety of typologies have been produced (Johnston, 1980b). Most of these typologies focus on the functions of the state, and Clark and Dear (1981) identify six particular characterizations of the state that have been developed by a number of authors. First, and perhaps most simply, the state has been viewed as a *supplier of public goods and services.* The provision of public goods is regarded as an allocative function of government, and consideration is given to the optimal rules for distributing public goods. In particular, the state is seen as providing those goods and services that the majority of the population require but are unable to provide for themselves.

Second, the state is also seen as a mechanism for *regulating and facilitating* the operation of the market economy. The state intervenes in the private market to ensure that the market creates the best possible allocation of resources, and to achieve the approximately equilibrium conditions that are characterized by high employment and low inflation. Within this context, the state also tries to maintain the "rules" of the free-market economy by enacting antitrust and antimonopoly legislation.

Third, part of the state's behavior is designed to adjust market outcomes in order to achieve some kind of policy goal. In this way the state engages in what might be called *social engineering,* which involves subjective judgments about what society ought to be rather than what it is. Although still accepting the marketplace as the major means of distribution, the state attempts to redress socioeconomic imbalances and to protect the interests of certain disadvantaged, or minority groups. More specifically, the state tends to set minimum thresholds with respect to standards of living and provides the facilities to ensure that nobody falls below these designated thresholds.

Fourth, the state acts as an *arbiter* in disputes between different interest groups in society. In this context the state has a number of options. For example, it can try to act as a neutral umpire, it can try to be rational and achieve some optimal outcome that benefits all the parties involved in the dispute, or it can be elitist and merely reflect the interests of the ruling power groups (Dye, 1972). This characterization of the state emphasizes the power vested in the state and its ability to use that power to further its own ends.

Fifth, the *instrumentalist* view of the state regards the state as being simply an instrument of the business elite. This viewpoint is perhaps best exemplified by the work of Miliband (1977), who explored the "conspiracy" between the ruling class and the state. He argues that the social backgrounds of the top decision makers in the government, judiciary, and law enforcement agencies ensure that the interests of major business, or capital, will always receive a sympathetic hearing. Thus the link between captial and the major state institutions tends to maintain the status quo of the socioeconomic and political system.

Sixth and finally, a *structuralist* perspective would argue that the functions of the state are determined by the structure of society itself rather than by a few key people within that society. The state responds to the prevailing balance of class forces within society, and attempts to alleviate persistent class contradictions. In this respect, the state is not an autonomous entity but rather, a reflection of the balance of power among competing social classes at any particular time.

Although it is convenient to distinguish among these different viewpoints, it is obvious that the categories are not mutually exclusive; some of them may subsume others. For example, both the structuralist and instrumentalist positions can be derived from Marxist theory (Harvey, 1976). What is most important, however, is that all six approaches contain both useful insights and inherent weaknesses. Their different theoretical perspectives are not easily reconciled, and it is best to adopt a position of theoretical pluralism (Saunders, 1979).

Forms of Urban Government

These various theories of the state are partly manifested at the local level by different forms of urban government. Most city governments fall into one of three categories:

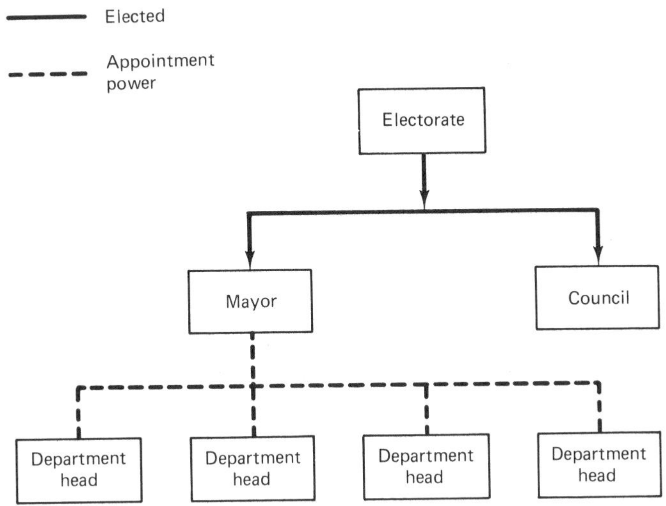

Figure 10.1 Mayor-council form of government. (From *City Lights: An Introduction to Urban Studies* by Barbara E. Phillips and Richard T. LeGates, Fig. 10.1, p. 262. Copyright © 1981 by E. Barbara Phillips and Richard T. LeGates. Reprinted by permission of Oxford University Press, Inc.)

the mayor-council form, the council-manager form, and the commission form. Fifty-two percent of all U.S. cities with populations of more than 50,000 had a council-manager form of government in 1970, while 40 percent had a mayor-council form of government (Caputo, 1976, p. 95). It is also true, however, that the council-manager form of government is not often found in cities with populations of more than 500,000.

In the *mayor-council* form of government, both the mayor and the city council are directly elected by the public. The mayor is regarded as the chief executive, while the council is the legislative body. Unlike the mayor, the council members usually have other jobs and can devote only a limited amount of time to their council duties. As shown in the organizational chart (Figure 10.1), the mayor typically has the power to appoint the individual department heads.

It is conventional to distinguish between strong and weak mayor-council forms of government. A mayor-council form of government is considered to be *strong* if it has some or all of the following characteristics. First, the mayor can veto ordinances passed by the council. Second, the mayor has significant power over the city budget, such as the right to submit an executive budget or have veto power over individual items in the budget. Third, the mayor has the power to appoint or remove department heads, or city commissioners, without council approval. Fourth, the mayor has a four-year term of office with the possibility of reelection for many terms, and enjoys the support of powerful local interest groups and an effective political organization.

On the other hand, a *weak* mayor-council system exists in those situations where many department heads, such as city treasurer, city assessor, or city attorney, are either elected directly by the public, or are appointed by the city council rather than by the mayor. Such situations are characterized by a diffusion of power and responsibilities, and individual department heads often have conflicting political philosophies. The power of the mayor also tends to be rather weak if he or she can only be elected to a comparatively short term of office, for example two years, and if other layers of local government, such as counties or special districts, have significant authority.

As one might expect, there has been considerable debate over the merits of council versus mayoral power. Most council members are elected from individual districts within the city, so it is often argued that the mayor should asume increased power and responsibility, as he or she is elected on a citywide basis and presumably represents the general interests of the entire city. On the other hand, others argue that a strong mayor can lead to the overpoliticization of local decision making, whereby public policy is designated to benefit those interest groups who have direct access to the mayor. The decentralization of power tends to benefit those economic, racial, or ethnic minorities who are represented by council members elected from their own neighborhoods.

Under the *council-manager* form of government, which is common in many medium-sized American cities, the mayor has much less power and authority than in a mayor-council government (Phillips and LeGates, 1981, p. 262). The most important individual figure in this form of government is the city manager, who is appointed by the city council (Figure 10.2). In most instances the city manager is responsible to a

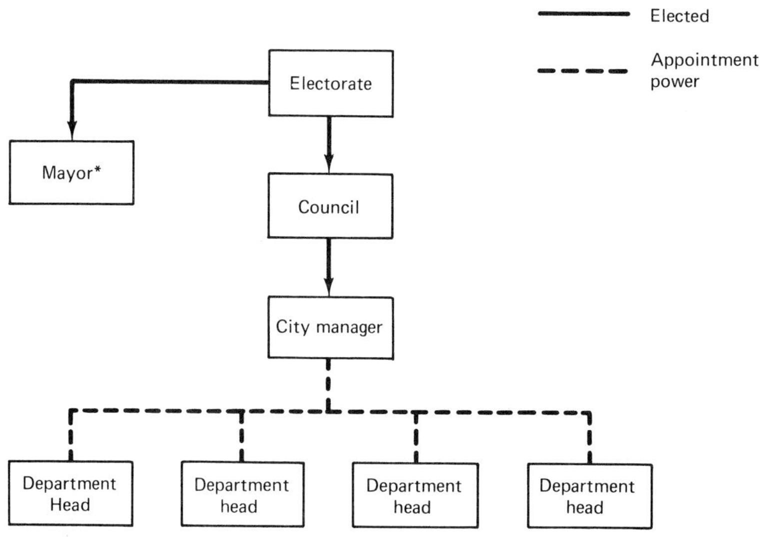

Figure 10.2 Council-manager form of government. (From *City Lights: An Introduction to Urban Studies* by Barbara E. Phillips and Richard T. LeGates, Fig. 10.2, p. 263. Copyright © 1981 by E. Barbara Phillips and Richard T. LeGates. Reprinted by permission of Oxford University Press, Inc.)

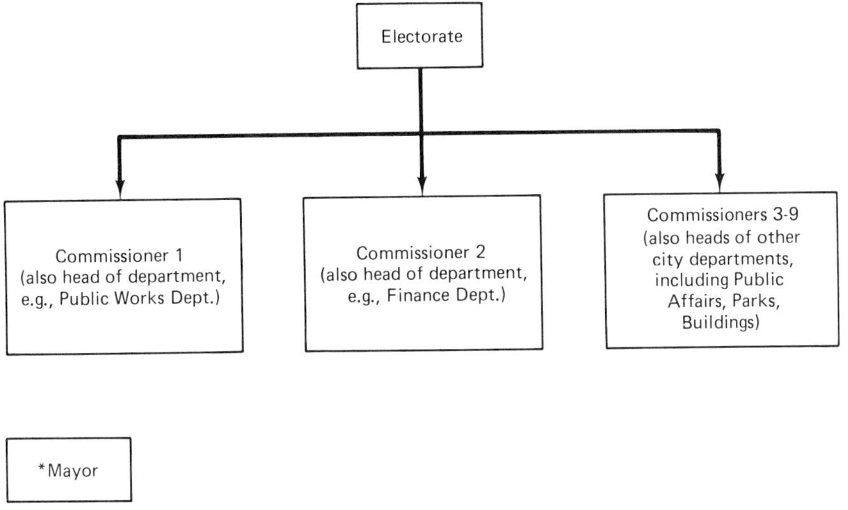

Figure 10.3 Commission form of government. (From *City Lights: An Introduction to Urban Studies* by Barbara E. Phillips and Richard T. LeGates, Fig. 10.3, p. 264. Copyright © 1981 by E. Barbara Phillips and Richard T. LeGates. Reprinted by permission of Oxford University Press, Inc.)

directly elected city council and has the power to appoint and remove department heads. The manager is responsible for the day-to-day running of the city, and although the council retains general legislative power, the manager generally prepares the city budget and develops policy recommendations for the council's action. Also, the combination of professional expertise, and access to detailed information, tends to give city managers considerable power.

Finally, under the *commission* form of urban government, the voters elect a relatively small number of commissioners, who function as both legislators and executives (Figure 10.3). In other words, there is no separation of power similar to that between the council and a mayor. The commission form was introduced in Galveston, Texas, in the early 1900s (Abrams, 1971, p. 57), but it has not been widely adopted. In particular, this form of government suffers from the fact that there is no executive leader, and thus it is very difficult to coordinate individual policy initiatives. One of the commissioners usually serves as mayor, but his or her function is largely ceremonial.

Public Participation

The idea of direct citizen input into urban government, and planning in general, received its greatest stimulus during the early 1960's. Both the Ford foundation projects and the Model Cities Program, of 1966, emphasized the idea of local public involvement (Kasperson and Breitbart, 1974). The introduction of public participation was viewed as a means by which some of the power could be transferred from the bureaucracy to the people. In addition, it was argued that local government officials would benefit from the increased flow of information, and thus be in a position to make more rational decisions. A more cynical view, however, would suggest that the formal recognition of public participation simply legitimizes the activity of planners, while giving the public the impression that their opinion counts (Knox, 1982, p. 209). Also, the socioeconomic characteristics of those citizens who do become involved in the local decision-making process suggest that it is local business interests that are likely to benefit most.

In any event, it is not hard to imagine why local officials have been less than enthusiastically receptive to the notion of extensive public participation in the planning process. Most bureaucracies try to preserve money and time by considering a minimum number of alternatives and restricting participation to a small number of decision makers (Downs, 1964). Also, planners tend to feel that too much public participation undermines their professional expertise, and that the different interest groups will tend to cancel each other out anyway.

Perhaps one of the most effective forms of public participation falls under the heading of advocacy planning. *Advocacy planning* involves the use of experts by neighborhood organizations, and other local groups, to ensure that their interests and needs are articulated in the technical language of professional planners. Kasperson and Breitbart (1974, p. 43) suggest that there are really two types of advocacy planning. One is where an advocate directly represents a particular client, or neighborhood, on a specific issue, while the other type involves an advocate working on his or her own initiative to help a particular group of citizens, but no formal arrangements are involved. In the latter instance, the advocate proceeds solely on the basis of his or her own ideological judgment, so the principle of advocacy planning explicitly recognizes that planning goals are value statements that are not objectively verifiable, and so public decision making must reflect the will of the people (Davidoff and Reiner, 1962). In other words, conflicting interest groups must be directly represented, as planners cannot truly arrive at "objective" solutions. Advocate planners disavow the view that planning is merely the application of technical expertise to society's problems, and suggest that the advocate must identify his or her position with respect to a particular issue, and then represent the interests of a clientele that has similar views.

Most advocacy planning has tended to focus on the issues of urban renewal and freeway construction through low-income neighborhoods (Corey, 1972), and although this kind of approach has had some success in blocking, or at least modifying, the official plans, it has been criticized on a number of grounds. In particular, critics have identified three key problems: a neighborhood's susceptibility to the advocate's personal values, the exclusion of neighborhood members from the more technical processes of plan preparation and data manipulation, and the focus of advocacy planning on short-term issues rather than on long-term goals (Kasperson and Breitbart, 1974, p. 48). These first two points suggest that the advocate planner can sometimes assume, either knowingly or unknowingly, the role of community manipulator (Peattie, 1968).

Location of Public Facilities

Public input would seem to be especially appropriate in the context of locating public facilities, such as waste treatment plants, parks, museums, art galleries, libraries, and public hospitals (Kirby, 1982). The allocation of public facilities requires not only the computation of demand levels, but also the calculation of *externality* effects, which summarize the effects of a location decision on those not directly involved with the facility (Palm, 1981, p. 243). A positive externality, or spillover effect, occurs when the residents of an area gain from a particular location decision, such as a new public park. A negative externality, however, will lower the quality of life in an area, such as when a new freeway divides an existing community and increases the amount of noise and air pollution. It is in the context of these negative externalities, of course, that most conflicts tend to occur, and Harvey (1973) has drawn a distinction between accessibility and proximity. *Accessibility* to a public facility is generally regarded as a positive asset, but *proximity* refers to the effect of being close to a facility that is not directly utilized, thus imposing a cost on those households involved.

In essence, the public facility locational decision is inherently a *political act,* representing a compromise between various interest groups (Dear, 1974). The political nature of the decision occurs for three main reasons. First, the lack of clear theory for locating public facilities ensures that the decision is the subject of various political pressures, although much recent work has been devoted to the question of maximizing accessibility (Hodgart, 1978). Second, the lack of detailed information concerning potential demand, and budget restrictions, does not encourage the development of a purely criteria-based decision-making process. Third, because financial resources are limited and priorities must be established, decisions concerning the location of public facilities are unavoidably forced into the political arena.

A good example of the problems associated with locating public facilities is provided by *mental health care* establishments. Dear (1978) has suggested that such establishments generate two types of externalities. First, there are the tangible effects which involve clearly identifiable, and usually quantifiable impacts. For example, most residents fear that community mental health centers result in declining property values. This situation can often result in a self-fulfilling prophecy syndrome, although there is in fact some evidence that property values are unrelated to the siting of such facilities. In a study of Philadelphia neighborhoods (Dear, 1977), both positive and negative property value fluctuations were observed, and since many public facilities are often in superior physical condition to their surrounding neighborhoods, there are justifiable reasons to expect some instances of increasing property values. The intangible effects, on the other hand, are associated with such things as the fear for personal safety, the stigma attached to mental illness, and the dislike of loitering clients.

The perceptions of the neighborhood residents themselves play an extremely important role in the identification of externality effects. In a household survey conducted in metropolitan Toronto, it was found that a strongly neutral group of respondents did not anticipate any impact on their neighborhood from the introduction of mental health facilities (Dear et al., 1980). In general, respondents who claimed to be aware of a local mental health care facility were relatively more tolerant in their estimation of the neighborhood impact of such facilities. Also, the spatial extent of the negative externality field appeared to be remarkably confined. As proximity to a potential facility increased, so did the perceived undesirability of that facility, but the most negative responses occurred within one block of a facility location; beyond six blocks there was a far more tolerant attitude.

Planners appear to have developed three major conflict-avoidance strategies when dealing with community opposition to plans for mental health facilities. The simplest involves finding locations where no community opposition is expected, or where controversial facilities would generally be unnoticed (Dear and Wittman, 1980). Such locations are usually found within areas of the inner city that are characterized by rental accommodation and transient residents. If such locations are not appropriate, one of two other approaches tends to be adopted. Either a community is educated and coerced into accepting a facility before it is actually introduced, or a facility is set up without prior warning, in the hope that it will go unnoticed until it can be demonstrated that it does not generate any harmful spillover effects (Wolpert et al., 1975).

10.2 THE PLANNING PROCESS

Berry (1973) has postulated an urban policy model (Figure 10.4) and suggested a sequence of four modes of planning that are variants of this general model. In essence one can distinguish between two categories of inputs—external forces, and policies and programs—that produce change in the urban system. This change can generate two different types of outputs: undesirable results or desirable results: that is, either problems, or the goals or objectives that are being sought. Box 1 represents the existing urban system which has to be acted on to achieve the goals contained in box 2. In general, urban planning can either be consciously directed toward achieving these

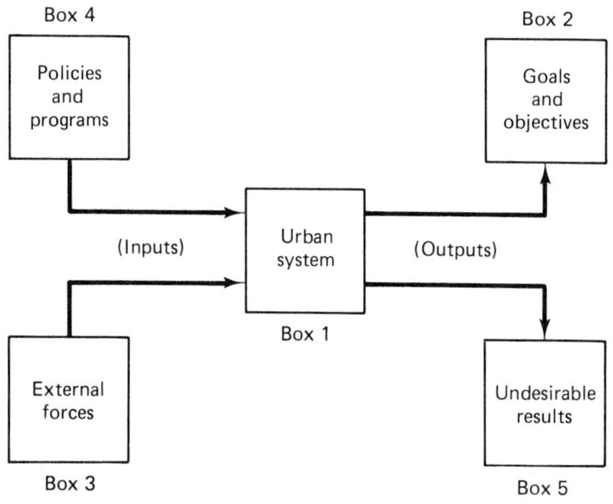

Figure 10.4 Urban policy model. (Reprinted from *The Human Consequences of Urbanization: Divergent Paths in the Urban Experience of the Twentieth Century* by B. J. L. Berry, Fig. 17, p. 173. Copyright © 1973 by St. Martin's Press, Inc. Reprinted by permission of the publisher.)

long-range goals, or it can simply react to the problems or crises represented by box 5. Box 3 contains the exogenous forces that influence the urban system, but whose causes lie outside the influence of the urban policymaker. Such forces include the behavior of the birthrate and the gross national product, which often affect the growth of urban areas far more than the policies of individual city planning departments. Finally, box 4 represents the policies and programs generated by government planning agencies. These programs can be likened to levers that are pulled in order to cause desired changes in the urban system.

Four Modes of Planning

Within this general framework, Berry identified four modes or styles of planning: ameliorative problem solving, allocative trend modifying, exploitive opportunity-seeking, and normative goal oriented. The simplest and perhaps most common form of planning is the *ameliorative problem-solving* form (Figure 10.5a), in which nothing is done until the problems reach crisis proportions. This strategy is very present oriented, and little thought is given to long-run goals or objectives. American local authorities are often forced into this essentially reactive mode of planning because of their reliance on elected officials with short terms of office, their restricted budgets, and their limited legal jurisdictions (LaGory and Pipkin, 1981, p. 276).

The *allocative trend-modifying* form of planning (Figure 10.5b) is more future oriented, and uses projections of existing trends to forecast problems that will arise in the future. Based on the prediction of these future problems, available resources are allocated to promote the most desirable outcomes. In this scenario, the regulatory mechanisms are devised to modify and make the best of existing trends. Traffic forecasting demand models provide an excellent example of this strategy of predicting the future and then trying gently to modify it.

The *exploitive opportunity-seeking* planning style (Figure 10.5c) does not identify future problems, but seeks out new growth opportunities. These new growth opportunities are identified by imaginative leaders in both the public and private sectors of the economy. As well as planners themselves, the individual actors are corporate managers, real estate developers, and industrialists. Whereas the trend-modifying approach seeks to make the best out of existing trends, the opportunity-seeking approach merely aims to maximize profits while it can, with less concern for the future.

Finally, *normative goal-oriented* planning (Figure 10.5d) is explicitly future oriented, and seeks to identify a desired future state for the urban system. Specific goals are set in accordance with the kind of future that is desired, and plans are implemented to guide the system toward those goals. This approach is more long term in nature, and assumes that consensus can be reached with respect to what an ideal urban system should be.

In reality, of course, planning policy in most countries represents a mixture of these four major types. However, normative goal-oriented planning is really possible only in those countries which have a centralized form of government, with sufficient

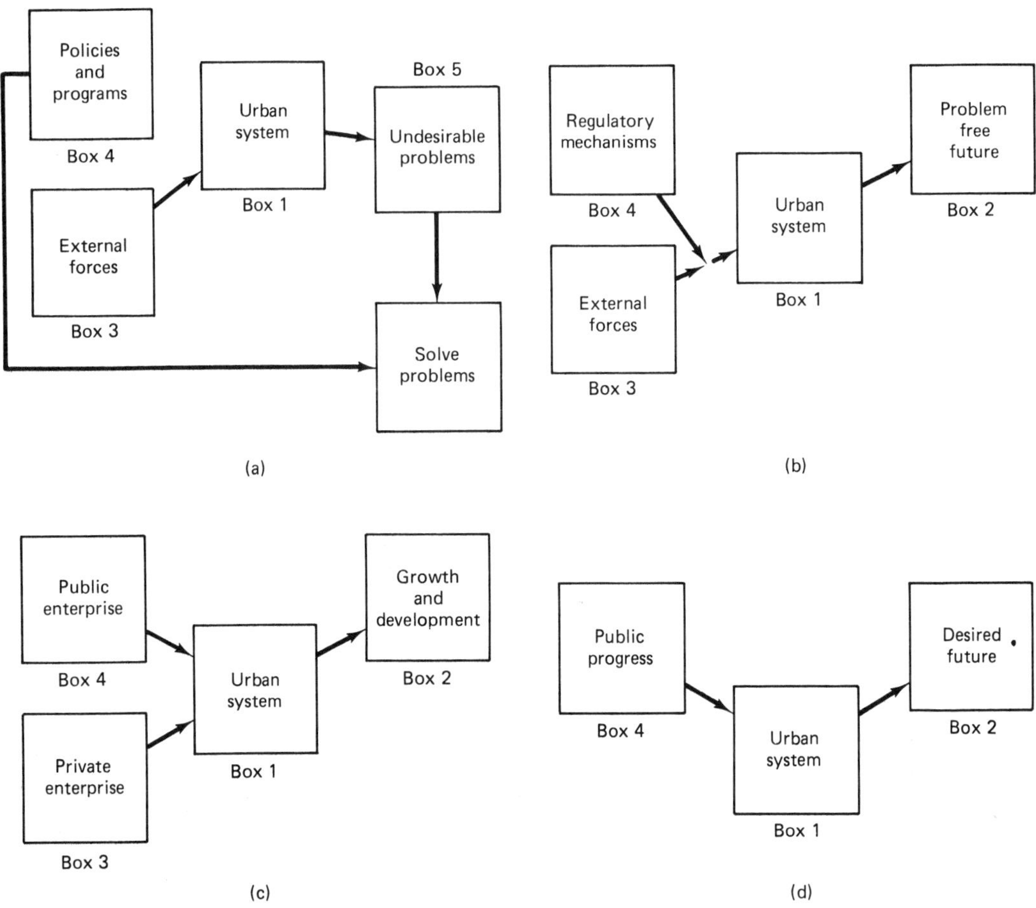

Figure 10.5 Four urban policy-making styles: (a) ameliorative problem solving; (b) allocative trend modifying; (c) exploitive opportunity seeking; (d) normative goal-oriented. (Reprinted from *The Human Consequences of Urbanization: Divergent Paths in the Urban Experience of the Twentieth Century* by B. J. L. Berry, Fig. 18, pp. 175–176. Copyright © 1973 by St. Martin's Press, Inc. Reprinted by permission of the publisher.)

control over the different sectors of the economy. Thus this style of planning is characteristic of the Soviet Union and to a lesser extent of democratic countries with strong central governments, such as Sweden and Great Britain. At the other extreme, countries such as the United States and Canada tend to exemplify the ameliorative problem-solving and the allocative trend-modifying forms of planning.

Stages in the Planning Process

A variety of schematic summaries of the various stages in the planning process have been devised (McLoughlin, 1969; Wilson, 1974; Batty, 1979; Oppenheim, 1980). The

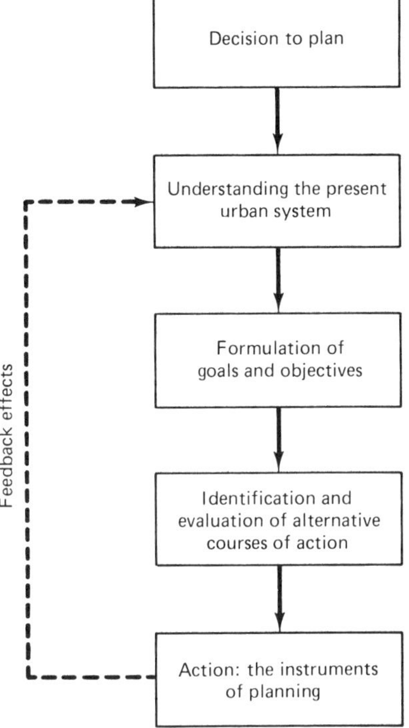

Figure 10.6 Planning process.

one presented here (Figure 10.6) is a simplified composite of these, and like them, falls within the genre of systems planning. Fundamental to the concept of systems planning is the idea of interaction between two types of systems: the controlling system, represented by the planners themselves, and the urban system, which it seeks to control (Hall, 1975, p. 271). In other words, just as cities and regions can be usefully conceptualized in terms of interacting systems, so can planners themselves, thus creating a planning system (Wilson, 1968).

The first stage in the overall planning process is the actual *decision to plan.* Planning, as we understand it today, is of relatively recent origin, and should not be taken for granted. The decision to plan requires moving from a society dominated by laissez-faire principles to one that accepts the need for at least a certain amount of state intervention. Such a decision is a major step, as it involves the restriction of individual freedoms, such as the right to do what one likes with one's own property. In this respect, the need for planning, and the definitions of its roles and purposes, should be kept under constant review by all sections of society.

Having made the decision to plan, the next step is to *understand the operation of the present urban system.* The system must be represented in summary form, and that representation can be either purely descriptive, without providing an explanation of the underlying processes at work in the system, or causal, identifying the constituent cause-and-effect relationships (Oppenheim, 1980, p. 2). The bulk of the present book has been devoted to describing a number of theories and models that contribute to our understanding of the present urban system. For the most part these models have been partial rather than general, in that they are concerned only with one identifiable subsystem, such as the housing market, within the overall urban system.

Batty (1978) has suggested that the models used in this stage of the planning process can be categorized according to a number of major characteristics. First, in terms of the temporal dimension, they range from static, through quasi-dynamic, to fully dynamic. Because of the unavailability of true time-series data, however, most urban models are static in nature, which creates a serious problem, as planning is concerned with change over time. Second, models have been constructed at different levels of both sectoral and spatial aggregation. Sectoral aggregation involves aggregating different occupational or ethnic groups, for example, while spatial aggregation involves aggregating different spatial units, such as blocks and census tracts. Third, from a technical perspective, models incorporate either linear or nonlinear forms of relationships, with linear models usually being regarded as special forms of nonlinear models. Because linear mathematics has been more thoroughly developed than its nonlinear counterpart, most urban models are linear, although a pursuasive argument can be made that most real-world relationships are nonlinear. Finally, models entail either direct or indirect solution procedures. Direct procedures involve some kind of immediate solution, whereas indirect methods are sequential and involve iterative or simulation techniques.

Having attempted to understand the nature of the urban system as it is presently constituted, usually through the construction of appropriate urban models, the next step is to *formulate a series of goals and objectives.* Chapin (1965, pp. 349–351) has suggested that a hierarchy of policy decisions can be identified. For example, a first-order policy decision might be to contain urban development at a particular level. A second-order policy decision might involve decisions concerning concentration versus dispersal, or a few large nuclei versus several smaller ones. Third-order decisions would then get down to the specifics of land use patterns, residential densities, and transportation networks.

In a similar vein, McLoughlin (1969, p. 97) distinguished between goals and objectives. Goals are typically rather vague and general, and progress toward a particular goal requires the attainment of certain more precise objectives. For example, a stated goal might be to increase the opportunities for outdoor recreation in the city, while the associated objectives might be to double the acreage of parks within the next 10 years, and to acquire 5000 acres of river and lakeside land within the next 20 years. Similarly, a goal of providing a convenient pattern of major shopping centers might be matched with the particular objective of ensuring that the average distance of households from their nearest major shopping centers is no more than 5 miles.

Wilson (1974, p. 16) has chosen to characterize the concept of goals as representing general areas of concern. In this way he introduces (1) political goals, such as the maintenance of efficient and democratic government; (2) economic goals, such as accessibility to goods and services; (3) social goals, such as safety; and (4) environmental goals, such as environmental quality. There is always the thorny problem, however, of who should be responsible for identifying the particular goals towards which an urban system is directed. The broad goals for society are generally a matter for the politicians, but politicians are often involved with acute short-term issues (Hall, 1975, p. 276). Somehow, then, goals must be formulated via cooperative effort involving direct participation by the public, perhaps through public opinion polls and referendums, local politicians, and professional planners.

Once the goals and objectives have been defined, *alternative courses of action for achieving those goals must be identified and evaluated.* In particular, the proposed alternative courses of action must be related specifically to the original goals and objectives. For example, alternatives related to the physical form of the city, such as whether it should be linear, circular, or polynuclear, might have very little to do with stated objectives concerning employment opportunities and accessibility to shopping centers. Once a set of feasible alternatives have been suggested, however, there are three major principles of program evaluation that should be adhered to (Krueckeberg and Silvers, 1974, p. 194): first, the various impacts of a program over time should be clearly identified; second, the seriousness of these impacts, both good and bad, should be estimated; and third, the costs of the program should be considered in the light of available funds.

Three relatively formal methods for evaluating alternative courses of action, or planning programs, have been established in the planning literature. The most popular methodology can be generally labeled as *cost-benefit analysis,* whereby the anticipated benefits to be generated by a given program are compared to its anticipated costs. The costs and benefits are usually itemized in money terms, and it is assumed that the best alternative is the one that provides the greatest quantity of economic benefits in relation to economic costs. One of the obvious problems of this approach, however, is that many planning elements, such as a beautiful landscape or building, cannot be evaluated in financial terms. In other words, notions of social costs and benefits must also be included in the overall analysis. Somewhat less formal evaluative devices that try to deal with this problem are the planning balance sheet (Lichfield et al., 1975) and the goals' achievement matrix (Hill, 1968).

After particular courses of action have been chosen, they are implemented, or put into practice, using the *instruments of planning.* Scott (1980, p. 61) has suggested that there are three major ways that urban governments, or planning agencies, have intervened in urban affairs: by using fiscal policies, land regulation policies, and development policies. One of the major instruments of fiscal policy has been the property tax, which is ubiquitous in the United States. Also, monetary variables are manipulated by controlling the prices of certain urban goods and services, such as legislating limits on housing mortgage rates, and rent controls. Finally, urban governments often directly subsidize, or provide grants for, mass transit systems, low-income housing programs, and industrial location incentives. Many would argue, however, that such subsidies are merely palliative, and simply contribute to the inefficient production of a variety of urban services.

One of the most popular types of land regulation policy has been the use of zoning ordinances, which we discussed in the context of land use and land value theory (see Section 2.3). Other legal restrictions on the use of land include such devices as subdivision controls, construction codes, and building height limitations. Often, however, such restrictions have been lifted in those situations where some kind of political pressure has been brought to bear. For example, exceptions are sometimes made to land use zoning ordinances in order to placate a particular interest group. In particular, land use restrictions are often relaxed in those situations where they threaten to depress land prices.

The final type of policy instrument is represented by the direct development or redevelopment of targeted areas by government agencies. Examples of such development projects include public housing construction, urban renewal, and the initial development of industrial estates. These projects all play important roles in terms of guiding the urban land market, and thus shaping the spatial patterns of land use and land value.

The effect of manipulating these policy instruments is then monitored in order to calibrate their influence on the urban system. Sometimes the *feedback effects* are in the anticipated, positive direction, but often there are unanticipated side effects. These unanticipated side effects are comparable to those sometimes produced by surgical intervention in the case of hospital patients. The overall planning process has a certain trial-and-error element to it, and the systems approach allows it to be viewed in terms of a functioning system, with internal feedback effects that can be induced by manipulating certain exogenous factors. In particular, the systems model of planning contains two major assumptions, one explicit and the other more implicit (Hall, 1979, p. 5). First, it is explicitly stated that this is a scientific approach to planning, which assumes that the urban system can be understood to such a degree that is possible to forecast accurately both of the direct and indirect effects of government intervention on the operation of that system. Second, and more implicitly, it is assumed that the urban planner can act in a value-free manner, with all the detachment of a physical scientist.

As can be imagined, these assumptions have been rather harshly criticized by some authors, especially in terms of what is seen as the inability to place the process of urban planning within the overall activity of the capitalist state (Scott, 1980, p. 231). As a result of this and other criticisms of mainstream planning theory, a series of alternative approaches have been suggested. Most of these alternatives focus on the role of public participation in the planning process and emphasize the fact that planning can be viewed as a political act of redistribution. In this latter context, it has been shown how the existing distribution of income and resources is often simply reinforced by the distribution of public goods (Harvey, 1973).

The Comprehensive City Plan

On the most local scale, much of the planning effort is devoted to producing, and implementing, a comprehensive city plan. Such plans are intended to provide a blueprint of how the city should develop, and they are long range in the sense that they often project up to 20 years into the future. Most of the following objectives tend to be incorporated into these plans (Chapin, 1965, p. 360). First, there should be provision for an orderly physical growth and development of the city. Second, land should be allocated among various alternative uses in order to maximize its potential benefits. Third, facilities should be provided to satisfy the various needs of a society with increasing amounts of leisure time. Fourth, an attempt should be made to provide a range of neighborhood environments. Fifth, economic development should be promoted in an effort to ensure sufficient employment opportunities for all sectors of the labor force. Sixth, plans should be made to ensure the provision of certain public services, such as transportation and education facilities.

Generally, the overall plan is divided into a number of components, or elements (Northam, 1979, pp. 474–476). *Population studies* are used to project the future demand for city services. Independent projections are made for various subgroups, based on age, income, and sex, so that the demand for particular types of services, such as transportation for the elderly, can be anticipated. These projections are also disaggregated for different parts of the city, as future demands will obviously vary across different types of neighborhoods.

Housing studies are conducted in conjunction with the population studies to ensure that sufficient amounts of different types of housing will be available in the future. For example, there should be an appropriate mix of single-family and multifamily dwelling units, and attention should be paid to the spatial distribution of different kinds of housing. Often, the private sector tends to be aimed at providing high-income housing, so the future need for low-income housing must be accurately assessed, including the feasibility of subsidizing low-income housing projects.

Aspects of the economic structure of the city are considered in *economic studies*. These studies project future demand for different parts of the labor force, and try to anticipate the need for particular specialized skills. Job retraining programs might be advocated to generate these skills, or attempts made to attract appropriate migrants from other cities. The interrelationships between the local economy and the state and national economies are also explored, in order to assess the impact of national fluctuations. The economic base and input–output analysis procedures described in Chapter 6 are important methodological tools in this context.

Land use studies are a key element of the overall planning process, and an inventory of existing land use is essential to the development of a city plan. Trends in land use, and current land use densities, serve as guides to future requirements, and land regulation policies are implemented to minimize the effects of negative externalities. Particular attention is paid to problems that might develop in the rural-urban fringe, where the competition for land between urban and agricultural uses is the most intense.

Finally, all comprehensive city plans involve a series of *transportation studies*. The obvious relationship between land use and traffic flow is utilized to estimate future traffic demands, often using some form of gravity model (see Section 8.1). Consideration must also be given to the future provision of mass transit systems and parking facilities for private automobiles. For example, the future use of the downtown area by private automobiles can be manipulated, to a certain extent, by the structure of parking costs.

10.3 URBAN DEPRIVATION

A number of urbanists have conceptualized a "cycle of poverty" that is especially associated with the central areas of North American cities. In the present section we discuss one such conceptualization (Johnston, 1982, pp. 253–261), especially as it relates to the interrelationships between different manifestations of poverty and the concept of multiple deprivation. We will then describe and evaluate the idea of tackling these problems by means of area-based positive discrimination, and conclude by exploring some alternative explanations of the cycle of poverty.

The Cycle of Poverty

Johnston's (1982) view of a cycle of poverty is represented in Figure 10.7. This diagram shows how the problems are linked in a cumulative fashion, thus creating a chain of situations that is difficult to break. *Poverty* is experienced by those members of society who are unable to find employment, or who are excessively poorly paid. The greatest single item of expenditure is generally housing, so those with the lowest incomes tend to live in *poor-quality housing,* both because they cannot afford high rents and because they are unable to qualify for mortgages. Often, the rents demanded are even higher than what might be suggested by prevailing market conditions because of the oligopolistic control of the housing supply by a few, very powerful landlords.

Poverty, especially through its relationship to poor housing, creates certain *stresses and strains* for the households concerned. This stress often generates certain kinds of chronic *health problems* that are related to poor diet, cold, and exposure to vermins. Sometimes severe mental illness can result from the problem of trying to cope with inadequate resources, and interpersonal disputes are accentuated by the high-density living. Palm (1981, p. 245) has pointed to the association between poverty and

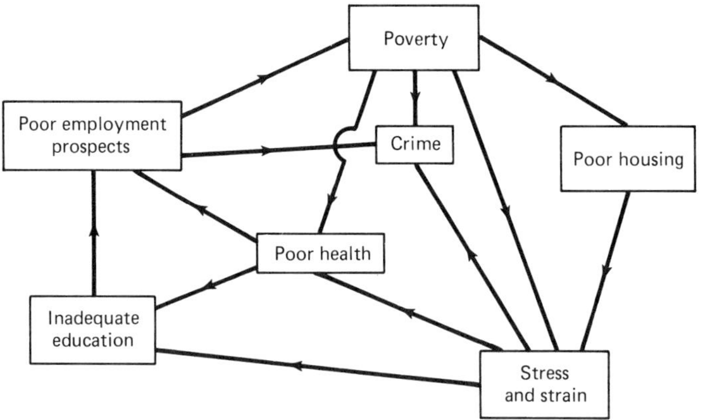

Figure 10.7 Cycle of poverty. (Reprinted from *The American Urban System: A Geographical Perspective* by R. J. Johnston, Fig. 9.2, p. 257. Copyright © by St. Martin's Press, Inc. Reprinted by permission of the publisher.)

particular health problems, and points out that health care facilities are often unequally distributed and discriminatory.

The cycle of poverty is further strengthened by the *inadequate educational facilities* that are characteristic of many inner-city areas. The school buildings are often obsolete, and the financial resources available to local school boards are relatively meager compared to their suburban counterparts. It is also true that unhealthy children are less likely to reach their full potential than are those who are well fed and housed. This relative deprivation in terms of educational opportunities tends to translate into *poor employment prospects*. Without certain qualifications, most of the school graduates are destined to end up in low-skilled, poorly paid jobs that provide little opportunity for advancement. The employment problem is compounded by the fact that in recent years many types of industry have been moving to the suburbs (see Section 6.2), thus generating high levels of unemployment in inner-city areas, especially with respect to blue-collar occupations.

A central element in this cycle of poverty is the incident of *crime*. Two types of crime appear to be particularly prevalent in this context. First, there are high rates of crimes against property, or economic crimes, that tend to be stimulated by high rates of poverty. Second, the stresses and strains associated with high unemployment also tend to be associated with crimes against the person, such as spouse beating and child abuse. Unemployment also tends to encourage the formation of youth gangs and associated turf rivalries.

Most of these problems described within the cycle of poverty tend to be concentrated in particular parts of the city. Thus Smith (1973, p. 125) has identified areas of Tampa, Florida, which are characterized by low economic status, poor housing, high disease rates, low educational attainment, and high rates of social disorganization. This overlapping and interpenetration of problems, in a spatial sense, has led to a concept of multiple deprivation, in order to indicate those parts of the city that are deprived in a variety of ways (Herbert, 1975). There is some evidence, however, that different problems do not always spatially coincide to the extent that is implied by such concepts as multiple deprivation (Smith, 1979).

Area-Based Positive Discrimination

Given the spatial concentration of poverty, and associated problems, it was perhaps natural that solutions should be sought in terms of providing help on a local basis. Area-based policies were introduced to complement existing welfare programs, which did not provide long-term help for the most deprived segments of the population and were unable to break the cycle of poverty in inner-city areas. Much of the initial impetus for this strategy was provided by the Ford Foundation, which during the 1950s was especially concerned with the problems of metropolitan government and urban renewal (Eyles, 1979). In particular, the Foundation started a gray-areas program, which was specifically aimed at decaying neighborhoods in the central city. A series of demonstration projects were undertaken in Boston, New Haven, North Carolina, Oakland, Philadelphia, and Washington. Similar experimental community action programs were instigated by the President's Committee on Juvenile Delinquency. In both cases the importance of educational and employment opportunities were stressed, and resources were concentrated into a few demonstration or experimental projects. It is probably fair to say, however, that these projects were not conspicuously successful, with public involvement remaining rather minimal, and few jobs being produced.

These initiatives were later adopted by the federal government in its War on Poverty program during the Kennedy administration, and the associated Economic Opportunity Act and Office of Economic Opportunity (Eyles, 1979). A series of community action programs stressed the need to coordinate services and to encourage the participation of the poor (Kramer, 1969). The provision of employment opportunities was seen as a primary goal, and Kasperson (1977) has argued that significant contributions were made in terms of creating jobs for the urban poor. The Model Cities program, set up in 1966, was also based on the area projects. Grants and technical assistance were provided to help communities establish demonstration programs which would reduce social and economic disadvantages. The program eventually involved about 150 cities, although the emphasis was placed on physical blight and urban renewal rather than on the poor themselves.

Despite some limited success, however, there is a growing feeling that such area-based programs do not get to the root of the poverty problem, in that it is unrealistic to abstract the problems of particular neighborhoods from their wider social context (Maclaran, 1981). Hamnett (1979), and others, have criticized what they call the fetishism of space, whereby spatial causes are inferred from spatial manifestations. They argue that deprived neighborhoods are merely the setting for a number of deprived persons who happen to reside there, and that the problems experienced by such persons arise from nonareal causes. In other words, if the problems are not areally caused, area-based solutions are unlikely to eliminate those problems. Eyles (1979) argues that although area effects can intensify or compound individual deprivations, they are not the source of those deprivations, which lie in the broader socioeconomic structure of capitalist society. Smith (1979) reminds us, however, that the economic and socially deprived are located in geographical space, as well as within an economic system and a class structure, so the spatial location of resources is clearly a relevant factor.

Alternative Explanations

Rather than simply focussing on the cycle of poverty and area-based solutions, it is advisable, then, to think in terms of a variety of possible explanations of urban deprivation (Knox, 1982, p. 207). In this context, there appear to be at least five major candidates (Hamnett, 1979). First, the idea of a *culture of poverty* was initially put forward by Lewis (1966), who argued that problems arise from the internal pathology of deviant groups, who suffer from a lack of opportunity and aspiration. Consequently, strategies to improve the situation should concentrate on social education in general rather than on particular projects with respect to housing and income maintenance.

Second, the concept of *transmitted deprivation* has been invoked to suggest that social maladjustment is transmitted from one generation to the next. The emphasis is on the relationships between persons, families, and groups. Thus the home environment is seen to be the major culprit rather than the problems of low wages and poor housing. For adherents of this idea, the solution lies in using professionals such as social workers to help parents improve the home environment.

Third, it has been suggested that the problems of the socioeconomically deprived can be blamed on *institutional malfunctioning*. In this scenario it is aruged that problems have arisen due to the failure of planning and administrative bureaucracies. Such bureaucracies have tended to generate a series of separate departments concerned with education, housing, and the like, and so have been unable to fashion a coherent public policy that is capable of addressing the interrelated problems that together lead to multideprived persons and households. The solution to institutional malfunctioning apparently lies in a more coordinated approach to rational social planning.

Fourth, it has been argued that problems of urban deprivation simply arise from the *unequal distribution of resources and opportunities*. The underprivileged are unable to obtain their fair share of society's resources, as they are not represented, or allowed to participate fully, in the political process (Eyles, 1978). The solution to this inequitable distribution of resources is seen to lie in positive discrimination policies and greater public participation in the planning process.

Finally, Marxist theory suggests that problems of urban deprivation can be utlimately explained in terms of the overall socioeconomic structure of capitalist society. In particular, problems arise from *class conflict*, whereby certain class divisions are necessary to maintain an economic system based on private profit. The key concept here is inequality, and the proposed solution lies in the redistribution of power and political control. Although these explanations of deprivation are by no means mutually exclusive, it is certainly clear that while policies of positive discrimination might make sense in the context of some explanatory frameworks, they are regarded as nothing more than short-term cosmetic devices by those who are pursuaded by the class conflict model of explanation.

10.4 POSSIBLE URBAN SPATIAL PLANS

A variety of possible urban spatial plans, or patterns, have been suggested (Albers, 1974). One of the earliest conceptions of an ideal city was formulated by *Ebenezer Howard* in 1902, in a book that has since been republished (Howard, 1965). Howard tried to incorporate the best of rural and urban living in a series of potentially self-sufficient communities of approximately 30,000 people that would be surrounded by permanent green belts. These cities were called *garden cities*, and he emphasized the need for relatively low population densities. The overall city would be about 1000 acres, of which the central 5 acres was designed to include commercial and entertainment activities. Beyond the central area were a series of residential rings, including a grand avenue, within an industrial area just within the surrounding green belt. Two garden cities were built near London, Letchworth and Welwyn, and garden cities became fashionable in the United States after 1910. But many of these cities, like Forest Hills Gardens, New York, which was designed by Olmsted and financed by the Russell Sage Foundation, became affluent suburbs for commuters rather than self-contained communities (Phillips and LeGates, 1981, p. 408).

Another visionary in terms of ideal urban form was *Frank Lloyd Wright.* He planned a hypothetical city called Broadacre which encouraged a completely low-density urban spread (Hall, 1975, p. 67). Each home would be surrounded by an acre of land to grow crops on. These homes would then be connected by superhighways, thus creating an automobile-based city, complete with suburban shopping centers. A major drawback of Wright's semiagrarian conception, however, was that it paid insufficient attention to the economic base of the city. Industry was to be decentralized to a series of scattered nodes, thus inhibiting the development of economies of scale (see Section 6.1).

The Swiss-born architect *LeCorbusier* had very different ideas from Wright, in that he favored a very centralized city, with business activity concentrated downtown in multistory office buildings. In terms of the residential areas, most families would live in multistory apartment complexes, surrounded by open, parklike spaces. Thus LeCorbusier advocated very high overall population densities, while leaving the bulk of the land unbuilt (Hall, 1975, p. 73). His impact is especially clear in numerous multi-story projects in Europe, where slums were cleared to make way for high-rise residential developments with open space between them. These high-rise housing projects, however, were often criticized as being worse than the slums they replaced, in

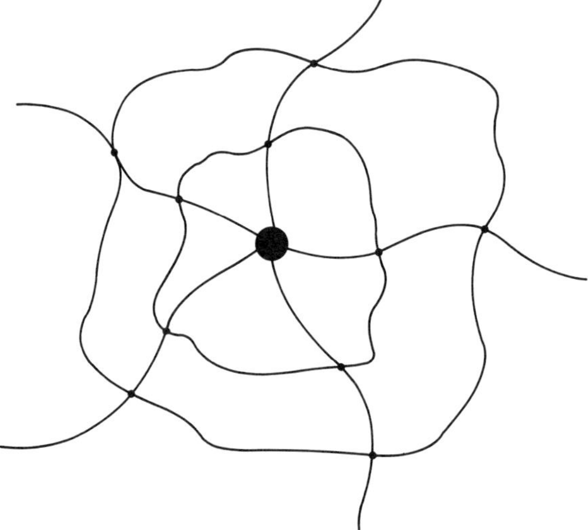

Figure 10.8 Circular plan.

that they tended to inhibit community feeling and the supervision of children's playtime activity (LaGory and Pipkin, 1981, p. 295).

The more recent planning literature tends to have been concerned with three basic forms of plan: the circular, the linear, and the sectoral (Reynolds, 1961). The *circular* plan is based on a set of ring and radial roads, which focus on a central business district (Figure 10.8). Many cities have tended naturally to follow this type of radial-concentric growth, with individual neighborhoods developing in the interstices between each radial and ring road. Green belts have been suggested as a major technique for controlling the outward expansion of such cities, although the urban sprawl often begins just outside the green belt. Besides being unable to contain the spatial spread of cities, green belt policies have also been criticized because they favor higher-income families, who tend to live at the edge of the city.

The *linear* plan was proposed as a planning framework for London, and is characterized by a central corridor containing the major areas of employment and economic activity (Figure 10.9). Residential areas are located along roads that run at right angles from the central corridor, and these are also connected by a circumferential highway. This plan provides for an orderly arrangement of land use, while maintaining the potential for industrial economies of scale along the central corridor. Open land is preserved between the residential areas, and the form of the plan is ideal for towns located on major rivers such as the Thames.

Finally, the *sectoral*, or radial plan, has a downtown nucleus with a series of radial corridors (Figure 10.10). Along these corridors are various-sized urban subcenters, with their own array of goods and services. Rather like central place theory (see Section 4.2), a hierarchy of service centers is postulated, with the downtown providing certain highly specialized goods and services for the whole urban area, while the subcenters cater to the more local, less specialized demands. Open space is preserved between the radial corridors, and the corridors themselves are especially conducive to the establishment of mass-transit systems. One of the drawbacks of this formulation, however, is the relative difficulty of moving from one radial to another and the associated potential for downtown congestion.

Speculation as to the most appropriate form for future cities has tended to highlight the importance of anticipating significant energy shortages. In this context,

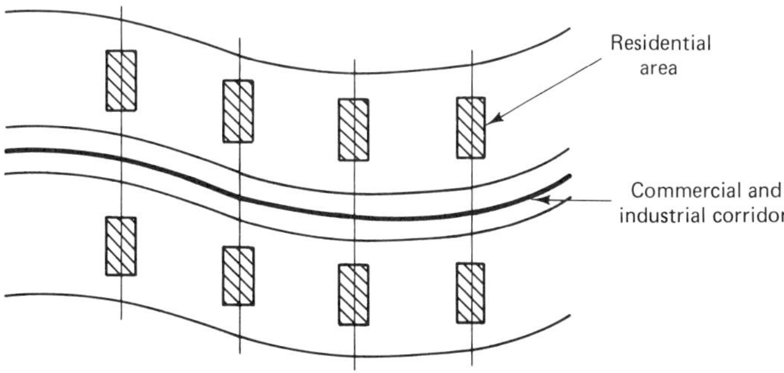

Figure 10.9 Linear plan.

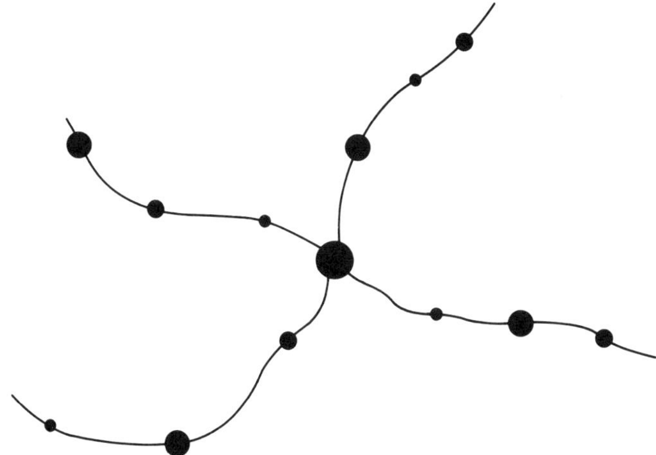

Figure 10.10 Sectoral plan.

van Til (1980) has suggested that future cities might emphasize regional subcenters within which most transportation is confined. These subcenters would develop where there is a particularly high density of commercial and industrial activity, and in those locations that are central to the circulation system of an energy-poor society. They would be as autonomous as possible, and would become the most preferred places of residence in a new, relatively immobile urban world.

Similar sentiments to those of van Til have been expressed by Birdsall (1980), who also foresees multiple commercial nodes and travel patterns that reflect higher energy costs. In addition, Birdsall expects a different form of urban political organization to emerge in the future, with the essential administrative functions of government encompassing the entire urbanized areas. Within this overall political structure, however, smaller communities within the city will develop and be responsible for the provision of local services, such as recreation, health care facilities, and primary education. The higher political jurisdiction will attempt to coordinate these local efforts, and collect and redistribute taxes in order to minimize neighborhood fiscal disparities.

References

Abrams, C., *The Language of Cities,* Viking Press, New York, 1971.

Abler, R., J. S. Adams, and P. R. Gould, *Spatial Organization: The Geographer's View of the World,* Prentice-Hall, Englewood Cliffs, N.J., 1971.

Abu-Lughod, J., and M. M. Foley, "The consumer votes by moving," in N. N. Foote, J. Abu-Lughod, M. M. Foley, and L. Winnick, Eds., *Housing Choices and Housing Constraints,* McGraw-Hill, New York, 1960, pp. 134–178.

Adams, J. S., "Directional bias in intra-urban migration," *Economic Geography,* 45 (1969), pp. 302–323.

Adams, J. S., "Residential structure of midwestern cities," *Annals of the Association of American Geographers,* 60 (1970), pp. 37–62.

Adams, J. S., and K. A. Gilder, "Household location and intra-urban migration," in D. T. Herbert and R. J. Johnston, Eds., *Social Areas in Cities,* Vol. 1: *Spatial Processes and Forms,* Wiley, New York, 1976, pp. 159–192.

Albers, G., "A town planner's view of urban structure as an object of physical planning," in J. G. Rothenberg and I. G. Heggie, Eds., *Transport and the Urban Environment,* Wiley, New York, 1974, pp. 209–216.

Alonso, W., "The historic and structural theories of urban form: Their implications for urban renewal," *Land Economics,* 40 (1964a), pp. 227–231.

Alonso, W., *Location and Land Use,* Harvard University Press, Cambridge, Mass., 1964b.

Alonso, W., "A theory of the urban land market," in L. S. Bourne, Ed., *Internal Structure of the City: Readings on Space and Environment,* Oxford University Press, New York, 1971, pp. 154–159.

Amedeo, D., and R. G. Golledge, *An Introduction to Scientific Reasoning in Geography,* Wiley, New York, 1975.

Appleyard, D. "City designers and the pluralistic city," in L. Rodwin, Ed., *Planning Urban*

Growth and Regional Development: The Experience of the Guayana Program of Venezuela, MIT Press, Cambridge, Mass., 1969, pp. 422–452.

Appleyard, D., "Styles and methods of structuring a city," *Environment and Behavior,* 2 (1970), pp. 100–117.

Artle, R., *The Structure of the Stockholm Economy,* Cornell University Press, Ithaca, N.Y., 1965.

Asher, H. B., *Causal Modeling,* Sage, Beverly Hills, Calif., 1976.

Babcock, R. F., and F. P. Bosselman, *Exclusionary Zoning: Land Use Regulation and Housing in the 1970's,* Praeger, New York, 1973.

Baerwald, T. J. "The site selection process of suburban residential builders," *Urban Geography,* 2 (1981), pp. 339–357.

Baird, J. C., *Psychophysical Analysis of Visual Space,* Pergamon Press, Elmsford, N.Y., 1970.

Baird, J. C., M. Wagner, and E. Noma, "Impossible cognitive spaces," *Geographical Analysis,* 14 (1982), pp. 204–216.

Baldwin, J., "Social area analysis and studies of delinquency," *Social Science Research,* 3 (1974), pp. 151–168.

Barrett, F., "The search process in residential relocation," *Environment and Behavior,* 8 (1976), pp. 169–198.

Bassett, K. A., and J. R. Short, *Housing and Residential Structures: Alternative Approaches,* Routledge & Kegan Paul, Boston, 1980.

Batty, M., "Urban models in the planning process," in D. T. Herbert and R. J. Johnston, Eds., *Geography and the Urban Environment,* Vol. 1, Wiley, New York, 1978, pp. 63–134.

Batty, M. "On planning processes," in B. Goodall and A. Kirby, Eds., *Resources and Planning,* Pergamon Press, Elmsford, N.Y., 1979, pp. 17–45.

Beavon, K. S. O., *Central Place Theory: A Reinterpretation,* Longman, Harlow, England, 1977.

Berry, B. J. L., *Commercial Structure and Commercial Blight: Retail Patterns and Processes in the City of Chicago,* Research Paper 85, Department of Geography, University of Chicago, Chicago, 1963.

Berry, B. J. L., *Geography of Market Centers and Retail Distribution,* Prentice-Hall, Englewood Cliffs, N.J., 1967.

Berry, B. J. L., *The Human Consequences of Urbanization: Divergent Paths in the Urban Experience of the Twentieth Century,* St. Martin's Press, New York, 1973.

Berry, B. J. L., and A. M. Baker, "Geographic sampling," in B. J. L. Berry and D. F. Marble, Eds., *Spatial Analysis: A Reader in Statistical Geography,* Prentice-Hall, Englewood Cliffs, N.J., 1968, pp. 91–100.

Berry, B. J. L. and R. S. Bednarz, "A hedonic model of prices and assessments for single-family homes: Does the assessor follow the market or the market follow the assessor?" *Land Economics,* 51 (1975), pp. 21–40.

Berry, B. J. L., and W. L. Garrison, "The functional bases of the central place hierarchy," *Economic Geography,* 34 (1958), pp. 145–154.

Berry, B. J. L., and F. E. Horton, Eds., *Geographic Perspectives on Urban Systems,* Prentice-Hall, Englewood Cliffs, N.J., 1970.

Berry, B. J. L., and J. D. Kasarda, *Contemporary Urban Ecology,* Macmillan, New York, 1977.

Berry, B. J. L., E. C. Conkling, and D. M. Ray, *The Geography of Economic Systems,* Prentice-Hall, Englewood Cliffs, N.J., 1976.

Birdsall, S. S., "Alternative prospects for America's urban future," in S. D. Brunn and J. O. Wheeler, Eds., *The American Metropolitan System: Present and Future,* Wiley, New York, 1980, pp. 201–211.

Blalock, H. M., Jr., *Causal Inferences in Nonexperimental Research,* University of North Carolina Press, Chapel Hill, N.C., 1964.

Blalock, H. M., Jr., *Social Statistics,* Rev. 2nd ed., McGraw-Hill, New York, 1979.

Blumner, S. M., and V. M. Johnson, "The effects of selected variables on housing values in Pomona, California," *Geographical Analysis,* 7 (1975), pp. 303–310.

Boal, F. W., "Ethnic residential segregation," in D. T. Herbert and R. J. Johnston, Eds., *Social Areas in Cities,* Vol. 1: *Spatial Processes and Forms,* Wiley, New York, 1976, pp. 41–79.

Boddy, M. J., "The structure of mortgage finance: Building societies and the British social formation," *Transactions of the Institute of British Geographers,* New Series, 1 (1976), pp. 58–71.

Bourne, L. S., "Housing supply and housing market behavior in residential development," in D. T. Herbert and R. J. Johnston, Eds., *Social Areas in Cities,* Vol. 1: *Spatial Processes and Forms,* Wiley, New York, 1976, pp. 111–158.

Bourne, L. S., *The Geography of Housing,* Wiley, New York, 1981.

Bourne, L. S., Ed., *Internal Structure of the City: Readings on Urban Form, Growth, and Policy,* 2nd ed., Oxford University Press, New York, 1982.

Boyce, R. R., "Residential mobility and its implications for urban spatial change," *Proceedings of the Association of American Geographers,* 1 (1969), pp. 22–26.

Briggs, R., "Urban cognitive distance," in R. M. Downs and D. Stea, Eds., *Image and Environment: Cognitive Mapping and Spatial Behavior,* Aldine, Chicago, 1973, pp. 361–388.

Brigham, E. F., "The determinants of residential land values," *Land Economics,* 41 (1965), pp. 325–334.

Brown, D. M., "The location decision of the firm: An overview of theory and evidence," *Papers of the Regional Science Association,* 43 (1979), pp. 23–39.

Brown, L. A., and J. Holmes, "Search behavior in an intra-urban migration context: A spatial perspective," *Environment and Planning,* 3 (1971), pp. 307–326.

Brown, L. A., and E. G. Moore, "The intra-urban migration process: A perspective," in L. S. Bourne, Ed., *Internal Structure of the City: Readings on Space and Environment,* Oxford University Press, New York, 1971, pp. 200–209.

Brummell, A. C., "A method of measuring residential stress," *Geographical Analysis,* 13 (1981), pp. 248–261.

Buck, W. P., "The industrial park," in D. F. Walker, Ed., *Planning Industrial Development,* Wiley, New York, 1980, pp. 291–321.

Bucklin, L. P., "Retail gravity models and consumer choice: A theoretical and empirical critique," *Economic Geography,* 47 (1971), pp. 489–498.

Burgess, E. W., "The growth of the city," in R. E. Park, E. W. Burgess, and R. D. Mackenzie, Eds., *The City,* University of Chicago Press, Chicago, 1925, pp. 47–62.

Burroughs, W. J., and E. K. Sadalla, "Asymmetries in distance cognition," *Geographical Analysis,* 11 (1979), pp. 414–421.

Cadwallader, M. T., "A methodological examination of cognitive distance," in W. F. E. Preiser, Ed., *Environmental Design Research,* Vol. 2, Dowden, Hutchinson & Ross, Stroudsburg, Pa., 1973, pp. 193–199.

Cadwallader, M. T., "A behavioral model of consumer spatial decision making," *Economic Geography,* 51 (1975), pp. 339–349.

CADWALLADER, M. T., "Cognitive distance in intraurban space," in G. T. Moore and R. G. Golledge, Eds., *Environmental Knowing: Theories, Research, and Methods,* Dowden, Hutchinson & Ross, Stroudsburg, Pa., 1976, pp. 316–324.

CADWALLADER, M. T., "Frame dependency in cognitive maps: An analysis using directional statistics," *Geographical Analysis,* 9 (1977), pp. 284–292.

CADWALLADER, M. T., "The model-building process in introductory college geography: An illustrative example," *Journal of Geography,* 77 (1978a), pp. 100–102.

CADWALLADER, M. T., "Urban information and preference surfaces: Their patterns, structures, and interrelationships," *Geografiska Annaler,* 60 B (1978b), pp. 97–106.

CADWALLADER, M. T., "Problems in cognitive distance: Implications for cognitive mapping," *Environment and Behavior,* 11 (1979a), pp. 559–576.

CADWALLADER, M. T., "Neighborhood evaluation in residential mobility," *Environment and Planning A,* 11 (1979b), pp. 393–401.

CADWALLADER, M. T., "The process of neighborhood choice," paper presented at the International Conference on Environmental Psychology, University of Surrey, Guildford, England, 1979c.

CADWALLADER, M. T., "Towards a cognitive gravity model: The case of consumer spatial behavior," *Regional Studies,* 15 (1981a), pp. 275–284.

CADWALLADER, M. T., "A unified model of urban housing patterns, social patterns, and residential mobility," *Urban Geography,* 2 (1981b), pp. 115–130.

CADWALLADER, M. T., "Urban residential mobility: A simultaneous equations approach," *Transactions of the Institute of British Geographers,* New Series, 7 (1982), pp. 458–473.

CALHOUN, J. B., "Population density and social pathology," *Scientific American,* 206 (1962), pp. 139–148.

CANTER, D., *The Psychology of Place,* St. Martin's Press, New York, 1977.

CANTER, D., and S. K. TAGG, "Distance estimation in cities," *Environment and Behavior,* 7 (1975), pp. 59–80.

CAPUTO, D. A., *Urban America: The Policy Alternatives,* W. H. Freeman, San Francisco, 1976.

CARTER, H., *The Study of Urban Geography,* 3rd ed., Edward Arnold, London, 1981.

CASTELLS, M., *The Urban Question,* Edward Arnold, London, 1977.

CATANESE, A. J., and J. C. SNYDER, Eds., *Introduction to Urban Planning,* McGraw-Hill, New York, 1979.

CHAPIN, F. S., Jr., *Urban Land Use Planning,* 2nd ed., University of Illinois Press, Urbana, Ill., 1965.

CHAPIN, F. S., Jr., *Human Activity Patterns in the City,* Wiley, New York, 1974.

CHARNEY, A. H., "Intraurban manufacturing location decisions and local tax differentials," *Journal of Urban Economics,* 14 (1983), pp. 184–205.

CHISHOLM, M., *Rural Settlement and Land Use: An Essay in Location,* 3rd ed., Hutchinson, London, 1979.

CHORLEY, R. J., and P. HAGGETT, "Trend-surface mapping in geographical research," *Transactions of the Institute of British Geographers,* 37 (1965), pp. 47–67.

CLARK, C., "Urban population densities," *Journal of the Royal Statistical Society,* Series A, 114 (1951), pp. 490–496.

CLARK, G., and M. J. DEAR, "The state in capitalism and the capitalist state," in M. J. Dear and A. J. Scott, Eds., *Urbanization and Urban Planning in Capitalist Society,* Methuen, New York, 1981, pp. 45–61.

CLARK, W. A. V., "A test of directional bias in residential mobility," in H. McConnell and D. W.

Yaseen, Eds., *Models of Spatial Variation,* Northern Illinois University Press, De Kalb, Ill., 1971, pp. 2–27.

Clark, W. A. V., "Behavior and constraints of spatial structure," *New Zealand Geographer,* 28 (1972), pp. 171–180.

Clark, W. A. V., "Migration in Milwaukee," *Economic Geography,* 52 (1976), pp. 171–180.

Clark, W. A. V., "On modelling search behavior," in D. Griffith and R. MacKinnon, Eds., *Dynamic Spatial Models,* Sijthoff en Noordhoff, Alphen aan den Rijn, The Netherlands, 1981, pp. 102–131.

Clark, W. A. V., "Recent research on migration and mobility: A review and interpretation," *Progress in Planning,* 18 (1982a), pp. 1–56.

Clark, W. A. V., Ed., *Modelling Housing Market Search,* Croom Helm, London, 1982b.

Clark, W. A. V., and J. E. Burt, "The impact of workplace on residential relocation," *Annals of the Association of American Geographers,* 70 (1980), pp. 59–67.

Clark, W. A. V., and M. T. Cadwallader, "Locational stress and residential mobility," *Environment and Behavior,* 5 (1973a), pp. 29–41.

Clark, W. A. V., and M. T. Cadwallader, "Residential preferences: An alternate view of the intraurban space," *Environment and Planning,* 5 (1973b), pp. 693–703.

Clark, W. A. V., and J. O. Huff, "Some empirical tests of duration-of-stay effects in intraurban migration," *Environment and Planning A,* 9 (1977), pp. 1357–1374.

Clark, W. A. V. and J. L. Onaka, "Life cycle and housing adjustment as explanations of residential mobility," *Urban Studies,* 20 (1983), pp. 47–57.

Clark, W. A. V., and G. Rushton, "Models of intra-urban consumer behavior and their implications for central place theory," *Economic Geography,* 46 (1970), pp. 486–497.

Clark, W. A. V., and T. R. Smith, "Modeling information use in a spatial context," *Annals of the Association of American Geographers,* 69 (1979), pp. 575–588.

Clark, W. A. V., and T. R. Smith, "Housing market search behavior and expected utility theory: 2. The process of search," *Environment and Planning A,* 14 (1982), pp. 717–737.

Clarke, M., and A. G. Wilson, "The dynamics of urban spatial structure: Progress and problems," *Journal of Regional Science,* 23 (1983), pp. 1–18.

Comrey, A. L., *A First Course in Factor Analysis,* Academic Press, New York, 1973.

Converse, P. D., "New laws of retail gravitation," *Journal of Marketing,* 14 (1949), pp. 379–384.

Coombs, C. H., *A Theory of Data,* Wiley, New York, 1964.

Corey, K., "Advocacy in planning: A reflective analysis," *Antipode,* 4 (1972), pp. 46–63.

Cox, K. R., "Bourgeois thought and the behavioral geography debate," in K. R. Cox and R. G. Golledge, Eds., *Behavioral Problems in Geography Revisited,* Methuen, New York, 1981, pp. 256–279.

Cox, K. R., and F. Z. Nartowicz, "Jurisdictional fragmentation in the American metropolis: Alternative perspectives," *International Journal of Urban and Regional Research,* 4 (1980), pp. 196–209.

Cox, K. R., and G. Zannaras, "Designative perceptions of macrospaces: Concepts, a methodology, and applications," in R. M. Downs and D. Stea, Eds., *Image and Environment: Cognitive Mapping and Spatial Behavior,* Aldine, Chicago, 1973, pp. 162–178.

Daniels, P. W., and A. M. Warnes, *Movement in Cities: Spatial Perspectives on Urban Transport and Travel,* Methuen, New York, 1980.

Darden, J. T., "Lending practices and policies affecting the American metropolitan system," in S. D. Brunn and J. O. Wheeler, Eds., *The American Metropolitan System: Present and Future,* Wiley, New York, 1980, pp. 93–110.

DAVID, H. A., *The Method of Paired Comparisons,* Charles Griffin, London, 1963.

DAVIDOFF, P., and T. REINER, "A choice theory of planning," *Journal of American Institute of Planners,* 28 (1962), pp. 108–115.

DAVIES, W. K., "Alternative factorial solutions and urban social character," *Canadian Geographer,* 22 (1978), pp. 273–297.

DAWES, R. M., and B. CORRIGAN, "Linear models in decision making," *Psychological Bulletin,* 81 (1974), pp. 95–106.

DAY, R. A., "Urban distance cognition: Review and contribution," *Australian Geographer,* 13 (1976), pp. 193–200.

DAY, R. A., and D. J. WALMSLEY, "Residential preferences in Sydney's inner suburbs: A study in diversity," *Applied Geography,* 1 (1981), pp. 185–197.

DEAR, M. J., "A paradigm for public facility location theory," *Antipode,* 6 (1974), pp. 46–50.

DEAR, M. J., "Abandoned housing," in J. S. Adams, Ed., *Urban Policymaking and Metropolitan Dynamics: A Comparative Geographical Analysis,* Ballinger, Cambridge, Mass., 1976, pp. 59–99.

DEAR, M. J., "Impact of mental health facilities on property values," *Community Mental Health Journal,* 13 (1977), pp. 150–157.

DEAR, M. J., "Planning for mental health care: A reconsideration of public facility location theory," *International Regional Science Review,* 3 (1978), pp. 93–111.

DEAR, M. J., and A. J. SCOTT, Eds., *Urbanization and Planning in Capitalist Societies,* Methuen, New York, 1981.

DEAR, M. J., and I. WITTMAN, "Conflict over the location of mental health facilities," in D. T. Herbert and R. J. Johnston, Eds., *Geography and the Urban Environment,* Vol. 3, Wiley, New York, 1980, pp. 345–362.

DEAR, M. J., S. M. TAYLOR, and G. B. HALL, "External effects of mental health facilites," *Annals of the Association of American Geographers,* 70 (1980), pp. 342–352.

DE VISE, P., "The suburbanization of jobs and minority employment," *Economic Geography,* 52 (1976), pp. 348–363.

DINGEMANS, D., "Redlining and mortgage lending in Sacramento," *Annals of the Association of American Geographers,* 69 (1979), pp. 225–239.

DOLING, J., and P. WILLIAMS, "Building societies and local lending behaviour," *Environment and Planning A,* 15 (1983), pp. 663–673.

DOWNS, A., *Inside Bureaucracy,* Rand, Chicago, 1964.

DOWNS, R. M., "The cognitive structure of an urban shopping center," *Environment and Behavior,* 2 (1970), pp. 13–39.

DOWNS, R. M., "Cognitive mapping: A thematic analysis," in K. R. Cox and R. G. Golledge, Eds., *Behavioral Problems in Geography Revisited,* Methuen, New York, 1981, pp. 95–122.

DOWNS, R. M. and D. STEA, Eds., *Image and Environment: Cognitive Mapping and Spatial Behavior,* Aldine, Chicago, 1973.

DOWNS, R. M., and D. STEA, *Maps in Minds: Reflections on Cognitive Mapping,* Harper & Row, New York, 1977.

DUNCAN, O. D., *Introduction to Structural Equation Models,* Academic Press, New York, 1975.

DUNCAN, O. D., and B. DUNCAN, "Residential distribution and occupational stratification," *American Journal of Sociology,* 60 (1955), pp. 493–503.

DUNCAN, O. D., and S. LIEBERSON, "Ethnic segregation and assimilation," *American Journal of Sociology,* 64 (1959), pp. 364–374.

DYE, T., *Understanding Public Policy,* Prentice-Hall, Englewood Cliffs, N.J., 1972.

DYOS, H. J., *The Study of Urban History,* Edward Arnold, London, 1968.

Edmonston, B., *Population Distribution in American Cities,* Lexington Books, Lexington, Mass., 1975.

Entrikin, J. N., "Contemporary humanism in geography," *Annals of the Association of American Geographers,* 66 (1976), pp. 615–632.

Erickson, R. A., "The evolution of the suburban space economy," *Urban Geography,* 4 (1983), pp. 95–121.

Ermuth, F., *Residential Satisfaction and Urban Environmental Preferences,* Geographic Monograph 3, Atkinson College, York University, Toronto, 1974.

Evans, A. W., "The determination of the price of land," *Urban Studies,* 20 (1983), pp. 119–129.

Everitt, J. C., "Community and propinquity in a city," *Annals of the Association of American Geographers,* 66 (1976), pp. 104–116.

Everitt, J. C., and M. T. Cadwallader, "Husband–wife role variation as a factor in home area definition," *Geografiska Annaler,* 63 B (1981), pp. 23–34.

Eyles, J., "Social theory and social geography," *Progress in Geography,* Vol. 6. Edward Arnold, London, 1974, pp. 27–88.

Eyles, J., "Social geography and the study of the capitalist city: A review," *Tijdschrift voor Economische en Sociale Geografie,* 69 (1978), pp. 296–305.

Eyles, J., "Area-based policies for the inner city: Context, problems, and prospects," in D. T. Herbert and D. M. Smith, Eds., *Social Problems and the City: Geographical Perspectives,* Oxford University Press, New York, 1979, pp. 226–243.

Festinger, L., "Cognitive dissonance," in S. Coopersmith, Ed., *Frontiers in Psychological Research: Readings from Scientific American,* W. H. Freeman, San Francisco, 1964, pp. 207–213.

Firey, W., "Sentiment and symbolism as ecological variables," *American Sociological Review,* 10 (1945), pp. 140–148.

Fischer, C. S., *The Urban Experience,* Harcourt Brace Jovanovich, New York, 1976.

Fisher, F. M., *The Identification Problem in Econometrics,* McGraw-Hill, New York, 1966.

Flowerdew, R., "Search strategies and stopping rules in residential mobility," *Transactions of the Institute of British Geographers,* New Series, 1 (1976), pp. 47–57.

Fredland, D. R., *Residential Mobility and Home Purchase: A Longitudinal Perspective on the Family Life Cycle and the Housing Market,* Lexington Books, Lexington, Mass., 1974.

Galle, O. R., W. R. Grove, and J. M. McPherson, "Population density and pathology: What are the relations for man?" *Science,* 176 (1972), pp. 23–30.

Golant, S. M., "Housing and transportation problems of the urban elderly," in J. S. Adams, Ed., *Urban Policymaking and Metropolitan Dynamics: A Comparative Geographical Analysis,* Ballinger, Cambridge, Mass., 1976, pp. 379–422.

Gold, J. R., *An Introduction to Behavioral Geography,* Oxford University Press, New York, 1980.

Goldberg, M., and P. Horwood, *Zoning: Its Costs and Relevance for the 1980's,* The Fraser Institute, Vancouver, British Columbia, 1980.

Golledge, R. G., "Some equilibrium models of consumer behavior," *Economic Geography,* 46 (1970), pp. 417–424.

Golledge, R. G., "Learning about urban environments," in T. Carlstein, D. Parkes, and N. Thrift, Eds., *Making Sense of Time,* Edward Arnold, London, 1978, pp. 76–98.

Golledge, R. G., "The geographical relevance of some learning theories," in K. R. Cox and R. G. Golledge, Eds., *Behavioral Problems in Geography Revisited,* Methuen, New York, 1981a, pp. 43–66.

GOLLEDGE, R. G., "Misconceptions, misinterpretations, and misrepresentations of behavioral approaches in human geography," *Environment and Planning A,* 13 (1981b), pp. 1325-1344.

GOLLEDGE, R. G., and L. A. BROWN, "Search, learning, and the market decision process," *Geografiska Annaler,* 49 B (1967), pp. 116-124.

GOLLEDGE, R. G., and L. J. HUBERT, "Some comments on non-Euclidean mental maps," *Environment and Planning A,* 14 (1982), pp. 107-118.

GOLLEDGE, R. G., R. BRIGGS, and D. DEMKO, "The configuration of distances in intra-urban space," *Proceedings of the Association of American Geographers,* 1 (1969), pp. 60-65.

GORDON, G., "The historico-geographic explanation of urban morphology: A discussion of some Scottish evidence," *Scottish Geographical Magazine,* 97 (1981), pp. 16-26.

GOULD, P. R., "Acquiring spatial information," *Economic Geography,* 51 (1975), pp. 87-99.

GOULD, P. R. and R. WHITE, *Mental Maps,* Penguin, London, 1974.

GRANFIELD, M. L., *An Econometric Model of Residential Location,* Ballinger, Cambridge, Mass., 1975.

GRAY, F., "Non-explanation in urban geography," *Area,* 7 (1975), pp. 228-235.

GREGORY, D., *Ideology, Science and Human Geography,* St. Martin's Press, New York, 1978.

GRIFFIN, E., and L. FORD, "A model of Latin American city structure," *Geographical Review,* 70 (1980), pp. 397-422.

GRIFFITH, D. A., "Evaluating the transformation from a monocentric to a polycentric city," *Professional Geographer,* 33 (1981), pp. 189-196.

GUEST, A. M., "Patterns of family location," *Demography,* 9 (1972), pp. 159-172.

HAGGETT, P., "Spatial forecasting—a view from the touchline," in R. L. Martin, N. J. Thrift, and R. J. Bennett, Eds., *Towards the Dynamic Analysis of Spatial Systems,* Pion, London, 1978, pp. 205-210.

HAGGETT, P., and K. A. BASSETT, "The use of trend-surface parameters in inter-urban comparisons," *Environment and Planning,* 2 (1970), pp. 225-237.

HAGGETT, P., and R. J. CHORLEY, "Models, paradigms, and the new geography," in R. J. Chorley and P. Haggett, Eds., *Models in Geography,* Methuen, London, 1967, pp. 19-41.

HALL, P., Ed., *Von Thunen's Isolated State,* Pergamon Press, Oxford, 1966.

HALL, P., *Urban and Regional Planning,* Wiley, New York, 1975.

HALL, P., "Planning: A geographer's view," in B. Goodall and A. Kirby, Eds., *Resources and Planning,* Pergamon Press, New York, 1979, pp. 3-15.

HAMNETT, C., "Area-based explanations: A critical appraisal," in D. T. Herbert and D. M. Smith, Eds., *Social Problems and the City: Geographical Perspectives,* Oxford University Press, New York, 1979, pp. 244-260.

HARMAN, H. H., *Modern Factor Analysis,* 2nd ed., University of Chicago Press, Chicago, 1967.

HARTSHORN, T. A., *Interpreting the City: An Urban Geography,* Wiley, New York, 1980.

HARVEY, D., *Explanation in Geography,* Edward Arnold, London, 1969.

HARVEY, D., *Society, the City and the Space-Economy of Urbanism,* Commission on College Geography, Resource Paper 18, Association of American Geographers, Washington, D.C., 1972.

HARVEY, D., *Social Justice and the City,* Johns Hopkins University Press, Baltimore, 1973.

HARVEY, D., "Class-monopoly rent, finance capital and the urban revolution," *Regional Studies,* 8 (1974), pp. 239-255.

HARVEY, D., "The Marxian theory of the state," *Antipode,* 8 (1976), pp. 80-98.

HARVEY, D., "Government policies, financial institutions and neighborhood change in U.S. cities," in D. R. Deskins, Jr., G. Kish, J. D. Nystuen, and G. Olsson, Eds., *Geographic*

Humanism, Analysis and Social Action, Michigan Geographical Publication 17, Department of Geography, University of Michigan, Ann Arbor, Mich., 1977, pp. 291–320.

HARVEY, D., "Conceptual and measurement problems in the cognitive-behavioral approach to location theory," in K. R. Cox and R. G. Golledge, Eds., *Behavioral Problems in Geography Revisited,* Methuen, New York, 1981, pp. 18–42.

HARVEY, R. O., and W. A. V. CLARK, "The nature and economics of urban sprawl," in L. S. Bourne, Ed., *Internal Structure of the City: Readings on Space and Environment,* Oxford University Press, New York, 1971, pp. 475–482.

HAWLEY, A. H., and O. D. DUNCAN, "Social area analysis: A critical appraisal," *Land Economics,* 33 (1957), pp. 337–345.

HAY, A., "Positivism in human geography: Response to critics," in D. T. Herbert and R. J. Johnston, Eds., *Geography and the Urban Environment,* Vol. 2, Wiley, New York, 1979, pp. 1–26.

HERBERT, D. T., *Urban Geography: A Social Perspective,* Praeger, New York, 1972.

HERBERT, D. T., "Urban deprivation: Definition, measurement, and spatial qualities," *The Geographical Journal,* 141 (1975), pp. 362–372.

HERBERT, D. T., "Social deviance in the city: A spatial perspective," in D. T. Herbert and R. J. Johnston, Eds., *Social Areas in Cities,* Vol. 2: *Spatial Perspectives on Problems and Policies,* Wiley, New York, 1976, pp. 89–121.

HERBERT, D. T., "Introduction: Geographical perspectives and urban problems," in D. T. Herbert and D. M. Smith, Eds., *Social Problems and the City: Goegraphical Perspectives,* Oxford University Press, New York, 1979a, pp. 1–9.

HERBERT, D. T., "Urban crime: A geographical perspective," in D. T. Herbert and D. M. Smith, Eds., *Social Problems and the City: Geographical Perspectives,* Oxford University Press, New York, 1979b, pp. 117–138.

HERBERT, D. T., *The Geography of Urban Crime,* Longman, New York, 1982.

HERBERT, D. T., and R. J. JOHNSTON, "Geography and the urban environment," in D. T. Herbert and R. J. Johnston, Eds., *Geography and the Urban Environment,* Vol. 1, Wiley, New York, 1978, pp. 1–33.

HERBERT, D. T., and C. J. THOMAS, *Urban Geography: A First Approach,* Wiley, New York, 1982.

HILL, F., "Spatio-temporal trends in urban population density: A trend surface analysis," in L. S. Bourne, R. D. Mackinnon, and J. W. Simmons, Eds., *The Form of Cities in Central Canada: Selected Papers,* Department of Geography Research Publication 11, University of Toronto, Toronto, 1973, pp. 103–119.

HILL, M., "A goals' achievement matrix for evaluating alternative plans," *Journal of the American Institute of Planners,* 34 (1968), pp. 19–29.

HODGART, R. L., "Optimizing access to public services: A review of problems, models and methods of locating central facilities," *Progress in Human Geography,* 2 (1978), pp. 17–48.

HONEY, R. D., "Metropolitan governance," in J. S. Adams, Ed., *Urban Policymaking and Metropolitan Dynamics: A Comparative Geographical Analysis,* Ballinger, Cambridge, Mass., 1976, pp. 425–462.

HORVATH, F. E., "Psychological stress," *General Systems Yearbook,* 4 (1959), pp. 203–230.

HORVATH, R. J., "Trend surface fitting to random data—an experimental test," *American Journal of Science,* 265 (1967), pp. 5869–5878.

HOURIHAN, K., "The evaluation of urban neighborhoods 1: Perception," *Environment and Planning A,* 11 (1979a), pp. 1337–1353.

HOURIHAN, K., "The evaluation of urban neighborhoods 2: Preference," *Environment and Planning A,* 11 (1979b), pp. 1356–1366.

HOWARD, E., *Garden Cities of Tomorrow,* MIT Press, Cambridge, Mass., 1965.

HOWARD, I. P., and W. B. TEMPLETON, *Human Spatial Orientation,* Wiley, New York, 1966.

HOYT, H., *The Structure and Growth of Residential Neighborhoods in American Cities,* Federal Housing Administration, Washington, D.C., 1939.

HUFF, D. L., "Defining and estimating a trading area," *Journal of Marketing,* 28 (1964), pp. 34–38.

INTRILIGATOR, M. D., *Econometric Models, Techniques, and Applications,* Prentice-Hall, Englewood Cliffs, N.J., 1978.

ISARD, W., *Introduction to Regional Science,* Prentice-Hall, Englewood Cliffs, N.J., 1975.

JOHNSTON, J., *Econometric Methods,* 2nd ed., McGraw-Hill, New York, 1972.

JOHNSTON, R. J., *Urban Residential Patterns: An Introductory Review,* Praeger, New York, 1971.

JOHNSTON, R. J., "Activity spaces and residential preferences: Some tests of the hypothesis of sectoral mental maps," *Economic Geography,* 48 (1972), pp. 199–211.

JOHNSTON, R. J., "Spatial patterns in suburban evaluations," *Environment and Planning,* 5 (1973), pp. 385–395.

JOHNSTON, R. J., "Urban geography: City structures," *Progress in Human Geography,* 2 (1977), pp. 118–129.

JOHNSTON, R. J., *Geography and Geographers: Anglo-American Human Geography since 1945,* Edward Arnold, London, 1979.

JOHNSTON, R. J., "On the nature of explanation in human geography," *Transactions of the Institute of British Geographers,* New Series, 5 (1980a), pp. 402–412.

JOHNSTON, R. J., "Political geography without politics," *Progress in Human Geography,* 4 (1980b), pp. 439–446.

JOHNSTON, R. J., *The American Urban System: A Geographical Perspective,* St. Martin's Press, New York, 1982.

JOHNSTON, R. J., "From description to explanation in urban geography," *Geography,* 68 (1983), pp. 11–15.

JOHNSTONE, J. W. C., "Social class, social areas and delinquency," *Sociology and Social Research,* 63 (1978), pp. 49–72.

KAIN, J. F., and J. M. QUIGLEY, "Measuring the value of housing quality," *Journal of the American Statistical Association,* 65 (1970), pp. 532–548.

KAIN, J. F., and J. M. QUIGLEY, "Housing market discrimination, homeownership, and savings behavior," *The American Economic Review,* 62 (1972), pp. 263–277.

KASPERSON, R. E., "Participation through centrally planned social change: Lessons from the American experience on the urban scene," in W. R. D. Sewell and J. T. Coppock, Eds., *Public Participation in Planning,* Wiley, London, 1977, pp. 173–190.

KASPERSON, R. E., and M. BREITBART, *Participation, Decentralization, and Advocacy Planning,* Commission on College Geography Resource Paper 25, Association of American Geographers, Washington, D.C., 1974.

KING, A. T., and P. MIESZKOWSKI, "Racial discrimination, segregation and the price of housing," *Journal of Political Economy,* 81 (1973), pp. 590–606.

KIRBY, A., *The Politics of Location: An Introduction,* Methuen, London, 1982.

KIRK, W., "Problems of geography," *Geography,* 48 (1963), pp. 357–371.

KMENTA, J., *Elements of Econometrics,* Macmillan, New York, 1971.

KNOX, P., *Urban Social Geography: An Introduction,* Longman, New York, 1982.

KOTLER, P., "Mathematical models of individual buyer behavior," *Behavioral Science,* 13 (1968), pp. 274–287.

KRAMER, R. M., *Participation and the Poor,* Prentice-Hall, Englewood Cliffs, N.J., 1969.

KRUECKEBERG, D. A., and A. L. SILVERS, *Urban Planning Analysis: Methods and Models,* Wiley, New York, 1974.

LAGORY, M., and J. S. PIPKIN, *Urban Social Space,* Wadsworth, Belmont, Calif., 1981.

LANE, R., T. POWELL, and P. SMITH, *Analytical Transport Planning,* Wiley, New York, 1973.

LAPHAM, V., "Do blacks pay more for housing?" *Journal of Political Economy,* 79 (1971), pp. 1244–1257.

LATHAM, R. F., and M. H. YEATES, "Population density growth in Metropolitan Toronto," *Geographical Analysis,* 2 (1970), pp. 177–185.

LEE, T., "Perceived distance as a function of direction in the city," *Environment and Behavior,* 2 (1970), pp. 40–51.

LEE, T., "Cities in the mind," in D. T. Herbert and R. J. Johnston, Eds., *Social Areas in Cities,* Vol. 2: *Spatial Perspectives on Problems and Policies,* Wiley, New York, 1976, pp. 159–187.

LEINBACH, T. R., "Locational trends in non-metropolitan industrial growth: Some evidence from Vermont," *Professional Geographer,* 30 (1978), pp. 30–36.

LEONE, R. A. and R. J. STRUYK, "The incubator hypothesis: Evidence from five S.M.S.A.'s," *Urban Studies,* 13 (1976), pp. 325–331.

LEONTIEF, W. W., "Input-output economics," *Scientific American,* 185 (1951), pp. 15–21.

LEWIS, O., "The culture of poverty," *Scientific American,* 215 (1966), pp. 19–25.

LEY, D., *The Black Inner City as Frontier Outpost: Images and Behavior of a Philadelphia Neighborhood,* Association of American Geographers, Washington, D.C., 1974.

LEY, D., "Behavioral geography and the philosophies of meaning," in K. R. Cox and R. G. Golledge, Eds., *Behavioral Problems in Geography Revisited,* Methuen, New York, 1981, pp. 209–230.

LEY, D., *A Social Geography of the City,* Harper & Row, New York, 1983.

LEY, D., and M. S. SAMUELS, Eds., *Humanistic Geography: Prospects and Problems,* Maaroufa Press, Chicago, 1978.

LICHFIELD, N., P. KETTLE, and M. WHITBREAD, *Evaluation in the Planning Process,* Pergamon Press, Oxford, 1975.

LIEBER, S. R., "An experimental approach for the migration decision process," *Tijdschrift voor Economische en Sociale Geografie,* 70 (1979), pp. 75–85.

LLOYD, P. E., and P. DICKEN, *Location in Space: A Theoretical Approach to Economic Geography,* Harper & Row, New York, 1972.

LLOYD, R., and D. JENNINGS, "Shopping behavior and income: Comparisons in an urban environment," *Economic Geography,* 54 (1978), pp. 157–167.

LONG, L. H., "The influence of number and ages of children on residential mobility," *Demography,* 9 (1972), pp. 317–382.

LOUVIERE, J. J., and D. A. HENLEY, "Information integration theory applied to student apartment selection decisions," *Geographical Analysis,* 9 (1977), pp. 130–141.

LOUVIERE, J. J., and K. L. NORMAN, "Applications of information-processing theory to the analysis of urban travel demand," *Environment and Behavior,* 9 (1977), pp. 91–106.

LUCE, R. D., and E. GALANTER, "Psychophysical scaling," in R. D. Luce, R. R. Bush, and E. Galanter, Eds., *Handbook of Mathematical Psychology,* Vol. 1, Wiley, New York, 1963, pp. 245–307.

LUNDBERG, U., "Emotional and geographical phenomena in psychophysical research," in R. M. Downs and D. Stea, Eds., *Image and Environment: Cognitive Mapping and Spatial Behavior,* Aldine, Chicago, 1973, pp. 322–337.

LYNCH, K., *The Image of the City,* MIT Press, Cambridge, Mass., 1960.

MACDONALD, K. I., "Path analysis," in C. A. O'Muircheartaigh and C. Payne, Eds., *The Analysis of Survey Data,* Vol. 2: *Model Fitting,* Wiley, London, 1977, pp. 81–104.

MACLARAN, A., "Area-based positive discrimination and the distribution of well-being," *Transactions of the Institute of British Geographers,* New Series, 6 (1981), pp. 53–67.

MACLENNAN, D., and N. J. WILLIAMS, "Revealed space preference theory—A cautionary note," *Tijdschrift voor Economische en Sociale Geografie,* 70 (1979), pp. 307–309.

MANN, P., *An Approach to Urban Sociology,* Routledge & Kegan Paul, London, 1965.

MARK, J., "Determinants of urban house prices: A methodological comment," *Urban Studies,* 14 (1977), pp. 359–363.

MCDONALD, J. F., and H. W. BOWMAN, "Some tests of alternative urban population density functions," *Journal of Urban Economics,* 3 (1976), pp. 242–252.

MCDONALD, J. F., and H. W. BOWMAN, "Land value functions: A reevaluation," *Journal of Urban Economics,* 6 (1979), pp. 25–41.

MCGINNIS, R., "A stochastic model of social mobility," *American Sociological Review,* 33 (1968), pp. 712–722.

MCGRATH, J. E., Ed., *Social and Psychological Factors in Stress,* Holt, Rinehart and Winston, New York, 1970.

MCLOUGHLIN, J. B., *Urban and Regional Planning: A Systems Approach,* Faber & Faber, London, 1969.

MERCER, C., *Living in Cities: Psychology and the Urban Environment,* Penguin, London, 1975.

MERCER, J., "Metropolitan housing quality and an application of causal modeling," *Geographical Analysis,* 7 (1975), pp. 295–302.

MERCER, J., "On continentalism, distinctiveness, and comparative urban geography: Canadian and American cities," *Canadian Geographer,* 23 (1979), pp. 119–139.

MICHELSON, W., *Environmental Choice, Human Behavior and Residential Satisfaction,* Oxford University Press, New York, 1977.

MILIBAND, R., *Marxism and Politics,* Oxford University Press, London, 1977.

MILLS, E. S., *Studies in the Structure of the Urban Economy,* Johns Hopkins University Press, Baltimore, 1972.

MILLS, E. S., *Urban Economics,* 2nd ed., Scott, Foresman, Glenview, Ill., 1980.

MITCHELL, R. E., "Some social implications of high-density housing," *American Sociological Review,* 36 (1971), pp. 18–29.

MOORE, E. G., "Comments on the use of ecological models in the study of residential mobility in the city," *Economic Geography,* 47 (1971), pp. 73–85.

MOORE, E. G., *Residential Mobility in the City,* Commission on College Geography Resource Paper 13, Association of American Geographers, Washington, D.C., 1972.

MOORE, E. G., and S. CLATWORTHY, "The role of urban data systems in the analysis of housing issues," in L. S. Bourne and J. R. Hitchcock, Eds., *Urban Housing Markets,* University of Toronto Press, Toronto, 1978, pp. 228–258.

MORRILL, R. L., "The Negro ghetto: Problems and alternatives," *Geographical Review,* 55 (1965), pp. 339–361.

MORRILL, R. L., and F. R. PITTS, "Marriage, migration, and the mean information field: A study in uniqueness and generality," *Annals of the Association of American Geographers,* 57 (1967), pp. 401–422.

Morrison, W. I., and P. Smith, "Input–output methods in urban and regional planning: A practical guide," *Progress in Planning,* 7 (1977), pp. 59–151.

Murdie, R. A., *Factorial Ecology of Metropolitan Toronto, 1951–61,* Research Paper 116, Department of Geography, University of Chicago, Chicago, 1969.

Muth, R. F., *Cities and Housing: The Spatial Pattern of Urban Residential Land Use,* University of Chicago Press, Chicago, 1969.

Myers, J. H., and M. Alpert, "Determinant buying attitudes: Meaning and measurement," *Journal of Marketing,* 32 (1968), pp. 13–20.

Myrdal, G., *Rich Lands and Poor,* Harper & Row, New York, 1957.

Namboodiri, N. K., L. F. Carter, and H. M. Blalock, Jr., *Applied Multivariate Analysis and Experimental Designs,* McGraw-Hill, New York, 1975.

Newling, B. E., "The spatial variation of urban population densities," *Geographical Review,* 59 (1969), pp. 242–252.

Norcliffe, G. B., "Territorial influences in urban political space: A study of perception in Kitchener–Waterloo," *Canadian Geographer,* 18 (1974), pp. 311–329.

Northam, R. M., *Urban Geography,* 2nd ed., Wiley, New York, 1979.

Norton, R. D., and J. Rees, "The product cycle and the spatial decentralization of American manufacturing," *Regional Studies,* 13 (1979), pp. 141–151.

Odland, J., and J. Jakubs, "Urban travel alternatives: A class of models for individual and collective preferences," *Socio-Economic Planning Sciences,* 11 (1977), pp. 265–271.

Oppenheim, N., *Applied Models in Urban and Regional Analysis,* Prentice-Hall, Englewood Cliffs, N.J., 1980.

Orleans, P., "Differential cognition of urban residents: Effects of social scale on mapping," in R. M. Downs and D. Stea, Eds., *Image and Environment: Cognitive Mapping and Spatial Behavior,* Aldine, Chicago, 1973, pp. 115–130.

Osgood, C. E., G. J. Suci, and P. H. Tannenbaum, *The Measurement of Meaning,* University of Illinois Press, Urbana, Ill., 1957.

Pahl, R. E., *Whose City?* 2nd ed., Penguin, London, 1975.

Palm, R. I., "The telephone and the organization of urban space," *Proceedings of the Association of American Geographers,* 5 (1973a), pp. 207–210.

Palm, R. I., "Factorial ecology and the community of outlook," *Annals of the Association of American Geographers,* 63 (1973b), pp. 341–346.

Palm, R. I., "The role of real estate agents as information mediators in two American cities," *Geografiska Annaler,* 58 B (1976), pp. 28–41.

Palm, R. I., "Financial and real estate institutions in the housing market," in D. T. Herbert and R. J. Johnston, Eds., *Geography and the Urban Environment,* Vol. 2, Wiley, New York, 1979, pp. 83–123.

Palm, R. I., *The Geography of American Cities,* Oxford University Press, New York, 1981.

Palm, R. I., and D. Caruso, "Factor labelling in factorial ecology," *Annals of the Association of American Geographers,* 62 (1972), pp. 122–133.

Papageorgiou, G. J., and E. Casetti, "Spatial equilibrium residential land values in a multicenter setting," *Journal of Regional Science,* 11 (1971), pp. 385–389.

Peach, C., V. Robinson, and S. Smith, Eds., *Ethnic Segregation in Cities,* Croom Helm, London, 1981.

Peattie, L., "Reflections on advocacy planning," *Journal of the American Institute of Planners,* 34 (1968), pp. 80–88.

Phillips, E. B., and R. T., LeGates, *City Lights: An Introduction to Urban Studies,* Oxford University Press, New York, 1981.

PHIPPS, A. G., "Scaling problems in the cognition of urban distances," *Transactions of the Institute of British Geographers,* New Series, 4 (1979), pp. 94–102.

PHIPPS, A. G., "Utility function switching during residential search," *Geografiska Annaler,* 65 B (1983), pp. 23–38.

PHIPPS, A. G., and W. H. LAVERTY, "Optimal stopping and residential search behavior," *Geographical Analysis,* 15 (1983), pp. 187–204.

PIPKIN, J. S., "Problems in the psychological modelling of revealed destination choice," in S. Gale and G. Olsson, Eds., *Philosophy in Geography,* D. Reidel, Dordrecht, The Netherlands, 1979, pp. 309–328.

PIPKIN, J. S., "Cognitive behavioral geography and repetitive travel," in K. R. Cox and R. G. Golledge, Eds., *Behavioral Problems in Geography Revisited,* Methuen, New York, 1981, pp. 145–181.

PIRIE, G. H., "Thoughts on revealed preference and spatial behavior," *Environment and Planning A,* 8 (1976), pp. 947–955.

POCOCK, D., and R. HUDSON, *Images of the Urban Environment,* Macmillan, London, 1978.

POLK, K., "Urban social areas and delinquency," *Social Problems,* 14 (1967), pp. 320–325.

POPP, H., "The residential location decision process: Some empirical and theoretical considerations," *Tijdschrift voor Economische en Sociale Geografie,* 67 (1976), pp. 300–305.

PRED, A. R., "The intrametropolitan location of American manufacturing," *Annals of the Association of American Geographers,* 54 (1964), pp. 165–180.

PRED, A. R., *City-Systems in Advanced Economies: Past Growth, Present Processes, and Future Development Options,* Wiley, New York, 1977.

PRESTON, V., "A multidimensional scaling analysis of individual differences in residential area evaluation," *Geografiska Annaler,* 64 B (1982), pp. 17–26.

PROSPERI, D. C., and H. J. SCHULER, "An alternative method to identify rules of spatial choice," *Geographical Perspectives,* 38 (1976), pp. 33–38.

QUIGLEY, J. M., "Housing demand in the short run: An analysis of polytomous choice," *Explorations in Economic Research,* 3 (1976), pp. 76–102.

QUIGLEY, J. M., and D. H. WEINBERG, "Intra-metropolitan residential mobility: A review and synthesis," *International Regional Science Review,* 2 (1977), pp. 41–66.

REES, P. H., "Concepts of social space: Toward an urban social geography," in B. J. L. Berry and F. E. Horton, Eds., *Geographic Perspectives on Urban Systems,* Prentice-Hall, Englewood Cliffs, N.J., 1970, pp. 306–394.

REILLY, W. J., *The Law of Retail Gravitation,* W. J. Reilly, New York, 1931.

REYNOLDS, J. P., "The plan," *Town Planning Review,* 32 (1961), pp. 151–184.

ROBINSON, G., "Trials on trends through clusters of cirques," *Area,* 4 (1972), pp. 104–113.

ROGERS, A., *Statistical Analysis of Spatial Dispersion: The Quadrat Method,* Pion, London, 1974.

ROOT, J. D., "Intransitivity of preferences: A neglected concept," *Proceedings of the Association of American Geographers,* 7 (1975), pp. 185–189.

ROSE, H. M., *Social Processes in the City: Race and Urban Residential Choice,* Commission on College Geography Resource Paper 6, Association of American Geographers, Washington, D.C., 1969.

ROSSI, P. H., *Why Families Move,* 2nd ed., Sage, Beverly Hills, Calif., 1980.

ROWLES, G. D., "Reflections on experiential field work," in D. Ley and M. S. Samuels, Eds., *Humanistic Geography: Prospects and Problems,* Maaroufa Press, Chicago, 1978, pp. 173–193.

RUMMELL, R. J., *Applied Factor Analysis,* Northwestern University Press, Evanston, Ill., 1970.

RUSHTON, G., "Analysis of spatial behavior by revealed space preference," *Annals of the Association of American Geographers,* 59 (1969), pp. 391–400.

RUSHTON, G., "The scaling of locational preferences," in K. R. Cox and R. G. Golledge, Eds., *Behavioral Problems in Geography Revisited,* Methuen, New York, 1981, pp. 67–92.

SACK, R. D., *Conceptions of Space in Social Thought: A Geographic Perspective,* Macmillan Press, London, 1980.

SAMUELSON, P. A., "Consumption theory in terms of revealed preference," *Economica,* 15 (1948), pp. 243–253.

SARGENT, C. S., JR., "Land speculation and urban morphology," in J. S. Adams, Ed., Urban Policymaking and Metropolitan Dynamics: A Comparative Geographical Analysis, Ballinger, Cambridge, Mass., 1976, pp. 21–57.

SAUNDERS, P., *Urban Politics: A Sociological Interpretation,* Hutchinson, London, 1979.

SAYER, A., "Explanation in economic geography: Abstraction versus generalization," *Progress in Human Geography,* 6 (1982), pp. 68–88.

SCHMID, C. F., "Urban crime areas: Part II," *American Sociological Review,* 25 (1960), pp. 655–678.

SCHULER, H. J., "A disaggregate store-choice model of spatial decision-making," *Professional Geographer,* 31 (1979), pp. 146–156.

SCHUSKY, J., "Public awareness and concern with air pollution in the St. Louis Metropolitan area," *Journal of Air Pollution Control Association,* 16 (1966), pp. 72–76.

SCOTT, A. J., *The Urban Land Nexus and the State,* Pion, London, 1980.

SCOTT, A. J., "Locational patterns and dynamics of industrial activity in the modern metropolis," *Urban Studies,* 19 (1982), pp. 111–141.

SCOTT, A. J., "Location and linkage systems: A survey and reassessment," *Annals of Regional Science,* 17 (1983), pp. 1–39.

SELYE, H., *The Stress of Life,* McGraw-Hill, New York, 1956.

SEYFRIED, W. R., "The centrality of urban land values," *Land Economics,* 39 (1963), pp. 275–284.

SHEPPARD, E. S., "Theoretical underpinnings of the gravity hypothesis," *Geographical Analysis,* 10 (1978), pp. 386–402.

SHERRATT, G. G., "A model for general urban growth," in C. W. Churchman and M. Verhulst, Eds., *Management Sciences, Model and Techniques,* Vol. 2, Pergamon Press, Elmsford, N.Y., 1960, pp. 147–159.

SHEVKY, E., and W. BELL, *Social Area Analysis,* Stanford University Press, Stanford, Calif., 1955.

SHEVKY, E., and M. WILLIAMS, *The Social Areas of Los Angeles,* University of California Press, Los Angeles, 1949.

SHINN, A. M., "Relations between scales," in H. M. Blalock, Jr., Ed., *Measurement in the Social Sciences: Theories and Strategies,* Aldine, Chicago, 1974, pp. 121–158.

SIMKUS, A. A., "Residential segregation by occupation and race in ten urbanized areas, 1950–1970," *American Sociological Review,* 43 (1978), pp. 81–93.

SIMMONS, J. W., "Changing residence in the city: A review of intra-urban mobility," *Geographical Review,* 58 (1968), pp. 622–651.

SIMON, H. A., *Models of Man,* Wiley, New York, 1957.

SMITH, D. M., *The Geography of Social Well-Being in the United States: An Introduction to Territorial Social Indicators,* McGraw-Hill, New York, 1973.

SMITH, D. M., "The identification of problems in cities: Applications of social indicators," in D. T. Herbert and D. M. Smith, Eds., *Social Problems and the City: Geographical Perspectives,* Oxford University Press, New York, 1979, pp. 12–32.

SMITH, D. M., *Industrial Location Theory,* 2nd ed., Wiley, New York, 1981.

SMITH, T., W. A. V. CLARK, J. O. HUFF, and P. SHAPIRO, "A decision-making and search model for intraurban migration," *Geographical Analysis,* 11 (1979), pp. 1–22.

SØRENSEN, A., K. E. TAEUBER, and L. J. HOLLINGSWORTH, JR., "Indexes of racial residential segregation for 109 cities in the United States, 1940 to 1970," *Sociological Focus,* 8 (1975), pp. 125–142.

SPEARE, A., S. GOLDSTEIN, and W. H. FREY, *Residential Mobility, Migration and Metropolitan Change,* Ballinger, Cambridge, Mass., 1974.

SPENCER, C., and M. WEETMAN, "The microgenesis of cognitive maps: A longitudinal study of new residents of an urban area," *Transactions of the Institute of British Geographers,* New Series, 6 (1981), pp. 375–384.

STEED, G. P. F., "Intrametropolitan manufacturing: Spatial distribution and locational dynamics in Greater Vancouver," *Canadian Geographer,* 17 (1973), pp. 235–258.

STEVENS, S. S., "The direct estimation of sensory magnitudes—loudness," *American Journal of Psychology,* 69 (1956), pp. 1–25.

STOKOLS, D., "A social-psychological model of human crowding phenomena," *Journal of the American Institute of Planners,* 38 (1972), pp. 72–83.

STOPHER, P. R., and A. H. MEYBURG, *Urban Transportation Modeling and Planning,* Lexington Books, Lexington, Mass., 1975.

STRASZHEIM, M. R., "Housing market discrimination and black housing consumption," *The Quarterly Journal of Economics,* 88 (1974), pp. 19–43.

STRUYK, R. J., and F. J. JAMES, *Intrametropolitan Industrial Location: The Pattern and Process of Change,* Lexington Books, Lexington, Mass., 1975.

SYMANSKI, R., and J. AGNEW, *Order and Skepticism: Human Geography and the Dialectic of Science,* Association of American Geographers, Washington, D.C., 1981.

TANNER, J. C., *Factors Affecting the Amount of Travel,* Road Research Technical Paper 51, Department of Scientific and Industrial Research, London, 1961.

TAYLOR, P. J., "Distance transformation and distance decay functions," *Geographical Analysis,* 3 (1971), pp. 221–238.

TAYLOR, P. J., *Quantitative Methods in Geography: An Introduction to Spatial Analysis,* Houghton Mifflin, Boston, 1977.

THOMAS, R. W., and R. J. HUGGETT, *Modelling in Geography: A Mathematical Approach,* Barnes & Noble, New York, 1980.

THOMPSON, D. L., "New concept: Subjective distance. Store impressions affect estimates of travel time," *Journal of Retailing,* 39 (1963), pp. 1–6.

THOMPSON, W. R., *A Preface to Urban Economics,* Johns Hopkins University Press, Baltimore, 1965.

THORNDYKE, P. W., "Distance estimation from cognitive maps," *Cognitive Psychology,* 13 (1981), pp. 526–550.

TIMMERMANS, H., "A spatial preference model of regional shopping behavior," *Tijdschrift voor Economische en Sociale Geografie,* 70 (1979), pp. 45–48.

TIMMERMANS, H., and G. RUSHTON, "Revealed space preference theory—A rejoinder," *Tijdschrift voor Economische en Sociale Geografie,* 70 (1979), pp. 309–312.

TIMMS, D. W. G., *The Urban Mosaic: Towards a Theory of Residential Differentiation,* Cambridge University Press, Cambridge, 1971.

TINKLER, K. J., "Trend surface with 'low explanations'; the assessment of their significance," *American Journal of Science,* 267 (1969), pp. 114–123.

TOCALIS, T. R., "Changing theoretical foundations of the gravity concept of human interaction," in B. J. L. Berry, Ed., *The Nature of Change in Geographical Ideas,* Northern Illinois University Press, De Kalb, Ill., 1978, pp. 65–124.

TOLMAN, E. C., "Cognitive maps in rats and men," *Psychological Review,* 55 (1948), pp. 189–208.

TROWBRIDGE, C. C., "On fundamental methods of orienting and imaginary maps," *Science,* 38 (1913), pp. 888–897.

TUAN, Y. F., *Space and Place: The Perspective of Experience,* University of Minnesota Press, Minneapolis, Minn., 1977.

UDRY, J. R., "Increasing scale and spatial differentiation: New tests of two theories from Shevky and Bell," *Social Forces,* 42 (1964), pp. 403–413.

UNWIN, D. J., "Percentage RSS in trend surface analysis," *Area,* 2 (1970), pp. 25–28.

UNWIN, D. J., *Introductory Spatial Analysis,* Methuen, New York, 1981.

VAN ARSDOL, M. D., JR., S. F. CAMILLERI, and C. F. SCHMID, "The generality of urban social area indexes," *American Sociological Review,* 23 (1958), pp. 277–284.

VAN TIL, J., "A new type of city for an energy-short world," *The Futurist,* 14 (1980), pp. 64–70.

VAN VALEY, T. L., W. C. ROOF, and J. E. WILCOX, "Trends in residential segregation: 1960–1970," *American Journal of Sociology,* 82 (1977), pp. 826–844.

WALKER, R. A., "The transformation of urban structure in the nineteenth century and the beginnings of suburbanization," in K. R. Cox, Ed., *Urbanization and Conflict in Market Societies,* Methuen, London, 1978, pp. 165–212.

WARD, D., *Cities and Immigrants: A Geography of Change in Nineteenth-Century America,* Oxford University Press, New York, 1971.

WARNES, A. M., and P. W. DANIELS, "Spatial aspects of an intrametropolitan central place hierarchy," *Progress in Human Geography,* 3 (1979), pp. 384–406.

WEAVER, C. L., and R. F. BABCOCK, *City Zoning: The Once and Future Frontier,* American Planning Association, Chicago, 1979.

WEBBER, M. J., "Life-cycle stages, mobility, and metropolitan change: 1. Theoretical issues," *Environment and Planning A,* 15 (1983), pp. 293–306.

WEBBER, M. J., R. SYMANSKI, and J. ROOT, "Toward a cognitive spatial theory," *Economic Geography,* 51 (1975), pp. 100–116.

WILKIE, W. L., and E. A. PESSEMIER, "Issues in marketing's use of multi-attribute attitude models," *Journal of Marketing Research,* 10 (1973), pp. 428–441.

WILLIE, C. V., "The relative contribution of family status and economic status to juvenile delinquency," *Social Problems,* 14 (1967), pp. 326–335.

WILSON, A. G., "Models in urban planning: A synoptic review of recent literature," *Urban Studies,* 5 (1968), pp. 249–276.

WILSON, A. G., "A family of spatial interaction models, and associated developments," *Environment and Planning,* 3 (1971), pp. 1–32.

WILSON, A. G., *Urban and Regional Models in Geography and Planning,* Wiley, New York, 1974.

WILSON, A. G., *Geography and the Environment: Systems Analytical Methods,* Wiley, Chichester, England, 1981.

WOLPERT, J., M. J. DEAR, and R. CRAWFORD, "Satellite mental health facilities," *Annals of the Association of American Geographers,* 65 (1975), pp. 23–35.

YEATES, M. H., "Some factors affecting the spatial distribution of Chicago land values, 1910–1960," *Economic Geography,* 41 (1965), pp. 55–70.

YEATES, M. H., *An Introduction to Quantitative Analysis in Human Geography,* McGraw-Hill, New York, 1974.

YEATES, M. H., and B. J. GARNER, *The North American City,* Harper & Row, New York, 1971.

YEATES, M. H., and B. J. GARNER, *The North American City,* 3rd ed., Harper & Row, New York, 1980.

YUILL, R. S., "Spatial behavior of retail customers: Some empirical measurements," *Geografiska Annaler,* 49 B (1967), pp. 105–115.

ZIELINKSI, K., "The modelling of urban population density: A survey," *Environment and Planning A,* 12 (1980), pp. 135–154.

ZORBAUGH, H. W., *The Gold Coast and the Slum,* Univeristy of Chicago Press, Chicago, 1929.

Index